PROJECT MANAGEMENT IN PRACTICE

PROJECT MANAGEMENT IN PRACTICE

Samuel J. Mantel, Jr.
Jack R. Meredith
Scott M. Shafer
Margaret M. Sutton

JOHN WILEY & SONS, INC.
New York • Chichester • Weinheim
Brisbane • Singapore • Toronto
http://www.wiley.com/college

ACQUISITIONS EDITOR   Beth Golub
MARKETING MANAGER   Jessica Garcia
PRODUCTION EDITOR   Patricia McFadden
SENIOR DESIGNER   Harry Nolan
OUTSIDE PRODUCTION MANAGEMENT   Suzanne Ingrao/Ingrao Assoc.
COVER DESIGN   Howard Grossman
COVER PHOTOGRAPH   ©Andrew Sacks/Stone

This book was set in 10½/12 Goudy by UG / GGS Information Services, Inc. and printed and bound by R. R. Donnelley & Sons. The cover was printed by Phoenix Color.

This book is printed on acid-free paper.

ISBN 0-471-37162-9

Printed in the United States of America

10 9 8 7 6 5 4 3 2 1

To Dotti: gentle critic, careful editor, loving wife.
S. J. M. Jr.

To a brave 15-year-old traveling alone from Wales
to Virginia: Robert Meredith 1662–1727.
J. R. M.

To Brianna and Sammy G., my most important
and rewarding projects.
S. M. S.

To Frank, Kyle, and Ali for their support, encouragement, and tolerance.
And to Bobbi, leader and coach, who helped me discover why I love my career
as a project manager.
M. M. S.

P R E F A C E

THE APPROACH

Over the past several decades, more and more work has been accomplished through the use of projects and project management. The use of projects has been growing at an accelerated rate. The exponential growth of membership in the Project Management Institute (PMI) is convincing evidence, as are the sales of computer software devoted to project management. Several societal forces are driving this growth, and many economic factors are reinforcing it. We describe these in Chapter 1 of this book.

A secondary effect has also been a major contributor to the use of project activity. As the use of projects has grown, its very success as a way of getting complex activities carried out successfully has become well established. The result has been a striking increase in the use of projects to accomplish jobs that in the past would simply have been turned over to someone with the comment, "Take care of it."

What happened then was that some individual undertook to carry out the job with little or no planning, little or no assistance, few resources, and often with only a vague notion of what was really wanted. The simple application of routine project management techniques significantly improved the consistency with which the outcomes resembled what the organization had in mind when the chore was assigned. Later, this sort of activity came to be known as "enterprise project management," "management by projects," and several other names, all of which are described as the project-oriented organization.

Some of these projects were large, but most were quite small. Some were complex, but most were relatively straightforward. Some required the full panoply of project management techniques, but most did not. All of them, however, had to be managed and thus required a great many people to take on the role of project manager in spite of little or no education in the science or art of project management.

One result was rising demand for education in project management. The number of college courses grew apace, as did the number of consulting firms offering seminars and workshops. Perhaps most striking was the growth in educational opportunities through post-secondary schools offering "short courses"—schools such as DeVry Institute, ITT, and others. In addition, short courses were offered by colleges and community colleges concentrating on both part-time and full-time education for individuals already in the work force. An exemplar of this approach is the University of Phoenix.

Communications from some instructors in these institutions told us that they would like a textbook that was shorter and focused more directly on the "technical" aspects of project management than those currently available. They were willing to forego most of the theoretical aspects of management, particularly if such were not directly tied to practice. Their students, who were not apt to take advanced course work in project management, had little use for understanding the historical development of the field. They felt no need to read about the latest academic research on the management of knowledge-based projects in a manufacturing environment. Finally, instructors asked for increased use of project management application software, though they added that they did not want a replacement for the many excellent "step-by-step" and "computing-for-dummies" types of books that were readily available. They wanted the emphasis to be on project management, not on project management software.

These requests sounded sensible to us and we have tried to write such a book.

ORGANIZATION AND CONTENT

With few exceptions, both readers and instructors are most comfortable with project management texts that are organized around the project life cycle, and this book is so organized. We start by defining in Chapter 1 a project and differentiating project management from general management. After discussing the project life cycle, we briefly cover project selection. We feel strongly that project managers who understand why a project was selected by senior management also understand the firm's objectives for the project. Understanding those things, we know, will be of value in making the inevitable trade-offs between time, budget, and performance.

Chapter 2 is devoted to the various roles the project manager must play and to the skills required to play them effectively. In addition, we cover the various ways in which projects can be organized. The nature of the project team and the behavorial aspects of projects are also briefly discussed.

Project planning, budgeting, and scheduling are covered in Chapters 3–5. Beginning with planning in Chapter 3 and budgeting in Chapter 4, the use of project management software is covered in increasing detail. Software is used throughout the book, where relevant, to illustrate the use and power of such software to aid in managing projects. Chapter 5 uses standard manual methods for building project schedules, and Microsoft Project® is demonstrated in parallel. Risk management software, Crystal Ball® 2000, is referenced in several chapters. Excel® is used in Chapter 6 to solve a problem on crashing a project. Detailed instructions are given. Chapter 6 also deals with resource allocation problems in a multiproject setting. A major section of this chapter is devoted to the insights of E. Goldratt in his book *Critical Chain.**

Chapter 7 concerns monitoring and controlling the project. Earned value analysis is covered in some detail. The final chapter deals with auditing, evaluating, and terminating projects.

Interest in risk management has grown rapidly in recent years, but the subject gets only minimal attention in most introductory level project management textbooks. We deal with risk throughout this book, introducing methods of risk management where relevant to the subject at hand. For example, simulation is referred to in Chapter 1 during our discussion of project selection models and is demonstrated in Chapter 5 by using Microsoft Excel® for the purpose. Simulation is also demonstrated in Appendix C using Crystal Ball® 2000. Detailed applications are made to project selection, budgeting, and scheduling problems. Crystal Ball® 2000 also simulates networks discussed in the section on the *Critical Chain* (see Chapter 6).

We are certainly aware that no text on project management could be structured to reflect the chaos that seems to surround some projects throughout their lives, and a large majority of projects now and then. The organization of this book reflects a tidiness and sense of order that is nonexistent in reality. Nonetheless, we make repeated references to the technical, interpersonal, and organizational glitches that impact the true day-to-day life of the project manager.

---

*Goldratt, E. M. *Critical Chain*. Great Barrington, MA: North River, 1997.

PEDAGOGY

The book includes several pedagogical aids. The end-of-chapter material includes *Review Questions* that focus on the textual material. *Discussion Questions* emphasize the implications and applications of ideas and techniques covered in the text. Where appropriate, there are *Problems* that are primarily directed at developing skills in the technical areas of project management as well as familiarizing the student with the use of relevant software.

In addition to the above, we have included *Incidents for Discussion* in the form of caselettes. In the main, these caselettes focus on one or more elements of the chapter to which they are appended. Several of them, however, require the application of concepts and techniques covered in earlier chapters so that they also serve an integrative function.

More comprehensive cases are also appended to each chapter. A set of these beginning in Chapter 3 is associated with the same project—the planning, building, and marketing of an assisted living facility for people whose state of health makes it difficult for them to live independently, but who are not yet ill enough to require nursing home care. Each chapter is followed by another major case calling upon the ideas and methods covered in the chapter. With all these cases, integration with material in other chapters is apt to be required.

We have used Excel® spreadsheets where appropriate throughout the book. Microsoft Office® is widely available, and with few exceptions students and professional project managers are familiar with its operation. We include instructions in the body of the text for running Excel's® Random Number Generation and its Solver tools.

A free 120-day trial edition of Microsoft Project 2000® is included in each copy of the book. The attached CD-ROM includes a complete version of Project 2000® as well as a comprehensive user's guide to the software and an overview of how to "get started" using it. The CD-ROM also contains a complete tutorial with step-by-step instructions on how to use the software including several case studies and descriptions of how specific companies use software to manage their projects. Preprogrammed, standard printouts are shown as illustrations throughout the text.

Microsoft Project® was chosen because it is a competent piece of software that is used by a large majority of all project management software users. While Project 2000® comes with this book, schools and professionals with access to earlier versions (specifically Project 4.0® and Project 98®) are not at a disadvantage. Almost all the relevant commands are the same in all three versions, and the standard printouts are very similar. One exception is found in the case of earned value calculations and reports. There are slight variations among versions, and all three vary slightly from the Project Management Institute standards. The differences are easily handled and are explained in Chapter 7. With this exception, we do not differentiate between the versions and refer to them all as Microsoft Project (MSP).

A free trial edition of Decisioneering's Crystal Ball® 2000 is also included in each copy of the book. We have noted in Chapters 1, 4, 5, and 6 some of the problems where the use of statistical decision models and simulation can be very helpful in managing risk. Because we felt that some instructors might desire an option to delay consideration of applied risk analysis to more advanced courses, applications of Crystal Ball® 2000 are not integrated into the various chapters, but they are grouped in Appendix C. Detailed instructions are given. In addition, a number of the end-of-chapter problems have been rewritten to adapt them for solution by Crystal Ball®. These can be found in the *Instructor's Resource Guide* along with added instructions for use of the software. Crystal Ball® was chosen because it works seamlessly with Excel® and is user friendly.

As we have noted elsewhere, projects have failed because the project manager attempted to manage the software rather than the project. We feel strongly that students and professionals should learn to use the basic project management techniques by hand—and only then turn to software for relief from their manual efforts.

As is true with any textbook, we have made some assumptions about both the students and professionals who will be reading this book. We assume that they have all had some elementary training in management, or have had equivalent experience. We also assume that, as managers, they have some slight acquaintance with the fundamentals of accounting, behavioral science, finance, and statistics. We even assume that they have forgotten most of the statistics they once learned; therefore, we have included an Appendix on relevant elementary statistics and probability as a memory refresher.

SUPPLEMENTS

The *Instructor's Resource Guide* will provide assistance to the project management instructor in the form of answers/solutions to the questions, problems, incidents for discussion, and end-of-chapter cases. This guide will also reference relevant Harvard Business School type cases and readings, teaching tips, and other pedagogically helpful material. The publisher maintains a web site for this and other books. The address is *www.wiley.com/college/projectmgt*. The site contains an electronic version of the *Instructor's Resource Guide*, an extensive set of PowerPoint slides, sample course outlines, links to relevant material organized by chapter, and sample test questions to test student understanding.

ACKNOWLEDGMENTS

There is no possible way to repay the scores of project managers and students who have contributed to this book, often unknowingly. The professionals have given us ideas about how to manage projects and students have taught us how to teach project management. We are grateful beyond our ability to express it.

We are also grateful to a small group of individuals, both close friends and acquaintances, who have been extraordinarily willing to let us "pick" their brains. They graciously shared their time and knowledge without stint. We send our thanks to: James Cochran, *Louisiana Tech University*; James Evans, *University of Cincinnati*; Karen Garrison, *3X Consulting Corporation*; Timothy Kloppenborg, *Xavier University, Ohio*; Samuel Mantel, III, *Cisco Systems, Inc.*; Gerhard Rosegger, *Case Western Reserve University*; and above all to Suzanne Ingrao, *Ingrao Associates*, without whom this book would have been unreadable.

Finally, we owe a massive debt to those colleagues who reviewed the manuscript for this book: George R. Dean, *DeVry Institute of Technology, DuPage*; William C. Giauque, *Brigham Young University*; Bill Leban, *Keller Graduate School of Management*; J. Wayne Patterson, *Clemson University*; Patrick Philipoom, *University of South Carolina*; Arthur C. Rogers, *City University*; Dean T. Scott, *DeVry Institute of Technology, Pomona*; Richard V. Sheng, *DeVry Institute of Technology, Long Beach*; William A. Sherrard, *San Diego State University*; Louis C. Terminello, *Stevens Institute of Technology*; and Jeffrey L. Williams, *University of Phoenix*. We owe a special thanks to Byron Finch, *Miami University*, for a number of particularly thoughtful suggestions for improvement. While we give these reviewers our thanks, we absolve each and all of blame for our errors, omissions, and wrong-headed notions.

Samuel J. Mantel, Jr.
Joseph S. Stern Professor
    Emeritus of Operations Management
College of Business Administration
University of Cincinnati
608 Flagstaff Drive
Cincinnati, OH 45215
mantelsj@email.uc.edu
(513) 931-2465

Jack R. Meredith
Broyhill Distinguished Scholar
    and Chair of Operations
Babcock Graduate School
    of Management
Wake Forest University
Winston Salem, NC 27109
jack.meredith@mba.wfu.edu
(336) 758-4467

Scott M. Shafer
Babcock Graduate School
    of Management
Wake Forest University
P.O. Box 7659
Winston Salem, NC 27109
scott.shafer@mba.wfu.edu
(336) 758-3687
www.mba.wfu.edu/faculty/shafer

Margaret M. Sutton
Sutton Associates
46 North Lake Avenue
Cincinnati, OH 45246
mmsutton@fuse.net
(513) 543-2806

C O N T E N T S

7   MONITORING AND CONTROLLING THE PROJECT   204

8   EVALUATING AND TERMINATING THE PROJECT   238

PROJECT MANAGEMENT IN PRACTICE

1

The World of Project Management

Once upon a time there was a heroine project manager. Her projects were never late. They never ran over budget. They always met contract specifications and invariably satisfied the expectations of her clients. And you know as well as we do, anything that begins with "Once upon a time . . ." is just a fairy tale.

This book is not about fairy tales. Throughout these pages we will be as realistic as we know how to be. We will explain project management practices that we know will work. We will describe project management tools that we know can help the project manager come as close as Mother Nature and Lady Luck will allow to meeting the expectations of all who have a stake in the outcome of the project.

1.1 WHAT IS A PROJECT?

Why this emphasis on project management? The answer is simple: Daily, organizations are asked to accomplish tasks that do not fit neatly into business-as-usual. A software group may be asked to develop an application program that will access U.S. government data on certain commodity prices and generate records on the value of commodity inventories held by a firm; the software must be available for use on April 1, 2004. The Illinois State Bureau for Children's Services may require an annually updated census of all Illinois resident children, aged 17 years or younger, living with an illiterate single parent; the census must begin in 18 months.

Note that each task is *specific* and *unique* with a specific *deliverable* aimed at meeting a *specific need or purpose*. These are *projects*. The routine issuance of reports on the value of commodity inventories, the routine counseling of single parents on nurturing their offspring—these are not projects. The difference between a project and a *nonproject* is not always crystal clear. For almost any precise definition, we can point to exceptions. At base, however, projects are unique, have a specific deliverable, and have a specific due date. Note that our examples have all those characteristics. The Project Management Institute (PMI) defines a project as "A temporary endeavor undertaken to create a unique product or service." [12, p. 167]

Projects vary widely in size and type. The writing of this book is a project. The reorganization of Procter & Gamble (P&G) into a global enterprise is a project, or more accurately a program, a large integrated set of projects. The construction of a fly-in fishing lodge in northern Manitoba, Canada is a project. The organization of "Cat-in-the-Hat Day" so that Mrs. Chaney's third grade class can celebrate Dr. Suess's birthday is also a project.

Both the hypothetical projects we mentioned earlier and the real-world projects listed just above have the same characteristics. They are unique, specific, and have desired completion dates. They all qualify as projects under the PMI's definition. They have an additional characteristic in common—they are multidisciplinary. They require input from people with different kinds of knowledge and expertise. This multidisciplinary nature of projects means that they are complex, that is, composed of many interconnected elements and requiring input from groups outside the project. The various areas of knowledge required for the construction of the fly-in fishing lodge are not difficult to imagine. The knowledge needed for globalization of a large conglomerate like P&G is quite beyond the imagination of any one individual and requires input from a diversified group of specialists. Working as a team, the specialists investigate the problem to discover what information, skills, and knowledge are needed to accomplish the overall task. It may take weeks, months, or even years to find the correct inputs and understand how they fit together.

A secondary effect of using multidisciplinary teams to deal with complex problems is conflict. Projects are characterized by conflict. As we will see in later chapters, the project schedule, budget, and specifications conflict with each other. The needs and desires of the client conflict with those of the project team, the senior management of the organization conducting the project and others who may have a less direct stake in the project. Some of the most intense and intractable conflicts are those between members of the project team. Much more will be said about this in later chapters. For the moment, it is sufficient to recognize that projects and conflict seem to be inseparable companions.

It is also important to note that projects do not exist in isolation. They are often parts of a larger entity or program, just as projects to develop a new engine and an improved suspension system are parts of the program to develop a new automobile. The overall activity is called a *program*. Projects are subdivisions of programs. Likewise, projects are composed of *tasks*, which can be further divided into *subtasks* that can be broken down further still. The purpose of these subdivisions is to allow the project to be viewed at various levels of detail. The fact that projects are typically parts of larger organizational programs is important for another reason, as is explained in Section 1.5.

Finally, it is appropriate to ask, "Why projects?" The reason is simple. We form projects in order to fix the responsibility and authority for the achievement of an organizational goal on an individual or small group when the job does not clearly fall within the definition of routine work.

> A project, then, is a temporary endeavor undertaken to create a unique product or service. It is specific, timely, usually multidisciplinary, and always conflict ridden. Projects are parts of overall programs and may be broken down into tasks, subtasks, and further if desired.

1.2 PROJECT MANAGEMENT VS. GENERAL MANAGEMENT

Project management differs from general management largely because projects differ from what we have referred to as "nonprojects." The naturally high level of conflict present in projects means that the project manager (PM) must have special skills in conflict resolution. The fact the projects are unique means that the PM must be creative and flexible, and have the ability to adjust rapidly to changes. When managing nonprojects, the general manager tries to "manage by exception." In other words, for nonprojects almost everything is routine and is handled routinely by subordinates. The manager deals only with the exceptions. For the PM, almost everything is an exception.

Certainly, general management's success is dependent on good planning. For projects, however, planning is much more carefully detailed and project success is absolutely dependent on such planning. The project plan is the immediate source of the project's budget, schedule, control, and evaluation. Detailed planning is critically important. One should not, of course, take so much time planning that nothing ever gets done, but careful planning is a major contributor to project success. Project planning is discussed in Chapter 3.

Project budgeting differs from standard budgeting, not in accounting techniques, but in the way budgets are constructed. Budgets for nonprojects are primarily modifications of budgets for the same activity in the previous period. Project budgets are newly created for each project and often cover several periods in the future. The project budget is derived directly from the project plan that calls for specific activities. These activities require resources, and such resources are the heart of the project budget. Similarly, the project schedule is also derived from the project plan.

In a nonproject manufacturing line, the sequence in which various things are done is set when the production line is designed. The sequence of activities usually is not altered when new models are produced. On the other hand, each project has a schedule of its own. Previous projects with deliverables similar to the one at hand may provide a rough template for the current project, but its schedule will be set by the project's unique plan and by the date on which the project is due for delivery to the client. As we will see in later chapters, the special requirements associated with projects have led to the creation of special managerial tools for budgeting and scheduling.

The routine work of most organizations takes place within a well-defined structure of divisions, departments, sections, and similar subdivisions of the total unit. The typical project cannot thrive under such restrictions. The need for technical knowledge, information, and special skills almost always requires that departmental lines be crossed. This is simply another way of describing the transdisciplinary character of projects. When projects are conducted side-by-side with routine activities, chaos tends to result—the nonprojects rarely crossing organizational boundaries and the projects crossing them freely. These problems and recommended actions are discussed at greater length in Chapter 2.

The discussion of structure leads to consideration of another difference between project and general management. In general management, there is a reasonably well-defined managerial hierarchy. Superior-subordinate relationships are known and lines of authority are clear. In project management this is rarely true. The PM may be relatively low in the hierarchical chain of command. This does not, however, reduce his or her responsibility of completing a project successfully. Responsibility without the authority of rank or position is so common in project management as to be the rule, not the exception.

With little legitimate authority, the PM depends on negotiation skills to gain the cooperation of the many departments in the organization that may be asked to supply technology, information, resources, and personnel to the project. The parent organization's standard departments have their own objectives, priorities, and personnel. The project is not their responsibility, and the project tends to get the leftovers, if any, after the departments have satisfied their own need for resources. Without any real command authority, the PM must negotiate for almost everything the project needs.

It is important to note that there are two different types of negotiation, *win-win* negotiation and *win-lose* negotiation. When you negotiate the purchase of a car or a home, you are usually engaging in win-lose negotiation. The less you pay for home or car, the less profit the seller makes. Your savings are the other party's losses—win-lose negotiation. This type of negotiation is never appropriate when dealing with other members of your organization. If you manage to "defeat" a department head and get resources or commitments that the department head did not wish to give you, imagine what will happen the next time you need something from this individual. The PM simply cannot risk win-lose situations when negotiating with other members of the organization.

Within the organization, win-win negotiation is mandatory. In essence, in win-win negotiation both parties must try to understand what the other party needs. The problem you face as a negotiator is how to help other parties meet their needs in return for their help in meeting the needs of your project. When negotiation takes place repeatedly between the same individuals, win-win negotiation is the only sensible procedure. PMs spend a great deal of their time negotiating. General managers spend relatively little. Skill at win-win negotiating is a requirement for successful project managing. (See [2, 7, and 13].)

One final point about negotiating: Successful win-win negotiation often involves taking a synergistic approach by searching for the "third alternative." For example, consider a product development project focusing on the development of a new inkjet printer. A design engineer working on the project suggests adding more memory to the printer. The PM initially opposes this suggestion feeling that the added memory will make the printer too costly. Rather than rejecting the suggestion, however, the PM tries to gain a better understanding of the design engineer's concern.

Based on their discussion, the PM learns that the engineer's purpose in requesting additional memory is to increase the printer's speed. After benchmarking the competition, the design engineer feels the printer will not be competitive as it is currently configured. The PM explains his fear that adding the extra memory will increase the cost of the printer to the point that it also will no longer be cost competitive. Based on this discussion the design engineer and PM agree that they need to search for another (third) alternative that will increase the printer's speed without increasing its costs. A couple of days later, the design engineer identifies a new ink that can simultaneously increase the printer's speed and actually lower its total and operating costs.

Project management differs greatly from general management. Every project is planned, budgeted, scheduled, and controlled as a unique task. Unlike nonprojects, projects are often multidisciplinary and usually have considerable need to cross departmental boundaries for technology, information, resources, and personnel. Crossing these boundaries tends to lead to intergroup conflict.

Unlike their general management counterparts, project managers have responsibility for accomplishing a project, but little or no legitimate authority to command the required resources from the functional departments. The PM must be skilled at win-win negotiation to obtain these resources.

1.3   WHAT IS MANAGED? THE THREE GOALS OF A PROJECT

The performance of a project is measured by three criteria. Is the project on time or early? Is the project on or under budget? Does the project meet the agreed-upon specifications to the satisfaction of the customer? Figure 1-1 shows the three goals for any project. The performance of the project, and the PM, is measured by the degree to which these goals are achieved.

One of these goals, specifications, is set primarily by the client (although the client agrees to all three when contracting for the project). It is the client who must decide what capabilities are required of the project's deliverables—and this is what makes the project unique. Some writers insist that "quality" is a separate and distinct goal of the project along with time, cost, and specifications. We do not agree because we consider quality an inherent part of the project specifications, not separable from them.

If we did not live in an uncertain world in which the best made plans often go awry, managing projects would be relatively simple, requiring only careful planning. Unfortunately, we do not live in a perfectly predictable (*deterministic*) world, but one characterized by chance events (*uncertainty*). This ensures that projects travel a rough road. Murphy's Law seems as universal as death and taxes, and the result is that the most skilled planning is upset by uncertainty. Thus, the PM spends a great deal of time adapting to unpredicted change. The primary method of adapting is to *trade-off* one objective for another. If a construction project falls behind schedule because of bad weather, it may be possible to get back on schedule by adding resources—in this case, probably labor and some equipment. If the budget cannot be raised to cover the additional resources, the PM may have to negotiate with the client for a later delivery date. If neither cost nor schedule can be negotiated, the contractor may have to "swallow" the added costs (or pay a penalty for late delivery), and accept lower profits.

All projects are always carried out under conditions of uncertainty. Well-tested software routines may not perform properly when integrated with other well-tested routines. A chemical compound may destroy cancer cells in a test tube—and even in the bodies of test animals—but may kill the host as well as the cancer. Where one cannot

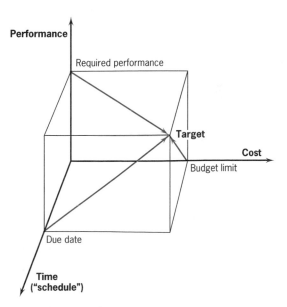

Figure 1-1   Performance, cost, and time project targets.

find an acceptable way to deal with a problem, the only alternative may be to stop the project and start afresh to achieve the desired deliverables. In the past, it was popular to label these technical uncertainties "technological risk." This is not very helpful, however, because it is not the technology that is uncertain. We can, in fact, do almost anything we wish, excepting perhaps faster-than-light travel and perpetual motion. What is uncertain is not technological success, but rather how much it will cost and how long it will take to reach success.

Most of the trade-offs PMs make are reasonably straightforward and are discussed during the planning, budgeting, and scheduling phases of the project. Usually they involve trading time and cost, but if we cannot alter either the schedule or the budget, the specifications of the project may be altered. Frills on the finished product may be foregone, capabilities not badly needed may be compromised. From the early stages of the project, it is the PM's duty to know which elements of project performance are sacrosanct and which are not.

One final comment on this subject: Projects must have some flexibility. Again, this is because we do not live in a deterministic world. Occasionally, a senior manager (who does not have to manage the project) presents the PM with a document precisely listing a set of deliverables, a fixed budget, and a firm schedule. This is failure in the making for the PM. Unless the budget is overly generous, the schedule overlong, and the specifications easily accomplished, the system is, as mathematicians say, "overdetermined." If Mother Nature so much as burps, the project will fail to meet its rigid parameters. A PM cannot be successful without flexibility.

> Projects have three interrelated objectives: to (1) meet the budget, (2) finish on schedule, and (3) meet specifications that satisfy the client. Because we live in an uncertain world, as work on the project proceeds, unexpected problems are bound to arise. These chance events will threaten the project's schedule or budget or specifications. The PM must now decide how to trade off one project goal against another (e.g., to stay on schedule by assigning extra resources to the project may mean it will run over the predetermined budget.) If the schedule, budget, and specifications are rigidly predetermined, the project is probably doomed to failure unless the preset schedule and budget are overly generous or the difficulty in meeting the specifications has been seriously overestimated.

1.4   THE LIFE CYCLES OF PROJECTS

All organisms have a *life cycle*. They are born, grow, wane, and die. This is true for all living things, for stars and planets, for the products we buy and sell, for our organizations, and for our projects as well. A project's life cycle measures project completion as a function of either time (schedule) or resources (budget). This life cycle must be understood because the PM's managerial focus subtly shifts at different stages of the cycle [1, 8]. During the early stages, the PM must make sure that the project plan really reflects the wishes of the client as well as the abilities of the project team and is designed to be consistent with the goals and objectives of the parent firm.

As the project goes into the implementation stage of its life cycle, the PM's attention turns to the job of keeping the project on budget and schedule—or, when chance interferes with progress, to negotiating the appropriate trade-offs to correct or minimize the damage. At the end of the project, the PM turns into a "fuss-budget" to assure that the specifications of the project are truly met, handling all the details of closing out the

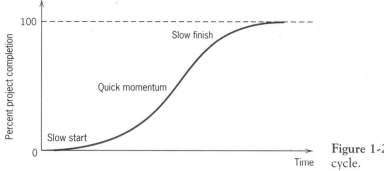

Figure 1-2   The project life cycle.

books on the project, making sure there are no loose ends, and that every "i" is dotted and "t" crossed.

Many projects are like building a house. A house-building project starts slowly with a lot of discussion and planning. Then construction begins and progress is rapid. When the house is built, but not finished inside, progress appears to slow down and it seemingly takes forever to paint everything, to finish all the trim, and to assemble and install the built-in appliances. Progress is slow-fast-slow as shown in Figure 1-2.

It used to be thought that the S-shaped curve of Figure 1-2 represented the life cycle for all projects. While this is true of many projects, there are important exceptions. Anyone who has baked a cake has dealt with a project that approaches completion by a very different route than the traditional S-curve, as shown in Figure 1-3.

The process of baking a cake is straightforward. The ingredients are mixed while the oven is preheated, usually to 350°F. The mixture (technically called "goop") is placed in a greased pan, inserted in the oven and the baking process begins. Assume that the entire process from assembling the ingredients to finished cake requires about 45 minutes—15 minutes for assembling the materials and mixing, and 30 minutes for baking. At the end of 15 minutes we have goop. Even after 40 minutes, having baked for 25 minutes, it may look like cake but, as any baker knows, it is still largely goop inside. If a toothpick (our grandmothers used a broom straw) is inserted into the middle of the "cake" and then removed, it does not come out clean. In the last few minutes of the process, the goop in the middle becomes cake. If left a few minutes too long in the oven, the cake will begin to burn on the bottom. Project Cake follows a path to completion much like Figure 1-3.

There are many projects that are similar to cake—the production of computer software, and many chemical engineering projects, for instance. In these cases the PM's job begins with great attention to having all the correct project resources at hand or guaranteed to be available when needed. Once the "baking" process is underway—the integra-

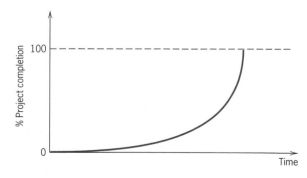

Figure 1-3   An alternate project life cycle.

tion of various sets of code or chemicals—one can usually not add missing ingredients. As the process continues, the PM must concentrate on determining when the project is complete—"done" in the case of cake, or a fully debugged program in the case of software.

In later chapters, we will also see the importance of the shape of the project's life cycle on how management allocates resources or reacts to potential delays in a project. Management does not need to know the precise shape of the life cycle, but merely whether its completion phase is concave (Figure 1-2) or convex (Figure 1-3) to the baseline.

> There are two different paths (life cycles) along which projects progress from start to completion. One is S-shaped and the other is J-shaped. It is an important distinction because identifying the different life cycles helps the PM to focus attention on appropriate matters to ensure successful project completion.

1.5   SELECTING PROJECTS

Before a project begins its life cycle, it must have been *selected* for funding by the parent organization. Whether the project was proposed by someone within the organization or an outside client, it is subject to approval by a more or less formal selection process. Often conducted by a committee of senior managers, the major function of the selection process is to ensure that several conditions are considered before a commitment is made to undertake any project. These conditions vary widely from firm to firm, but several are quite common: (1) Is the project potentially profitable? Does it have a chance of meeting our return-on-investment hurdle rate? (2) Does the firm have, or can it easily acquire, the knowledge and skills to carry out the project successfully? (3) Does the project involve building competencies that are considered consistent with our firm's strategic plan? (4) Does the organization currently have the capacity to carry out the project on its proposed schedule? This list could be greatly extended.

The selection process is usually complete before a PM is appointed to the project. Why, then, should the PM be concerned? Quite simply, the PM should know exactly why the organization selected the specific project because this sheds considerable light on what the project (and hence the PM) is expected to accomplish, from senior management's point of view, with the project. The project may have been selected because it appeared to be profitable, or was a way of entering a new area of business, or a way of building a reputation of competency with a new client or in a new market. This knowledge can be very helpful to the PM by indicating senior management's goals for the project, which will point to the desirability of some trade-offs and the undesirability of others.

There are many different methods for selecting projects, but they may be grouped into two fundamental types, nonnumeric and numeric. The former does not use numbers for evaluation. The latter does.

Nonnumeric Selection Methods

The Sacred Cow   At times, the organization's Chief Executive Officer (CEO) or other senior executive casually suggests a potential product or service that the organization might offer to its customers. The suggestion often starts, "You know, I was thinking that we might . . ." and concludes with ". . . Take a look at it and see if it looks sensible. If not, we'll drop the whole thing."

Whatever the selection process, the aforementioned project will be approved. It becomes a "Sacred Cow" and will be shown to be technically, if not economically, feasible. This may seem irrational to new students of project management, but such a judgment ignores senior management's intelligence and valuable years of experience—as well as the subordinate's desire for long-run employment. It also overlooks the value of support from the top of the organization, a condition that is necessary for project success [3].

The Operating/Competitive Necessity This method selects any project that is necessary for continued operation of a group or facility. If the answer to the "Is it necessary. . . .?" question is "yes," and if we wish to continue using the facility or system to stay in business, the project is selected. The Investment Committee of a large manufacturing company started to debate the advisability of purchasing and installing pumps to remove 18 inches of flood water from the floor of a small, but critical production facility. The debate stopped immediately when one officer pointed out that without the facility, the firm was out of business.

The same questions can be directed toward the maintenance of a competitive position. Some years ago, General Electric almost decided to sell a facility that manufactured the large, mercury vapor light bulbs used for streetlights and lighting large parking lots. The lighting industry had considerable excess capacity for this type of bulb and the resulting depressed prices meant they could not be sold profitably. GE, however, felt that if they dropped these bulbs from their line of lighting products, they might lose a significant portion of all lightbulb sales to municipalities. The profits from such sales were far in excess of the losses on the mercury vapor bulbs.

Comparative Benefits Many organizations have to select from a list of projects that are complex, difficult to assess, and often noncomparable, e.g., United Way organizations and R&D organizations. Such institutions often appoint a selection committee made up of knowledgeable individuals. Each person is asked to arrange a set of potential projects into a rank-ordered set. Typically, each individual judge may use whatever criteria he or she wishes to evaluate projects. Some may use carefully determined technical criteria, but others may try to estimate the project's probable impact on the ability of the organization to meet its goals. While the use of various criteria by different judges may trouble some, it results from a purposeful attempt to get as broad a set of evaluations as possible.

Rank-ordering a small number of projects is not inherently difficult, but when the number of projects exceeds 15 or 20, the difficulty of ordering the group rises rapidly. A *Q-sort* is a convenient way to handle the task [6]. First, separate the projects into three subsets, "good," "fair," and "poor," using whatever criteria you have chosen—or been instructed to use. If there are more than seven or eight members in any one classification, divide the group into two subsets, for instance, "good-plus" and "good-minus." Continue subdividing until no set has more than seven or eight members (see Figure 1-4). Now, rank-order the items in each subset. Arrange the subsets in order of rank, and the entire list will be in order.

The committee can make a composite ranking from the individual lists any way it chooses. One way would be to number the items on each individual list in order of rank, and add the ranks given to each project by each of the judges. Projects may then be approved in the order of their composite ranks, at least until the organization runs out of available funds.

Numeric Selection Methods

Financial Assessment Methods Most firms select projects on the basis of their expected economic value to the firm. Although there are many economic assessment

Steps	Results at Each Step

1. For each participant in the exercise, assemble a deck of cards, with the name and description of one project on each card.
2. Instruct each participant to divide the deck into two piles, one representing a high priority, the other a low-priority level. (The piles need not be equal.)
3. Instruct each participant to select cards from each pile to form a third pile representing the medium-priority level.
4. Instruct each participant to select cards from the high-level pile to yield another pile representing the very high level of priority; select cards from the low-level pile representing the very low level of priority.
5. Finally, instruct each participant to survey the selections and shift any cards that seem out of place until the classifications are satisfactory.

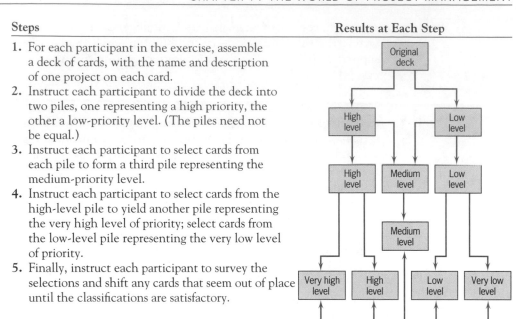

Figure 1-4 The Q-Sort method [6].

methods available—payback period, average annual rate of return, internal rate of return, and so on—we will describe here two of the most widely used methods: *payback period* and *discounted cash flow.**

The payback period for a project is the initial fixed investment in the project divided by the estimated annual net cash inflows from the project (which include the cash inflows from depreciation of the investment). The ratio of these quantities is the number of years required for the project to return its initial investment. Because of this perspective, the payback period is often considered a surrogate measure of risk to the firm: the longer the payback period, the greater the risk to the firm. To illustrate, if a project requires an investment of $100,000 and is expected to return a net cash inflow of $25,000 each year, then the payback period is simply 100,000/25,000 = 4 years, assuming the $25,000 annual inflow continues at least 4 years. Although this is a popular financial assessment method, it ignores any returns beyond the payback period as well as the time value of money. For these reasons, it is not usually recommended as a project selection method, though it is valuable for cash budgeting. Of the financial assessment methods, the discounted cash flow method discussed next is recommended instead.

The discounted cash flow method considers the time value of money, the inflation rate, and the firm's return-on-investment hurdle rate for projects. The annual cash inflows and outflows are collected and discounted to their *net present value* (NPV) using the organization's *required rate of return* (a.k.a. the *hurdle rate* or *cutoff rate*).

$$NPV \text{ (project)} = -I_0 + \sum_{t=1}^{n} F_t/(1 + k)^t$$

*Explanations of the theory and methods of calculating the net present value of cash inflows is beyond the scope of this book. We recommend that the reader who could benefit from an explanation turn to any standard college textbook on finance [e.g., 11].

where

I_0 = the initial investment, which will be negative because it is an outflow

F_t = the net cash flow in period, t

k = the required rate of return or hurdle rate

If one wishes to include the potential effects of inflation or deflation in the calculation, it is quite easily done. The discounting term, $(1 + k)^t$, simply becomes, $(1 + k + p_t)^t$, where p_t is the estimated rate of inflation or deflation for period t. If the required rate of return is 10 percent and we expect the rate of inflation will be 3 percent, then the discount factor becomes $(1 + .10 + .03)^t = (1.13)^t$ for that period.

In the early years of a project when outflows usually exceed inflows, the NPV of the project for those years will be negative. If the project becomes profitable, inflows become larger than outflows and the NPV for those later years will be positive. If we add up the present value of the net cash flows for all years, we have the NPV of the project. If this sum is positive, the project may be accepted because it earns more than the required rate of return. The following boxed example illustrates these calculations.

PsychoCeramic Sciences, Inc.*

PsychoCeramic Sciences, Inc. (PSI) is a large producer of cracked pots and other cracked items. The firm is considering the installation of a new manufacturing line that will, it is hoped, allow more precise quality control on the size, shape, and location of the cracks in its pots as well as in vases designed to hold artificial flowers.

The plant engineering department has submitted a project proposal that estimates the following investment requirements: an initial investment of $125,000 to be paid up-front to the Pocketa-Pocketa Machine Corporation, an additional investment of $100,000 to install the machines, and another $90,000 to add new material handling systems and integrate the new equipment into the overall production system. Delivery and installation is estimated to take one year, and integrating the entire system should require an additional year. Thereafter, the engineers predict that scheduled machine overhauls will require further expenditures of about $15,000 every second year, beginning in the fourth year. They will not, however, overhaul the machinery in the last year of its life.

The project schedule calls for the line to begin production in the third year, and to be up-to-speed by the end of that year. Projected manufacturing cost savings and added profits resulting from higher quality are estimated to be $50,000 in the first year of operation and are expected to peak at $120,000 in the second year of operation, and then to follow the gradually declining pattern shown in the table at the end of this box.

Project life is expected to be 10 years from project inception, at which time the proposed system will be obsolete and will have to be replaced. It is estimated that the machinery will have a salvage value of $35,000. PSI has a 12 percent hurdle rate for capital investments and expects the rate of inflation to be about 3 percent per year over the life of the project. Assuming that the initial expenditure occurs at the beginning of the year and that all other receipts and expenditures occur as lump sums at the end of the year, we can prepare the Net Present Value analysis for the project as shown in the table on the following page.

Microsoft Excel's® **NPV** function can be used to compute the Net Present Value of a series of future cash flows. The function requires two arguments that are enclosed in parentheses and separated by a comma: the discount rate to be used, and a range corresponding to the actual cash flows (see the spreadsheet below). The range of the cash flows contains the period by period cash flows. Each cash flow contained in the range is assumed to occur at the end of the period. If the initial investment, the first cash flow, occurs at the beginning of the first period, it should be added to the result of the net present value calculation and not included in the range of cash flows associated with the second argument.

Referring to the spreadsheet below, the **NPV** function was entered in cell **D16**. Since the first cash flow of −$125,000 occurs at the beginning of the first period, there is no need to discount it as it is already in present value terms. The remaining cash flows are assumed to occur at the end of their respective periods. For example, the $115,000 cash flow associated with 2005 is assumed to occur at the end of the fifth period. According to the results, the Net Present Value of the project is positive and, thus, the project can be accepted. (The project would have been rejected if the hurdle rate had been 14 percent, resulting in a discount rate of 17 percent.)

*Source: [10, pp. 49–50]

	A	B	C	D	E	F	G	H	I
1	**Discount Rate**	15.0%				*Key Formulas:*			
2						Cell B14	=65,000+35,000		
3	**Year**	**Inflow**	**Outflow**	**Net Flow**		Cell D4	=B4−C4 (copy to cells D5:D14)		
4	2000*	$0	$125,000	−$125,000		Cell D16	=D4+NPV(B1,D5:D14)		
5	2001	$0	$100,000	−$100,000					
6	2002	$0	$90,000	−$90,000		*All cash flows assumed to occur at the			
7	2003	$50,000	$0	$50,000		end of the year except the initial			
8	2004	$120,000	$15,000	$105,000		investment of $125,000 which occurs at			
9	2005	$115,000	$0	$115,000		the beginning of 2000.			
10	2006	$105,000	$15,000	$90,000					
11	2007	$97,000	$0	$97,000					
12	2008	$90,000	$15,000	$75,000					
13	2009	$82,000	$0	$82,000					
14	2010	$100,000	$0	$100,000					
15									
16	**Net Present Value**			$17,997					
17									
18			$65,000 cost savings						
19			and added profits + $35,000 slavage						
20			value						
21									
22									

Perhaps the most difficult aspect related to the proper use of discounted cash flow is determining the appropriate discount rate to use. While this determination is made by senior management, it has a major impact on project selection, and therefore, on the life of the PM. For most projects the hurdle rate selected is the organization's cost of capital though it is often arbitrarily set too high as a general allowance for risk. In the case of particularly risky projects, a higher hurdle rate may be justified, but it is not a good general practice. Another common, but misguided practice is to set the hurdle rate high as an allowance for resource costs increases. Neither risk nor inflation should be treated so casually. Specific corrections for each should be made if the firm's management feels it is required. If a project is competing for funds with another investment, the hurdle rate may be the *opportunity cost of capital*, that is, the rate of return the firm must forego if it invests in a project instead.

Because the present value of future returns decreases as the discount rate rises, a high hurdle rate biases the analysis strongly in favor of short-run projects. For example, given a rate of 20 percent, a dollar ten years from now has a present value of only $.16, $(1/1.20)^{10} = .16$. The critical feature of long-run projects is that costs associated with them are spent early in the project and have high present values while revenues are delayed for several years and have low present values.

This effect may have far-reaching implications. The high interest rates during the 1970s and 1980s forced many firms to focus on short-run projects. The resulting disregard for long-term technological advancement led to a deterioration in the ability of some United States firms to compete in world markets [5].

The discounted cash flow method's of calculation are simple and straightforward. Like the other financial assessment methods, it has a serious defect. First, it ignores all nonmonetary factors except risk. Second, because of the nature of discounting, all the discounted methods bias the selection system by favoring short-run projects. Let us now examine a selection method that goes beyond assessing only financial profitability.

Scoring Methods The scoring methods were developed to overcome some of the disadvantages of the simple financial profitability methods, especially their focus on a single criterion. The simplest scoring approach, the *unweighted 0-1 factor method*, lists multiple criteria of significant interest to management. Given a list of the organization's goals, a selection committee, usually senior managers, familiar with both the organization's criteria and potential project portfolio check off, for each project, which of the criteria would be satisfied; for example, see Figure 1-5. Those projects that exceed a certain number of check-marks may be selected for funding.

All the criteria, however, may not be equally important and the various projects may satisfy each criterion to different degrees. To correct for these drawbacks, the *weighted factor scoring method* was developed. In this method, a number of criteria, n, are considered for evaluating each project and their relative importance weights, w_j, are estimated. The sum of the weights over all the j criteria is usually set arbitrarily at 1.00, though this is not mandatory. It is helpful to limit the criteria to just the major factors and not include criteria that are only marginal to the decision such as representing only 2 or 3% importance. A rule of thumb might be to keep n less than eight factors because the higher weights, say 20 percent or more, tend to force the smaller weights to be insignificant. Their importance weights, w_j, can be determined in any of a number of ways: a particular individual's subjective belief, available objective factors such as surveys or reports, group composite beliefs such as simple averaging among the group members, and so on.

In addition, a score, s_{ij}, must be determined for how well each project i satisfies each criterion j. The sum of these scores over all the criteria gives the total score, S_i, for each project, i, from which the best project is then selected. Typically, a 5-point scale is used to ascertain these scores, through 3-, 7-, and even 9-point scales are sometimes used.

Project _____

Rater _____ Date _____

	Qualifies	Does Not Qualify
No increase in energy requirements	x	
Potential market size, dollars	x	
Potential market share, percent	x	
No new facility required	x	
No new technical expertise required		x
No decrease in quality of final product	x	
Ability to manage project with current personnel		x
No requirement for reorganization	x	
Impact on work force safety	x	
Impact on environmental standards	x	
Profitability		
Rate of return more than 15% after tax	x	
Estimated annual profits more than $250,000	x	
Time to break-even less than 3 years	x	
No need for external consultants		x
Consistency with current line of business		x
Impact on company image		
With customers	x	
With our industry		x
Totals	12	5

Figure 1-5
A sample project
selection form, an
unweighted 0–1
scoring model.

The top score, such as 5, is reserved for excellent performance on that criterion such as a return on investment (ROI) of 50% or more, or a reliability rating of "superior." The bottom score of 1 is for "poor performance," such as an ROI of 5 percent or less, or a reliability rating of "poor." The middle score of 3 is usually for average or nominal performance (e.g., 15–20% ROI), and 4 is "above average" (21–49% ROI) while 2 is "below average" (6–14% ROI). Notice that the bottom score, 1, on one category may be offset by very high scores on other categories. Any condition which is so bad that it makes a project unacceptable irrespective of how good it may be on other criteria, is a *constraint*. If a project violates a constraint, it is removed from the set and not scored.

Note two characteristics in these descriptions. First, the categories for each scale need not be in equal intervals—they should correspond to the subjective beliefs about what constitutes excellent, below average, and so on. Second, the five-point scales can be based on either quantitative or qualitative data, thus allowing the inclusion of financial and other "hard" data (cash flows, net present value, market share growth, costs) as well as "soft" subjective data (fit with the organization's goals, personal preferences, attractiveness, comfort). And again, the soft data also need not be of equal intervals. For example, "superior" may rate a 5 but "OK" may rate only a 2.

The general mathematical form of the weighted factor scoring method is

$$S_i = \sum_{j=1}^{n} s_{ij} \, w_j$$

where

    S_i = the total score of the *i*th project

    s_{ij} = the score of the *i*th project on the *j*th criterion

    w_j = the weight or importance of the *j*th criterion

Using a Weighted Scoring Model to Select Wheels

As a junior in college, you now find that you need to purchase a car in order to get to your new part-time job and around town more quickly. This is not going to be your "forever" car, and your income is limited; basically, you need reliable wheels. You have two primary criteria of equal importance, cost and reliability. You have a limited budget and would like to spend no more than $3,500 on the car. In terms of reliability, you can't afford to have the car break down on your way to work, or for that matter, cost a lot to repair. Beyond these two major criteria, you consider everything else a "nicety" such as comfort, heat and air, appearance, handling, and so on. Such niceties you consider only half as important as either cost or reliability. Table A shows a set of scales you created for your three criteria, converted into quantitative scores.

Table A: Criteria Scales and Equivalent Scores

	Scores				
Criterion	1	2	3	4	5
Cost	>$3,500	$3,000–3,499	$2,500–2,999	2,000–2,499	<$2,000
Reliability	poor	mediocre	ok	good	great
Niceties	none	few	some	many	lots

You have identified three possible cars to purchase. One of your sorority sisters is graduating this semester and is looking to replace "Betsy," her nice subcompact. She was going to trade it in but would let you have it for $2,800, a fair deal, except the auto magazines rate its reliability as poor. You have also seen an ad in the paper for a more reliable Minicar for $3,400 but the ad indicates it needs some body work. Last, you tore off a phone number from a campus poster for an old Japanese Import for only $2,200.

In Table B, you have scored each of the cars on each of the criteria, calculated their weighted scores, and summed them to get a total. The weights for the criteria were obtained from the following logic: If Y is the importance weight for Cost, then Y is also the importance for Reliability and $\frac{1}{2}$Y is the importance for Niceties. This results in the formula

$$Y + Y + \tfrac{1}{2}Y = 1.00 \qquad \text{or} \qquad Y = 0.4$$

Thus, Cost has 0.4 importance weight, as does Reliability, and Niceties has 0.2 importance.

Table B: Weighted Total Scores for Each Car

	Criteria (and Weights)			
Alternative Car	Cost (0.4)	Reliability (0.4)	Niceties (0.2)	Total
Betsy	3 × 0.4 = 1.2	2 × 0.4 = 0.8	4 × 0.2 = 0.8	2.8
Minicar	2 × 0.4 = 0.8	4 × 0.4 = 1.6	1 × 0.2 = 0.2	2.6
Import	4 × 0.4 = 1.6	3 × 0.4 = 1.2	1 × 0.2 = 0.2	3.0

Based on this assessment, it appears that the Import with a total weighted score of 3.0 may best satisfy your need for basic transportation. As shown in

Table C, spreadsheets are a particularly useful tool for comparing options using a weighted scoring model.

Table C: Creating a Weighted Scoring Model in a Spreadsheet

	A	B	C	D	E
1	Criteria	Cost	Reliability	Niceties	
2	Weights	0.4	0.4	0.2	
3					
4	Alternative Car	Cost	Reliability	Niceties	Total
5	Betsy	3	2	4	2.8
6	Minicar	2	4	1	2.6
7	Import	4	3	1	3.0
8					
9	Key Formulas:				
10	Cell E5	=SUMPRODUCT(B$2:D$2,B5:D5)			
11		(copy to cells E6:E7)			

Project selection is an inherently risky process. Throughout this section we have treated risk by "making allowance" for it. Managing and analyzing risk can be handled in a more straightforward manner. By estimating the highest, lowest, and most likely values that costs, revenues, and other relevant variables may have, and by making some other assumptions about the world, we can estimate outcomes for the projects among which we are trying to make selections. This is accomplished by simulating project outcomes. Appendix C demonstrates how to do this using Crystal Ball® 2000 on a sample selection problem.

> The PM should understand why a project is selected for funding so that the project can be managed to optimize its advantages and achieve its objectives. There are two types of project selection methods: numeric and nonnumeric. Both have their advantages. Of the numeric methods there are two subtypes, methods that assess the profits associated with a project and more general methods that measure nonmonetary advantages in addition to the monetary pluses. Of the financial methods, the discounted cash flow is best. In our judgment, however, the weighted scoring method is the most useful.

1.6   THE AGGREGATE PROJECT PLAN

As we noted early in this chapter, projects are usually subdivisions of a major program that an organization wishes to accomplish such as a new information systems development program or an innovative product development program. For example, a project to develop a new dashboard control system or a new engine—both might be parts of a program to develop a new automobile platform or model. It is not a single project that determines the organization's long-run success, but rather the set of projects pursued by the organization, the *project portfolio*, (or even the portfolio of programs). Therefore, in

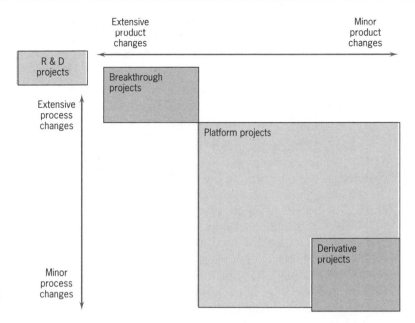

Figure 1-6
The aggregate project plan.

making project selection decisions, it is vital to consider the interactions among various projects and to manage the projects as a set. This is in stark contrast to the common practice of simply setting a project budget and specified return on investment (ROI) hurdle rate, then funding projects until either the budget or supply of acceptable projects is exhausted. Organizations that fund all projects that meet their ROI criterion typically end up with significantly more ongoing projects than they can competently manage. Because ROI is an insufficient selection criterion, the set of projects chosen may not be close to an optimal portfolio.

To address this issue of effectively choosing and managing a set of projects, Professors Wheelwright and Clark of the Harvard Business School developed a framework for categorizing projects that they call the Aggregate Project Plan [14]. Their framework dealt with product and process development projects and categorized them along two dimensions: (1) the extent of changes made to the product and (2) the degree of process change. Based on these two dimensions, projects can be categorized into the following four categories as shown in Figure 1-6.

1. *Derivative projects.* Derivative projects seek to make incremental improvements in the product and/or process. Projects that seek to reduce the product's cost or make minor product line extensions exemplify these types of projects. Developing a stripped down version of an existing modem would qualify as a derivative project. This category accounts for a large majority of all innovations.

2. *Breakthrough projects.* These projects are at the opposite end of the continuum from derivative projects and typically seek the development of a new generation of products. Developing a modem that would work with fiber-optic cable as opposed to copper wire is an example of a breakthrough project.

3. *Platform projects.* Platform projects fall between derivative and breakthrough projects. In general, the result of these projects is a product that can serve as the *platform* for an entire line of products, that is, the platform for a program. A key difference between platform projects and breakthrough projects is that platform projects stick with existing technology. As an example, the development of a new modem

capable of sending and receiving data at 256 Kb would qualify as a platform project. If this modem succeeds, it could serve as the basis for a number of derivative projects focusing on cost improvements and the development of other modems with different features.

1. *R&D projects*   R&D projects entail working with basic technology to develop new knowledge. Depending on its focus, an R&D project might lead to breakthrough, platform, or derivative innovations.

Use of the aggregate project plan requires that all projects be identified and plotted. The size of the points plotted for each project should be proportional to the amount of resources the project will require. In Figure 1-7, we have used different shapes to indicate different types of projects. Internal projects are plotted using circles while projects pursued as part of a strategic alliance with other firms are plotted using squares.

There are a number of ways the aggregate project plan can be used. The identification of gaps in the types of projects being undertaken is probably most important. For example, are the types of projects undertaken too heavily skewed toward derivative type projects? This might indicate an inadequate consideration of the firm's long-run competitive position. Also, the aggregate project plan facilitates evaluation of the resource commitments of the ongoing or proposed projects. Finally, this framework can serve as a model for employee development. New employees can initially be assigned to work on derivative projects. After gaining experience, employees can be assigned to a platform project, then assigned to manage a derivative project. As managerial skill accumulates, the employee will qualify for larger and more valuable projects. Of course, we must remember that the fundamental purpose of this entire process is to ensure that the set of projects accurately reflects the organization's strategic goals and objectives.

Another approach to the problem of developing a research portfolio was developed at SmithKline Beecham, a pharmaceutical company [14]. Each R&D project is evaluated under four different assumptions about funding levels; current scale, scale-up, scale-down, and minimal. Using decision tree analysis, the expected values of the outcomes associated with each funding level are determined. Projects are ranked by ex-

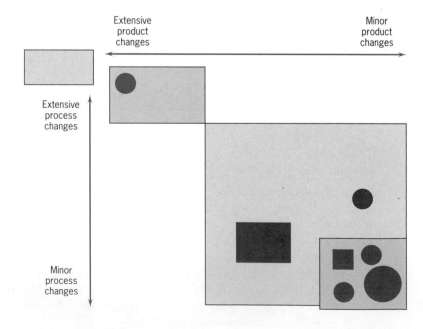

Figure 1-7   An example aggregate project plan.

pected return and the highest expected value portfolio is then constructed. This approach to building an R&D or product portfolio is not simple to implement, but is a powerful tool for exercising the highest level of corporate strategy.

> Projects are often subdivisions of major programs. Long-run success is determined by the organization's portfolio of projects. Classified by the extent of innovation in product and process, there are four types of projects: derivative, breakthrough, platform, and R&D projects. The actual mix of projects is a direct expression of the organization's competitive strategy. A proper mix of project categories can help ensure its long-run competitive position.

1.7   THE MATERIALS IN THIS TEXT

When reading a text, it is helpful to understand how the book is organized and where it will take the reader. Following this introductory chapter, our attention goes to the various roles the PM must play and the ways projects are organized. Chapter 2 focuses on the behavioral and structural aspects of projects and their management. It describes the PM's roles as communicator, negotiator, and manager. It also includes a discussion of project management as a profession and reports briefly on the Project Management Institute (PMI), the PM's professional organization. Then attention turns to the ways in which projects can be organized within the parent establishment. *Matrix organization* is discussed at length as are the conflicts and managerial problems that matrix organizations tend to foster. Finally, the chapter moves to the *project team*: its purposes and the widespread use of transdisciplinary teams. Using transdisciplinary teams to plan and carry out the project is a source of both creativity and conflict. The management of conflict is briefly covered.

The remainder of the book is designed to conform to the life cycle of any project, whatever the shape of the life cycle curve. Chapter 3 covers the process of *planning and launching the project*, construction of the *work breakdown structure* (WBS), and *responsibility charts*. These activities require the project team to estimate resource and time requirements for accomplishing what the project plan has described. Chapter 4 not only discusses the construction of a *project budget*, it also presents a method of improving one's estimating skills. Because any estimate is a forecast, the allied subject of risk management is introduced.

Chapter 5 covers scheduling, the Program Evaluation Review Technique (PERT), the Critical Path Method (CPM), and Gantt charts, the most common ways of illustrating the *project schedule*. Schedules will be calculated under conditions of uncertainty in two ways: (1) using standard probability theory, and (2) using simulation. In Chapter 6, *resource allocation* is discussed. To begin, we consider the problem of *crashing* a project, i.e., using additional resources in order to shorten project duration. Then we deal with two fundamental problems of resource management. First, a schedule of resource usage must be prepared, (a.k.a., *resource loading*). Second, we adjust the resource loads to avoid gluts and shortages of valuable resources, (a.k.a., *resource leveling*). The problems of resource usage when there are multiple projects competing for a limited resource pool are then covered, as are ways of dealing with these problems. The chapter ends with a discussion of Goldratt's *Critical Chain*.[3]

The subject of Chapter 7 is monitoring and controlling projects. The nature of project data collection is explained and various types of project reports, including *earned value reports*, are illustrated and discussed. Following this, we cover the general purposes and mechanisms for project control. The chapter ends with a section devoted to the *control of change* on a project. It is here that we discuss "*scope creep*" and how to control it.

Chapter 8 deals with *evaluating*, *auditing*, and *terminating* projects. The project team often fears evaluation and auditing. Team members usually equate these activities with fault finding, but when correctly used they are valuable aids for the PM and team. Project termination is usually ignored or treated as a trivial problem in practice—and in most works on project management. We feel it is an important and complex process that may cause serious problems if not handled properly.

Throughout this book there are illustrations of the tools and reports used by project managers. Many of these were produced using Microsoft Project® (MSP), Crystal Ball® 2000, and Excel®* (All illustrations and applications generated by MSP, Crystal Ball®, and Excel®, or any other application software will be clearly identified.) There are a large number of spreadsheets and literally hundreds of project management software packages on the market. Most of them perform with reasonable competence in the tasks for which they were designed. Of the packages intended for overall project management, MSP is by far the favorite with roughly half the total market. There are also a large number of specialized software packages, for example, report generators, and special risk management packages. Most are compatible with MSP or Excel®, often seamlessly so, and we mention some of them when relevant. In the past decade or two, spreadsheet software has become highly sophisticated. Excel®, for example, can perform simulations and statistical analysis as well as handle the usual arithmetic, accounting, and financial calculations.

When one reads the literature of project management, one sees much about *risk management*. Too often, it may seem to the reader that risk management is a highly specific task. It isn't. Risk management is a reference to a class of ideas, methods, and techniques that aids the management of projects being carried out in an uncertain world. Outside factors can affect projects in a wide variety of ways and so our discussions of risk management cannot be restricted to a chapter on the subject. They appear throughout the book. Tools and techniques are introduced as they are needed to deal with specific problems. The reader should note that these tools have wide application beyond project management and most are valuable for the general manager as well as the PM.

With this introduction, let us begin our study of project management.

REVIEW QUESTIONS

1. Use the characteristics of a project to differentiate it from a nonproject.

2. Contrast win-lose negotiation with win-win negotiation and explain why the latter is so important in project management.

3. Identify the three goals of a project and describe how the project manager achieves them. What does it mean for a project to be "overdetermined?"

4. Contrast the two types of project life cycles and discuss why it is important to know which type the current project is following.

5. How does the weighted scoring approach avoid the drawbacks of the NPV approach? Can the two approaches be combined? How? What weights would be appropriate if they were combined?

6. What advantages are lost if the sum of the weights in a

---

*As noted in the preface, for the illustrations used in this book the outputs from Microsoft Project versions 4.1, 98, and 2000 do not vary significantly. Thus, references to the Microsoft project management software will not distinguish versions except where noted.

weighted scoring approach does not add to 1.0? Why is it suggested that factors with less than 2 percent or 3 percent impact not be considered in this approach?

7. Draw a distinction between a project and a program. Why is the distinction important?

8. Why is it important for a project to have "flexibility"?

9. Why are R&D projects in a company's Aggregate Project Plan significantly different in type from the firm's Derivative, Breakthrough, and Platform projects?

DISCUSSION QUESTIONS

10. Contrast the three types of nonnumeric project selection methods. Could any specific case combine two of them, such as the sacred cow and the operating necessity, or the comparative benefits and the competitive necessity?

11. What errors in a firm's project portfolio might the Wheelwright and Clark aggregate project plan graphically identify?

12. You are the project manager of a team of software specialists working on a project to produce a piece of application software in the field of project management. Give some examples of things that might go wrong on such a project and the sorts of trade-offs you might have to make.

13. In Figure 1-7, what distribution of large and small circles and squares across the four boxes would characterize a strong, well-positioned product development business? A weak business?

14. Give several examples of projects found in your city, region, or country—avoiding those used as examples in the chapter.

15. For each of the projects identified in the answer to Question 14, is the life cycle for the project S-shaped or J-shaped?

16. Construct a list of factors, conditions, and circumstances you think might be important for a manufacturing firm to evaluate during the project selection process. Do the same for a computer repair shop.

17. How might you use project management for doing a major school work assignment?

PROBLEMS

18. A four-year financial project has net cash inflows of $20,000; $25,000; $30,000; and $50,000 in the next four years. It will cost $75,000 to implement the project. If the required rate of return is 0.2, conduct a discounted cash flow calculation to determine the NPV.

19. What would happen to the NPV of the above project if the inflation rate was expected to be 4 percent in each of the next four years?

20. Use a weighted scoring model to choose between three locations (A, B, C) for setting up a factory. The relative weights for each criterion are shown in the following table. A score of 1 represents unfavorable, 2 satisfactory, and 3 favorable.

		Location		
Category	Weight	A	B	C
Labor costs	20	1	2	3
Labor productivity	20	2	3	1
Labor supply	10	2	1	3
Union relations	10	3	3	2
Material supply	10	2	1	1
Transport costs	25	1	2	3
Infrastructure	5	2	2	2

21. Using a spreadsheet for Problem 20, find the following:
(a) What would be your recommendation if the weight for the transportation cost went down to 10 and the weight for union relations went up to 25?
(b) Suppose location A received a score of 3 for transport cost and location C received a score of 2 for transport cost. Would your recommendation change under these circumstances?
(c) The VP of Finance has looked at your scoring model and feels that tax considerations should be included in the model with a weight of 15. In addition, the VP has scored the locations on tax considerations as follows: A-3, B-2, and C-1. How does this affect your recommendation?

22. Nina is trying to decide in which of four shopping centers to locate her new boutique. Some cater to a higher class of clientele than others, some are in an indoor mall, some have a much greater volume than others, and, of course, rent varies considerably. Because of the nature of her store, she has decided that the class of clientele is the most important consideration. Following this, however, she must pay attention to her expenses and rent is a major

item, probably 90 percent as important as clientele. An indoor, temperature-controlled mall is a big help for stores such as hers where 70 percent of sales are from passersby slowly strolling and window shopping. Thus, she rates this as about 95 percent as important as rent. Last, a higher volume of shoppers means more potential sales; she thus rates this factor as 80 percent as important as rent.

As an aid in visualizing her location alternatives, she has constructed the following table. A "good" is scored as 3, "fair" as 2, and "poor" as 1. Use a weighted score model to help Nina come to a decision.

	Location			
	1	2	3	4
Class of clientele	fair	good	poor	good
Rent	good	fair	poor	good
Indoor mall	good	poor	good	poor
Volume	good	fair	good	poor

23. Using a spreadsheet for Problem 22, determine how Nina's ability to negotiate a lower rent at location 3, thereby raising its ranking to "good," will affect the overall rankings of the four locations.

INCIDENT FOR DISCUSSION

Bouncing Garage Door Openers

A large manufacturer of garage door openers designed an automated system to cut checks to vendors. The company was very pleased with the system. They have been using the automated system for three years. They average over 250 checks cut, 2–3 times per week. The system was designed to calculate how much was owed to each supplier, then electronically notify the bank to transfer the exact total amount needed from the company's holding account to their clearing account. Once the money was transferred, the system printed the vendor's checks which were manually mailed to the vendor.

Recently, two of the company's checks bounced—returned marked "Insufficient Funds." The president got wind of this and notified the Information Services Project Leader, Karen Kelso to stop everything, reprioritize all of her team's projects, and redesign the automated check-cutting system to include safeguards so that this could never happen again.

Karen knew the president had a tendency to panic, so she decided to investigate what had happened before beginning this project. She spoke to the bank and found out that twice someone had reproduced the company's checks and cashed them for a greater amount than they were originally. This caused the checks to bounce because insufficient funds had been transferred to the clearing account to cover the increased value of the checks.

The bank told Karen that they could help safeguard her computer system. They could create a Positive Pay Run. This was a system whereby the bank would verify every check that was cut against the checks that the vendors tried to deposit or cash. The bank would take all liability if a check got through that was not verified. To create this system Karen would need to have her people reprogram the current system to create a file for the bank containing each check number, vendor name, and check amount. The bank would then be able to provide Positive Pay Run verification. The bank charged a penny a check for this service. Karen thought that it would take one of her people about a day to reprogram the system to create such a file.

Questions: What should Karen do, follow the President's instructions, follow the bank's suggestion, or nothing? Why? What information should Karen give the president to justify her decision?

C A S E

United Screen Printers

United Screen Printers (USP) produces a wide range of decals for displaying promotional messages on fleet vehicles (including delivery vans, eighteen-wheelers and aircraft). Its decals range from flat-color designs to full-color photographic reproductions.

Although it is one of the oldest forms of printing, screen printing is superior to most of the more modern approaches because it permits making heavier deposits of ink onto a surface resulting in more vibrant and longer lasting finishes. Screen printing works by blocking out areas on a silk screen so that ink passes through only the unblocked areas to make an impression on the vinyl decal.

Many in the industry believe that the economics of fleet graphics make them an extremely attractive form of advertising and should lead to their continued penetration of a largely untapped market. One industry source estimated that the cost of fleet graphics works out to be $2.84 per 1,000,000 visual impressions. Given the highly cost effective nature of using fleet graphics as a form of advertising, it is speculated that organizations will increasingly exploit this form of advertising. In addition, as organizations become better aware of this advertising medium, it is likely they will want to change their message more frequently. According to managers at USP, this may be one of the major factors that is apparently driving the competition to focus more on short leadtimes and prices, and less on decal durability.

USP is about to begin its annual evaluation of proposed projects. Six projects have been proposed as described below.

1. *Purchase new large press.* There is currently a three-and-half to four-week backlog in the screen printing department. The result of this is that USP's total leadtime is 4 to 6 weeks in comparison to an industry average leadtime of 3.5 to 4 weeks. In a typical month, USP ships 13 percent of its orders early, 38 percent on-time, and 49 percent late. It has been estimated that 75 percent of the backlog is waiting for press 6, the largest press in the shop. Furthermore, press 6 is in dire need of replacement parts but USP has been unable thus far to locate a source for these parts. Given the problem of finding replacement parts and the fact that the press is somewhat outdated, this proposal calls for purchasing a new large press for $160,000. Based on estimates that a new large press could process jobs 50 percent to 100 percent faster than press 6, it is calculated that the payback period for a new large press would be one year.

2. *Build new headquarters.* USP's CEO fervently believes that the company needs to have a strong corporate identity. He therefore purchased land and had plans drawn up for the construction of a new corporate headquarters. Analysis of the new headquarters indicated that although it would improve operating efficiencies, the savings generated would not pay for the new building (estimated to cost $4 million). Many of the board members viewed the project as too risky since it would increase the company's debt as a percent of capital from almost zero to 50 percent.

3. *Pursue ISO 9000 certification.* This proposal also comes from USP's CEO. ISO 9000 is a set of standards that provides customers with some assurance that a supplier follows accepted business practices. In some industries obtaining ISO 9000 certification is essential, such as in industries that export to Europe and the domestic automobile industry. It was less clear what competitive advantage pursuing ISO 9000 would provide USP at this time. On the other hand, the process alone would help it document and perhaps improve its processes. The cost of this initiative was estimated to be $250,000 to $300,000 and would take one year to complete.

4. *Develop formal procedure for mixing inks.* This proposal comes from USP's plant manager. At present, mixing inks is a highly specialized skill that consumes 2–3 hours of the team leader's time each day. This project would focus on developing ink formulas to make the task of mixing inks more routine, and less specialized and subjective. The team leader is paid $25,000 annually. The cost of pursuing this project is estimated to be $10,000.

5. *Purchase and install equipment to produce four-color positives in-house.* The lead time to have positives made by an outside supplier is typically one week and costs $1,500 to $6,000. According to this proposal, the cost of purchasing the equipment to produce four-color positives in-house would be approximately $150,000 plus $25,000 for installation and training. The variable costs of producing positives in house are estimated to be $375 per job. If produced in-house, the leadtime for the four-color positives would be approximately an hour-and-a-half.

6. *Purchase inkjet printers.* An alternative to purchasing a new screen printing press is to add capacity based on newer technology. Given the inkjet's production rate, six inkjet printers at a cost of $140,000 would be needed to provide the equivalent capacity of a new large screen printing press. The major disadvantage of the inkjet printers is that compared to the screen printing process, the outdoor durability is more limited. In general, inkjet printers are more economical for small orders, while screen printing presses are more economical for large orders.

USP currently has annual sales of approximately $7 million. It typically allocates up to 10 percent of sales to these types of projects.

QUESTIONS:

1. Construct an aggregate project plan for USP.
2. What criteria would you recommend USP use in selecting its projects this year?
3. Based on your recommended criteria and the aggregate project plan, what projects would you recommend USP fund this year? Are there any types of projects you would recommend USP pursue that were not proposed?
4. What, if any, additional information would you want in making your recommendations? How would you go about obtaining this information?

C A S E

Handstar Inc.

Handstar Inc. was created a little over four years ago by two college roommates to develop software applications for handheld computing devices. It has since grown to ten employees with annual sales approaching $1.5 million. Handstar's original product was an expense report application that allowed users to record expenses on their handheld computer and then import these expenses into a spreadsheet that then created an expense report in one of five standard formats. Based on the success of its first product, Handstar subsequently developed three additional software products: a program for tracking and measuring the performance of investment portfolios, a calendar program, and a program that allowed users to download their email messages from their PC and read them on their handheld computer.

The two founders of Handstar have recently become concerned about the competitiveness of the firm's offerings, particularly since none of them has been updated since their initial launch. Therefore, they asked the directors of product development and marketing to work together and prepare a list of potential projects for updating Handstar's current offerings as well as to develop ideas for additional offerings. The directors were also asked to estimate the development costs of the various projects, product revenues, and the likelihood that Handstar could retain or obtain a leadership position for the given product. Also, with the increasing popularity of the Internet, the founders asked the directors to evaluate the extent to which the products made use of the Internet.

The product development and marketing directors identified three projects related to updating Handstar's existing products. The first project would integrate Handstar's current calendar program with its email program. Integrating these two applications into a single program would provide a number of benefits to users such as allowing them to automatically enter the dates of meetings into the calendar based on the content of an email message. The directors estimated that this project would require 1250 hours of software development time. Revenues in the first year of the product's launch were estimated to be $750,000. However, because the directors expected that a large percentage of the users would likely upgrade to this new product soon after its introduction, they projected that annual sales would decline by 10 percent annually in subsequent years. The directors speculated that Handstar was moderately likely to obtain a leadership position in email/calendar programs if this project were undertaken and felt this program made moderate use of the Internet.

The second project related to updating the expense report program. The directors estimated that this project would require 400 hours of development time. Sales were estimated to be $250,000 in the first year and to increase 5 percent annually in subsequent years. The directors speculated that completing this project would almost certainly maintain Handstar's leadership position in the expense report category, although it made little use of the Internet.

The last product enhancement project related to enhancing the existing portfolio tracking program. This project would require 750 hours of development time and would generate first-year sales of $500,000. Sales were projected to increase 5 percent annually in subsequent years. The directors felt this project would have a high probability of maintaining Handstar's leadership position in this category and the product would make moderate use of the Internet.

The directors also identified three opportunities for new products. One project was the development of a spreadsheet program that could share files with spreadsheet programs written for PCs. Developing this product would require 2500 hours of development time. First-year sales were estimated to be $1,000,000 with an annual growth rate of 10 percent. While this product did not make use of the Internet, the directors felt that Handstar had a moderate chance of obtaining a leadership position in this product category.

The second new product opportunity identified was a Web browser. Developing this product would require 1875 development hours. First-year sales were estimated to be $2,500,000 with an annual growth rate of 15 percent. Although this application made extensive use of the Internet, the directors felt that there was a very low probability that Handstar could obtain a leadership position in this product category.

The final product opportunity identified was a trip planner program that would work in conjunction with a PC connected to the Web and download travel instructions to the user's handheld computer. This product would require 6250 hours of development time. First-year sales were projected to be $1,300,000 with an annual growth rate of 5 percent. Like the Web browser program, the directors felt that there was a low probability that Handstar could obtain a leadership position in this category, although the program would make extensive use of the Internet.

In evaluating the projects, the founders believed it was reasonable to assume each product had a three-year life. They also felt that a discount rate of 12 percent fairly reflected the company's cost of capital. An analysis of payroll records indicated that the cost of software developers is $52 per hour including salary and fringe benefits. Currently there are four software developers on staff, and each works 2500 hours per year.

QUESTIONS:

1. Which projects would you recommend Handstar pursue based on the NPV approach?
2. Assume the founders weigh a project's NPV twice as much as both obtaining/retaining a leadership position and making use of the Internet. Use the weighted factor scoring method to rank these projects. Which projects would you recommend Handstar pursue?
3. In your opinion is hiring an additional software development engineer justified?

BIBLIOGRAPHY

1. ADAMS, J. R., and S. E. BARNDT. "Behavioral Implications of the Project Life Cycle." In D. I. Cleland, and W. R. King, eds., *Project Management Handbook.* New York: Van Nostrand Reinhold, 1983.
2. FISHER, R., and W. URY. *Getting to Yes.* Harmondsworth, Middlesex, G. B.: Penguin Books, 1983. (This is a classic book on win-win negotiations, in addition to being good reading.)
3. GOLDRATT, E. M. *Critical Chain.* Great Banington, MA: North River, 1997.
4. GREEN, S. G. "Top Management Support of R&D Projects: A Strategic Leadership Perspective." *IEEE Transactions on Engineering Management,* August 1995. (What Prof. Green has to say about the role of a project champion in support of R&D projects applies equally well to all sorts of projects.)
5. HAYES, R., and W. J. ABERNATHY. "Managing Our Way to Economic Decline." *Harvard Business Review,* July–August 1980. (An excellent, persuasive, and timeless blast at those who focus their business decisions solely on short-run profits.)
6. HELIN, A. F., and W. E. SOUDER. "Experimental Test of a Q-Sort Procedure for Prioritizing R&D Projects." *IEEE Transactions on Engineering Management,* November 1974. (The Q-Sort is a handy, useful, and easy-to-use technique.)
7. JANDT, F. E. *Win-Win Negotiating.* New York: John Wiley, 1987.
8. KAPLAN, R. S. "Must CIM be Justified by Faith Alone?" *Harvard Business Review,* March–April 1986.
9. KLOPPENBORG, T. J., and S. J. MANTEL, JR. "Trade-offs on Projects: They May Not Be What You Think." *Project Management Journal,* March 1990.
10. MEREDITH, J. R., and S. J. MANTEL, JR. *Project Management: A Managerial Approach,* 4th ed. New York: John Wiley, 2000.
11. MOYER, R. C., J. R. McGUIGAN, and W. J. KRETLOW. *Contemporary Financial Management,* 7th ed., Cincinnati: South-Western, 1998.
12. Project Management Institute Standards Committee. *A Guide to the Project Management Body of Knowledge.* Upper Darby, PA: Project Management Institute, 1996. (A must own, and read, by every project manager.)
13. RAIFFA, H. *The Art and Science of Negotiation.* Cambridge: Belknap/Harvard Press, 1982. (Like [2], this is a classic on the subject of win-win negotiation. Probably the most influential book in its field, and justly so.)
14. SHARPE, P., and T. KEELIN. "How SmithKline Beecham Makes Better Resource-Allocation Decisions." *Harvard Business Review,* March–April 1998. (An excellent process for selecting projects as well as for constructing a project portfolio. The ability to implement the process depends on a fairly sophisticated senior management team.)
15. WHEELWRIGHT, S. C., and K. B. CLARK. "Creating Project Plans to Focus Product Development." *Harvard Business Review,* March–April 1992.

2

The Manager, the Organization, and the Team

Once a project has been selected, the next step is for senior management to choose a project manager (PM). It is the PM's job to make sure that the project is properly planned, implemented, and completed—and these activities will be the subjects of the chapters that follow this one.

While PMs are sometimes chosen prior to a project's selection, the more typical case is that the selection is announced following a meeting between senior management and the prospective PM. This appointment sometimes comes as a complete surprise to the candidate whose only obvious qualification for the job is not being otherwise fully occupied on a task more important than the project [17]. At this meeting, the senior manager describes the project and emphasizes its importance to the parent organization, and also to the future career of the prospective PM. (In the language of the Mafia, "It's an offer you can't refuse.")

After a brief consideration of the project, the PM comes to a tentative decision about what talents and knowledge are apt to be required. The PM then calls a meeting of people who have the requisite talent and knowledge, and the planning begins. This is the *launch meeting*, and we will delay further consideration of it until Chapter 3 in which we take up the planning process in detail. First, we must examine the skills required by the person who will lead a team of individuals to carry out a carefully coordinated set of activities in an organizational setting seemingly designed expressly to prevent cooperation. It is helpful if we make a few mild assumptions to ease the following discussions. First, assume that the project's parent organization is medium- to large-size, and is functionally organized (i.e., organized into functions such as marketing, manufacturing, R&D, human resources, and the like). Further assume that the project has some well-defined components or technologies and that the project's output is being delivered to an arm's-length client. These assumptions are not critical. They merely give a context to our discussions.

Before we proceed, an experienced project manager has suggested that we share with the reader one of her reactions to the materials in this book. To the student or the inexperienced PM, it is the project budgets, the schedules with Gantt charts and PERT/CPM networks, the reports and project management software, and the mysteries of resource allocation to multiple projects that appear to be the meat of the PM's job. But these things are not hard to learn, and once understood can, for the most part, be managed by making appropriate inputs to project management software. The hard part of project management is playing the many roles of the PM. The hard part is negotiating with stubborn functional managers and clients who have their own legitimate axes to grind. The hard part is keeping the peace among project team members each of whom know, and are quick to tell, the proper ways to do things. The hard part is being surrounded by the chaos of trying to run a project in the midst of a confused mass of activity representing the normal business of the organization. These are the things we discuss in this chapter, because *these are the hard parts.*

2.1 THE PM'S ROLES

Facilitator

First, to understand the PM's roles, it is useful to compare the PM with a functional manager. The head of a function such as manufacturing or marketing directs the activities of a well-established unit or department of the firm. Presumably trained or risen from the ranks, the functional manager has expertise in the technology being managed. He is an accountant, or an industrial engineer, or a marketing researcher, or a shop foreman, or a . . . . The functional manager's role, therefore, is mainly that of *supervisor* (literally "overseer"). Because the project's place in the parent organization is often not well defined and does not seem to fit neatly in any one functional division, neither is the PM's place neatly defined. Because projects are multidisciplinary, the PM rarely has technical competence in more than one or two of the several technologies involved in the project. As a result, the PM is not a competent overseer and thus has a different role. The PM is a *facilitator*.

The PM must ensure that those who work on the project have the appropriate knowledge and resources, including that most precious resource, time, to accomplish their assigned responsibilities. The work of a facilitator does not stop with these tasks. For reasons that will be apparent later in this chapter, the project is often beset with conflict—conflict between members of the project team, conflict between the team and senior managers (particularly managers of the functional divisions), conflict with the client and other outsiders. The PM must manage these conflicts by negotiating resolution of them.

Actually, the once sharp distinction between the manager-as-facilitator and the manager-as-supervisor has been softened in recent years. With the slow but steady adoption of the participative management philosophy, the general manager has become more and more like the project manager. In particular, responsibility for the planning and organization of specific tasks is given to the individuals or groups that must perform them, always constrained, of course, by company policy and legality. The manager's responsibility is to make sure that the required resources are available and that the task is properly concluded. The transition from traditional authoritarian management to facilitation continues because facilitation is more effective as a managerial style.

A second important distinction between the PM and the traditional manager is that the former uses the *systems approach* and the latter adopts the *analytical approach* to understanding and solving problems. The analytical approach centers on understanding the bits and pieces in a system. It prompts study of the molecules, then atoms, then electrons, and so forth. The systems approach includes study of the bits and pieces, but also an understanding of how they fit together, how they interact, and how they affect and are affected by their environment. The traditionalist manages his or her group (a *subsystem* of the organization) with a desire to optimize the group's performance. The systems approach manager conducts the group so that it contributes to total system optimization. It has been well demonstrated that if all subsystems are optimized, a condition known as *suboptimization*, the total system is not even close to optimum performance. (Perhaps the ultimate example of suboptimization is "The operation was a success, but the patient died.") We take this opportunity to recommend to you an outstanding book on business, *The Goal*, by Goldratt and Cox [10]. It is an easy-to-read novel and a forceful statement on the power of the systems approach as well as the dangers of suboptimization.

To be successful, the PM must adopt the systems approach. Consider that the project is a system composed of tasks (subsystems) which are, in turn, composed of subtasks, and so on. The system, a project, exists as a subsystem of the larger system, a program, that is a subsystem in the larger system, a firm, which is . . . and so on. Just as the project's objectives influence the nature of the tasks and the tasks influence the nature of the subtasks, so does the program and, above it, the organization influence the nature of the project. To be effective, the PM must understand these influences and their impacts on the project and its deliverables. (For an excellent introduction to systems thinking, see [5 or 21].)

Think for a moment about designing a new airplane—a massive product development project—without knowing a great deal about its power plant, its instrumentation, its electronics, its fuel subsystems—or about the plane's desired mission, the intended takeoff and landing facilities, the intended carrying capacity and intended range. One cannot even start the design process without a clear understanding of the subsystems that might be a part of the plane and the larger systems of which it will be a part as well as those that comprise its environment.

Given a project and a deliverable with specifications that result from its intended use in a larger system within a known or assumed environment, the PM's job is straightforward. Find out what tasks must be accomplished to produce the deliverable. Find out what resources are required and how those resources may be obtained. Find out what personnel are needed to carry out production and where they may be obtained. Find out when the deliverable must be completed. All of which is to say that the PM is responsible for planning, organizing, staffing, budgeting, directing, and controlling the project. In other words, the PM "manages" it. But others, the functional managers for example, will staff the project by selecting the people who will be assigned to work on the project. The functional managers also may develop the technical aspects of the project's design and dictate the technology used to produce it. The logic and illogic of this arrangement will be revisited later in this chapter.

At times, the PM may work for a program manager who closely supervises and second-guesses every decision the PM makes. Such bosses are also quite willing to help by instructing the PM about exactly what to do. This unfortunate condition is known as *micromanagement* and is one of the deadly managerial sins. The PM's boss rationalizes this overcontrol with such statements as "Don't forget, I'm responsible for this project," "This project is very important to the firm," or "I have to keep my eye on everything that goes on around here." Such statements deny the value of delegation and assume that everyone except the boss is incompetent. This overwhelming self-importance practically ensures mediocre performance, if not outright project failure. Any project successes will be claimed by the boss. Failures will be blamed on the subordinate PM.

There is little a PM can do about the "My way or the highway" boss except to polish the résumé or request a transfer. (It is a poor career choice to work for a boss who will not allow you to succeed.) As we will see later in this chapter, the most successful project teams tend to adopt a *collegial style*. Intrateam conflict is minimized, cooperation is the norm, and the likelihood of success is high.

Communicator

The PM must be a person who can handle responsibility. The PM is responsible to the project team, to senior management, to the client, and to anyone else who may have a stake in the project's performance or outcomes. Consider, if you will, the Central Arizona Project (CAP). This public utility moves water from the Colorado River to Phoenix, several other Arizona municipalities, and to some American Indian reservations. The water is transported by a system of aqueducts, reservoirs, pipes, and pumping stations. Besides the routine delivery of water, almost everything done at CAP is a project. Most of the projects are devoted to the construction, repair, and maintenance of their system. Now consider a PM's responsibilities. A maintenance team, for instance, needs resources in a timely fashion so that maintenance can be carried out according to a precise schedule. The PM's clients are municipalities. The drinking public (water, of course) is a highly interested stakeholder. The system is even subject to partisan political turmoil because CAP-supplied water is used as a political football in Tucson.

The PM is in the middle of this muddle of responsibility and must manage the project in the face of all these often-conflicting interests. CAP administration, the project teams, the municipalities (and their Native American counterparts), and the public all communicate with each other —often contentiously.

Figure 2-1 shows the PM's position and highlights the communication problem involved in any project. The solid lines denote the PM's communication channels. The dotted lines denote communication paths for the other parties-at-interest in the project. Problems arise when some of these parties propagate communications that may mislead other parties, or directly conflict with other messages in the system. It is the PM's responsibility to introduce some order into this communication mess.

For example, assume that senior management calls for tighter cost control or even for a cost reduction. The project team may react (screaming or whining) with a complaint that "They want us to cut back on project quality!" The PM must intervene to calm ruffled team feathers and, perhaps, ask a senior manager to reassure the project team that high quality is an organizational objective though not every gear, cog, and cam needs to be gold-plated.

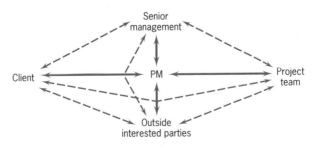

Figure 2-1 Communication paths between a project's parties-at-interest.

Similarly, the client may drop in to check on a project and blithely ask a team member, "Would it be possible to alter the specs to include such-and-such?" The team member may think for a moment about the technical problems involved and then answer quite honestly, "Yeah, that could be done." Again, the PM must intervene—if and when the question and answer come to light—to determine the cost of making such a change, as well as the added time that would be required. The PM must then ask whether the client wishes to alter the project scope given the added cost and delayed delivery. This scenario is so common it has a name, *scope creep*. It is the PM's nightmare.

Virtual Project Manager

More and more often, project teams are geographically dispersed. Many projects are international, and team members may be on different continents, for example, aircraft engine design and engine construction. Many are carried out by different organizations in different locations, for example, the development of composite material automobile bodies or large-scale communication systems. Many are the product of different divisions of one firm where the divisions are in different cities. Geographically dispersed projects are referred to as *virtual projects*—possibly because so much of the communication is conducted by email, through Web sites, by telephone or video conferencing, and other high technology methods. An interesting view of "virtual" people who work in one country but live in another (often on another continent) is given in a *Wall Street Journal* article [8].

Long-distance communication is commonplace and no longer prohibitively expensive. It may, however, be beset with special problems. In the case of written and voice-only communication (and even in video conferencing when the camera is not correctly aimed), the communicators cannot see one another. In such cases we realize how much we depend on feedback—the facial expression and body language that let us know if our messages are received and with what level of acceptance. Two-way, real-time communication is the most effective way to transmit information or instructions. For virtual projects, communication between PM and project team must be frequent, open, and two-way.

The PM's responsibility for communication with senior management poses special problems for any PM without fairly high levels of self-confidence. Formal and routine progress reports aside (cf. Chapter 7), it is the PM's job to keep senior management up to date on the state of the project. It is particularly important that the PM keep management informed of any problems affecting the project—or any problem likely to affect the project in the future. A golden rule for anyone is ***"Never let the boss be surprised!"*** Violations of this rule will cost the PM credibility, trust, and possibly his or her job. Where there is no trust, effective communication ceases. Senior management must be informed about a problem in order to assist in its solution. The timing of this information should be at the earliest point a problem seems likely to occur. Any later is too late. This builds trust between the PM and senior managers. The PM who is trusted by the *project champion* and can count on assistance when organizational clout is needed is twice blessed.

The PM is also responsible to the client. Clients are motivated to stay in close touch with a project they have commissioned. Because they support the project, they feel they have a right to intercede with suggestions (requests, alterations, demands). Cost, schedule, and performance changes are the most common outcome of client intercession, and the costs of these changes often exceed the client's expectations. Note that it is not the PM's job to dissuade the client from changes in the project's scope, but the PM must be certain that the client understands the impact of the changes on the project's goals of delivery time, cost, and performance.

The PM is responsible to the project team just as team members are responsible to the PM. As we will see shortly, it is very common for project team members to be assigned to work on the project, but to report to a superior who is not connected with the project. Thus, the PM will have people working on the project who are not "direct reports." Nonetheless, the relationship between the team and the PM may be closer to boss-subordinate than one might suspect. The reason for this is that both PM and team members often develop a mutual commitment to the project and to its successful conclusion. The PM facilitates the work of the team, and helps them succeed. As we will see in the final chapter, the PM may also take an active interest in fostering team members' future careers. Like any good boss, the PM may serve as advisor, counselor, confessor, and interested friend.

Meetings, Convenor and Chair

The two areas in which the PM communicates most frequently are reports to senior management and instructions to the project team. We discuss management reports in Chapter 7 on monitoring and controlling the project. We also set out some rules for conducting successful meetings in Chapter 7. Communication with the project team typically takes place in the form of project team meetings. When humorist Dave Barry reached 50 years of age, he wrote a column listing 25 things he had learned in his first 50 years of living. Sixteenth on the list is "If you had to identify, in one word, the reason why the human race has not and never will achieve its full potential, that word would be 'meetings'."

Most of the causes of meeting-dread are associated with failure to adopt common sense about when to call meetings and how to run them. As we have said, one of the first things the PM must do is to call a "launch meeting." Make sure that the meeting starts on time and has a prearranged stopping time. As convenor of the meeting, the PM is responsible for taking minutes, and keeping the meeting on track. The PM should also make sure that the invitation to the meeting includes a written agenda. This allows the invitees to come prepared—and they are expected to do so. For some rules on conducting effective meetings that do not result in angry colleagues, see the subsection on meetings in Chapter 7.

> The PM is a facilitator, unlike the traditional manager who is a supervisor. The PM must adopt the systems approach to making decisions and managing projects. Trying to optimize each part of a project, suboptimization, does not produce an optimized project. Multiple communication paths exist in any project and some paths bypass the PM causing problems. Much project communication takes place in meetings that may be run effectively if some simple rules are followed. In virtual projects much communication is via high technology channels. Above all, the PM must keep senior management informed about the current state of the project.

2.2 THE PM'S RESPONSIBILITIES TO THE PROJECT

The PM has three overriding responsibilities to the project. First is the acquisition of resources and personnel. Second is dealing with the obstacles that arise during the course of the project. Third is exercising the leadership needed to bring the project to a successful conclusion and making the trade-offs necessary to do so.

Acquiring Resources

Acquiring resources and personnel is not difficult. Acquiring the necessary quality and quantity of resources and personnel is. Senior management typically suffers from a mental condition known as "irrational optimism." While the disease is rarely painful to anyone except PMs, the suffering among this group may be quite severe.

It has long been known that the further one proceeds up the managerial ladder, the easier, faster, and cheaper a job appears to be compared to the opinion of the person who has to do the work [9]. The result is that the work plan developed by the project team may have its budget and schedule cut and then cut again as the project is checked and approved at successively higher levels of the organization. At times, an executive in the organization will have a strong interest in a pet project. In order to improve the chance that the pet project will be selected, the executive may deliberately (or subconsciously) understate the resource and personnel commitments required by the project. Whatever the cause, it is the PM's responsibility to ensure that the project has the appropriate level of resources. When the project team needs specific resources to succeed, there is no acceptable excuse for not getting them—though there may be temporary setbacks.

When a human resource is needed, the problem is further complicated. Most human resources come to the project on temporary assignment from the functional departments of the organization. The PM's wants are simple—the individual in the organization who is most competent on the specific task to be accomplished. Such individuals are, of course, precisely the people that the functional managers are least happy to release from their departmental jobs for work on the project, either full- or part-time. Those workers the functional manager is prone to offer are usually those whom the PM would least like to have.

Lack of functional manager enthusiasm for cooperation with the project has another source. In many organizations, projects are seen as glamorous, interesting, and high-visibility activities. The functional manager may be jealous or even suspicious of the PM who is perceived to have little or no interest in the routine work that is the bread and butter for the parent organization.

Fighting Fires and Obstacles

Still another key responsibility of the PM is to deal with obstacles. All projects have their crises—fires that must be quenched. The successful PM is also a talented and seasoned fire fighter. Early in the project's life cycle, fires are often linked to the need for resources. Budgets get cut and the general cuts must be transformed into highly specific cuts in the quantities of highly specific resources. An X percent cut must be translated into Y units of this commodity or Z hours of that engineer's time. (An obvious reaction by the PM is to pad the next budget submitted. As we argue in Chapters 4 and 6, this is a bad idea and tends to cause more problems than it solves.)

As work on the project progresses, most fires are associated with technical problems, supplier problems, and client problems. Technical problems occur, for example, when some subsystem (e.g., a computer routine) is supposed to work but fails. A typical supplier problem occurs when subcontracted parts are late or do not meet specifications. Client problems tend to be far more serious. Most often, they begin when the client asks "Would it be possible for this thing to . . .?" Again, scope creep.

Most experienced PMs are good fire fighters. If they do not develop this skill they do not last as PMs. People tend to enjoy doing what they are skilled at doing. Be warned: When you find a skilled fire fighter who fights a lot of fires and enjoys the activity, you may have found an arsonist. At one large, highly respected industrial firm we know, there is a wisecrack commonly made by PMs. "The way to get ahead around here is to get a project, screw it up, and then fix it. If it didn't get screwed up, it couldn't have been very hard or very important." We do not believe that anyone purposely botches projects (or knowingly allows them to be botched). We do, however, suspect that the attitude breeds carelessness because of the belief that they can fix any problem.

Leadership and Making Trade-Offs

In addition to being responsible for acquiring resources for the project and for fighting the project's fires, the PM is also responsible for making the trade-offs necessary to lead the project to a successful conclusion. The issue of trade-offs is a key feature of the remainder of this book. In each of the following chapters and particularly in the chapters on budgeting, scheduling, resource allocation, and control, we will deal with many examples of trade-offs. They will be specific. At this point, however, we should establish some general principles.

The PM is the key figure in making trade-offs between project cost, schedule, and performance. Which of these has higher priority than the others is dependent on many factors having to do with the project, the client, and the parent organization. If cost is more important than time for a given project, the PM will allow the project to be late rather than incur added costs. If a project has successfully completed most of its specifications, and if the client is willing, both time and cost may be saved by not pursuing some remaining specifications. It is the client's choice.

Of the three project goals, performance (specifications and client satisfaction) is usually the most important. Schedule is a close second, and cost is usually subordinate to the other two. Note the word "usually." There are many exceptions and this is another case where the political acuity of the PM is of primary importance. While performance is almost always paramount when dealing with an "arm's-length" client, it is not invariably so for an inside client. If the parent firm has inadequate profits, specifications may be sacrificed for cost savings. Organizational policy may influence trade-offs. Grumman Aircraft (now a part of Northrop-Grumman) had a longstanding policy of on-time delivery. If a Grumman project for an outside client fell behind on its schedule, resources (costs) were added to ensure on-time delivery.

Another type of trade-off occurs between projects. At times, two or more projects may compete for access to the same resources. This is a major subject in Chapter 6, but the upshot is that added progress on one project may be traded off for less progress on another. If a single PM has two projects in the same part of the project life cycle and makes such a trade-off, it does not matter which project wins, the PM will lose. We strongly recommend that any PM managing two or more projects do everything possible to avoid this problem by making sure that the projects are in different phases of their life cycles. We urge this with the same fervor we would urge parents never to act so as to make it appear that one child is favored over another.

Negotiation, Conflict Resolution, and Persuasion

It is not possible for the PM to meet these responsibilities without being a skilled negotiator and resolver of conflict. The acquisition of resources requires negotiation. Dealing with problems, conflict, and fires requires negotiation and conflict resolution. The same skills are needed when the PM is asked to lead the project to a successful conclusion—and to make the trade-offs required along the way.

In Chapter 1 we emphasized the presence of conflict in all projects and the resultant need for win-win negotiation and conflict resolution. A PM without these skills cannot be successful. There is no stage of the project life cycle that is not characterized by specific types of conflict. If these are not resolved, the project will suffer and possibly die. For new PMs, training in win-win negotiation is just as important as training in PERT/CPM, budgeting, project management software, and project reporting. Such training is not merely useful, it is a necessary requirement for success. While an individual who is not (yet) skilled in negotiation may be chosen as PM for a project, the training should start immediately. A precondition is the ability to handle stress. (The bibliography for Chapter 1 contains references on win-win negotiation.)

Projects must be selected for funding, and they begin when senior management has been persuaded that they are worthwhile. Projects almost never proceed through their life cycles without change. Changes in scope are common. Trade-offs may change what deliverable is made, how it is made, and when it is delivered. Success at any of these stages depends on the PM's skill at persuading others to accept the project as well as changes in its methods and scope once it has been accepted. Any suggested change will have supporters and opponents. If the PM suggests a change, others will need to be persuaded that the change is for the better. Senior management must be persuaded to support the change just as the client and the project team may need to be persuaded to accept change in the deliverables or in the project's methods or timing.

Persuasion is rarely accomplished by "my way or the highway" commands. Neither can it be achieved by locker-room motivational speeches. In an excellent article in the *Harvard Business Review* [6], Jay Conger describes the skill of persuasion as having four essential parts: (1) effective persuaders must be credible to those they are trying to persuade; (2) they must find goals held in common with those being persuaded; (3) they must use "vivid" language and compelling evidence; and (4) they must connect with the emotions of those they are trying to persuade. The article is complete with examples of each of the four essential parts.

> The PM is responsible for acquiring the human and material resources needed by the project. The PM is also responsible for exercising leadership, fire fighting, and dealing with obstacles that impede the project's progress. Finally, the PM is responsible for making the trade-offs between budget, schedule, and specifications that are needed to ensure project success. To be successful at meeting these responsibilities, the PM must be skilled at negotiation, conflict resolution, and persuasion.

2.3 SELECTION OF A PROJECT MANAGER

A note to senior management: It is rarely a good idea to select a project manager from a list of engineers (or other technical specialists) who can be spared from their current jobs at the moment. Unfortunately, in many firms this appears to be the primary criterion for choice. We do not argue that current availability is not one among several appropriate criteria, but that it is only one of several—and never the most important. Neither does the list of criteria begin with "Can leap over tall buildings with a single bound."

The most important criterion, by far, is that the prospective PM, in the language of sales people, is a "closer." Find individuals who complete the tasks they are given. As any senior manager knows, hard workers are easy to find. What is rare is an individual who is driven to finish the job. Given a set of such people, select those who meet the following criteria at reasonably high levels.

Credibility

For the PM, credibility is critical. In essence, it means that the PM is believable. There are two areas in which the PM needs believability. The first is *technical credibility*, and the second is *administrative credibility*. The PM is not expected to have an expert's knowledge of each of the technologies that may be germane to the project. The PM should, however, be able to explain the current state of the project, its progress, and its problems to senior management. The PM should also be able to interpret the wishes of management and the client to the project team [11 and 16].

While quite different, administrative credibility is just as significant to the project. For management and the client to have faith in the viability of the project, reports, appraisals, audits, and evaluations must be timely and accurate. For the team, resources, personnel, and knowledge must be available when needed. For all parties, the PM must be able to make the difficult trade-offs that allow the project to meet its objectives as well as possible. This requires mature judgment and considerable courage.

Sensitivity

There is no need to belabor what should, by now, be obvious. The PM needs a finely tuned set of political antennae as well as an equally sensitive sensor of interpersonal conflict between team members, or between team members (including himself or herself) and other parties-at-interest to the project. Also needed are technical sensors that indicate when technical problems are being swept under the rug or when the project is about to fall behind its schedule.

Leadership, Style, Ethics

A leader is someone who indicates to other individuals or groups the direction in which they should proceed. When complex projects are decomposed into a set of tasks and subtasks, it is common for members of the project to focus on their individual tasks, thereby ignoring the project as a whole. This fosters the dreaded suboptimization that we mentioned early in this chapter. Only the PM is in a position to keep team members working toward completion of the whole project rather than its parts. In practice, leaders keep their people energized, enthusiastic, well organized, and well informed. This, in turn, will keep the team well motivated.

At the beginning of this chapter we noted that the PM's role should be facilitative rather than authoritarian. Now let us consider the style with which that role is played. There has been much research on the best managerial style for general management, and it has been assumed that the findings apply to PMs as well. Recent work has raised some questions about this assumption. While there is little doubt that the most effective overall style is participative, Professor Shenhar of the Stevens Institute of Technology adds another dimension to style [22]. He found that as the level of technological uncertainty of a project went from "low tech" to "very high tech," the appropriate management style (while being fundamentally participative) went from "firm" to "highly flexible." In addition, he found that the complexity of the project, ranked from "simple" to "highly complex," called for styles varying from "informal" to "highly formal." To sum up, the more technically uncertain a project, the more flexible the style of management should be. The more complex a project, the more formal the style should be. In this context, flexibility applies primarily to the degree that new ideas and approaches are considered. Formality applies primarily to the degree to which the project operates in a structured environment.

Professor Shenhar's work has the feeling of good sense. When faced with technological uncertainty, the PM must be open to experimentation. In the same way, if a project is highly complex with many parts that must be combined with great care, the PM cannot allow a haphazard approach by the project team. In the end, the one reasonably sure conclusion about an effective management style for PMs is that it must be participative. Autocrats do not make good project managers.

Another aspect of leadership is for the PM to have—and to communicate—a strong sense of ethics. Because projects differ from one to another, there are few standard procedures that can be installed to ensure honest and ethical behavior from all parties-at-interest to the project. One has only to read a daily paper to find examples of kickbacks, bribery, covering up mistakes, use of substandard materials, theft, fraud, and outright lies on project status or performance. Dishonesty on anyone's part should not be permitted in projects. The Project Management Institute (PMI) has developed a Code of Ethics for the profession (see Table 2-1).

> Successful PMs have some common characteristics. They are "closers." They also have high administrative and technical credibility, show sensitivity to interpersonal conflict, and possess the political know-how to get help from senior management when needed. In addition, the PM should be a leader, and adopt a participatory management style that may have to be modified depending on the level of technological sophistication and uncertainty involved in the project. Another critical project management skill is the ability to direct the project in an ethical manner.

2.4 PROJECT MANAGEMENT AS A PROFESSION

It should be obvious to the reader that project management is a demanding job. Planning and controlling the complexities of a project's activities, schedule, and budget would be difficult even if the project had the highest claim on the parent organization's knowledge and resources, and if the PM had full authority to take any action required to keep the project on course for successful completion. Such is never the case, but all is not lost because there are tools available to bring some order to the chaos of life as a PM—to cope with the difficulties of planning and the uncertainties that affect budgets and schedules. Also, as we have indicated, it is possible to compensate for missing authority through negotiation. Mastering the use of project management tools requires specialized knowledge that is often acquired through academic preparation, which is to say that *project management is a profession*. The profession comes complete with career paths and an excellent professional organization.

The Project Management Institute (PMI) was founded in 1969. By 1990 the PMI had 7500 members. It grew to 17,000 by 1995, but five years later, by mid-2000, membership had exploded to more than 64,000. The exponential growth of the PMI is the result of the exponential growth in the use of projects and PMs as a way of getting things done. For example, a senior vice president of an international chemical firm installed project management as a way of controlling the workloads on his technical specialists and on a few overloaded facilities—project management having tools to handle the allocation of scarce resources. In another instance, a new CEO of a large hospital mandated that all nonroutine, one-time operations be managed as projects so that she could have information on the nature and status of all such activities.

Table 2-1 Code of Ethics for the Project Management Profession*

PREAMBLE: Project Management Professionals, in the pursuit of the profession, affect the quality of life for all people in our society. Therefore, it is vital that Project Management Professionals conduct their work in an ethical manner to earn and maintain the confidence of team members, colleagues, employees, employers, clients and the public.

ARTICLE I: Project Management Professionals shall maintain high standards of personal and professional conduct and:
   a. Accept responsibility for their actions.
   b. Undertake projects and accept responsibility only if qualified by training or experience, or after full disclosure to their employers or clients of pertinent qualifications.
   c. Maintain their professional skills at the state of the art and recognize the importance of continued personal development and education.
   d. Advance the integrity and prestige of the profession by practicing in a dignified manner.
   e. Support this code and encourage colleagues and co-workers to act in accordance with this code.
   f. Support the professional society by actively participating and encouraging colleagues and co-workers to participate.
   g. Obey the laws of the country in which work is being performed.

ARTICLE II: Project Management Professionals shall, in their work:
   a. Provide necessary project leadership to promote maximum productivity while striving to minimize cost.
   b. Apply state of the art project management tools and techniques to ensure quality, cost and time objectives, as set forth in the project plan, are met.
   c. Treat fairly all project team members, colleagues and co-workers, regardless of race, religion, sex, age or national origin.
   d. Protect project team members from physical and mental harm.
   e. Provide suitable working conditions and opportunities for project team members.
   f. Seek, accept and offer honest criticism of work, and properly credit the contribution of others.
   g. Assist project team members, colleagues and co-workers in their professional development.

ARTICLE III: Project Management Professionals shall, in their relations with their employers and clients:
   a. Act as faithful agents or trustees for their employers and clients in professional business matters.
   b. Keep information on the business affairs or technical processes of an employer or client in confidence while employed, and later, until such information is properly released.
   c. Inform their employers, clients, professional societies or public agencies of which they are members or to which they may make any presentations, of any circumstances that could lead to a conflict of interest.
   d. Neither give nor accept, directly or indirectly, any gift, payment or service of more than nominal value to or from those having business relationships with their employers or clients.
   e. Be honest and realistic in reporting project quality, cost and time.

ARTICLE IV: Project Management Professionals shall, in fulfilling their responsibilities to the community:
   a. Protect the safety, health and welfare of the public and speak out against abuses in these areas affecting the public interest.
   b. Seek and extend public knowledge and appreciation of the project management profession and its achievements.

Source: Project Management Institute.

In recent years, a new kind of organization has emerged—the *project-oriented organization* (a.k.a. "management of projects" [4], "enterprise project management" [15], and similar names). In these firms all nonroutine activities are organized as projects. In addition, the process of instituting change in routine operations is also commonly organized as a project. The motives behind this approach to handling change are the same as those motivating the chemical firm VP and the hospital CEO, the need to control and to have information about what is happening in the organization.

To establish standards for project management and to foster professionalism in the field, the PMI has codified the areas of learning required to manage projects. This *Pro-*

ject Management Body of Knowledge (PMBOK) has been compiled into a book published by the PMI and serves as a basis for practice and education in the field [20]. The PMI also publishes two important periodicals: first, the *Project Management Journal,* oriented to project management theory, though its articles are almost uniformly related to the actual practice of project management; and second, the *PM Network* magazine, which is a trade journal aimed at practitioners. Both publications are valuable for the experienced PM as well as the neophyte or student.

The fantastic variety of projects being conducted today ranges from esoteric research on gene identification to routine maintenance of machine tools. On one page of a daily newspaper (*USA Today,* September 29, 1999, p. 3A), we find the following: Goodwill Industries hiring 10,000 people to help compile the 2000 Census for a project funded by the U.S. Department of Commerce; the state of Florida, together with Miami-Dade county, creating a project to preserve an ancient stone circle believed to have been carved by the Tequesta Indians; New York city approval of a Donald Trump project to build the world's tallest residential building. There are several other projects reported on this page and throughout the rest of the paper.

Opportunities for careers in project management abound, but where can people competent to manage projects be found, or how can they be trained? A rapidly growing number of colleges, universities, and technical institutes have developed courses and degree programs in project management. It is still true, however, that a majority of people currently managing projects have no formal training except for occasional project management seminars and workshops lasting from one-half day to two weeks. In recent years, many local chapters of the PMI have also offered training programs of varying length and depth. On-the-job training and coaching by experienced PMs is still the primary source of learning for the beginner.

The career path for the PM usually starts with work on a small project, and then on some larger projects. If the individual survives life as a project worker, graduation to the next level comes in the form of duty as a "project engineer" or as a "deputy" PM for a project. Then comes duty as the manager of a small project, and then as PM of larger ones. All of this, of course, presumes a track record of success.

> A professional organization, the Project Management Institute (PMI) has been devoted to project management. The growth in the field has been exponential. Among other reasons for this growth is the project-oriented organization. The PMI has published the *Project Management Body of Knowledge* (PMBOK). It also publishes two professional periodicals. Many courses and degree programs in project management are available.

2.5 FITTING PROJECTS INTO THE PARENT ORGANIZATION

Earlier in this chapter we referred several times to problems caused by the way projects are organized as a part of the parent organization. It is now time to deal with this subject. It would be most unusual for a PM to have any influence over the interface between the project and the parent organization. This arrangement is a matter of company policy and usually is decided by senior management. The nature of the interface, however, has a major impact on the PM's life, and it is necessary that the PM understand why senior managers make what appears to be the worst of all possible choices for the interface.

More on "Why Projects?"

Before examining the alternative ways in which a project can interface with the organization, it is useful to add to our understanding of just why organizations choose to conduct so much of their work as projects. We spoke above of project-oriented firms. In addition to the managerial reasons that caused the rapid spread of such organizations, there were also strong economic reasons. First, devising product development programs by integrating product design, engineering, manufacturing, and marketing functions in one team not only improved the product, it also allowed significant cuts in the *time-to-market* for the product. For example, Chrysler (now Daimler-Chrysler) cut almost 18 months from the new product development time required for design-to-street and produced designs that have been widely rated as outstanding. This brought the LH sedans (as well as Chrysler's small car, the Neon, and their sport car, the Viper) to market much faster than normal in the automotive industry. Quite apart from the value of a fine design, the economic value of the time saved is immense and derives from both reduced design labor and overhead, plus earlier sales and return on the investment—in this case amounting to hundreds of millions of dollars. This same process also allows a firm to tailor special versions of standard products for individual clients. We will have more to say about this process at the end of this chapter.

Second, the product development/design process requires input from different areas of specialized knowledge. The exact mix of knowledge varies from product to product or service to service. Teams of specialists can be formed, do their work, and disband. The make-up of such teams can easily be augmented or changed.

Third, the explosive expansion of technical capabilities in almost every area of the organization tends to destabilize the structure of the enterprise. Consider almost any industry. It has gone through the earthquakes of changed technology, revamped software systems, altered communication systems, followed by mergers, downsizing, spin-offs, and other catastrophes—all of which require system-wide responsiveness. Traditional organizations cannot handle rapid, large-scale change, but project organizations can.

Last, like our hospital CEO, many upper-level managers we know lack confidence in their ability to cope with and respond to such large-scale, rapid change in their organizations. Organizing these changes as projects gives the managers some sense of accountability and control.

All these factors fostered the expanded use of projects, but traditional ways of organizing projects were too costly and too slow, largely because of how they linked to the parent firm. In the years following World War II, projects came into common use. Most of the early projects were created to solve large-scale government problems, many of which were related to national defense—the building of an intercontinental ballistic missile, the construction of an interstate highway system, the development and deployment of a missile defense system, and similar massive projects [13]. At the same time, private industry tentatively began to use projects to develop new medicinal drugs, larger and faster commercial airliners, large-scale computing machines, shopping malls, and apartment complexes with hundreds of units. All such projects had several things in common: they were large, complex, and often required the services of hundreds of people. The natural way to organize such projects is what came to be known as the *pure project organization*.

Pure Project Organization

Consider the construction of a football stadium or a shopping mall. Assume that the land has been acquired and the design approved. Having won a competitive bid, a contractor assigns a project manager and a team of construction specialists to the project.

Each specialist, working from the architectural drawings, develops a set of plans to deal with his or her particular specialty area. One may design and plan the electrical systems, another the mechanicals, still another the parking and landscaping, and so forth. In the meantime, someone is arranging for the timely delivery of cranes, earth movers, excavation equipment, lumber, cement, brick, and other materials. And someone is hiring a suitable number of local construction workers with the appropriate skills. See Figure 2-2 for a typical pure project organization.

The supplies and equipment and workers arrive when they are needed (in a perfect world), do the work, complete the project, and disband. The PM is, in effect, the CEO of the project. When the project is completed, accepted by the client, equipment returned, and local workers paid off, then the PM and the specialists return to their parent firm and await the next job.

For large projects, the pure project organization is effective and efficient, but for small projects it is a very expensive way to operate. In the preceding example, we assumed that there was always work for each member of the labor force. On a very large project, that assumption is approximately true. On a small project, the normal ebb and flow of work is not evened out as it is on large projects with a large number of workers. On small projects, therefore, it is common to find personnel shortages one week and overages the next. Second, on small projects the human resources person or the accountant is rarely needed full-time. Often such staff persons may be needed one-quarter or one-half time; but humans do not come in fractions. They are always integers. Remember also that pure projects are often carried out at some distance from the home office, and a quarter-time accountant cannot go back to the home office when work on the project slacks off. Part-time workers are not satisfactory either. They never seem to be on site when they are needed.

There are other drawbacks to the pure project. While they have a broad range of specialists, they have limited technological depth. If the project's resident specialist in a given area of knowledge happens to be lacking in a specific subset of that area, the project must hire a consultant, add another specialist, or do without. If the parent organization has several concurrent projects drawing on the same specialty areas, they develop fairly high levels of duplication in these specialties. This is expensive.

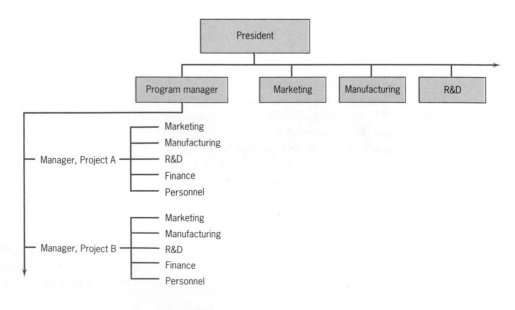

Figure 2-2 Pure project organization.

There are other problems, and one of the most serious is seen in R&D projects or in projects that have fairly long lives. People assigned to the project tend to form strong attachments to it. The project begins to take on a life of its own. A disease called "projectitis" develops. One pronounced symptom is worry about "Is there life after the project?" Foot dragging as the project end draws near is common, as is the submission of proposals for follow-up projects in the same area of interest—and, of course, using the same project team.

Functional Project Organization

Some projects have a very different type of structure. Assume, for example, that a project is formed to install a new production machine in an operating production line. The project includes the removal of the old machine and the integration of the new machine into the production system. In such a case, we would probably organize the project as an appendage to the Manufacturing division where the production system is located. Figure 2-3 shows a typical example of functional project organization.

Quite unlike pure projects that are generally separated from the day-to-day operations of the parent organization, functionally organized projects are embedded in the functional group where the project will be used. This immediately corrects some of the problems associated with pure projects. First, the functional project has immediate, direct, and complete contact with the most important technologies it may need, and it has in-depth access. Second, the fractional resource problem is minimized for anyone working in the project's home functional group. Functionally organized projects do not have the high personnel costs associated with pure projects because they can easily assign people to the project on a part-time basis. Finally, even projectitis will be minimal because the project is not removed from the parent organization and specialists are not divorced from their normal career tracks.

There are, however, two major problems with functionally organized projects. First, communications across functional department boundaries are rarely as simple as most firms think they are. When technological assistance is needed from another division, it may or may not be forthcoming on a timely basis. Technological depth is certainly present, but technological breadth is missing. The same problem exists with communication outside the function. In the pure project, communication lines are short and messages move rapidly. This is particularly important when the client is sending or receiving messages. In most functionally organized projects, the lines of communication to people or units outside the functional division are slow and tortuous. Traditionally, messages are not to be sent outside the division without clearing through the division's senior management. Insisting that project communications follow the organizational

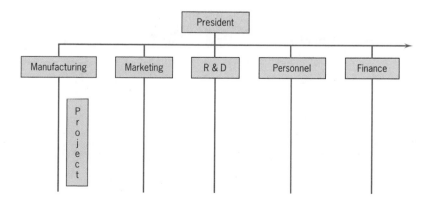

Figure 2-3
Functional project
organization.

chain of command imposes impossible delays on most projects. It most certainly impedes frank and open communication between project team members and the project client.

Another major problem besets functionally organized projects. The project is rarely a high-priority item in the life of the division. The task of Manufacturing is to produce product. The job of Marketing is to sell. Manufacturing may have a sincere interest in a new machine or Marketing in a new product, but those projects do not make "here and now" contributions to the major objectives of the divisions. We have already noted the tendency of managers to focus on short-run goals. After all, managerial bonuses are usually linked to short-run performance. Given this bias, functionally organized projects often get short shrift from their sponsoring divisions.

Matrix Project Organization

In an attempt to capture the advantages of both the pure project and the functionally organized project as well as to avoid the problems associated with each type, a new type of project organization—more accurately, a combination of the two—was developed. To form a matrix organized project, a pure project is superimposed on a functionally organized system as in Figure 2-4. The PM reports to a program manager or a vice-president of projects or some senior individual with a similar title whose job it is to coordinate the activities of several or all of the projects. These projects may or may not be related, but they all demand the parent's resources and the use of resources must be coordinated, if not the projects themselves. This method of organizing the interface between projects and the parent organization succeeds in capturing the major advantages of both pure and functional projects. It does, however, create some problems that are unique to this matrix form. To understand both the advantages and disadvantages, we will examine matrix management more closely.

As the figure illustrates, there are two distinct levels of responsibility in a matrix organization. First, there is the normal functional hierarchy that runs vertically in the figure and consists of the regular departments such as marketing, finance, manufacturing, human resources, and so on. (We could have illustrated a bank or university or an enterprise organized on some other principle. The departmental names would differ, but the structure of the system would be the same.) Second, there are horizontal structures, the projects that overlay the functional departments and, presumably, have some access to the functional department's competencies. Heading up these horizontal projects are the project managers.

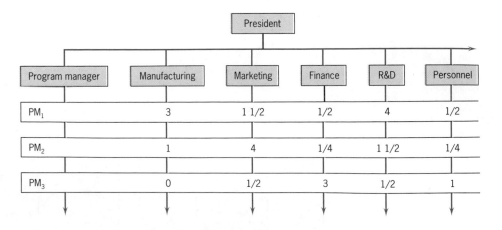

Figure 2-4   Matrix project organization.

	Program manager	Manufacturing	Marketing	Finance	R&D	Personnel
PM$_1$		3	1 1/2	1/2	4	1/2
PM$_2$		1	4	1/4	1 1/2	1/4
PM$_3$		0	1/2	3	1/2	1

A close examination of Figure 2-4 shows some interesting details. Project 1 has assigned to it three people from the Manufacturing division, one and one-half from Marketing, a half-time person from Finance, four from R&D, and one-half from Personnel, plus an unknown number from other divisions not shown in the figure. Other projects have different make-ups of people assigned. This is typical of projects that have different objectives. Project 2, for example, appears to be aimed at the development of a new product with its concentration of Marketing representation, plus significant assistance from R&D, representation from Manufacturing, and staff assistance from Finance and Personnel. The PM controls what these people do and when they do it. The head of a functional group controls who from the group is assigned to the project and what technology is appropriate for use on the project.

We can disregard the problems raised by the split authority for the moment and concentrate on the strong points of this arrangement. Because there are many possible combinations of the pure project and the functional project, the matrix project may have some characteristics of each organizational type. If the matrix project closely resembles the pure project with many individuals assigned full-time to the project, it is referred to as a "strong" matrix or a "project" matrix. If, on the other hand, functional departments assign resource capacity to the project rather than people, the matrix is referred to as a "weak" matrix or a "functional" matrix. The project might, of course, have some people and some capacity assigned to it, in which case it is sometimes referred to as a "balanced" matrix. (The *Random House Unabridged Dictionary* defines "balanced" as "being in harmonious or proper arrangement . . ." In no way does the balanced matrix qualify as "balanced.") None of the terms—strong, weak, balanced—is precise, and matrix projects may be anywhere along the continuum from strong to weak. It may even be stronger or weaker at various times during the project's life.

The primary reason for choosing a strong or weak matrix depends on the needs of both the project and the various functional groups. If the project is likely to require complex technical problem solving, it will probably have the appropriate technical specialists assigned to it. If the project's technology is less demanding, it will be a weaker matrix that is able to draw on a functional group's capacity when needed. A firm manufacturing household oven cleaners might borrow chemists from the R&D department to develop cleaning compounds that could dissolve baked-on grease. The project might also test whether such products were toxic to humans by using the capacity of the firm's Toxicity Laboratory rather than having individual toxicity testers assigned to the project team.

One of the most important strengths of the matrix form is this flexibility in the way it can interface with the parent organization. Because it is, or can be, connected to any and all of the parent organization's functional units, it has access to any and all of the parent organization's technology. The way it utilizes the services of the several technical units need not be the same for each unit. This allows the functional departments to optimize their contributions to any project. They can meet a project's needs in a way that is most efficient. Being able to share expertise with several projects during a limited time period makes the matrix arrangement far less expensive than the pure project with its duplication of competencies, and just as technologically "deep" as the functional project. The matrix has a strong focus on the project itself just as does the pure project. In this, it is clearly superior to the functional project that often is subordinate to the regular work of the functional group. In general, matrix organized projects have the advantages of both pure and functional projects. For the most part, they avoid the major disadvantages of each. Close contact with functional groups tends to mitigate "projectitis." Individuals involved with matrix projects are never far from their home department and do not develop the detached feelings that sometimes strike those involved with pure projects.

With all their advantages, matrix projects have their own, unique problems. By far the most significant of these is the violation of an old dictum of the military and of management theory, the Unity of Command principle: For each subordinate, there shall be one, and only one, superior. In matrix projects, the individual specialist borrowed from a function has two bosses. The PM is in charge of what the individual does and when it is done. Functional managers decide who will work on the project, and what specific technologies will be used to complete the project's tasks. The project manager may control which tasks the specialist undertakes, but the specialist reports to a functional manager who makes decisions about the specialist's performance evaluation, promotion, and salary. Thus, project workers are often faced with conflicting orders from the PM and the functional manager. The result is conflicting demands on their time and activities. The project manager is in charge of the project, but the functional manager is usually superior to the PM on the firm's organizational chart, and may have far more political clout in the parent organization. Life on a matrix project is rarely comfortable for anyone, PM or worker.

As we have said, in matrix organizations the PM controls administrative decisions and the functional heads control technological decisions. This distinction is simple enough when writing about project management, but for the operating PM the distinction, and partial division of authority and responsibility, is complex indeed. The ability of the PM to negotiate anything from resources to technical assistance to delivery dates is a key contributor to project success. As we have said before and will certainly say again, success is doubtful for a PM without strong negotiating skills.

While the ability to balance time, cost, and performance between several projects is an advantage of matrix organization, that ability has its dark side. The organization's full set of projects must be carefully monitored by the program manager, a tough job. Further, the movement of resources from project to project in order to satisfy the individual schedules of the multiple projects may foster political infighting among the several PMs. As usual, there are no winners in these battles. Naturally, each PM is more interested in ensuring success for his or her individual project than in maintaining general organization-wide goals. In Chapter 1 we discussed some of the issues involved in aggregate planning, and we will have much more to say on this matter in Chapter 6.

Intrateam conflict is a characteristic of all projects, but the conflicts seem to us to be particularly numerous and contentious in matrix projects. In addition to conflicts arising from the split authority and from the violation of Unity of Command, another major source of conflict appears to be inherent in the nature of the transdisciplinary teams in a matrix setting. Functional projects have such teams, but team members have a strong common interest, their common functional home. Pure projects have transdisciplinary teams, but the entire team is full-time and committed to the project. Matrix project teams are transdisciplinary, but team members are often not full-time, have different functional homes, and have other commitments than the project. They are often committed to their functional area or to their career specialty, rather than to the project.

A young man of our acquaintance works one-quarter time on each of two projects and half-time in his functional group, the mechanical engineering group in an R&D division. He estimates that approximately three-quarters of the time he is expected to be in two or more places at the same time. He indicated that this is normal.

With all its problems, there is no real choice about project organization for most firms. Functional projects are too limited and too slow. Pure projects are far too expensive. Matrix projects are both effective and efficient. They are here to stay, conflict and all.

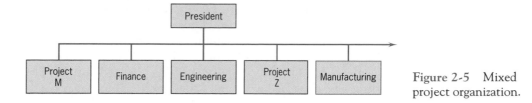

Figure 2-5   Mixed project organization.

Mixed Organizational Systems

Functional, matrix, and pure projects exist side by side in some organizations (see Figure 2-5). In reality, they are never quite as neatly defined as they appear here. Matrix or functional projects may be organized, become very successful and expand into pure projects. It may not stop there, with the pure project growing into an operating division of the parent firm, perhaps becoming a subsidiary or even a stand-alone, venture firm. There are many such cases (e.g., Texas Instruments and the Speak and Spell toy developed by one of its employees).

The ability to organize projects to fit the needs of the parent firm has allowed projects to be used under conditions that might be quite difficult were project organization constrained to one or two specific forms. As the hybridization increases, though, the firm risks increasing the level of conflict in and between projects because of duplication, overlapping authority, and increased friction between project and functional management.

The Project Staff Office

There is another way of solving some of the problems of choosing one or another organizational form for projects. The parent organization can set up a project staff office, more or less like a functional group. This group acts as staff to all projects [2, 3]. The project office may handle some or all of the budgeting, scheduling, and reporting activities while the functional units supply the technical work. This approach is useful when the system operates many small projects with short lives. For example, facility maintenance projects may be operated this way. Maintenance team leaders act as PMs, and the project office keeps the records and makes reports. Because the teams are semipermanent groups, they develop techniques for working together and often specialize in specific types of maintenance problems. Reports and records are standardized, and the system has few of the administrative problems of many maintenance systems.

At times the project office is effective, and at times it is not. Based on limited observation, it appears to us that the system works well when the functional specialists have fairly routine projects. If this is not the case, the team must be involved in generating the project's budget, schedule, and specifications, and kept well informed about the progress of the project measured against its goals. Some years ago, a large pharmaceutical firm used a similar arrangement on R&D projects, the purpose being to "protect" their scientists from having to deal with project schedules, budgets, and progress reports, all of which were handled by the project office. The scientists were not even bothered with having to read the reports. The result was precisely what one might expect. All projects were late and over budget—very late and far over budget.

> The rapid growth in the use of projects has made the traditional ways of creating an interface between projects and the parent organization inadequate in many cases. Pure project organizations, unless very large, are too costly and

lack technological depth. Functionally organized projects lack technological breadth, are slow to act, and have other faults. Linking the two forms into matrix organized projects combines the strengths of the traditional forms and avoids most of their weaknesses. It has severe problems of its own, however, caused by split responsibility for the project with the PM controlling what must be done and when, and the functional manager controlling who will do things and how. It also violates the principle of Unity of Command. Some organizations operate all three types of projects simultaneously. A project management office may be set up to achieve consistent project administration when the firm is operating a number of differently organized projects.

2.6 THE PROJECT TEAM

We have mentioned the project team several times in the foregoing sections. Effective team members have some characteristics in common. Only the first of these is usually taken into account.

1. They must be *technically competent*. This is so obvious that it is often the only criterion applied. While the functional departments will always remain the ultimate source of technological problem solving for the project, it requires a technically competent person to know exactly when additional technical knowledge may be required by the project.

2. Senior members of the project team must be *politically sensitive*. It is rarely possible to complete a project of reasonable size and complexity without incurring problems that require aid from the upper echelons of executive row; that is, from a *project champion* [18]. Getting such aid depends on the PM's ability to proceed without threatening, insulting, or bullying important people in the functional groups. To ensure cooperation and assistance, there is a delicate balance of power that must be maintained between the project and the functional departments, and between one project and others.

3. Members of the project team need a strong *problem orientation*. This characteristic will be explained in more detail shortly. For now, take the phrase to mean that the team's members should be concerned about solving any problems posed by the project, not merely about those subproblems that concern their specific academic or technical training.

4. Team members need a strong *goal orientation*. Projects are uncomfortable environments for people with a 9-to-5 view of work. In particular, PMs cannot succeed if their focus is on activity rather than results. One project team member of our acquaintance was bemoaning a series of 60+ hour weeks. "They told me that I would work about 50 hours in an average week. I've been on this project almost 18 months, and we haven't had an average week yet."

5. Project workers need *high self-esteem*. Project members who hide mistakes and failure are disasters waiting to happen. Team members must be sufficiently self-confident that they can immediately acknowledge their own errors and point out problems caused by the errors of others. PMs should note that "shooting the messenger" who brings bad news will instantly stop the flow of negative information. The result is that the golden rule we stated above, "Never let the boss be surprised," will be violated, too.

Gathering such a team is a nontrivial job. If it is done well, motivation of team members is rarely a problem. Remember that the functional managers control the pay and promotion of project workers in a matrix system. Fortunately, it has been shown that a sense of achievement, growth, learning, responsibility, and the work itself are strong motivators, and the project is a high-visibility source of these [12].

In a large project, the PM will have a number of "assistant managers" on the project team—a senior engineer, field manager, contract administrator, support services manager, and several other individuals who can help the PM determine the project's needs for staff and resources. (In the next chapter we will see precisely how the staff and resource requirements are determined.) They can also help to manage the project's schedule, budget, and technical performance. For a large project, such assistance is necessary. For a small project the PM will probably play all these roles.

Matrix Team Problems

The smaller the project, the more likely it is to be organized as a weak (functional) matrix. In such projects the PM may have no direct reports. The PM contracts with functional managers for capacity, but often knows most of the individuals who are doing the actual work. Thus, the PM can usually communicate directly with project workers, even in the weakest of matrices. In the case of small projects, this ability to communicate directly with members of the project team (even though they are not officially a team at all) is important. It is the only way the PM can keep the project a coordinated effort and on course. Again, the ability to communicate with and direct functional specialists working on project tasks is dependent on the PM's ability to negotiate with the functional manager. Actually, the negotiation is not too difficult because the PM is tacitly taking responsibility to direct the workers' performance. If the PM is getting good performance from the functional specialists, this relieves the functional manager of some responsibility and accountability.

For matrix projects, it is particularly important to maintain good morale for the few project workers that may be assigned to the team. A project office (a.k.a. a project "war room") is helpful, serving as a control center, conference room for project meetings, a coffee shop, technical discussion center, and crisis center. Earlier in this chapter, we noted the use of a project staff office with a purpose of supplying the project with administrative assistance. The war room may also provide such a purpose, but its ability to serve as a focal point for project team activity and heighten the project's *esprit de corps* makes a significant contribution to matrix projects. The Walt Disney Co. sets up division-wide project war rooms and expects the PMs, the functional managers, and the division executive team to use the war room to stay abreast of project timelines and to identify areas of organizational impact on the project or vice versa.

A number of factors make matrix project teams unusually difficult to manage. Such teams are seen by their members to be temporary so the tendency to develop team loyalty is limited. The technical specialists working on the teams are often perfectionists and have a strong desire to keep tinkering with a project deliverable that already meets the client's specifications and expectations. While project managers usually blame the client for scope creep, it is not uncommon for the project team to be the primary cause. The principal source of management problems for the PM, however, is the level of conflict in project teams.

Intrateam Conflict

Conflict is no stranger to any workplace, but matrix projects seem to have far more than their share. The causes are many, but in 1975 Thamhain and Wilemon published their research on conflict in projects and this work remains absolutely relevant today [23].

They identified several different sources of conflict and noted that the sources seemed to differ when the project was in different stages of its life cycle. They also made some recommendations for dealing with the conflicts. These are shown in Table 2-2. Table 2-3 shows the relative frequency of the various sources of conflict.

A reading of the recommendations Thamhain and Wilemon made for reducing or preventing these conflicts reveals four common threads: (1) many of the recommendations feature careful project planning; (2) many are based on the practice of participative management; (3) many require interaction and negotiation between the PM and the functional departments; and (4) there is great emphasis on communication between the PM and all parties-at-interest to the project. Our next chapter is devoted to careful project planning, and we have already discussed the need for negotiation and communication. Participative management is a requirement for proper project planning, and it will be covered in the project-planning chapter. We will continue to mention, if not belabor, these four themes throughout the rest of this book.

Certain aspects of the data in Table 2-3 are significant. Schedules are a major source of conflict throughout the project's life. Priorities are a close second, particularly

Table 2-2 Major Sources of Conflict During Various Stages of the Project Life Cycle*

| Life Cycle Phase | Conflict Source | Major Conflict Source and Recommendations for Minimizing Dysfunctional Consequences |
		Recommendations
Project formation	Priorities	Clearly defined plans. Joint decision making and/or consultation with affected parties. Stress importance of project to organization goals.
	Procedures	Develop detailed administrative operating procedures to be followed in conduct of project.
		Secure approval from key administrators.
		Develop statement of understanding or charter.
	Schedules	Develop schedule commitments in advance of actual project commencement.
		Forecast other departmental priorities and possible impact on project.
Buildup phase	Priorities	Provide effective feedback to support areas on forecasted project plans and needs via status review sessions.
	Schedules	Schedule work breakdown packages (project subunits) in cooperation with functional groups.
	Procedures	Contingency planning on key administrative issues.
Main program	Schedules	Continually monitor work in progress.
		Communicate results to affected parties.
		Forecast problems and consider alternatives.
		Identify potential trouble spots needing closer surveillance.
	Technical	Early resolution of technical problems.
		Communication of schedule and budget restraints to technical personnel.
		Emphasize adequate, early technical testing.
		Facilitate early agreement on final designs.
	Labor	Forecast and communicate staffing requirements early.
		Establish staffing requirements and priorities with functional and staff groups.
Phaseout	Schedules	Close schedule monitoring in project life cycle.
		Consider reallocation of available staff to critical project areas prone to schedule slippages.
		Attain prompt resolution of technical issues which may affect schedules.
	Personality and labor	Develop plans for reallocation of people upon project completion.
		Maintain harmonious working relationships with project team and support groups. Try to loosen up high-stress environment.

*Source: [23].

Table 2-3 Number of Conflicts During a Sample Project*

Sources of Conflict	Phase of Project				Total
	Start	Early	Main	Late	
Project priorities	27	35	24	16	102
Admin. procedures	26	27	15	9	77
Technical trade-offs	18	26	31	11	86
Staffing	21	25	25	17	88
Support cost estimates	20	13	15	11	59
Schedules	25	29	36	30	120
Personalities	16	19	15	17	67
Total	**153**	**174**	**161**	**111**	

*Source: [23].

in the first two stages of the project's life. Because the distinction between the project's "start" and the "early" phase of its life is probably unclear, we can lump them together for the observation that a lion's share of the conflicts will come near the beginning of the project—and the PM must be prepared to deal with them.

Certain aspects of the data in Table 2-3 seem significant. Schedules are a major source of conflict throughout the project's life. Priorities are a close second, particularly in the first two stages of the project's life. Because the distinction between the project's "start" and the "early" phase of its life is not apt to be clear, we can lump them together for the observation that a lion's share of the conflicts will come near the beginning of the project—and the PM had better be prepared to deal with them.

One should not get the idea that conflict in the project team is all bad. Intrateam conflict often enhances team creativity. Out of arguments about competing good ideas come better ideas. For this to happen, however, parties to the conflict must be more interested in solving the problems at hand than they are about winning a victory for "their side." As we have already noted, some people are discipline oriented and others are problem oriented. Discipline-oriented individuals form what one writer calls a "NOT" (Name-Only Team), which he defines as a group of individuals working independently [7]. The intrateam conflict caused by such people is usually perceived to be "interpersonal" or "political." If such conflicts are the major force in project decisions, the project is apt to have problems. Again, we emphasize our earlier advice to the PM to recruit problem-oriented team members whenever possible.

A great deal has been written about conflict resolution as well as about negotiation (see [7] for example). Those two literatures have much in common. Both make it clear that the key to resolving conflict lies in the mediator's ability to transform win-lose situations into win-win solutions. This is also true when the mediator (usually the PM) is one of the parties to the conflict. One of the most important things a PM can do is develop sensitivity for conflict and then intervene at the earliest chance. Conflict avoidance, while it may appear to provide short-term comfort, is never a useful course of action for the PM.

Interpersonal conflict, unfortunately, never stays interpersonal. It impacts on the relationships between various groups and spills over to affect the ways in which these groups cooperate or fail to cooperate with each other. This, in turn, affects the ability of the PM to keep the project on course. The most difficult aspect of managing a project is the coordination and integration of its various elements so that they meet their joint goals of performance, schedule, and budget in such a way that the total project meets its goals.

When the project is complex, involving input and work from several departments or groups and possibly other contributions from several outside contractors, the intricate process of coordinating the work and timing of these inputs is difficult. When the groups are in conflict, the process is almost impossible. The task of bringing the work of all these groups together to make a harmonious whole is called *integration management*, (a.k.a. *systems engineering*). The job of managing this work across multiple groups is called *interface coordination* (a.k.a. *interface management*). Both integration management and interface management are deferred until Chapter 3 because they are critical to high-quality project planning and best understood as a part of the planning process as carried out by transdisciplinary teams.

> A PM should strive to acquire project team members who are technically competent, politically sensitive, problem- and goal oriented, and have high self-esteem. On small projects with a matrix organization, the project may be supplied with functional capacity, rather than full- or part-time people to do the work. It is important for the PM to establish good communication with the people doing the work. A project war room will help with coordination and morale. Intrateam conflict is common on matrix projects. Different sources of conflict occur at differing stages of the project's life cycle. Careful planning, participative management, win-win negotiation with functional groups, and open communication between all parties will help resolve conflict.

We hope that nothing in this chapter has made the PM's job seem simple. The best descriptor we can apply is "messy." The PM is surrounded by conflict and usually trapped in an irrational management structure, matrix management. It is most certainly a high-stress occupation. Why on earth would any sane person select such a risky and demanding profession by choice? Perhaps because it is demanding, and because it is risky, and because when the PM has finished a job, has completed the project on time, on budget, and on specification, there is such a powerful sense of achievement. In many managerial jobs the only way that one knows one has done good work is when the boss says so—and bosses often forget to make such statements. PMs know when they have done good work. Managing a project is a high-visibility task, complete with high rewards, but it is no place for managerial wimps.

It is now time to consider planning.

REVIEW QUESTIONS

1. Explain why the systems approach is necessary to manage projects.

2. Can you think of any other desirable characteristics for team members than those listed in Section 2.6?

3. Explain the meaning and implications of "projectitis."

4. Review the chapter and make a list of all the advantages and disadvantages of matrix project organization you can find. Then add to the list any additional advantages or disadvantages that may have occurred to you.

5. What is meant by "micromanagement?" Why is it such a managerial sin?

6. List five reasons to organize a new product development project as a functionally organized project in the parent firm's Marketing department.

7. List five reasons to organize a new product development project as a transdisciplinary, matrix-organized project.

8. Exactly why were projects in the pharmaceutical company mentioned at the end of Section 2.5 always late and over budget?

9. Why would the members of a "NOT" work independently if they were members of a designated team? What does "independently" mean in this context?

DISCUSSION QUESTIONS

10. The chapter mentions that regular functional managers are moving from their classic authoritarian style to a facilitative, participatory style because it is more effective. Do you think it took managers 200 years to learn that, or is something else driving the change?

11. There is danger in letting the client "visit" the project operation too frequently, not the least of which is "scope creep" or informal change to the project's performance specifications. What other dangers might arise? How might the danger of scope creep be monitored and controlled?

12. How should a PM decide which problems (or potential problems) deserve being reported to management and which are not worth the trouble when attempting to "never surprise the boss?"

13. Discuss how you would go about getting competent staff from a functional department.

14. Another trade-off PMs have to make is between team process and progress—the purpose being to keep the peace, give the team an occasional rest, protect the larger organization or other projects, and so on. What might happen if the PM does not anticipate these trade-offs?

15. Usually projects involving high levels of technological uncertainty are quite complex. Yet Shenhar says to use a *flexible* management style with high-uncertainty projects, but a formal style with complex projects. Explain.

16. In many project-oriented organizations, even routine processes are treated as projects. Why do you think this happened? How is it accomplished?

17. A matrix organization is difficult to manage all by itself. What do you think the problems would be in managing mixed organizational systems?

18. Can you think of any circumstances where deferring conflict might be a wise course of action?

19. Give an example of a case in which project management could be important in your personal life. Explain why, as well as how and why you might organize such a project.

INCIDENTS FOR DISCUSSION

Frankson Inc.

Harold Frankson is the CEO of Frankson Inc., a privately owned, medium size manufacturing company. The company is 17 years old, and until recently has experienced rapid growth. Mr. Frankson credits the depressed Asian economy with his company's recent problems.

Six months ago Mr. Frankson hired Elizabeth Baresak as the director of corporate planning for the company. After reviewing the company's financial statements and performance records for the last few years, Ms. Baresak came to the conclusion that the Asian economy was not the real problem impacting Frankson's recent performance. Ms. Baresak felt that the Frankson Company's products were out of date and the company had not done a good job of responding to their market. She found examples of the company not moving quickly enough when faced with a market threat or an opportunity. Ms. Baresak met with Mr. Frankson and told him this, and added that she believed that the strong functional organization of the company impeded the kind of action required to fix problems. Accordingly, she recommended that Mr. Frankson create a new position, *Projects and Programs Officer*, to use and promote project management principals and techniques at Frankson. The new PPO would also act as project manager for several current critical projects.

Mr. Frankson was pleased that Ms. Baresak found something that he could fix, but he did not care much for her solution. He believed that his functional department managers were capable professional people who should be able to work together efficiently and effectively. He thought that he should work with his management team to provide them with the direction they needed—what to do, when to do it, and who should do it. He would then put the functional manager most closely related to the problem in charge of the group. He was sure that a little directed push from himself would be just the thing to "get the projects rolling."

Questions: After this explanation by Mr. Frankson, Ms. Baresak is more convinced than ever that a separate, nonfunctional project manager is necessary. Is she right? If you were Ms. Baresak, how would you sell your idea to Mr. Frankson? If a new position is created, what other changes would you recommend making?

Toledo Medical Center

A 450 bed hospital in northwestern Ohio is in the planning and design phase of adding a new Psychiatric and Substance Abuse Outpatient service building. Construction is set to begin in three months. The Facilities Management department is normally responsible for assigning a project manager and overseeing projects for the medical center. The Facilities Management department does not currently have anyone on staff with direct experience in management of a building construction project. As a result, the president of the Medical Center is considering hiring a project manager from the architectural firm that is currently designing the building. The Director of Facilities Management believes his senior facilities engineer can handle the project for three reasons: she has a good

technical background, she pays meticulous attention to detail, and she is currently available for the job.

Questions: If you were the President, what would be your choice? Why? What additional information would you try to obtain before making the decision? Would someone with experience in building construction be a better choice?

C A S E

The Quantum Bank

Quantum Bank Inc. is a regional bank with branches throughout the southeast. In early 1999 the bank launched a Web site that provides its customers with the ability to check account balances, obtain information about the bank's various services, obtain contact information and email questions, and link to a variety of other useful sources of information. Given the site's tremendous success, competition from both traditional and nontraditional organizations, and the desire to expand its presence beyond its current geographical area, Quantum decided to expand its online offerings significantly. More specifically, Quantum would like to expand its Web site to include an online bill payment service, allow customers to apply for credit cards and loans online, open accounts online, and manage their investment portfolios online.

Vice-President of Information Systems, Stacey Thomas, has been charged with overseeing the project. One of her first tasks was to select the project manager. Because of the strategic importance of the project, she had a strong preference for staffing the project internally as opposed to employing the services of one of the many consulting firms available that specialize in these types of projects. After developing a list of ten or so possible candidates to serve as project manager, she was finally able to pare the list down to the two finalists described below.

Bill Fence

Bill joined Quantum in 1995 after graduating from a well-respected small private school with a degree in computer science. His first assignment as a member of the bank's help desk provided him with exposure to a variety of areas in the bank. He quickly gained a reputation for being able to solve difficult technical problems. In addition, users of the bank's various computer systems were often heard commenting on how service oriented Bill was and on his ability to describe concepts in nontechnical terms.

Because of both his technical knowledge related to hardware and his ability to program, Bill was selected to develop the bank's Web site in 1998. Bill worked alone

on this project and had frequent meetings with one of the bank's directors of Information Systems, who supervised the project. Initially, the director did most of the design work and Bill did the computer programming. Bill often proposed alternative ways for incorporating key features into the Web site, and the director would choose among the options Bill identified. Toward the end of the development project, Bill began to take a more active role in proposing features to include in the site.

The development project was largely completed on time and on budget considering the changes in the scope of the project that were made as the project progressed. Several suggestions that would have extended the site's functionality were tabled to be considered after the site was officially launched.

In his current position as Webmaster, Bill is in charge of maintaining the bank's Web site. Although Bill's staff now includes a programmer and a hardware specialist, his approach is very much hands on, staying involved with all technical aspects of the site. Bill has developed an excellent rapport with his two direct reports, and they have emulated much of Bill's style including working long hours and even competing to see who can accumulate the largest number of soft drink cans, empty candy wrappers, and computer printouts on one desk.

Andy Dover

Andy Dover also joined the bank in 1995 after completing his MBA at a large public university. Andy entered graduate school immediately after graduating with a Civil Engineering undergraduate degree at the same university.

Andy spent his first year rotating between various departments in the bank's management training program. After completing this training, Andy requested permanent assignment to the operations group. His initial assignment was to oversee the check encoding operation. After implementing several process improvements, Andy was eventually promoted to senior operations analyst and worked on several large process improvement projects.

Performance evaluations of Andy suggested that one of his greatest strengths was his ability to step back from a problem and understand how the various issues were interrelated. His evaluations further recognized him as "a highly motivated self-starter with very good organizational skills." His organizational skills also helped him effectively present information, and he was often requested to make short presentations related to a particular project's status to senior management.

By almost all accounts, Andy was considered highly competent, completing assigned tasks in a timely fashion with little or no direct supervision. At the same time, Andy always made it a point to communicate regularly with other project team members to keep them abreast of his progress. He was often passionate about his ideas and was typically able to get buy-in from other team members for his ideas.

Andy is almost always seen carrying his planner. As an avid stock investor, he makes it a point to stay abreast of trends in technology. He has a basic understanding of how the Internet works and knows all the important buzzwords. While he has fooled around and created a couple of Web pages, he knows very little about more sophisticated programming languages such as Java, and knows even less about computer hardware beyond its basic purpose.

QUESTIONS

1. Who would you recommend Stacey Thomas select to serve as project manager? Why?

2. How would you recommend this project be organized? Functional project? Pure project? Matrix? Why?

3. Do you agree with Ms. Thomas's decision that the project should be staffed internally? What are the major advantages of staffing the project with Quantum employees? Are there any advantages to utilizing the services of an outside consulting firm?

BIBLIOGRAPHY

1. AFZALUR, R. M. *Managing Conflict in Organizations.* Westport, CT: Praeger, 1992.

2. BLOCK, T. R. "The Project Office Phenomenon." *PM Network,* March 1998.

3. BOLLES, D. "The Project Support Office." *PM Network,* March 1998.

4. BOZNAK, R. G. "Management of Projects: A Giant Step Beyond Project Management." *PM Network,* January 1996.

5. CHURCHMAN, C. W. *The Systems Approach,* rev. ed. New York: Delta, 1979. (This book is a readable classic on the systems approach to understanding organizations as systems. The book is out of print, but widely available in university libraries.)

6. CONGER, J. A. "The Necessary Art of Persuasion." *Harvard Business Review,* May–June 1998.

7. DEWHURST, H. D. "Project Teams: What Have We Learned?" *PM Network,* April 1998.

8. FLYNN, J. "E-Mail, Cellphones and Frequent-Flier Miles Let 'Virtual' Expats Work Abroad but Live at Home." *The Wall Street Journal,* New York: Dow Jones, October 25, 1999.

9. GAGNON, R. J., and S. J. MANTEL, JR. "Strategies and Performance Improvement for Computer-Assisted Design." *IEEE Transactions on Engineering Management,* November 1987.

10. GOLDRATT, E. M., and J. COX. *The Goal,* 2nd rev. ed. Great Barrington, MA: North River Press, 1992. (One of the outstanding works in the entire literature of business. This novel is a powerful statement on the dangers of suboptimization. Many companies assign it as required reading for their managers.)

11. GRANT, K. P., C. R. BAUMGARDNER, and G. S. STONE. "The Perceived Importance of Technical Competence to Project Managers in the Defense Acquisition Community." *IEEE Transactions on Engineering Management,* February 1997.

12. HERZBERG, F. H. "One More Time: How Do You Motivate Employees?" *Harvard Business Review,* January–February 1968. (A widely reprinted article.)

13. HUGHES, T. P. *Rescuing Prometheus.* New York: Pantheon, 1998. (A wonderful book written by a historian. It is full of fascinating stories and valuable insights about the nature of complex projects and the management problems they raise.)

14. KOTTER, J. P. "What Effective General Managers Really Do." *Harvard Business Review,* November–December 1982. (An article that "tells it like it is." Most people who have never served as a manager do not believe it. Those who have managed, general or project management, know it is accurate.)

15. LEVINE, H. A. "Enterprise Project Management: What Do Users Need? What Can They Have?" *PM Network*, July 1998.

16. MATSON, E. "Congratulations, You're Promoted" and "Project: You." *Fast Company*, as reprinted in *Engineering Management Review*, Winter 1998. (Two excellent articles that report hard fact with wry humor.)

17. PATTERSON, N. "Selecting Project Managers: An Integrated List of Predictors." *Project Management Journal*, June 1991.

18. PINTO, J. K., and D. P. SLEVIN. "The Project Champion: Key to Implementation Success." *Project Management Journal*, December 1989. (See also Green, S. G., in Ch. 1 bibliography.)

19. PINTO, J. K., and O. P. KHARBANDA. "Lessons for an Accidental Profession." *Business Horizons*, March–April 1995. (An absolutely wonderful article on project management, including "the vital dozen" rules for the project manager.)

20. Project Management Institute Standards Committee. *A Guide to the Project Management Body of Knowledge*. Upper Darby, PA: Project Management Institute, 1996.

21. SCHODERBEK, P. P., C. G. SCHODERBEK, and A. G. KEFALAS. *Management Systems: Conceptual Considerations*. 4th ed. Homewood, IL: Irwin, 1990. (While this book is out of print, it should be available in most college and university libraries. It is worth the search.)

22. SHENHAR, A. J. "From Theory to Practice: Toward a Typology of Project-Management Styles." *IEEE Transactions on Engineering Management*, February 1998.

23. THAMHAIN, H. J., and D. L. WILEMON. "Conflict Management in Project Life Cycles." *Sloan Management Review*, Summer 1975. (A highly influential article, just as timely today as it was a quarter of a century ago.)

3

Planning the Project

If problems arise during the life of a project, our first hunch would be that the project was not properly planned. Most of the time our hunch would be correct. Inadequate planning is more the case than the exception. We can only guess why. Perhaps the reason is that senior management and/or the PM and/or the project team are impatient. They want "to get on with it." Possibly some of the people who should be engaged in planning have heard Tom Peters, well-known searcher-for-excellence and management guru, comment that good planning almost never cuts implementation time and that "Ready, Fire, Aim" is the way good businesses do it.

As a matter of fact, Peters is wrong. There is a ton of research that concludes that careful planning is strongly associated with project success—and to the best of our knowledge there is no research that supports the opposite position. Clearly, planning can be overdone, a condition often called "paralysis by analysis." Somewhere in between the extremes is the happy medium that everyone would like to strike, but this chapter does not seek to define the golden mean between no planning and over-planning [8]. We do, however, examine the nature of good planning, and we describe proven methods for generating plans that are adequate to the task of leading a project work force from the start of the project to its successful conclusion. We must start by deciding what things should be a part of a project plan.

3.1 THE CONTENTS OF A PROJECT PLAN

Before considering how to plan, we should decide why we are planning and what information the plan should contain. The primary function of a project plan is to serve the PM as a map of the route from project start to finish. The plan should contain sufficient information that, at any time, the PM knows what remains to be done, when, with what resources, by whom, when the task will be completed, and what specifications the output should meet. This information must be known at any level of detail from the most general overall level to the minutiae of the smallest subtask. As the project travels the route from start to finish, the PM needs also to know whether or not any changes in project plans are contemplated and whether or not any problems are likely to arise in the future. In other words, the PM needs to know the project's current state and its future expectations. Because PMs are sometimes appointed after the project has begun, the PM also needs to know the project's history to date.

There are several different types of project plans. The project *master plan* is outlined just below. A bit later we will describe the project *action plan*, the Work Breakdown Structure (WBS), and linear responsibility charts, which are also plans that serve special purposes. As we will see, each of these plays a different role in project management.

The elements required in the project master plan fall into one of the following nine categories.

1. *Overview.* This section contains a brief description of the project and its deliverables, together with a list of the major milestones or significant events in the project schedule. It is intended for senior management. It should also include expected profitability and competitive effects as well as the probable technical results.

2. *Objectives.* This is a more detailed description of the project's deliverables and outcomes. One approach to describing a project's objectives takes the form of a project *mission statement.* The intent of that mission statement is to communicate to project team members (and others) the purpose of the project so that they can make decisions that are consistent with the project's overall objectives. To foster team understanding of the project as a whole, a representative group of team members is often included in the process of developing the mission statement.

3. *General approach.* In this section, the technical and managerial approaches to the work are described. An identification of the project as "derivative," "platform," or "breakthrough" might be included, as might the relationship between this project and others being undertaken or contemplated by the organization. Also noted are plans that go beyond the organization's standard management practices. For example, some firms do not allow the use of consultants or subcontractors without special approval.

4. *Contractual aspects.* This section contains a complete description of all agreements made with the client or any third party. This list would include all reporting requirements; the technical specifications of all deliverables; agreements on delivery dates, incentives, and penalties (if any) for noncompliance; specific procedures for making changes in the deliverables; project review dates and procedures; and similar agreements.

5. *Schedules.* Included in this section is an outline of all schedules and milestones. Each task in the project is listed in a project *action plan* or a *WBS.* (The action plan and WBS are discussed later in this chapter.) Listed with each task is the time required to perform it. The project schedule is constructed from this data and is included in this section.

6. *Resource requirements.* Estimates of project expenses, both capital and operating, are included here. The costs associated with each task are shown, and overhead and fixed charges are listed. This becomes the *project budget,* though the PM may use a budget that deletes overhead and some fixed charges for day-to-day project management and control. (The details of budget preparation are covered in the next chapter.) In addition, cost monitoring and cost control procedures are described here.

7. *Personnel.* This section covers the details of the project work force. It notes any special skill requirements, necessary training, and special legal arrangements such as

security clearances or nondisclosure agreements. Combined with the schedule, it notes the time-phasing of all personnel requirements.

8. *Evaluation methods.* Descriptions of all project evaluation procedures and standards are found in this section. Also included are all procedures and requirements for monitoring, collecting, and storing data on project performance, together with a description of the required project history.

9. *Potential problems.* "Learn from experience" is a widely ignored adage. This section is an attempt to remedy that condition. Planners should list the reasonably frequent disasters that strike projects similar to the one being undertaken—late subcontractor deliveries, bad weather, unreasonable deadlines, equipment failure, complex coordination problems, and similar happenings. The argument is made that crises cannot be predicted. The only uncertainty, however, is which of the crises will occur and when. In any case, dealing with crises does not require a which-and-when prediction. In every project there are times when dependence on a subcontractor, or the good health of a software-code writer, or good weather, or machine availability is critical to progress on a project. Plans to deal with such potential crises should be a standard part of the project plan. It is well to remember that no amount of current planning can solve current crises—but preplanning may prevent or soften the impact of some.

Obviously, all of the plan contents listed above are necessary for large, nonroutine projects such as a major software development project. They are not all required for small, routine projects. Specific items such as task schedules, resource/personnel needs, and calendars are needed for any project, large or small, routine or not. Indeed, even if the project is both small and routine, a section dealing with contractual agreements is needed if the project is for an arm's-length client or if a subcontractor or consultant is involved.

One additional use for a careful, complete project plan is when the project may be small and routine, but it is also carried out frequently, as in some maintenance projects. The complete planning process may be conducted to form a template for such projects—with particular emphasis on evaluation methods. With this template, planning similar projects is simple—just fill in the blanks. If changes in the plan are contemplated, the prescribed evaluation methods can be employed. This allows a "continuous improvement" program to be implemented with ongoing evaluation of suggested changes.

> The project plan should contain nine elements: a project overview, a statement of objectives, a description of the technical and managerial approaches to the work, all contractual agreements, schedules of activities, a list of resource requirements or a project budget, personnel requirements, project evaluation methods, and preparations to meet potential problems.

3.2 THE PLANNING PROCESS—OVERVIEW

A great deal has been written about planning. Some of the literature focuses on the strategic aspect of planning [14, 15]—choosing and planning projects that contribute to the organization's goals (cf., Section 1.5, subsection on aggregate planning in Chapter 1). Another body of writing is directed at the techniques of how to plan rather than what to plan [9, 10, 12, and 13]. These techniques, if we are to believe what we read, differ from industry to industry, from subject to subject. Architecture has a planning process; so does software development, as does construction, as well as pharmaceutical R&D projects, and campaigns for raising funds for charity.

As far as we can determine, the way that planning techniques vary in these different cases has more to do with nomenclature than substance. Consider, for example, the following planning process that has been divided into eight distinct steps.

1. Develop and evaluate the concept of the project. Describe what it is you wish to develop, including its basic performance characteristics, and decide if getting such a deliverable is worthwhile. If so, continue.

2. Carefully identify and spell out the actual capabilities that the project's deliverable must have to be successful. Design a system (product or service) that will have the requisite capabilities.

3. Create such a system (product or service), which is to say, build a prototype deliverable.

4. Test the prototype to see if it does, in fact, have the desired capabilities. If necessary, cycle back to step 3 to modify the prototype and retest it. Continue until the deliverable meets the preset requirements.

5. Integrate the deliverable into the system for which it was designed. In other words, install the deliverable in its required setting.

6. Validate the deliverable—which answers the question, "Now that we have installed the deliverable, does it still work properly?"

7. If the deliverable has been validated, let the client test it. Can the client operate the system? If not, instruct the client.

8. If the client can operate (and accepts) the deliverable, make sure that the client understands all standard operating and maintenance requirements. Then shake the client's hand, present the client with a written copy of maintenance and operating instructions, give the client the bill, and leave.

Reread the eight steps. Are they not an adequate description of the planning process for any R&D project, for the design of a new pick-up truck, of a high-end hotel room, of a restaurant kitchen, of a machine tool, of a line of toys, etc.?

The eight steps above were originally written to describe the planning process for computer software [1]. There seem to be as many different planning sequences and steps as there are authors writing about planning. Almost all of them, regardless of the number of steps, meet the same criteria if they are meant to guide a project to a successful conclusion. The final plan must have the elements described in the previous section of this chapter.

> There are many techniques for developing a project plan. They are fundamentally similar. All of them use a systematic analysis to identify and list the things that must be undertaken in order to achieve the project's objectives, to test and validate the plan, and to deliver it to the user.

3.3 THE PLANNING PROCESS—NUTS AND BOLTS

This section deals with the problem of determining and listing the various tasks that must be accomplished in order to complete a project. The important matters of generating a project budget and developing a precise project schedule are left to succeeding chapters, though much of the raw material for doing those important things will come from the planning process described here.

The Launch Meeting—and Subsequent Meetings

Once senior management has decided to fund a major project, or a highly important small project, a *project launch meeting* should be called. Preparation for this meeting is required [7, 11].

When a PM is appointed to head a new project, the PM's first job is to review the project objectives (*project scope*) with the senior manager who has fundamental responsibility for the project. The purpose of this interview is threefold: (1) to make sure that the PM understands the expectations that the organization has for the project; (2) to identify who among the senior managers (in addition to the manager who is party to this interview) has a major interest in the project; and (3) to determine if anything about the project is atypical for projects of the same general kind (e.g., a product/service development project undertaken in order to extend the firm's market into a new area).

Armed with this background, the PM should briefly study the project with an eye to preparing an invitation list for the project launch meeting. At the top of the list should be at least one representative of senior management, a strong preference given to the individual with the strongest interest in the project, the probable project champion. (The champion is usually, but not necessarily, the person with responsibility for the project.) Recall in Chapter 2 we noted that the project champion could lend the political clout that is occasionally needed to overcome obstacles to cooperation from functional managers—if such obstacles were not amenable to dissolution by the PM.

Next on the invitation list come the managers from the functional areas that will be called upon to contribute competencies or capacities to the project. If highly specialized technical experts will be needed, the PM can add individuals with the required expertise to the list, after clearing the invitation with their immediate bosses, of course.

The PM may chair the launch meeting, but the senior manager introduces the project to the group, and discusses its contributions to the parent organization. If known and relevant, the project's tentative priority may be announced. If the due dates for deliverables have been contracted, this should also be made clear. The purpose of senior management's presence is to ensure that the group understands the firm's commitment to the project. It is particularly important for the functional managers to understand that management is making a real commitment, not merely paying lip service.

At this point, the PM can take over the meeting and begin a group discussion of the project. It is, however, important for the senior manager(s) to remain for this discussion. The continuing presence of these august persons more or less assures cooperation from the functional units. The purpose of the discussion is to develop a general understanding of what functional inputs the project will need.

Some launch meetings are restricted to brainstorming a problem. The output of such a meeting is shown in Table 3-1. In this case, the Director of Human Resources (HR) of a medium-size firm was asked by the Board of Directors to set up a program to improve employee retention. At the time, the firm had a turnover rate slightly above 60 percent per year among its technical employees. (A turnover rate of 50 percent was about average for the industry.) The HR Director held a launch meeting of all department heads, all senior corporate officers, and members of the Board. At this meeting, the group developed a list of "action items," each of which became a project.

When dealing with a single project, it is common for a preliminary plan to be generated at the launch meeting, but we question the advisability of this. For either functional managers or the PM to guess at budgets or schedules with no real study of the

Table 3-1   Program Launch Meeting Output, Human Resources Development

Goal of Program: Reduce employee turnover from 60 percent to 40 percent
Program Manager: Human Resources Director

Objective	Action Item

Improve employee morale	• Collect data from:
	   • Exit interviews
	   • Employee survey
	   • Cultural audit
	   • Interviewing "retained" employees
	• Seminars for all staff on personality types and working styles
	• Employee fitness center implemented
	• New employee luncheons with department heads
	• New hire "30-day" reunions
	• Complete pro forma for opening day care center
	• Overhaul of employee orientation program
	• Competitive salary analysis conducted and adjustments made

Broaden staff competencies	• Competencies for all positions completed and system established to maintain ongoing competencies
Attain stronger employee commitment to organizational standards for productivity, outcomes, and customer satisfaction	• Six-week series on management and leadership for managers • Leadership training for supervisors • Performance-based pay system developed • Job descriptions format redesigned around organizational effectiveness standards
Improve recruitment efforts	• Increase recruitment efforts, additional advertising, three job fairs • Hire recruiter • Implement defined contribution pension plan for new hires • Internet job hotline • Radio spots

project's deliverables is not prudent. First, the transition from a "tentative, wild guessti-mate" to "but you promised" is instantaneous in these cases. Second, there is no founda-tion for mutual discussion or negotiation about different positions taken publicly and based on so little knowledge or thought. It is sufficient, in our judgment, to get a firm commitment from functional managers to study the proposed project and return for an-other meeting with a technically (and politically) feasible plan for their group's input to the project.

It has been said, "If this means many planning meetings and extensive use of partic-ipatory decision making, then it is well worth the effort." [5, p. 316] If the emphasis is on "participative decision making," we agree. Actual planning at the launch meeting should not go beyond the most aggregated level unless the deliverables are well under-stood or the delivery date is cast in concrete and the organization has considerable ex-perience with similar projects. Of course, if this is the case, a major launch meeting may not be required.

The results of the launch meeting should be that: (1) the project's scope is under-stood and temporarily fixed, and (2) the various functional managers understand their responsibilities and have committed to develop an initial plan. In the meetings that fol-low, the project plan will become more and more detailed and firmer. When the group has developed what appears to be a workable plan with a schedule and budget that seem feasible, the plan moves through the appropriate management levels where it is approved, or altered and approved. If altered, it must be checked with those who did the planning. The planners may accept the alterations or a counter-proposal may be made. The project plan may cycle up and down the managerial ladder several times before it receives final approval, at which time no further changes may be made without a formal *change order* (a procedure also described in the plan).

Irrespective of who alters (or suggests alterations) to the project plan during the process described above, it is imperative that everyone be kept fully informed. It is no more equitable for a senior manager to change a plan without consultation with the PM (and, hence, the project team) than it would be for the PM or the team to alter the plan without consultation and approval from senior management. If an arm's-length client is involved, the client's approval is required for any changes that will have an effect on the schedule, cost, or deliverable.

Open, honest, and frequent communication between the interested parties is critical for successful planning. What emerges from this process is the project master plan, sometimes called the project *baseline plan*. It contains all the nine elements noted in Section 3.1 and all amendments to the plan adopted as the project is carried out. When senior management and the client have "signed-off" on the plan, it becomes the *project charter*, a contract-like document affirming that all major parties-at-interest to the project are in agreement on the deliverables, the cost, and the schedule.

Sorting Out the Project

The previous subsection discussed the planning process as seen from the outside. The PM and the functional managers developed plans as if by magic. It is now time to be specific about how such plans may be generated. In order to develop a project plan that will take us from start to finish of a project, we need to know precisely what must be done, by whom, when, and with what resources. Every task, however small, that must be completed in order to complete the project should be listed together with any required material or human resources.

Making such a list is a nontrivial job. It requires a systematic procedure. While there are several systematic procedures that may be used, we advise a straightforward and conceptually simple way to attack the problem—the *hierarchical planning process*.

To use this process, one must start with the project's objective(s). The planner, often the PM, makes a list of the major activities that must be completed to achieve the objective(s). The list may be as short as two or three activities, or as large as 20. Usually the number is between five and 15. We call these Level 1 activities. The planner now takes each Level 1 activity and delegates it to an individual or functional group. (The PM might delegate one or more Level 1 tasks to him- or herself.) The delegatee deals with the task as if it were itself a project and makes an action plan to accomplish it; that is, he or she lists the set of Level 2 tasks required to complete the Level 1 task. Again, the breakdown typically runs between five and 15 tasks, but a few more or less does not matter. The process continues. For each Level 2 task, someone or some group is delegated responsibility to prepare an action plan of Level 3 subtasks. The procedure of successively decomposing larger tasks into their component parts continues until the lowest level subtasks are sufficiently understood so that there is no reason to continue. As a rule of thumb, the lowest level tasks in a typical project will have a duration of two days to two weeks. If the team is quite familiar with the work, longer durations are acceptable for the lowest level tasks.

In doing hierarchical planning only one rule appears to be mandatory. At any given level, the "generality" or "degree of detail" of the tasks should be roughly at the same level. One should not use highly detailed tasks for Level 1 plans, and one should not add very general tasks at Level 3 or more. This can best be done by finding all Level 2 subtasks for each Level 1 task before moving one's attention to the Level 3 subtasks. Similarly, break all Level 2 tasks into their respective Level 3 tasks before considering any Level 4 subtasks, if the breakdown proceeds that far. A friend of ours who is an internationally known artist and teacher of industrial design explained why. When producing a painting or drawing, an artist first sketches in the main compositional lines in the scene. The artist then adds detail, bit by bit, over the whole drawing, continuing this process until the work is completed. If this is done, the finished work will have a "unity." Unity is not achieved if individual areas of the picture are completed in detail before moving on to other areas. A young art student then made a pen-and-ink sketch of a fellow student, showing her progress at three different stages, see Figure 3-1.

We have said that the breakdown of Level 1 tasks should be delegated to someone who will carry out the Level 2 tasks. It is the same with Level 2 tasks being delegated to someone who will design and carry out the required Level 3 tasks. A relevant question is "Who are all these delegatees?" Let's assume that the project in question is of reasonable size, neither very large nor small. Assume further that the PM and the functional managers are reasonably experienced in dealing with similar projects. In such a case, the PM would probably start by working on Level 1. Based on her background, the PM might work on Level 2 of one or more of the Level 1 tasks. Where recent experience was missing, she would delegate to the proper functional manager the task of specifying the Level 2 tasks. In the same way, the latter would delegate Level 3 task specification to the people who have the appropriate knowledge.

Figure 3-1 Three levels of detail in hierarchical planning.

In general, the job of planning should be delegated to the lowest competent level. At Level 1, this is usually the PM. At lower levels, functional managers and specialists are the best planners. In Chapter 2 (Section 2.1) we described that strange bugbear, the micromanager. It is common for micromanagers to preempt the planning function from subordinates or, as an alternative, to allow the subordinate to develop an initial plan that the micromanager will amend with potentially disastrous results. The latter is an event reported with some frequency (and accuracy) in *Dilbert©*.

The Project Action Plan

The collection of these plans, including all levels, buttressed with some additional data (see just below) is called the project's action plan. Figure 3-2 shows an action plan form that helps to organize the required information. The additional data in the columns are:

<table>
<tr><td colspan="5" align="center">ACTION PLAN</td></tr>
<tr><td colspan="5">Deliverables _____</td></tr>
<tr><td colspan="5"> </td></tr>
<tr><td colspan="5">_____</td></tr>
<tr><td colspan="5">Start date _____ Due date _____ Project duration _____</td></tr>
<tr><td colspan="5">Key constraints and assumptions _____</td></tr>
<tr><td colspan="5"> </td></tr>
<tr><td>Tasks</td><td>Immediate Predecessor Tasks</td><td>Estimated Time Duration</td><td>Estimated Resources</td><td>Assigned To</td></tr>
<tr><td> </td><td> </td><td> </td><td> </td><td> </td></tr>
</table>

Figure 3-2 A form to assist hierarchical planning.

(1) estimates of the resources required for each task in the plan, (2) the estimated time required to accomplish each task, (3) information about who has responsibility for the task, and (4) data that will allow tasks to be sequenced so that the set may be completed in the shortest possible time. Once the project starting date is known, item 2 in the preceding list may be changed from the time required for a subtask completion to the date on which the subtask is scheduled for completion.

To understand the importance of item 4 in the list, consider a set of subtasks, all of which must be completed to accomplish a parent task on a higher level. It is common in such a set that one or more subtasks (A) must be completed before one or more other subtasks (B) may be started. The former tasks (A) are said to be *predecessors* of the *successor* tasks (B). For instance, if our project is to paint the walls of a room, we know that before we apply paint to a wall, we must do a number of predecessor tasks. These predecessors include: clear the floor area near the wall to be painted and cover with drop cloths; remove pictures from the wall; clean loose dirt, oil, grease, stains, and the like from the wall; fill and smooth any cracks or holes in the wall; lightly sand or score the wall if it has previously been painted with a high-gloss paint; wipe with a damp cloth or sponge to remove dust from the sanding; and mask any surrounding areas where this paint is not wanted. All these tasks are predecessors to the task "Paint the walls."

The predecessor tasks for "paint the walls" have been listed in the order in which they might be done if only one person was working. If several people are available, several of these tasks might be done at the same time. Note that if three tasks can be done simultaneously, the total elapsed time required is the time needed for the longest of the three, not the sum of the three task times. This notion is critical for scheduling, so predecessors must be listed in the action plan. One convention is important. When listing predecessors, only the *immediate predecessors* are listed. If A precedes B and B precedes C, only B is a predecessor of C.

Table 3-1 illustrated the output of a project launch meeting (more accurately a *program* launch meeting). Table 3-2 shows an action plan for one of the action items resulting from the launch meeting. With the exception of tasks 3 and 4, it is a Level 1 plan. Three Level 2 items are shown for tasks 3 and 4. Because the HR Director is quite familiar with such projects, violating the one-level-only rule is forgivable. Note also that the HR Director has delegated some of the work to himself. Note also that instead of assumptions being shown at the beginning of the action plan, project evaluation measures were listed.

The action plan not only identifies the deliverable, but also notes the start date if it is known. Once the subtasks and their predecessors have been listed along with the estimated subtask activity times, the probable duration for the set of subtasks, and thus the task due date, can be determined as we will see in Chapter 5. If the estimates for the durations and resource requirements for accomplishing the subtasks are subject to constraints (e.g., no overtime work is allowed) or assumptions (e.g., there will be no work stoppage at our subcontractor's plant), these should be noted in the action plan.

If one wishes, the information in the form shown in Figure 3-2 can be entered directly into Microsoft Project® (MSP). Alternatively, one can produce an action plan using MSP, directly, as shown in Figure 3-3. The project title can be entered in a header or footer to the form, as can any other information such as a brief description of the deliverables, the name of the PM or the task manager, the project start and/or due dates, and the like.

Table 3-3 shows a MSP action plan with task durations and start and finish times for the Level 1 tasks in an infection control project. The project begins on Tuesday, September 12, 2000 and ends on November 30, 2000. As is customary, people work a

Table 3-2   An Action Plan for Improving Staff Orientation

Action Plan for Improving Staff Orientation

Project Objective: Enhance new employee orientation to improve retention and more effectively communicate organization's policies and procedures.
Measurable Outcomes: Increase in retention rate for new hires.
New hires better understand mission, vision, and core values of organization.
Competency level of new hires increased.

Task	Duration	Predecessor	Resources	Assigned To
1. Orientation task force launched	2 weeks	—	Education Manager, Education Staff (3), two Department Managers, three Staff representatives, facilitator	HR Director
2. Compile orientation evaluations for areas of improvement	4 weeks	—		Education Secretary
3. Enhancement proposal prepared (a) Draft recommended changes	2 weeks	1, 2	Orientation Task Force	Education Manager
(b) Recomendations presented to executive team	1 week	3(a)	Education Manager	HR Director
(c) Review and finalize orientation enhancements	2 weeks	3(b)	Orientation Task Force	Education Manager
4. Orientation presentations enhanced (a) Work with speakers to review presentations	4 weeks	3(c)	Speakers, Education Staff	Education Staff
(b) Facilitate preparation of Power Point presentation	6 weeks	4(a)	IS trainer, Education Staff, Speakers	Education Staff
(c) Facilitate acquisition of videos on certain subjects	6 weeks	4(a)	Education Staff, Speakers	Education Staff
5. Review evaluation tool to measure outcomes	2 weeks	1, 2, 3	Education Manager	Education Manager
6. Facilitate physical changes necessary to orientation room	4 weeks	4	Education Staff, AV staff, Facilities staff	Education Manager
7. Implement revised orientation program	0 days	5, 6, 7	Education staff, Speakers, HR staff	Education Manager
8. Evaluate feedback from first two orientation sessions	2 months	7	Education Staff	Education Manager
9. Present findings to executive team	1 week	8	Education Manager	HR Director
10. Evaluate feedback from first six orientation sessions	6 months	7	Education Manager	Education Manager
11. Develop continuous process improvement system for feedback results	4 weeks	7	Education Staff	Education Manager

Project deliverables:					
Project Manager:			**Project Title**		
ID	Task Name	Duration	Predecessors	Resource Names	Assigned To
1					
2					
3					
4					
5					
6					
7					
8					
9					
10					

Project start date:
Project due date:

Figure 3-3   An action plan as an output of MSP.

five-day week so a three-week task has 15 work days and 21 calendar days (three weeks), *assuming that the individual or team is working full-time on the task.* As we will see in Chapter 5, one usually dares not make that assumption and should check carefully to determine whether or not it is a fact. If the one performing the task is working part-time, a task that requires five days of work, for example, may require several weeks of calendar time. We will revisit this problem in Chapter 5.

Table 3-3   An Action Plan Showing Level 1 Tasks for an Infection Control Project (MSP)

Pulmonary Patient Infection Control Project
F. Nightengale, RN

ID	Task Name	Predecessors	Duration	Start	Finish	Resources
1	Form a task force to focus processes for pulmonary patients		2 wks	9/12/00	9/25/00	Infec. Control RN, Dr., Educator
2	Identify potential processes to decrease infection rate	1	3 wks	9/26/00	10/16/00	Team
3	Develop a treatment team process	1, 2	3 wks	9/26/00	10/16/00	Team
4	Education	3	1 wk	10/17/00	10/23/00	RNs, LPNs, CNAs
5	Implement processes on one unit as trial	4	3 wks	10/24/00	11/13/00	
6	Evaluate	5	1 wk	11/14/00	11/20/00	Infec. Control RN
7	Make necessary adjustments	6	1 wk	11/21/00	11/27/00	Infec. Control RN
8	Implement hospital-wide	7	3 days	11/28/00	11/30/00	

Table 3-4 A Template for a Brainstorming Planning Meeting

ID	Potential Steps	Objective	Success Measure	Barriers	Notes	Contact	E-mail address
1	Idea 1						
2	Idea 2						
3	Idea 3						
4	Idea 4						
5	Idea 5						
6	Idea 6						

MSP makes the task of Level 1 planning of the broad project tasks quite straightforward. The same is true when the planners wish to generate a more detailed listing of all the steps involved in a project. The PM merely lists the overall tasks identified by the planning team as the activities required to produce the project deliverables—for example, the output of a brainstorming session. The PM can then use MSP to take each of the "ideas" and create a hierarchical action plan, estimating required resources and durations. Table 3-4 shows a planning template used by a software company when they have their initial project brainstorming meetings about delivering on a customer request.

MSP has a planning wizard that guides the PM through the process of identifying all that is necessary to take an idea for a project activity and turn it into a useful action plan.

Table 3-5 is an example of a template developed by a computer systems support company. Company planners repeatedly performed the same steps when clients would ask for a local area network installation. They treated each job as if it were a new project, because costs and resource assignments varied with each assignment. To improve efficiency, they developed an action plan template using MSP. After meeting with a client, the project manager could add the agreed-upon project start date, and any constraints on the schedule required by the client. The steps to install the LAN remained the same. The start and finish dates, and the number of resources needed to meet the schedule were adjusted for each individual client, but the adjustments were usually small. Once the schedule of a specific job was decided, the PM could determine the resources needed to meet that schedule and find the cost of the project.

Creating this kind of template is simple. The software can calculate the cost of each different project which is most helpful to the project manager if cost, prices, or schedules must be negotiated. If the client wants the project to be completed earlier than scheduled, the PM can add the additional resources needed and project management software can determine the costs associated with the change.

If the PM wishes to include other information in the project's action plan, there is no reason not to do so. Some include a column to list the status of resource or personnel availability. Others list task start dates.

> The project launch meeting sets the project scope, elicits cooperation of others in the organization, demonstrates managerial commitment to the project, and initiates the project plan. The plan itself is generated through a hierarchical planning process by which parts of the plan are sequentially broken down into finer levels of detail by the individuals or groups that will implement them. The result is an action plan that lists all the tasks required to carry out the plan together with task resource requirements, durations, predecessors, and identification of the people responsible for each task.

Table 3-5 An MSP Template for a LAN Installation Project

Template for LAN Installation Project

ID	Task Name	Duration	Start	Finish	Predecessors	Resource Names
1	Phase I—Planning and design of LAN	13 days				
2	Project start	0 days				
3	Technical specifications determined	10 days			2	Project Manager, System Analysts, Systems Consultant, Writers, Chief Editor, Senior Programmer, Vice President-Management Information Systems, Senior Writers, Administrative Assistant
4	Design plan developed	3 days			3	Project Manager, System Analysts, Chief Editor, Vice President-Management Information Systems
5	Phase II—Preparation for installation	22 days				
6	Equipment ordering	2 days			4	Administrative Assistant
7	System prototype	20 days			6	System Analysts, Systems Consultant, Programmers, Senior Programmer, Junior Programmers
8	Configuration	10 days			6	System Analysts, Programmers, Tester, Senior Testers
9	Testing	5 days			8	Tester, Senior Testers
10	Site analysis	5 days			6	System Analysts, Programmers, Tester, Junior Programmers
11	Phase III—Installation	13 days				
12	Site installation	3 days			7, 8, 10	Tester, Project Manager, System Analysts, Systems Consultant, Senior Testers
13	Documentation set-up	10 days			12	Writers, Chief Editor, Senior Writers
14	Phase IV—Installation follow-up	12 days				
15	Orientation for client	2 days			13	Project Manager, System Analysts, Systems Consultant, Programmers, Administrative Assistant
16	Support to client	5 days			12	
17	Post-installation review	3 days			16	Project Manager, System Analysts, Systems Consultant, Chief Editor, Vice President-Management Information Systems
18	System acceptance	0 days			17, 15	

3.4 THE WORK BREAKDOWN STRUCTURE AND OTHER AIDS

At times, PMs seem to forget that many of the conventional forms, charts, and tables that they must fill out are intended to serve as aids, not punishments. They also forget that the forms, charts, and tables are not cast in bronze, but may be changed to fit the PMs' needs. In addition to the project action plan just discussed, two other useful aids are the *Work Breakdown Structure* (WBS) and the *Linear Responsibility Chart* (LRC).

The Work Breakdown Structure

Traditionally, the WBS is simply a set of all tasks in a project, usually arranged by task levels. It is sometimes presented as a tree, much like an organization chart, as in Figure 3-4. At the top of the tree is the project objective. Below it are the Level 1 tasks. Below each of these are the relevant Level 2 tasks, and so on. A WBS identifier number is in each task-box. A professor friend called this a "Gozinto chart." (He said it was named after a famous Italian mathematician, Prof. Zepartzat Gozinto. The name has stuck.)

Inadequate up-front planning, especially failing to identify all important tasks, is a primary contributor to the failure of a project to achieve its cost and time objectives. Therefore, a primary purpose for developing a WBS is to ensure that important tasks are not overlooked and thereby not accounted for and planned.

One simple approach for creating the WBS begins by gathering the project team together and providing each member with a pad of sticky-notes. Team members then write on the sticky-notes all the tasks they can think of that are required to complete the project. The sticky-notes can then be placed on the wall and arranged in various ways. One advantage of this approach is that it provides the entire team with a better understanding of the work needed to complete the project. The fact that it is a cooperative exercise also helps the project team to bond. Finally, this exercise is just as applicable to the construction of an action plan as it is to a WBS tree.

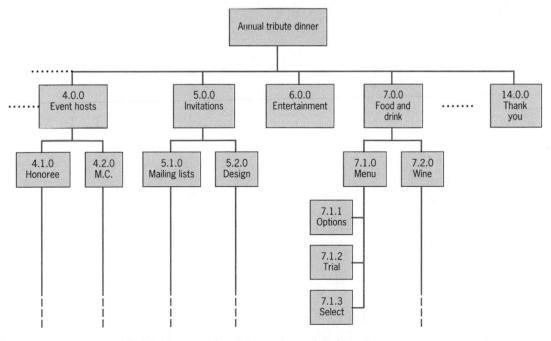

Figure 3-4   A partial WBS (Gozinto chart) for an Annual Tribute Dinner project.

MSP will make a WBS list (but not a tree-chart) at the touch of a key. The task levels are appropriately identified; for example, the WBS number "7.5.4" refers to the "Level 3, task Number 4" that is needed for "Level 2, task 5" that is a part of "Level 1, task 7." (The PM has the option of using any other identification system desired, but must enter the identifiers manually.)

Task levels are appropriately organized on the MSP printout, with Level 1 tasks to the left and others indented by level. If one uses a tree diagram and each task is represented by a box with the WBS identifier number, one can add any information one wishes—given that it will fit in the box. Such an entry might be the proper account number to charge for work done on that task, or the name of the individual (or department) with task responsibility, or with a space for the responsible party's signature denoting that the person has accepted accountability by "signing-off."

Table 3-6 shows the MSP printout for the entire Tribute Dinner project. The WBS identifier numbers are on the left, followed by tasks, predecessors, estimated durations and costs, and the individuals or groups responsible for the respective tasks.

The process of building an action plan and the resulting WBS is meaningful. Boss-subordinate pairs (remember that the boss-subordinate relationship is defined only in regard to the project and often does not exist outside the project) may differ on the technical approach to working on the task, the type and quantity of resources needed, or the duration for each subtask. If so, negotiation is apt to accompany the planning process. As usual, participatory management and negotiation often lead to improved project performance and better ways of meeting the project's goals. We have described the process to construct the project action plan above, but it bears repeating.

1. All project activities will be identified and arranged in successively finer detail, that is, by levels.

2. For each activity, the type and quantity of each required resource (including personnel) are identified.

3. For each activity, predecessors and task duration are estimated.

4. All project milestones are identified and located on the project schedule following their predecessor activities.

5. For each activity, the individual or group assigned to perform the work is identified. Acceptance of the assignment is noted by "signing-off."

In addition, we can determine several other pieces of information from the items listed above.

6. If project milestones, task durations, and predecessors are combined, the result is the project *master schedule*. (The master schedule will be illustrated in Chapter 5.) Additional time allowances for contingencies may be added, though we will later argue against this way of dealing with uncertainty.

7. The master schedule allows the PM to compare actual and planned task durations and resource usage at any level of activity, which is to say that the master schedule is also a control document. The need for such comparisons dictates what information about project performance should be monitored. This gives the PM the ability to control the project and take corrective action if the project is not proceeding according to plan. (More on project control in Chapter 7.)

The project action plan is the baseline document for managing a project. If all of the above information is contained in a WBS, the WBS is not distinguishable from the

Table 3-6   MSP Action Plan for an Annual Tribute Dinner Project

Foundation Annual Tribute Dinner
M. Stewart

WBS	Task Name	Predecessor	Estimated Duration	Estimated Cost	Resource Names
1	Begin preparations for tribute dinner		0 days	$0.00	
2	Select date & secure room	1	2 wks	$0.00	Event Coordinator
3	Obtain corporate sponsorships for event	2	20 days	$150.00	
3.1	Identify potential businesses to sponsor event		2 wks	$0.00	CEO, VP Marketing
3.2	Phone/write businesses	3.1	2 wks	$150.00	CEO, Event Coordinator
4	Event hosts/MC	2	46 days	$0.00	
4.1	Identify and secure honoree of event		3 wks	$0.00	CEO, PR
4.2	Identify and secure master of ceremonies		3 wks	$0.00	CEO, Event Coordinator, PR
4.3	Identify and secure person to introduce honoree		3 wks	$0.00	CEO, Event Coordinator, PR
4.4	Identify and secure event hosts and hostesses		3 wks	$0.00	CEO, Event Coordinator, PR
5	Invitations		179 days	$4,300.00	
5.1	Secure mailing lists		2 wks	$0.00	Secretary
5.2	Design invitation with PR firm	2, 3	4 wks	$1,500.00	PR, Marketing, Event Coordinator
5.3	Print invitation	5.2	3 days	$2,500.00	
5.4	Mail invitation	5.3	0 days	$300.00	
5.5	RSBP's back	5.4	9 wks	$0.00	Secretary
6	Event entertainment secured	2	2 wks	$1,000.00	
7	Food and drink		15 days	$750.00	
7.1	Finalize menu		5 days	$750.00	
7.1.1	Identify menu options	2	1 wk	$0.00	Secretary
7.1.2	Trial menus	7.1.1	1 day	$0.00	Secretary, Event Coordinator, CEO
7.1.3	Select final menu	7.1.2	1 wk	$750.00	Event Coordinator
7.2	Identify company to donate wine	3	3 wks	$0.00	Event Coordinator
8	Table decorations, gifts, cards, flowers, etc.		30 days	$2,800.00	
8.1	Identify and have made event gift to attendees	1	6 wks	$2,500.00	Event Coordinator, Secretary
8.2	Find florist to donate table arrangements	1	4 wks	$0.00	Event Coordinator
8.3	Hire calligrapher to make seating cards	5.5	2 wks	$300.00	Secretary
9	Develop PR exhibit to display at event	13	4 wks	$150.00	PR
10	Event and honoree publicity	2, 3	2 wks	$325.00	PR
11	Hire event photographer	2	1 wk	$450.00	Secretary
12	Finalize seating chart	5.5	3 wks	$0.00	Secretary, Event Coordinator, CEO
13	Hold tribute dinner	12	0 days	$0.00	
14	Send out 'thank you' notes to sponsors and donators	13	1 wk	$150.00	Secretary

All task detail shown

project action plan. WBSs, however, rarely contain so much information. Instead, they are typically designed for special purposes; for example, ensuring that all tasks are identified, and perhaps showing activity durations, sequencing, and due dates.

The Linear Responsibility Chart—and Derivatives

Like the WBS, *linear responsibility charts* (LRC) come in all sizes and shapes. Typically, the LRC is in the form of a matrix with the project tasks listed in the rows and departments or individuals in the columns. Thus, some people refer to the LRC as a *responsibility matrix*. (We use the term LRC to refer to any structured way of showing the roles and accountability existing between various people and project tasks.) For an example of a simple LRC, see Figure 3-5.

In Figure 3-5 shapes are used to indicate the nature of the responsibility link between a person and a task. Note that there must be at least one solid triangle, ▲, in every row, which means that someone must be accountable for completion of each task. For example, examine the row with the task "Solicit quotations." In this case the Project Engineer is accountable for carrying out the task. If needed, the Field Manager will support the process, helping the Project Engineer gather information or prepare the solicitation documents. The project's Contract Administrator must be kept informed about the solicitation process, and the PM must approve the documents before they are sent to potential vendors.

One can create as many different duties or responsibility links in an LRC as seem relevant to the situation. One can, for instance, indicate that some individuals or departments need to be notified about every task undertaken by a project, while other departments require notification only if certain conditions exist (e.g., an activity start will be delayed).

While one can construct LRCs manually, there are software packages that interact seamlessly with MSP that have several different LRC designs. All the PM needs to do is choose the types of linkages and fill in the blanks. As is the case with all of these tools, the purpose is to assist those who either work on the project or interface with it. One can use symbols or numbers to refer to different responsibility relationships, and the references may be to departments, job titles, or names. Only imagination and the needs of the project and PM bound the potential variety.

A final observation is needed on this subject. When we speak to functional managers about project management, one comment we often hear is anger about changes in

WBS / Responsibility		Project Office				Field Operator	
Subproject	Task	Project Manager	Contract Administrator	Project Engineer	Industrial Engineer	Field Manager	
Determine need	A1	○		●	▲		
	A2	▪	○	▲	●		
Solicit quotations	B1	○	▪	▲		●	
Write appropriate request	C1	▪	▲	○	●		
	C2		●	○	▲		
	C3	●	▪	▲		▪	
"	"						
"	"						
"	"						

Legend:
▲ Responsible   ▪ Notification
● Support   ○ Approval

Figure 3-5 A linear responsibility chart.

the project plan without notification to the people who are supposed to conduct the tasks or supply services to the project. One quote from the head of a statistics lab in a large consulting firm is typical. The head of the lab was speaking of the manager of a consulting project for a governmental agency when he said, "I pulled three of my best people off other work to reserve them for data analysis on the XYZ Project. They sat for days waiting for the data. That jerk [the PM] knew the data would be late and never bothered to let me know. Then the *%$#@% had the gall to come in here and ask me to speed up our analysis so he could make up lost time."

Make sure that the LRC has a "notify" category, and that it is properly used, not simply to report progress, but also to report changes in due dates, resource requirements, and the like.

> From the action plan one can extract a list of all tasks arranged by task level. This is the Work Breakdown Structure. The WBS will show numeric identifiers for each task plus other information as desired. The WBS may take a wide variety of forms. From the action plan one can also develop Linear Responsibility Charts. The LRC details the nature of responsibility of each individual or group involved in the project to the specific tasks required to complete the project.

3.5   MULTIDISCIPLINARY TEAMS—BALANCING PLEASURE AND PAIN

In Chapter 2 we promised further discussion of *multidisciplinary teams* (MT) on projects. We will now keep that promise. We delayed consideration of MTs until we discussed planning because planning is a primary use for such teams. Using MTs (or *transdisciplinary teams* as they are sometimes called) raises serious problems for the PM. When used on sizable, complex projects that necessitate inputs from several different departments or groups, the process of managing the way these groups work together is called *interface coordination*. It is an arduous and complicated job. Coordinating the work of these groups and the timing of their interaction is called *integration management*. Integration management is also arduous and complicated. Above all, MTs are almost certain to operate in an environment of conflict. As we will see, however, conflict is not an unmitigated disaster.

Integration Management and Concurrent Engineering

The problems of integration management are easily understood if we consider the traditional way in which products and services were designed and brought to market. The different groups involved in a product design project, for example, did not work together. They worked independently and sequentially. First, the product design group developed a design that seemed to meet the marketing group's specifications. This design was submitted to top management for approval, and possible redesign if needed. When the design was accepted, a prototype was constructed. The project was then transferred to the engineering group who tested the prototype product for quality, reliability, manufacturability, and possibly altered the design to use less expensive materials. There were certain to be changes, and all changes were submitted for management approval, at which time a new prototype was constructed and subjected to testing.

After qualifying on all tests, the project moved to the manufacturing group who proceeded to plan the actual steps required to manufacture the product in the most cost-effective way, given the machinery and equipment currently available. Again, changes were submitted for approval, often to speed up or improve the production process. If the project proceeded to the production stage, distribution channels had to be arranged, packaging designed and produced, marketing strategies developed, advertising campaigns developed, and the product shipped to the distribution centers for sale and delivery.

Conflicts between the various functional groups were legend. Each group tried to optimize its contribution, which led to nonoptimization for the system. This process worked reasonably well, if haltingly, in the past, but was extremely time consuming and expensive—conditions not tolerable in today's competitive environment.

To solve these problems, the entire project was changed from one that proceeded sequentially through each of the steps from design to sale to one where the steps were carried out concurrently. *Concurrent engineering* (CE) (a.k.a. *simultaneous engineering*) was invented as a response to the time and cost associated with the traditional method. (The word "engineering" is used here in a generic sense.) In addition to the Chrysler example noted near the beginning of Chapter 2, Section 2.6, Chrysler (now Daimler-Chrysler) used CE to make their PT Cruiser ready for sale in Japan four months after it was introduced in the United States. U.S. automobile manufacturers usually take about three years to modify a car or truck for the Japanese market (*Autoweek*, May 22, 2000, p. 9).

CE has been widely used for a great diversity of projects. For example, CE was used in the design and marketing of services by a social agency; to design, manufacture, and distribute ladies' sportswear; to design, plan, and carry out a campaign for political office; to plan the maintenance schedule for a public utility; and to design and construct the space shuttle. Concurrent engineering has been generally adopted as the proper way to tackle problems that are multidisciplinary in nature.

Monte Peterson, CEO of Thermos (now a subsidiary of Nippon Sanso, Inc.), formed a flexible interdisciplinary team with representatives from marketing, manufacturing, engineering, and finance to develop a new grill that would stand out in the market. The interdisciplinary approach was used primarily to reduce the time required to complete the project. For example, by including the manufacturing people in the design process from the beginning, the team avoided some costly mistakes later on. Initially, for instance, the designers opted for tapered legs on the grill. However, after manufacturing explained at an early meeting that tapered legs would have to be custom made, the design engineers changed the design to straight legs. Under the previous system, manufacturing would not have known about the problem with the tapered legs until the design was completed. The output of this project was a revolutionary electric grill that used a new technology to give food a barbecued taste. The grill won four design awards in its first year. This is concurrent engineering in action.

Again, the word "engineering" is used in its broadest sense, that is, the art of making practical application of science. Precisely *which* sciences is not specified. If the team members are problem-oriented, CE works very well. Some interesting research has shown that when problem-oriented people with different backgrounds enter conflicts about how to deal with a problem, they often produce very creative solutions—and without damage to project quality, cost, or schedule [6, p. 161]. The group itself typically resolves the conflicts arising in such cases when they recognize that they have solved the problem. For some highly effective teams, conflict becomes a favored style of problem solving.

When team members are both argumentative and oriented to their own discipline, CE appears to be no improvement on any other method of problem solving. The PM will have to use negotiation, persuasion, and conflict resolution skills, but there is no guarantee that these will be successful. Even when intragroup conflict is not a serious issue with discipline-oriented team members, they often adopt suboptimization as the preferred approach to problem solving. They argue that experts should be allowed to exercise their specialties without interference from those who lack expertise.

The use of MTs in product development and planning is not without its difficulties. Successfully involving transfunctional teams in project planning requires that some structure be imposed on the planning process. The most common structure is simply to define the group's responsibility as being the development of a plan to accomplish whatever is established as the project objective. There is considerable evidence, however, that this will not prevent conflict on complex projects.

Interface Coordination—Interface Management

One of the PM's more difficult problems when working with MTs is coordinating the work of different functional groups interacting as team members. The team members come from different functional areas and often are not used to dealing with one another directly. For the most part, they have no established dependencies on each other and being co-members of a team is not sufficient to cause them to associate—unless the team has a mission that makes it important for the members to develop relationships.

One approach to the problem of interface coordination is to expose the structure of the work assigned to the team [2]. One can identify and map the interdependencies between various members of the project team. Clearly, the way in which team members interact will differ during different phases of the project's work, so each major phase must be mapped separately. Figure 3-6 shows the mapping for the design of a silicon chip.

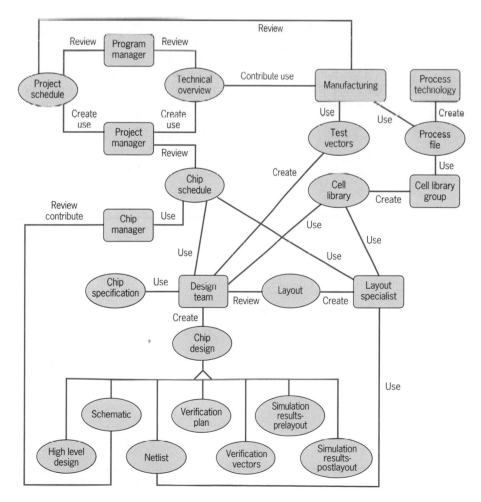

Figure 3-6   An interface mapping of a silicon chip design project. [2]

The logic of this approach to structuring MTs is reasonable. The original project plans and charts are a good initial source of information on interfaces, but project plans change during the execution of a large, complex project. Further, project plans assume, implicitly, that interfaces somehow change automatically during the different project phases—an assumption generally contrary to fact. This does not ignore the value of standard project planning and control tools of long-standing use; it simply uses interface maps to develop the coordination required to manage the interdependencies. The fundamental structure of this approach to interface management is shown in Figure 3-7.

No approach to interface coordination and management, taken alone, is sufficient. Mapping interfaces does not tell the PM what to do. The maps do, however, indicate which interfaces have a high potential for trouble. As usual, populating the project team with problem-oriented people will help. If a team member is strongly oriented toward making the project a success, rather than optimizing his or her individual contribution, it will be relatively easy for the PM to identify troublesome interfaces between members of the project team.

Comments on Empowerment and Work Teams

The use of a participatory management style has been, and will continue to be, emphasized in this book. In recent years several programs have been developed to institutionalize the participative style. Among these programs are Employee Involvement (EI), Quality Circles (QC), Total Quality Management (TQM), Self-Directed Work Teams (SDWT) [a.k.a. Self-Directed Teams (SDT) by dropping the word "work," which is what SDTs sometimes do], and Self-Managed Teams (SMT). While these programs differ somewhat in structure and in the degree to which authority is delegated to the team, they are all intended to empower workers to use their knowledge and creativity to improve products, services, and production methods.

There is no doubt that some of these teams meet their goals, and there is also no doubt that many of them do not. Research on the effectiveness of these programs yields mixed results [3]. The research (and our experience supports this) leads to the tentative conclusion that the success or failure of empowerment teams probably has more to do with the way in which the team program is implemented than with the team itself. When empowerment team programs are implemented with a well-designed plan for involvement in solving actual problems, and when the teams have full access to all rele-

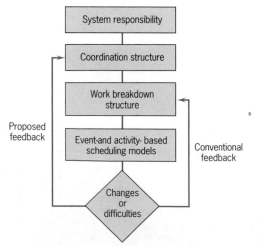

Figure 3-7 A coordination structure model for project management. [2]

vant information plus full support from senior management, the results seem to be quite good. When those conditions are not present, the results are mediocre at best.

Some of the more important advantages of empowerment are:

1. Teams generate high quality solutions to appropriate problems.
2. Micromanagement is avoided.
3. The team is given accountability for some part of the project deliverable.
4. Synergistic solutions are frequent.
5. The PM has a tool for timely team evaluation and feedback.

All of these advantages are strong motivators for team members. If the team is self-directed, however, an additional element must be present for the team to have a reasonable chance at success. Senior management needs to spell out the project's goals and to be quite clear about the range of authority and responsibility of the team. "Self-directed" does not mean "without direction"—nor does it apply to the team's mission. Furthermore, taking an active role in the team's work is not "voluntary" for team members. There must be a well-publicized way of "deselecting" team members who do not actively participate and do not carry a fair share of the team's workload.

For MT and CE to be successful, whether or not the teams are self-directed, the proper infrastructure must be in place, proper guidance must be given to the teams, and a reward structure that recognizes high-quality performance should be in place.

All of the potential problems that MT and CE can suffer notwithstanding, teams are extraordinarily valuable during the process of planning a project. They are certainly worth the effort of managing and coordinating.

> The task of managing the ways in which different groups interact during planning and implementation of projects is called "interface coordination." An important aid to interface coordination is mapping the interactions of the various groups. The task of integrating the work of these groups is called integration management. Concurrent engineering allows all groups involved in designing a project to work as a single group and join together to solve design problems simultaneously rather than separately and solving the problems sequentially.

In the next chapter, we use the project plan to develop a project budget. We discuss conflict surrounding the budgetary process. Then we deal with uncertainty, the project's (and PM's) constant companion.

REVIEW QUESTIONS

1. What are some of the benefits of setting up a project plan for routine, frequent projects?

2. Discuss the reasons for inviting the functional managers to a project launch meeting rather than their subordinates who may actually be doing the work.

3. Discuss the pros and cons of identifying and including the project team at the project launch meeting.

4. Why do so many "self-directed teams" perform poorly? What can be done to improve their performance?

5. Why is participatory management beneficial to project planning? How does the process of participatory management actually work in planning?

6. What is the difference between the *Resource* column on the action plan (that would include personnel needed by the project) and the *Assigned to* column?

7. Under what circumstances is it sensible to do without a project launch meeting?

DISCUSSION QUESTIONS

8. For each one of the nine components of a project master plan, discuss the problems that might be raised if the element was incomplete.

9. Give several examples of a type of project that would benefit from a template project action plan being developed.

10. Why is the hierarchical planning process useful for project planning? How might it influence the plan if the hierarchical planning process was not used?

11. What causes so much conflict on multidisciplinary teams? As a PM what would you try to do to prevent or reduce such conflict?

12. Of what help is a "map of interdependencies" to a PM who is managing a transdisciplinary team?

13. Develop an action plan with at least two levels for a project you are personally familiar with (e.g., moving away to college, registering for class, cleaning out a garage). (*Hint*: the plan will be more useful as a learning exercise if you have a subordinate or two—real or imaginary.) Be sure to include precedences, task durations, resource requirements, and milestones. Enter the plan in MSP.

14. Discuss the drawbacks of implementing a project plan without an LRC.

15. What are the potential ramifications of not utilizing integration management techniques or concurrent engineering while planning and implementing a project?

16. List the advantages of using an "empowered team" for planning. What conditions must be met for these advantages to accrue?

INCIDENTS FOR DISCUSSION

CompuDraw's Re-engineering Project:

The president of CompuDraw, a large computer graphics publishing firm was presented with a proposal by his Chief Operating Officer to hire a re-engineering consulting firm to come in and help cut costs through work re-design. The proposal outlined the cost of the consultants and the projected savings the firm could expect after the consultant's work was finished. The president was unclear about how the savings were determined and what would be the project specific deliverables.

Questions: What is your recommendation for the president to do next? What project planning tools would you suggest to ask the consultants to use to outline the project more specifically and address his concerns?

Movies of the Future

Movie Design, a manufacturer of movies on videotape, wants to get into the DVD business. They feel they must move into the DVD market to remain competitive. They are planning to take their top 50 selling videotape movie titles and convert them to DVD. This is a new manufacturing process for them. The company would like to manufacture 10,000–20,000 DVD movies per year beginning within nine months. The company has already selected the project manager and the project team. The project manager is ready to begin; he is most concerned about the project schedule, resources, and personnel.

Questions: If you were the project manager, which planning tools would you start with to resolve your concerns? Do these tools relate to each other? Explain.

C A S E

St. Dismas Assisted Living Facility—1

St. Dismas Medical Center, an urban, nonprofit, 450-bed rehabilitation hospital began to see a significant decline in admissions. St. Dismas' mission focuses on inpatient and outpatient rehabilitation of the severely injured and catastrophically ill. While the patient census varied from month to month, it appeared to the St. Dismas Board of Trustees that the inpatient population was slowly but steadily declining. The hospital's market researchers reported that fewer people were being severely injured due to the popularity of seat belts and bicycle/motorcycle helmets. In order to get a handle on the future of the organization, the Board and the CEO, Fred Splient M.D. called for a major strategic planning effort to take place.

In January 1999, St. Dismas held a planning retreat to identify future opportunities. The outcome of the retreat was that the Medical Center needed to focus its efforts around two major strategic initiatives. The first, a short-run initiative, was to be more cost-effective in the delivery of inpatient care. The second, a long-run strategy, was to develop new programs and services that would capitalize on the existing, highly competent rehabilitation therapy staff and St. Dismas's excellent reputation in the region.

At the time of the retreat, Fred Splient's parents were living with him and his family. Fred was an active member of the "sandwich generation." His parents were aging and developing many problems common to the geriatric populace. Their increased medical needs were beginning to wear on Fred and his family. It crossed Fred's mind that life might be more pleasant if the hospital Board approved an expansion of the Medical Center's campus to include an assisted living facility.

In March 1999, Fred had his Business Development team prepare a rough estimate of the potential return on investment of an assisted living facility. He asked the team to identify different options for facility construction and the associated costs. The team also did a complete competitive analysis and examined the options for services to be offered based on St. Dismas's potential population base and catchment area. The Business Development team visited several facilities across the country. The team also interviewed companies that could oversee the design, building, and operation of the facility for St. Dismas. The development team produced a preliminary business plan based on the recommended structure for the facility, estimated capital expenditure needs, estimated income from operation of the facility, as well as projected revenues to other Medical Center programs resulting from the facility's population.

The plan was presented at the May 1999 meeting of the Board of Trustees. Fred Splient and his team introduced the Board to the concept of opening an assisted living facility on St. Dismas's campus. The facility would be set up as a for-profit subsidiary of the Medical Center so that it could generate a profit and not be subjected to the strict guidelines of the hospital's accrediting agencies. As a subsidiary organization, however, the Board would still have control.

The chosen facility design was a freestanding apartment-like facility with a sheltered connection to the Hospital for access to the kitchen and hospital services. The facility would have 100 units with 15 to 30 of the units classified as "heavy-assisted" and built to code to house the physically and medically disabled. The rest of the units would be "light-assisted," larger apartments. The population would be approximately 110 to 150 residents, with most being single occupants rather than couples.

The light-assisted apartments could hold residents who required only minor medical and social interventions. The residents of the heavy-assisted section would have more medical needs and would require assistance getting around. The Business Development team recommended this type of programming model, because many

assisted living facilities were erected across the country, but few had a medical focus and offered the types of services that St. Dismas could offer—physical and occupational therapy programs, and behavior management programs to name a few.

The Board was assured that the facility would meet the strategic initiative of growing business. The business plan projected an immediate increase in the number of referrals to the outpatient therapy programs. Another projected deliverable of the project was to enable St. Dismas to strengthen its focus on reimbursable preventive and wellness programs for the healthier geriatric population. The project's longer term goal was to increase the census in the hospital's inpatient units by having a location where people could age in place until they were in need of hospitalization, and then such a facility would be right next door.

Depending on the exact size of the apartments, their equipment, and the actual ratio of heavy- to light-assisted units, Fred estimated that the entire project would cost between $8,500,000 and $11,000,000 for the facility construction. That estimate included the cost of land, furnishings, and a sheltered connection to the hospital. When up and running, it was estimated that the net income would range between $9,000 and $12,000 per unit per year. The team estimated the net cash flow for the entire project to be around $1,500,000 per year.

Fred requested the Board to approve the concept and allow his team to prepare a pro forma plan to the Board for approval. The plan would include a recommended design for both heavy- and light-assisted apartments. It would also include all costs of land, construction, furnishings, and staffing. Income estimates would be included and would be conservatively biased. A timetable would also be included.

The Board conducted several executive sessions, and by the middle of May voted to approve the concept. They approved the architectural-construction-management firm recommended by the team, and they requested Splient to proceed with developing a complete project plan. The Board appointed two Board members to sit on Fred's planning group.

In June, Dr. Splient gathered his executive team together and presented the project mission, scope and goals. He reported that the board had approved a small budget to finance the planning process. The Board also stipulated that construction could not begin until after the November 1999 city elections because two of the Board Members were running in that election, one for a city council seat and one as a county commissioner. The Board also stated that they would like a plan that would allow the facility to open by July 2000, as research has shown that many adult children find the summer the easiest time to assist their parents in finding an alternative to independent living arrangements. The CEO and executive team were now confident that they were ready to launch the project to plan, build, and open an assisted living facility at St. Dismas.

A few days later, Fred decided that it was time to set up the team that would take responsibility for what he called the ALF project. He quickly decided to include the following staff at the launch meeting:

- Chief Financial Officer (CFO)
- Vice President of Business Development and Marketing
- Rehab Services Medical Director
- Construction Project Manager for capital facilities projects
- Chief Operations Officer (COO) (nursing, facilities, food services, and housekeeping)
- Director of Information Services
- Director of Support Services (central supply, purchasing, and security)
- Two members of the Board of Trustees, one with construction experience and the other a probable electee to the city council.

Even though the department directors from Support Services and Information Services would not be involved until later, Fred decided to include them from the beginning. Fred knew some members of his team had a tendency to become obstacles to progress if they felt left out.

Fred named the group the ALF Project Steering Committee and held the first meeting. Fred presented his vision for the facility. He told the group that he personally would be managing this project. He led a discussion of all the major steps that must be included in the project plan, and asked each team member to identify the areas for which they would accept responsibility. The hospital's Construction Project Manager took responsibility for the construction of the facility, and the COO volunteered to oversee the building design, as well as define the needs for food services, housekeeping, staffing, and policy and procedure development. The CFO agreed to develop the budgets for each area of the project as well as the operating budget for the facility. The CFO also agreed to create the payroll and accounting systems necessary to operate the facility.

The IS director accepted responsibility to define and set up all the telecommunications and information system needs of the facility. The VP of Business Development agreed to create a preliminary marketing plan, and a communication package for the community and hospital staff. In addition she discussed organizing a major ground breaking event. The Medical Director said that he would design an assessment tool for determining residents' level of medical needs upon moving in to the facility. He felt this was the first step in defining what clinical services should be offered to residents. Fred told the team that he would develop the management structure for the new facility and work with in-house counsel to identify all governmental regulations as well as all industry standards that pertain to an assisted living facility and govern the facility's practices. Splient gave the team two months to come back with their detailed action plans for their areas of responsibility.

QUESTIONS

1. Define project deliverables.
2. Define project constraints and assumptions.
3. Develop a preliminary Level 1 action plan.
4. Is Dr. Splient a good choice for project manager? Support your position.

C A S E

John Wiley & Sons

John Wiley & Sons, Inc. publishes books, journals, and electronic products for the educational, professional, scientific, technical, and consumer markets. The oldest independent publisher in North America, Wiley is in the forefront of electronic publishing, with more than 200 products and services on disk, on CD-ROM, or available by network. Wiley has more than 11,000 active book titles and 400 journals. The company publishes 1500 new titles in a variety of formats each year. The company has approximately 2000 employees worldwide.

Wiley has U.S. publishing, marketing, and distribution centers in New York, Colorado, Maryland, New Jersey, and Illinois. A substantial portion of Wiley's business comes from international markets. In addition to offices in the United States, it has operations in Europe (England and Germany), Canada, Asia, and Australia to serve the needs of the local markets and explore opportunities for expanding its publishing programs.

In the early years, Wiley was best known for the works of Washington Irving, Edgar Allan Poe, Herman Melville, Nathaniel Hawthorne, and other nineteenth-century American literary giants. But by the turn of the century, the company was established as a leading publisher of works on science and technology.

Today its areas of specialization include the sciences, engineering, technology, mathematics, accounting, and business management, with a growing presence in general interest titles. Wiley is committed to providing information in those formats most accessible to its readers and is taking advantage of the rapid advances in digital information technology to enhance the speed and flexibility with which it delivers print publications as well as to develop a range of offerings in electronic formats.

The consulting firm you work for has been contacted by Wiley to support its textbook *Project Management in Practice*. Specifically, John Wiley and Sons is interested in contracting your consulting firm to develop the state-of-the-art website described above. Furthermore, Wiley would also like your firm to benchmark website state-of-the-art in terms of content, capabilities, and functionality prior to designing and developing this website.

Question: Develop a work breakdown structure for this project.

BIBLIOGRAPHY

1. AARON, J. M., C. P. BRATTA, and D. P. SMITH. "Achieving Total Project Control Using the Quality Gate Method." *Proceedings of the Annual Symposium of the Project Management Institute*, San Diego, October 4, 1993.

2. BAILETTI, A. J., J. R. CALLAHAN, and P. DiPIETRO. "A Coordination Structure Approach to the Management of Projects." *IEEE Transactions on Engineering Management*, November 1994.

3. BAILEY, D. E. "Comparison of Manufacturing Performance of Three Team Structures in Semiconductor Plants." *IEEE Transactions on Engineering Management*, February 1998.

4. BOWEN, H. K. *Project Management Manual*. Cambridge, MA: Harvard Business School, 9-697-034, October 6, 1997.

5. FORD, R. C., and F. S. McLAUGHLIN. "Successful Project Teams: A Study of MIS Managers." *IEEE Transactions on Engineering Management*, November 1992.

6. HAUPTMAN, O., and K. K. HIRJI. "The Influence of Process Concurrency on Project Outcomes in Product Development: An Empirical Study of Cross-Functional Teams." *IEEE Transactions on Engineering Management*. May 1996.

7. KNUTSON, J. "How to Manage a Project Launch Meeting." *PM Network*, July 1995.

8. LANGLEY, A. "Between 'Paralysis by Analysis' and 'Extinction by Instinct.'" *IEEE Engineering Management Review*, Fall 1995, reprinted from *Sloan Management Review*, Spring 1995. (This is a thoughtful article that speaks to both sides of the "How much planning should we do?" issue.)

9. LAVOLD, G. D. "Developing and Using the Work Breakdown Structure," in Cleland, D. I., and W. R. King, *Project Management Handbook*, New York: Van Nostrand Reinhold, 1983.

10. MARTIN, M. G. "Statement of Work: The Foundation for Delivering Successful Service Projects." *PM Network*, October 1998.

11. MARTIN, P. K., and K. TATE. "Kick Off the Smart Way." *PM Network*, October 1998.

12. PELLS, D. L. "Project Management Plans: An Approach to Comprehensive Planning for Complex Projects," in P. C. Dinsmore, ed., *The AMA Handbook of Project Management*, New York: AMACOM, 1993.

13. PRENTIS, E. L. "Master Project Planning: Scope, Time and Cost." *Project Management Journal*, March 1989.

14. WEBSTER, J. L., W. E. REIF, and J. S. BRACKER. "The Manager's Guide to Strategic Planning Tools and Techniques," *Planning Review*, November/December 1989, reprinted in *IEEE Engineering Management Review*, December 1990. (A fascinating compilation of planning techniques including such methods as the Delphi method, stakeholder analysis, benchmarking, critical success factors, focus group, and many others, 30 in all. It also has a short history of strategic planning. It does not, however, contain the Wheelwright-Clark method that was published after this article was written.)

15. WHEELWRIGHT, S. C., and K. B. CLARK. "Creating Project Plans to Focus Product Development." *Harvard Business Review*, March–April 1992.

4

Budgeting the Project

Having finished the planning for the technical aspects of the project, there is one more important element of planning to finish that then results in the go-ahead from top management to initiate the project. A budget must be developed in order to obtain the resources needed to accomplish the project's objectives. A budget is simply a plan for allocating organizational resources to the project activities.

But the budget also serves another purpose: It ties the project to the organization's aims and objectives through organizational policy. For example, NASA's Mars Pathfinder-Rover mission embedded a new NASA policy—to achieve a set of limited exploration opportunities at extremely limited cost. In 1976, NASA's two Viking-Mars Lander missions cost $3 billion to develop. In 1997, however, the Pathfinder-Rover mission cost only $175 million to develop, a whopping 94 percent reduction. The difference was the change in organizational policy from a design-to-performance orientation to a design-to-cost orientation.

In Chapter 3, we described the project planning process as a set of steps that began with the overall project plan and then divided and subdivided the plan's elements into smaller and smaller pieces that could finally be sequenced, assigned, scheduled, and budgeted. Hence, the project budget is nothing more than the project plan, based on the action plan or WBS, expressed in monetary terms.

Once the budget is developed, it acts as a tool for upper management to monitor and guide the project. Appropriate data must be collected and reported in a timely manner or the value of the budget to identify current financial problems or anticipate upcoming ones will be lost. This collection and reporting system must be as carefully designed as the initial project plans because late reporting, inaccurate reporting, or reporting to the wrong person will negate the main purpose of the budget. In one instance, the manager of a large computer company was supposed to receive quarterly results for the purpose of correcting problems in the following quarter. The results took four months to reach him, however, completely negating the value of the budgeting-reporting system.

In this chapter, we will first examine some different methods of budgeting and cost estimating, as used for projects. Then we will consider some ways to improve the cost estimation process, including some technical approaches such as learning curves and tracking signals. Last, we discuss the problem of budget uncertainty and the role of risk management when planning budgets.

4.1 METHODS OF BUDGETING

Budgeting is simply the process of forecasting what resources the project will require, how much will be needed, when they will be needed, and how much they will cost. Tables 4-1 and 4-2 depict the direct costs involved in making a video tape. Table 4-1 shows the cost per unit of usage (cost/hour) of seven different personnel categories and one facility. Note that the facility does not charge by the hour, but has a flat rate charge. Table 4-2 shows the resource categories and amounts used for each activity required to make the tape. The resource costs shown become part of the budget for producing the tape. As you will see below, overhead charges may be added to these direct charges.

Most businesses and professions employ experienced estimators who can forecast with amazingly small errors. For instance, a bricklayer can usually estimate within 1 or 2 percent the number of bricks required to construct a brick wall of given dimensions. In many fields, the methods of cost estimation are well documented based on the experience of estimators gathered over many years. The cost of a building, or house, is usually estimated by the square feet of floor area multiplied by an appropriate dollar value per square foot and then adjusted for any unusual factors.

Budgeting a project such as the development of a control system for a new computer, however, is often more difficult than budgeting more routine activities—and even more difficult than regular departmental budgeting which can always be estimated as: "Same as last year plus X percent." But project budgeters do not usually have tradition to guide them. Projects are, after all, unique activities. Of course, there may be somewhat similar past projects that can serve as a model, but these are rough guides at best. Forecasting a budget for a multiyear project such as a large product line or service

Table 4-1   Resource Cost per Unit for Producing a Videotape

	Producing a Videotape Resource Cost					
ID	Resource Name	Max. Units	Std. Rate	Ovt. Rate	Cost/Use	Accrue At
1	Scriptwriter	1	$25.00/hr	$40.00/hr	$0.00	Prorated
2	Producer	1	$45.00/hr	$60.00/hr	$0.00	Prorated
3	Client	0.2	$0.00/hr	$0.00/hr	$0.00	Prorated
4	Secretary	1	$10.00/hr	$20.00/hr	$0.00	Prorated
5	Editor	1	$25.00/hr	$45.00/hr	$0.00	Prorated
6	Production staff	1	$20.00/hr	$35.00/hr	$0.00	Prorated
7	Editing staff	1	$20.00/hr	$35.00/hr	$0.00	Prorated
8	Editing room	1	$0.00/hr	$0.00/hr	$250.00	Start

Table 4-2   Budget by Resource for Producing a Videotape

Producing a Videotape
Budget by Resource

ID	Task Name	Resource Work Hours	Cost	Task Duration
1	Project approval	0 hrs	$0.00	0 days
2	Scriptwriting	112 hrs	$2,800.00	14 days
	Scriptwriter	112 hrs	$2,800.00	
3	Schedule shoots	240 hrs	$5,400.00	15 days
4	Begin scheduling	0 hrs	$0.00	0 days
5	Propose shoots	120 hrs	$2,800.00	5 days
	Scriptwriter	40 hrs	$1,000.00	
	Producer	40 hrs	$1,800.00	
	Client	40 hrs	$0.00	
6	Hire secretary	40 hrs	$1,800.00	5 days
	Producer	40 hrs	$1,800.00	
7	Schedule shoots	80 hrs	$800.00	10 days
	Secretary	80 hrs	$800.00	
8	Scheduling comp	0 hrs	$0.00	0 days
9	Script approval	80 hrs	$1,800.00	5 days
	Producer	40 hrs	$1,800.00	
	Client	40 hrs	$0.00	
10	Revise script	80 hrs	$2,800.00	5 days
	Scriptwriter	40 hrs	$1,000.00	
	Producer	40 hrs	$1,800.00	
11	Shooting	160 hrs	$3,600.00	10 days
	Editor	80 hrs	$2,000.00	
	Production staff	80 hrs	$1,600.00	
12	Editing	168 hrs	$2,770.00	7 days
	Editor	56 hrs	$1,400.00	
	Editing staff	56 hrs	$1,120.00	
	Editing room	56 hrs	$250.00	
13	Final approval	160 hrs	$3,050.00	5 days
	Producer	40 hrs	$1,800.00	
	Client	40 hrs	$0.00	
	Editor	40 hrs	$1,000.00	
	Editing room	40 hrs	$250.00	
14	Deliver video to client	0 hrs	$0.00	0 days

development project is even more hazardous because the unknowns can escalate quickly with changes in technology, materials, and even the findings of the project up to that point.

Organizational tradition also impacts project budgeting, particularly in decisions about how overhead and other indirect costs are charged against the project. Every firm has its own accounting idiosyncrasies, and the PM cannot expect the accounting department to make special allowances for his or her individual project. Although accounting will charge normal expenditures against a particular activity's account number, as identified in the WBS, unexpected overhead or indirect expenses may suddenly appear when the PM least expects it, and probably at the worst possible time. There is no alternative—the PM must simply become completely familiar with the organization's accounting system, as painful as that may be.

In the process of gaining this familiarity, the PM will discover that cost may be viewed from three different perspectives [7]. The PM recognizes a cost once a commitment is made to pay someone for resources or services, for example when a machine is ordered. The accountant recognizes an expense when an invoice is received—not, as most people believe, when the invoice is paid. The controller perceives an expense when the check for the invoice is mailed. The PM is concerned with commitments made against the project budget. The accountant is concerned with costs when they are actually incurred. The controller is concerned with managing the organization's cash flows. Because the PM must manage the project, it is advisable for the PM to set up a system that will allow him or her to track the project's commitments.

Another aspect of accounting that will become important to the unaware PM is that accountants live in a linear world. When a project activity has an $8,000 charge and runs over a four-month period, the accounting department (or worse, their software) simply spreads the $8,000 evenly over the time period, resulting in a $2,000 allocation per month. If expenditures for this activity are planned to be $5,000, $1,000, $1,000, and $1,000, the PM should not be surprised when the organization's controller storms into the project office after the first month screaming about the unanticipated and unacceptable cash flow demands of the project!

Next, we look at two very different approaches for gathering the data for budgeting a project: top-down and bottom-up.

Top-Down Budgeting

The top-down approach to budgeting is based on the collective judgments and experiences of top and middle managers concerning similar past projects. These managers estimate the overall project cost by estimating the costs of the major tasks, which estimates are then given to the next lower level of managers to split up among the tasks under their control, and so on, until all the work is budgeted.

The advantage of this approach is that overall budget costs can be estimated quite accurately, though individual elements may be in substantial error. Another advantage is that errors in funding small tasks need not be individually identified because the overall budget allows for such exceptions. Similarly, the good chance that some small but important task was overlooked does not usually cause a serious budgetary problem. The experience and judgment of top management are presumed to include all such elements in the overall estimate.

Bottom-Up Budgeting

In bottom-up budgeting, the WBS or action plan identifies the elemental tasks, whose resource requirements are estimated by those responsible for executing them (e.g., programmer-hours in a software project). This results in much more accurate estimates. The resources, such as labor and materials, are then converted to costs and aggregated to different levels of the project, eventually resulting in an overall direct cost for the project. The PM then adds, according to organizational policy, indirect costs such as general and administrative, a reserve for contingencies, and a profit figure to arrive at a final project budget.

Bottom-up budgets are usually more accurate in the detailed tasks, but risk the chance of overlooking some small but costly tasks. Such an approach, however, is common in organizations with a participative management philosophy and leads to better morale, greater acceptance of the resulting budget, and heightened commitment by the project team. It is also a good managerial training technique for aspiring project and general managers.

Unfortunately, true bottom-up budgeting is rare. Upper level managers are reluctant to let the workers develop the budget, fearing the natural tendency to overstate costs, and fearing complaints if the budget must later be reduced to meet organizational resource limitations. Moreover, the budget is upper management's primary tool for control of the project, and they are reluctant to let others set the control limits.

We recommend that organizations employ both forms of developing budgets. They both have advantages, and the use of one does not exclude the use of the other. Making a single budget by combining the two depends on setting up a specific system to negotiate the differences. We discuss just such a system below. The only disadvantage of this approach is that it requires some extra time and trouble, a small price to pay for the advantages.

> Project budgeting is a difficult task due to the lack of precedent and experience with unique project undertakings. Yet, understanding the organization's accounting system is mandatory for a PM. The two major ways of generating a project budget are top-down and bottom-up. The former is usually accurate overall but possibly includes significant error for low-level tasks. The latter is usually accurate for low-level tasks but risks overlooking some small but potentially costly tasks. Most organizations use top-down budgeting in spite of the fact that bottom-up results in better acceptance and commitment to the budget.

4.2 COST ESTIMATING

In this section, we look at the details of the process of estimating costs and some dangers of arbitrary cuts in the project budget. We also describe and illustrate the difference between activity budgeting and program budgeting.

Work Element Costing

The task of building a budget is relatively straightforward but tedious. Each work element is evaluated for its resource requirements, and its costs are then determined. For example, suppose a certain task is expected to require 16 hours of labor at $10 per hour, and the required materials cost $235. In addition, the organization charges overhead for the use of utilities, indirect labor, and so forth at a rate of 50 percent of direct labor. Then, the total task cost will be

$$\$235 + (16 \text{ hr} \times \$10/\text{hr}) \times 1.5 = \$475.$$

In some organizations, the PM adds the overhead charges to the budget. In others, the labor time and materials are just sent to the accounting department and they run the numbers, add the appropriate overhead, and total the costs. Although overhead was charged here against direct labor, more recent accounting practices such as activity-based costing may charge portions of the overhead against other cost drivers such as machine time, weight of raw materials, or total time to project completion.

Direct resource costs such as for materials and machinery needed solely for a particular project are usually charged to the project without an overhead add-on. If machinery from elsewhere in the organization is used, this may be charged to the project at a certain rate (e.g., $/hr) that will include depreciation charges, and then will be credited to the budget of the department owning and paying for the machine. On top of this, there is often a charge for GS&A (general, sales, and administrative) costs that includes upper management, staff functions, sales and marketing, plus any other costs not included in the overhead charge. GS&A may be charged as a percentage of direct costs, all direct and indirect costs, or on other bases including total time to completion.

Thus, the fully costed task will include direct costs for labor, machinery, and resources such as materials, plus overhead charges, and finally, GS&A charges. The full cost budget is then used by accounting to estimate the profit to be earned by the project. The wise PM, however, will also construct a budget of direct costs for his or her own use. This budget provides the information required to manage the project without being confounded with costs over which he or she has no control.

Note that the overhead and GS&A effect can result in a severe penalty when a project runs late, adding significant additional and possibly unexpected costs to the project. Again, we stress the importance of the PM thoroughly understanding the organization's accounting system, and especially how overhead and other such costs are charged to the project.

Of course, this process can also be reversed to the benefit of the PM by minimizing the use of drivers of high cost. Sometimes clients will even put clauses in contracts to foster such behavior. For example, when the state of Pennsylvania contracted for the construction of the Limerick nuclear power generating facility in the late 1980s, they included such an incentive fee provision in the contract. This provision stated that any savings that resulted from finishing the project early would be split between the state and the contractor. As a result, the contractor went to extra expense and trouble to make sure the project was completed early. The project came in 8 months ahead of its 49-month due date and the state and the contractor split the $400 million savings out of the total $3.2 billion budget.

The Impact of Budget Cuts

In the previous chapter on planning, we described a process in which the PM plans Level 1 activities, setting a tentative budget and duration for each. Subordinates (and this term refers to anyone working on the project even though such individuals may not officially report to the PM and may be "above" the PM on the firm's organizational chart) then take responsibility for specifying the Level 2 activities required to produce the Level 1 task. As a part of the Level 2 specifications, tentative budgets and durations are noted for each Level 2 activity. The PM's initial budget and duration estimates are examples of top-down budgeting. The subordinate's estimates of the Level 2 task budgets and durations are bottom-up budgeting. As we promised, we now deal with combining the two budgets.

We will label the Level 1 task estimate of duration of the ith task as t_i, and the respective cost estimate as r_i, the t standing for "time" and the r for "resources." In the meantime, the subordinate has estimated task costs and durations for each of the Level 2 tasks that comprise Level 1 task i. We label the *aggregate* cost and duration of these Level 2 activities as r_i' and t_i', respectively. It would be nice if r_i equaled r_i', but the reality is rarely that neat. In general, $r_i << r_i'$. (The same is true of the time estimates, t_i and t_i'.) There are three reasons why this happens. First, jobs always look easier, faster, and cheaper to the boss than to the person who has to do them [6]. Second, bosses are usually optimistic and never admit that details have been forgotten or that anything can or will go wrong. Third, subordinates are naturally pessimistic and want to build in protection for everything that might possibly go wrong.

It is important that we make an assumption for the following discussion. We assume that both boss and subordinate are reasonably honest. What follows is a win-win negotiation, and it will fail if either party is dishonest. (We feel it is critically important to remind readers that it is never smart to view the other party in a negotiation as either stupid or ignorant. Almost without fail, such thoughts are obvious to the other party and the possibility of a win-win solution is dead.) The first step in reducing the difference between the superior's and subordinate's estimates occurs when the worker explains the reality of the task to the boss, and r_i rises. Encouraged by the fact that the boss seems to understand some of the problems, the subordinate responds to the boss's request to remove some of the protective padding. The result is that r_i' falls.

The conversation now shifts to the technology involved in the subordinate's work and the two parties search for efficiencies in the Level 2 work plan. If they find some, the two estimates get closer still, or, possibly, the need for resources may even drop below either party's estimate.

To complete our discussion, let's assume that after all improvements have been made, r_i' is still somewhat higher than r_i. Should the boss accept the subordinate's cost estimate or insist that the subordinate accept the boss's estimate? To answer this question, we must recall the discussion of project life cycles from Chapter 1. We discussed two different common forms of life cycles and these are illustrated again, for convenience, in Figure 4-1. One curve is S-shaped and the other is exponential, reaching upward toward infinity. As it happens, the shapes of these curves hold the key to our decision.

If the project life cycle is S-shaped, then with a somewhat reduced level of resources, a smaller than proportional cut will be made in the project's objectives or performance, likely not a big problem. If the project's life cycle is exponential, the impact of inadequate resources will be serious, a larger than proportional cut will be made in

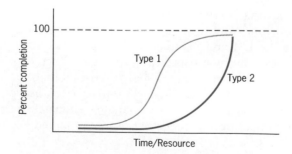

Figure 4-1   Two project life cycles (cf. Figures 1-2 and 1-3).

the project's performance. The same effect occurs during an "economy drive" when a senior manager decrees an across-the-board budget cut for all projects of say, 5 or 10 percent. For a project with an exponential life cycle, the result is disaster. It is not necessary to know the actual shape of a project's life cycle with any precision. One needs merely to know the probable curvature (concave or convex to the baseline) of the last stage of the cycle for the project being considered.

The message here is that for projects with S-shaped life cycles, the top-down budgeting process is probably acceptable. For exponential life-cycle projects, it is dangerous for upper management not to accept the bottom-up budget estimates. At the very least, management should pay attention when the PM complains that the budget is insufficient to complete the project. An example of this problem is NASA's Space Shuttle Program, projected by NASA to cost $10–13 billion but cut by Congress to $5.2 billion. Fearing a cancellation of the entire program if they pointed out the overwhelming developmental problems they faced, NASA acquiesced to the inadequate budget. As a result, portions of the program fell three years behind schedule and had cost overruns of 60 percent. As the program moved into the operational flight stage, problems stemming from the inadequate budget surfaced in multiple areas, culminating in the Challenger explosion in January 1986.

Activity vs. Program Budgeting

Traditional organizational budgets are typically *activity* oriented and based on historical data accumulated through an activity-based accounting system. Individual expenses are classified and assigned to basic budget lines such as phone, materials, fixed personnel types (salaried, exempt, etc.), or to production centers or processes. These lines are then aggregated and reported by organizational units such as departments or divisions.

Project budgets can also be presented as activity budgets, such as in Table 4-3 where one page of a six-page monthly budget report for a real estate management project is illustrated. When multiple projects draw resources from several different organizational units, the budget may be divided between these multiple units in some arbitrary fashion, thereby losing the ability to control project resources as well as the reporting of individual project expenditures against the budget.

This difficulty gave rise to *program budgeting*, illustrated in Table 4-4. Here the program-oriented project budget is divided by task and expected time of expenditure, thereby allowing aggregation across projects. Budget reports are shown both aggregated and disaggregated by "regular operations" and each of the projects has its own budget. For example, Table 4-3 would have a set of columns for regular operations as well as for each project.

> Cost estimating is more tedious than complex except where overhead and GS&A expenses are concerned. Thus, the wise PM will learn the organization's accounting system thoroughly. Low budget estimates or budget cuts will not usually be too serious for S-shaped life-cycle projects but can be disastrous for exponential life-cycle projects. Two kinds of project budget exist, usually depending on where projects report in the organization. Activity budgets show lines of standard activity by actual and budget for given time periods. Program budgets show expenses by task and time period. Program budgets are then aggregated by reporting unit.

Table 4-3   Typical Monthly Budget for a Real Estate Project (page 1 of 6)

	Current			
	Actual	**Budget**	**Variance**	**Pct.**
Corporate—Income Statement				
Revenue				
8430 Management fees				
8491 Prtnsp. reimb.—property mgmt.	7,410.00	6,222.00	1,188.00	119.0
8492 Prtnsp. reimb.—owner acquisition	.00	3,750.00	3,750.00—	.0
8493 Prtnsp. reimb.—rehab	.00	.00	.00	.0
8494 Other income	.00	.00	.00	.0
8495 Reimbursements—others	.00	.00	.00	.0
Total revenue	7,410.00	9,972.00	2,562.00—	74.3
Operating expenses				
Payroll & P/R benefits				
8511 Salaries	29,425.75	34,583.00	5,157.25	85.0
8512 Payroll taxes	1,789.88	3,458.00	1,668.12	51.7
8513 Group ins & med. reimb.	1,407.45	1,040.00	387.45—	135.3
8515 Workers' compensation	43.04	43.00	.04—	100.0
8516 Staff apartments	.00	.00	.00	.0
8517 Bonus	.00	.00	.00	.0
Total payroll & P/R benefits	32,668.12	39,124.00	6,457.88	83.5
Travel & entertainment expenses				
8512 Travel	456.65	300.00	156.65—	152.2
8522 Promotion, entertainment & gift	69.52	500.00	430.48	13.9
8523 Auto	1,295.90	1,729.00	433.10	75.0
Total travel & entertainment exp.	1,822.07	2,529.00	706.93	72.1
Professional fees				
8531 Legal fees	419.00	50.00	369.00—	838.0
8532 Accounting fees	289.00	.00	289.00—	.0
8534 Temporary help	234.58	200.00	34.58—	117.2

Table 4-4   Project Budget by Task and Month

Task	I	J	Estimate	Monthly Budget (£)							
				1	**2**	**3**	**4**	**5**	**6**	**7**	**8**
A	1	2	7000	5600	1400						
B	2	3	9000		3857	5143					
C	2	4	10000		3750	5000	1250				
D	2	5	6000		3600	2400					
E	3	7	12000				4800	4800	2400		
F	4	7	3000				3000				
G	5	6	9000			2571	5143	1286			
H	6	7	5000					3750	1250		
I	7	8	8000						2667	5333	
J	8	9	6000								6000
			75000	5600	12,607	15,114	14,193	9836	6317	5333	6000

4.3 IMPROVING COST ESTIMATES

In this section, we discuss a number of ways for improving the process of cost estimating. These range from better formalization of the process, using forms and other simple procedures, to more sophisticated techniques involving learning curves and tracking signals. We conclude with some miscellaneous topics, including behavioral issues that often lead to incorrect budget estimates.

Forms

The use of simple forms such as that in Figure 4-2 can be of considerable help to the PM in obtaining accurate estimates, not only of direct costs, but also when the resource is needed, how many are needed, who should be contacted, and if it will be available when needed. The information can be collected for each task on an individual form and then aggregated for the project as a whole.

Project name _____
Date _____
Task number _____

RESOURCES NEEDED

Resources	Person to Contact	How Many/ Much Needed	When Needed	Check (√) If Available
People: Managers, Supervisors				
Professional & Technical				
Nontechnical				
Money				
Materials: Facilities				
Equipment				
Tools				
Power				
Space				
Special Services: Research & Test				
Typing/clerical				
Reproduction				
Others				

Figure 4-2   Form for gathering data on project resource needs.

Not infrequently, organizations will approve projects that are forecast to lose money when fully costed and sometimes even when only direct costed. Such decisions by upper management are not necessarily foolish because there may be other, more important reasons for proceeding with a project, such as to:

- Acquire knowledge concerning a specific or new technology
- Get the organization's "foot in the door"
- Obtain the parts, service, or maintenance portion of the work
- Allow them to bid on a lucrative, follow-on contract
- Improve their competitive position
- Broaden a product line or line of business

Of course, such decisions are expected to lose money in the short term only and over the longer term will bring extra profits to the organization. It should be understood that "lowball" or "buy-in" bids (bidding low with the intent of cutting corners on work and material, or forcing subsequent contract changes) are unethical practices, violate the PMI Code of Ethics for Project Managers, and are clearly dishonest.

Learning Curves

Suppose a firm wins a contract to supply 25 units of a complex electronic device to a customer. Although the firm is competent to produce this device, it has never produced one as complex as this. Based on the firm's experience, it estimates that if it were to build many such devices it would take about four hours of direct labor per unit produced. With this estimate, and the wage and benefit rates the firm is paying, the PM can derive an estimate of the direct labor cost to complete the contract.

Unfortunately, the estimate will be in considerable error because the PM is underestimating the labor costs to produce the initial units that will take much longer than four hours each. Likewise, if the firm built a prototype of the device and recorded the direct labor hours, which may run as high as 10 hours for this device, this estimate applied to the contract of 25 units would give a result that is much too high.

In both cases, the reason for the error is the learning exhibited by humans when they repeat a task. In general, unit performance improves by a fixed percent each time the total production quantity doubles. More specifically, *each time the output doubles, the worker hours per unit decrease to a fixed percentage of their previous value.* This percentage is called the learning rate, and typical values run between 70 and 95 percent. The higher values are for more mechanical tasks, while the lower, faster-learning values are for more mental tasks such as solving problems. A common rate in manufacturing is 80 percent.

For example, if the device described in the earlier example required 10 hours to produce the first unit and this firm generally followed a typical 80 percent learning curve, then the second unit would require $.80 \times 10 = 8$ hours, the fourth unit would require 6.4 hours, the eighth unit 5.12 hours, and so on. Of course, after a certain number of repetitions, say 100 or 200, the time per unit levels out and little further improvement occurs.

Mathematically, this relationship we just described follows a negative exponential function. Using this function, the time required to produce the nth unit can be calculated as

$$T_n = T_1 n^r$$

where T_n is the time required to complete the nth unit, T_1 is time required to complete the very first unit, and r is the exponent of the learning curve and is calculated as the log(learning rate)/log(2). Tables are widely available for calculating the completion time of unit n and the cumulative time to produce units one through n for various learning rates; for example, see [14]. The impact of learning can also be incorporated into spreadsheets developed to help prepare the budget for a project as is illustrated in the example at the end of this section.

The use of learning curves in project management has increased greatly in recent years. For instance, methods have been developed to approximate composite learning curves for entire projects [1], for approximating total costs from the unit learning curve [4], and for including learning curve effects in critical resource diagramming [2]. The conclusion is that the effects of learning, even in "one-time" projects, should not be ignored. If costs are underestimated, the result will be an unprofitable project and senior management will be unhappy. If costs are overestimated, the bid will be lost to a savvier firm and senior management will be unhappy.

Media One Consultants

Media One Consultants is a small consulting firm that specializes in developing the electronic media that accompanies major textbooks. A typical project requires the development of an electronic testbank, PowerPoint lecture slides, and a website to support the textbook.

A team consisting of three of the firm's consultants just completed the content for the first of eighteen chapters of an operations management textbook for a major college textbook publisher. In total, it took the team 21 hours to complete this content. The consultants are each billed out at $65/hour plus 20 percent to cover overhead. Past experience indicates that projects of this type follow a 78 percent learning curve.

The publisher's developmental editor recently sent an email message to the team leader inquiring into when the project will be complete and what the cost will be. Should the team leader attempt to account for the impact of learning in answering these questions? How big a difference does incorporating learning into the budget make? What are the managerial implications of not incorporating learning into the time and cost estimates?

The team leader developed the spreadsheet below to estimate the budget and completion time for this project. The top of the spreadsheet contains key parameters such as the learning rate, the consultants' hourly billout rate, the overhead rate, and the time required to complete the first chapter. The middle of the spreadsheet contains formulas to calculate both the unit cost and time of each chapter and the cumulative cost and time.

According to the spreadsheet, the cost of the project is $14,910 and will require in total 191.2 hours. Had the impact of learning not been considered, the team leader would have likely grossly overestimated the project's cost to be $29,484 (1,638 × 18) and its duration to be 278 (21 × 18) hours. Clearly, several negative consequences could be incurred if these inflated time and cost estimates were used. For example, the publisher might decide to reevaluate its decision to award the contract to Media One. Furthermore, the time when the team members would be able to start on their next assignment would be incorrectly estimated. At a minimum, this would complicate the start of future projects. Perhaps more damaging, however, is that it could lead to lost business if potential clients were not willing to wait for their project to begin based on the inflated time estimates.

	A	B	C	D	E	F
1	Learning Rate	78.0%				
2	Hourly Rate	$65				
3	Overhead Rate	20.0%				
4	Time for First Unit	21				
5						
6			Cumulative	Chapter	Cumulative	
7	**Chapter Number**	**Unit Time**	**Time**	**Cost**	**Cost**	
8	1	21.0	21.0	$1,638	$1,638	
9	2	16.4	37.4	$1,278	$2,916	
10	3	14.2	51.5	$1,105	$4,020	
11	4	12.8	64.3	$997	$5,017	
12	5	11.8	76.1	$920	$5,937	
13	6	11.0	87.2	$862	$6,799	
14	7	10.5	97.6	$815	$7,614	
15	8	10.0	107.6	$777	$8,391	
16	9	9.6	117.1	$745	$9,137	
17	10	9.2	126.3	$718	$9,854	
18	11	8.9	135.2	$693	$10,548	
19	12	8.6	143.8	$672	$11,220	
20	13	8.4	152.2	$653	$11,873	
21	14	8.2	160.4	$636	$12,509	
22	15	8.0	168.3	$620	$13,130	
23	16	7.8	176.1	$606	$13,736	
24	17	7.6	183.7	$593	$14,329	
25	18	7.5	191.2	$581	$14,910	
26						
27	*Key Formulas:*					
28	B8	=B4				
29	B9	=B$8*(A9^(LOG(B$1)/LOG(2))) {copy to cells B10:B25}				
30	C8	=B8				
31	C9	=B9+C8 {copy to cells C10:C25}				
32	D8	=(B8*B$2)*(1+B$3)				
33	D9	=(B9*B$2)*(1+B$3) {copy to cells D10:D25}				
34	E8	=D8				
35	E9	=D9+E8 {copy to cells E10:E25}				

Tracking Signals

In Chapter 3, we noted that people do not seem to learn by experience, no matter how much they urge others to do so. PMs spend much time estimating—activity costs and durations, among many other things. There are two types of error in those estimates. First, there is *random error*. Errors are random when there is a roughly equal chance that estimates are above or below the true value of a variable, and the average size of the error is approximately equal for over and under estimates. If either of the above is not true for an estimator—either the chance of over or under estimates are not about equal or the size of over or under estimates are not approximately equal—the estimates are said to be *biased*. Random errors cancel out, which means that if we add them up the sum will approach zero. Errors caused by bias do not cancel out. They are *systematic* errors.

Calculation of a number called the *tracking signal* can reveal if there is systematic bias in cost and other estimates and whether the bias is positive or negative. Knowing this can then be quite helpful to a PM in making future estimates. Consider the spreadsheet data in Figure 4-3 where estimated and actual values for some factor are listed in the order they were made, indicated for ease of reference by "period." In order to compare estimates of different resources measured in different units and of different magnitudes, we will derive a tracking signal based on the *ratio* of actual to estimated values rather than the usual *difference* between the two.

To calculate the first period ratio in Figure 4-3, for example, we would take the ratio 163/155 = 1.052. This means that the actual was 5.2 percent higher than the estimate, a forecast that was biased low. In column D, we list these errors for each of the

	A	B	C	D	E	F	G
1	This is a template for improving one's estimating skills						
2							
3	MAR = Sum[|(At / Et)−1|] / n						
4	Tracking Signal = Sum[(At / Et)−1] / MAR						
5							Tracking
6	Period	Estimate	Actual	$(A_t / E_t) - 1$	$|(A_t / E_t) - 1|$	MAR	Signal
7	1	155	163	5.2%	5.2%		
8	2	242	240	−0.8%	0.8%	0.030	1.448
9	3	46	67	45.7%	45.7%	0.172	2.904
10	4	69	78	13.0%	13.0%	0.162	3.898
11	5	75	71	−5.3%	5.3%	0.140	4.120
12	6	344	423	23.0%	23.0%	0.155	5.205
13	7	56	49	−12.5%	12.5%	0.151	4.523
14	8	128	157	22.7%	22.7%	0.160	5.670
15							
16	Total			90.8%	128.1%		
17							
18	Formulas:						
19	Cell D7	=(C7/B7)−1 {copy to cells D8:D14}					
20	Cell E7	=ABS(D7) {copy to cells E8:E14}					
21	Cell F8	=SUM(E$7:E8)/COUNT(E$7:E8) {copy to cells F9:F14}					
22	Cell G8	=SUM(D$7:D8)/F8 {copy to cells G9:G14}					
23	Cell D16	=SUM(D7:D14) {copy to cell E16}					

Figure 4-3 Excel® template for finding bias in estimations.

periods and then cumulate them at the bottom of the spreadsheet. Note that in columns D and E we subtract 1 from the ratio. This centers the data around zero rather than 1.0, which makes some ratios positive, indicating an actual greater than the forecast, and other ratios negative, indicating an actual less than the forecast. If the cumulative percent error at the bottom of the spreadsheet is positive, which it is in this case, it means that the actuals are usually greater than the estimates, and vice versa, of course. The forecaster is biased, low if the ratio is positive and high if it is negative. The larger the percent error, the greater the bias.

Column E simply shows the absolute value of column D. Column F is the "mean absolute ratio," abbreviated MAR, which is the running average of the values in column E up to that period. (Check the formulas in the spreadsheet of Figure 4-3.) The tracking signal listed in column G is the ratio of the running sum of the values in column D divided by the MAR for that period. If the estimates are unbiased, the running sum of ratios in column D will be about zero and dividing this by the MAR will give a very small tracking signal, possibly zero. On the other hand, if there is considerable bias in the estimates, either positive or negative, the running sum of the ratios in column D will grow quite large. Then, when divided by the mean absolute ratio this will show whether it is greater than the variability in the estimates or not. If the bias is high, resulting in negative ratios, the resulting tracking signal will also be negative.

It should be noted that it is not simply the bias that is of interest to the PM, although that is very important. In addition, the MAR is important because this indicates the variability of the estimates compared with the resulting actual values. With experience, the MAR should decrease over time though it will never reach zero.

Other Factors

Studies consistently show that between 60 and 85 percent of projects fail to meet their time, cost, and/or performance objectives. The record for information system (IS) projects is particularly poor, it seems. For example, there are at least 45 estimating models available for IS projects but few IS managers use any of them [9, 12]. While the variety of problems that can plague project cost estimates seems to be unlimited, there are some that occur with high frequency and we will discuss each of these in turn.

Changes in resource prices, for example, are a common problem. The most common managerial approach to this problem is to increase all cost estimates by some fixed percentage. A better approach, however, is to identify each input that has a significant impact on the costs and to estimate the rate of price change for each one. The Bureau of Labor Statistics (BLS) in the U.S. Department of Commerce publishes price data and "inflators" for a wide range of commodities, machinery, equipment, and personnel specialities. (The BLS may be contacted at http://stats.bls.gov or www.bls.gov.)

Another problem is overlooking the need to factor into the estimated costs an adequate allowance for waste and spoilage. Again, the best approach is to determine the individual rates of waste and spoilage for each task rather than to use some fixed percentage.

A similar problem is not adding an allowance for increased personnel costs due to loss and replacement of skilled project team members. Not only will new members go through a learning period, which increases the time and cost of the relevant tasks, but professional salaries generally increase faster than the general average. Thus, it may cost substantially more to replace a team member with a newcomer who has about the same level of experience.

Then there is also Brooks's [3] "mythical man-month" effect which was discovered in the IS field but applies just as well in projects. As workers are hired, either for additional capacity or to replace those who leave, they require training in the project environment before they become productive. The training is, of course, informal on-the-job training conducted by their coworkers who must take time from their own project tasks, thus resulting in ever more reduced capacity as more workers are hired.

And there is the behavioral possibility that, in the excitement to get a project approved, or to win a bid, or perhaps even due to pressure from upper management, the project cost estimator gives a more "optimistic" picture than reality warrants. Inevitably, the estimate understates the cost. When the project is finally executed, the actual costs then result in a project that misses its profit goals, or worse, fails to make a profit at all.

Even organizational climate factors influence cost estimation. If the penalty for overestimating costs is much more severe than underestimating, almost all costs will be underestimated, and vice versa. A major manufacturer of airplane landing gear parts wondered why the firm was no longer successful, over several years, in winning competitive bids. An investigation was conducted and revealed that, three years earlier, the firm was late on a major delivery to an important customer and paid a huge penalty as well as being threatened with the loss of future business. The reason the firm was late was because an insufficient number of expensive, hard to obtain parts was purchased for the project and more could not be obtained without a long delay. The purchasing manager was demoted and replaced by his assistant. The assistant's solution to this problem was to include a 10 percent allowance for additional, hard to obtain parts in every cost proposal. This resulted in every proposal from the firm being significantly higher than their competitors' proposals in this narrow-margin business.

There is also a probabilistic element in most projects. For example, projects such as writing software require that every element work 100 percent correctly for the final product to perform to specifications. In programming software, if there are 1000 lines of code and each line has a 99.9 percent probability of being accurate, the likelihood of the final program working is only about 37 percent!

Finally, there is plain bad luck. What is indestructible, breaks. What is impenetrable, leaks. What is certified, guaranteed, and warranted, fails. The wise PM includes allowances for "unexpected contingencies."

There are many ways of estimating project costs; we suggest trying all of them and then using those that "work best" for your situation. The PM should take into consideration as many known influences as can be predicted, and those that cannot be predicted must then simply be "allowed for."

There are numerous ways to improve the process of cost estimation ranging from simple but useful forms and procedures to special techniques such as learning curves and tracking signals. Most estimates are in error, however, because of simpler reasons such as not using available tools, common sense, or failing to allow for problems and contingencies, such as having to replace workers midstream. In addition, there are behavioral and organizational reasons, such as informal incentive systems that reward inaccurate estimates.

4.4 BUDGET UNCERTAINTY AND RISK MANAGEMENT

In spite of the care and effort expended to create an accurate and fair budget, it is still only an estimate made under conditions of uncertainty. Because projects are unique, risk pervades all elements of the project, and particularly the project's goals of performance, schedule, and budget. We will discuss these issues of uncertainty and risk here, and offer some suggestions for dealing with them.

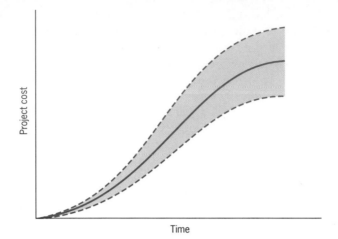

Figure 4-4
Estimate of project cost: estimate made at project start.

Budget Uncertainty

Perceptually, the PM sees the uncertainty of the budget somewhat like the shaded portion of Figure 4-4, where the actual project costs may be either higher or lower than the estimates the PM has derived. As we will describe later, however, it seems that more things can go wrong in a project and drive up the cost than can go right to keep down the cost. As the project unfolds, the cost uncertainty decreases as the project moves toward completion. Figures 4-5 (a), (b), and (c) illustrate this. An estimate at the beginning of the project as in Figure 4-4 is shown as the t_0 estimate in Figure 4-5(a). As work on the project progresses, the uncertainty decreases as the project moves toward completion. At time t_1 the cost to date is known and another estimate is made of the cost to complete the project, Figure 4-5(b). This is repeated at t_2, Figure 4-5(c). Each estimate, of course, begins at the actual cost to date and estimates only the remaining cost to completion. The further the project progresses, the less the uncertainty in the final project cost. It is common in project management to make new forecasts about project completion time and cost at fixed points in the project life cycle, or at special milestones.

The reasons for cost uncertainty in the project are many: prices may escalate, different resources may be required, the project may take a different amount of time than we expected thereby impacting overhead and indirect costs, and on and on. Earlier, we discussed ways to improve cost estimates, to anticipate such uncertainty, but change is a fact of life, including life on the project, and change invariably alters our previous budget estimates.

There are three basic causes for change in projects. Some changes are due to errors the cost estimator made about how to achieve the tasks identified in the project plan. Such changes are due to technological uncertainty: a building's foundation must be reinforced due to a fault in the ground that wasn't identified beforehand, a new innovation allows a project task to be completed easier than was anticipated, and so on.

Other changes result because the project team or client learns more about the nature of the performance goal of the project or the setting in which it is to be used. This derives from an increase in the team's or client's knowledge or sophistication about the project deliverables. The medical team plans to use a device in the field as well as in the hospital. The chemists find another application of the granulated bed process if it is altered to include additional minerals.

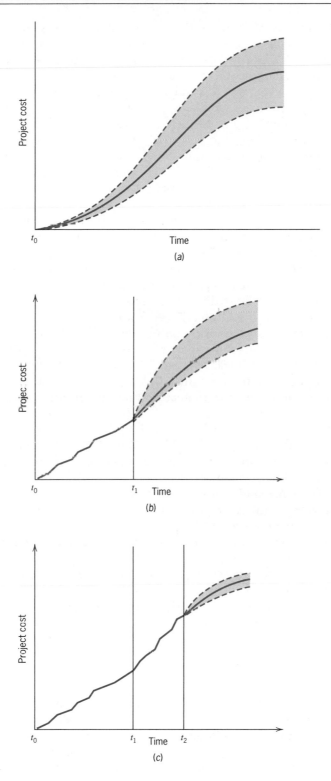

Figure 4-5 (a), (b), and (c) Estimates of project cost: estimates made at time t_0, t_1, and t_2.

The third source of change is the mandate: A new law is passed, a trade association sets a new standard, a governmental regulatory agency adopts a new policy. These changes alter the previous "rules of conduct" under which the project had been operating, usually to the detriment of the budget.

There are different ways to handle such changes. The least preferred way is simply to accept a negative change and take a loss on the project. The best approach is to prepare for change ahead of time by including provisions in the original contract for such changes. The easiest change to handle is when the change is the result of an increased specification by the client, yet even these kinds of changes are often mishandled by the project organization. Essentially, a formal change control procedure is included in the contract that allows for renegotiation of price and schedule for client-ordered changes in performance.

More difficult changes are those resulting from misunderstood assumptions, technological uncertainty, and mandates. Assumptions can be handled the easiest, and some technological uncertainties as well, by carefully listing all the assumptions, including those regarding technology, in the contract and stating that if these assumptions fail to hold, the contract will have to be renegotiated.

Mandates are the most difficult to accommodate because they can affect anything about the project and usually come without warning. The shorter the project duration, however, the less likely an unexpected mandate will impact the project. Thus, when contracting for a project of extended duration, it is best to divide it into shorter segments and contract for only one segment at a time. Of course, this also gives clients the opportunity to reconsider whether they want to complete the full project, as well as giving the competition an opportunity to steal the remainder of the project from you. Nevertheless, if a client wants to cancel a contract and is locked into a long-term agreement, the project will not have a happy ending anyway. At least with shorter segments the client may be willing to finish a segment before dropping the project. In any event, if the client is pleased with your performance on one segment of the contract, it is unlikely that a competitor will have the experience and cost efficiencies that you have gained and will be able to steal the next segment. At the least, the client would be obligated to give you an opportunity to match their bid.

As changes impact the project's costs, the budget for the remainder of the project will certainly have to be revised. There are three ways to revise a budget during the course of a project, each depending on the nature of the changes that have been experienced. If the changes are confined to early elements of the project and are not seen to impact the rest of the project, then the new budget can be estimated as the old budget plus the changes from the early elements.

More frequently, something systemic has changed that will impact the costs of the rest of the project tasks as well, such as a higher rate of inflation. In this case, the new budget estimate will be the accumulated costs to date plus the previous estimates of the rest of the budget multiplied by some correction factor for the systemic change. Recall that the BLS is an excellent source for such historical data that will aid the PM in estimating an appropriate correction factor.

Last, there may be some individual changes now perceived to impact specific elements of the remaining project tasks. The new budget estimate will then be the actual costs to date plus the expected costs for the remaining project tasks. Of course, in the most general case there may also be some systematic changes as well as the individual changes and these will also have to be added into the estimate, as described above.

Risk Management

The field of risk management has grown considerably over the last decade. The Project Management Institute's PMBOK [13] devotes a full chapter to this topic. In general, risk management includes three areas: (1) risk identification, (2) risk analysis, and (3) response to risk.

Risk Identification Risk identification consists of a thorough study of all sources of risk in the project. Common sources of risk include the organization of the project itself; senior management of the project organization; the client; the skills and character of the project team members, including the PM; acts of nature; and all of the three types of changes described earlier under budget uncertainty.

Scenario analysis is a well-known method for identifying serious risks. It involves identifying possible sequences of events or *scenarios* such as an earthquake in Tokyo, an extended labor strike, or the freezing of a river. Specific sources of these types of risk can often be determined by interviewing various parties either involved in the project as stakeholders or outside parties with previous experience in projects similar to the one at hand. Beyond this, a close analysis of the project plan and WBS and the linear responsibility chart (Chapter 3), as well as the PERT chart (Chapter 5) will often identify highly probable risks, extremely serious risks, or highly vulnerable areas, should anything go wrong.

After the major risks are identified, the following data should be obtained on each to facilitate further analysis: the probability of each risk event occurring, the range or distribution of possible outcomes if it does occur, the probabilities of each outcome, and the expected timing of each outcome. In most cases, good estimates will not be available, but getting as much data and as accurate estimates as possible will be crucial for the follow-on risk analysis.

Risk Analysis The topic of risk analysis has a long and well-established history. Two classic references in this topic are [8 and 15]. The essence of risk analysis is to state the various outcomes of a decision as probability distributions and to use these distributions to evaluate the desirability of certain managerial decisions. (A more detailed discussion related to the use of Crystal Ball,® an Excel® add-in, to address risk analysis in budgeting situations is provided in Appendix C.) The objective is to illustrate to the manager the distribution or *risk profile* of the outcomes (e.g., profits, completion dates, return on investment) of investing in some project. These risk profiles are one factor to be considered when making the decision, along with many others such as intangibles, strategic concerns, behavioral issues, fit with the organization, and so on. This is illustrated later in this chapter in Figure 4-6.

Before discussing the risk analysis techniques, we need to discuss some issues concerning the input data. We assume here that estimating the range and timing of possible outcomes of a risky event is not a problem but that the probabilities of each may be harder to establish. Given no actual data on the probabilities, the best guesses of people familiar with the problem is a reasonable substitute. An example of such guesses (a.k.a. estimates) can be seen in Table 4-5.

This table was derived from Table 3-4 in the previous chapter. The individuals who estimated task durations and budgets were asked for three estimates of the cost of each activity, a normal estimate plus optimistic and pessimistic estimates of the cost for each. From these an expected value for the cost of an activity can be found, but we will delay discussing this calculation until Chapter 5 where we show such calculations for either cost or durations.

Table 4-5 Optimistic, Normal, and Pessimistic Cost Estimates for the Annual Tribute Dinner

**Budget Information
Annual Tribute Dinner**

Task Name	Optimistic Cost = a	Normal Cost = m	Pessimistic Cost = b	Expected Cost = (a + 4m + b)/6
Begin preparations for tribute dinner				
Select date & secure room				
Obtain corporate sponsorships for event	$100.00	$150.00	$350.00	$175.00
Identify potential businesses to sponsor				
Phone/write businesses	$100.00	$150.00	$350.00	$175.00
Event hosts/MC				
Identify and secure honoree of event				
Identify and secure master of ceremonies				
Identify/secure person to introduce honoree				
Identify/secure event hosts & hostesses				
Invitations				
Secure mailing lists				
Design invitation with PR firm	$1,250.00	$1,500.00	$2,200.00	$1,575.00
Print invitation	$2,300.00	$2,500.00	$3,000.00	$2,550.00
Mail invitation	$250.00	$300.00	$410.00	$310.00
RSVP's back				
Event entertainment secured	$750.00	$1,000.00	$1,250.00	$1,000.00
Food and drink				
Finalize menu				
Identify menu options				
Trial menus				
Select final menu	$700.00	$750.00	$800.00	$750.00
Identify company to donate wine				
Table decorations, gifts, cards, flowers, etc.	$2,200.00	$2,800.00	$3,250.00	$2,775.00
Idenfity and have made event gift to attendees	$2,000.00	$2,500.00	$3,000.00	$2,500.00
Find florist to donate table arrangements				
Hire calligrapher to make seating cards	$200.00	$300.00	$400.00	$300.00
Develop PR exhibit to display at event	$75.00	$150.00	$225.00	$150.00
Event and honoree publicity	$200.00	$325.00	$450.00	$325.00
Hire event photographer	$400.00	$450.00	$500.00	$450.00
Finalize seating chart				
Hold tribute dinner				
Send out "thank you's" to sponsors & donators	$75.00	$150.00	$225.00	$150.00

Each person responsible for a task in this project was asked to take the estimated costs and determine a more accurate budget. The spreadsheet includes the cost information.

This project does not include any cost for staff time. Each member of the project team is considered part of General Salaries and Administration, and their associated time will not be expensed through this project.

If approximations cannot be made, there are other approaches that can be used. One approach is to assume that all outcomes are equally probable, though there is no more justification for this assumption than assuming any other arbitrarily chosen probability values.

Another approach is to assume that competitors and the environment are enemies, trying to do you in. This is the *game theory* approach. The decision maker takes a pessimistic mind-set and selects a course of action that minimizes the maximum harm (the *minimax* solution) any outcome can render regardless of the probabilities. With this approach, each decision possibility is evaluated for the worst possible outcome, all these worst outcomes are compared, and the decision with the "best" worst outcome is selected. For example, assume an investor would like to choose one of two mutual funds in which to invest. If interest rates rise, the return on mutual fund A will be 5 percent, while the return on mutual fund B will be 3 percent. On the other hand, if interest rates decrease, the return on A will be 7 percent while the return on B will be 12 percent. With the pessimistic approach, the worst outcome if mutual fund A is selected is a 5 percent return. Similarly, the worst return if B is selected is 3 percent. Since A has the better worst return (5 percent is better than 3 percent), the investor would choose to invest in mutual fund A using the pessimistic approach. Of course, by investing in A the investor is eliminating the chance of achieving a 12 percent return. There are other methods besides those we have mentioned, but these are representative of approaches when probability information is unavailable.

When probability information is available or can be estimated, many risk analysis techniques use the concept of *expected value* of an outcome—that is, the value of an outcome multiplied by the probability of that outcome occurring. For example, in a coin toss using a quarter, there are two possible outcomes and the expected value of the game is the sum of the expected values of all outcomes. It is easily calculated. Assume that if the coin comes up "head" you win a quarter, but if it is "tails" you lose a quarter. We also assume that the coin being flipped is a "fair" coin and has a .5 probability of coming up either heads or tails. The expected value of this game is

$$E(\text{coin toss}) = .5(\$.25) + .5(\$-.25) = 0$$

A decision table (a.k.a. a payoff-matrix), such as illustrated in Table 4-6, is one technique commonly used for single-period decision situations where there are a limited number of decision choices and a limited number of possible outcomes.

In the following decision table, there are four features:

- Three decision choices or alternatives, A_i
- Four states of nature, S_j, that may occur
- Each state of nature has its own probability of occurring, p_j, but the sum of the probabilities must be 1.0.
- The outcomes associated with each alternative and state of nature combination, O_{ij}, are shown in the body of the table.

Table 4-6   Decision Table (or payoff matrix) for Sample Problem

Alternatives	Probabilities	0.1	0.4	0.3	0.2	Expected Value
	States of Nature	High	Med.	Low	None	
Fast		14	10	6	1	7.4
Average		10	12	9	5	9.5*
Slow		5	8	12	7	8.7

*Maximum

If a particular alternative, i, is chosen, we calculate the expected value of that alternative as follows:

$$E(A_i) = p_1(O_{i1}) + p_2(O_{i2}) + p_3(O_{i3}) \ldots \text{ for all values of } j$$

For example, using the data below for alternative "Fast" we get

$$E(\text{Fast}) = 0.1(14) + 0.4(10) + 0.3(6) + 0.2(1) = 7.4$$

The reader may recall that we used a similar payoff matrix in Chapter 1, when we considered the problem of buying a car. In that example, the criteria weights played the same role as probabilities play in the example above. This technique has an interesting application for budgeting. Suppose there are two or more different technologies that can be adopted to produce a project deliverable (e.g., different conferencing methods to use for brainstorming a new product design, or different methods for conducting an R&D experiment). Not only would the costs be different, the risks associated with the costs and outcomes would also be different. While such cases are too complex to reproduce here, they are not uncommon, and are solvable by examining the expected values of the different budgets and outcomes.

The most useful and flexible technique for handling problems like the ones mentioned just above is Monte Carlo simulation [5]. (Again, for more details on simulation, see Appendix C.) In a simulation, a mathematical model is constructed of a situation and run to see what the outcomes will be under various circumstances. In a Monte Carlo simulation, the model is run many, many times starting from a different point each time based on the probability distributions of the variables. Equations in the model are then used to construct a statistical distribution of the outcomes of interest, such as costs and times. This approach was used to simulate the moving of a computer to a new location [16]. A computer run of 2000 trials was made, simulating various trials and variations in cost and time for each of three methods of moving the computer. A cost-probability distribution was then constructed, shown in Figure 4-6, to help identify the lowest-cost alternative as well as the alternative with the lowest risk of incurring a high cost. As seen in the figure, alternative 3 has the lowest expected cost (9) but also has the highest likelihood for a cost of 20 or more. Alternative 1 has the highest expected cost, but the lowest risk.

Response to Risk   Risk response typically involves a decision about which risks to prepare for and which to ignore and simply accept as potential threats. The main preparation for a risk is the development of a risk management plan. Such a plan includes contingency plans and logic charts detailing exactly what to do depending on particular events [11]. For example, Iceland is frequently subjected to unexpected avalanches and has thus prepared a detailed response plan for such events, stating who is in charge, the tasks that various agencies are to do at particular times, and so on.

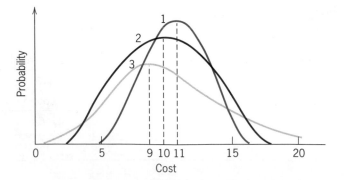

Figure 4-6
Probability distribution for three alternatives.

Beyond this, however, it is helpful to conduct actual tests of the risk management plan by conducting simulations such as tabletop exercises [11] or partial dress rehearsals. Tabletop exercises simulate the decision making and actions to be taken in the risk management plan. These are primarily soft simulations where the actions are just stated instead of being executed. More realism can be injected, at some cost, by partially (or fully) taking the actions, such as with fire drills. The practice in taking these actions can be very helpful in the event the risk actually comes to pass. More detailed simulations might include full dress rehearsals where even more fully realistic actions are taken.

In spite of the effort taken to make realistic budget estimates, it can still be useful to prepare for changes in the budget as the project unfolds. Such changes derive from multiple sources, including technology, economics, improved project understanding, and mandates. To the extent possible, it is best to try to include these contingencies in the contract in case they come to pass. Risk management consists of risk identification through scenario analysis and careful investigation for sources of risk. We deal with risk through such means as decision tables, simulation, and response, which entail identifying which risks will be prepared for and which will be ignored and simply accepted.

We are now ready to consider the scheduling problem. Because durations, like costs, are uncertain, we will continue our discussion of the matter, adding some very powerful but reasonably simple techniques for dealing with the uncertainty surrounding both project schedule and cost.

REVIEW QUESTIONS

1. Contrast the disadvantages of top-down budgeting and bottom-up budgeting.

2. What is the logic in charging administrative costs based on total time to project completion?

3. Would you expect a task in a manufacturing plant that uses lots of complex equipment to have a learning curve rate closer to 70 percent or 95 percent?

4. How does a tracking signal improve budget estimates?

5. Are there other kinds of changes in a project in addition to the three basic types described in Section 4.4? Might a change be the result of two types at the same time?

6. Distinguish among highly probable risks, extremely serious risks, and highly vulnerable areas in risk identification.

DISCUSSION QUESTIONS

7. Given the tendency of accountants to allocate a project's estimated costs evenly over the duration of the task, what danger might this pose for a project manager who faces the following situation? The major task for a $5 million project is budgeted at $3 million, mostly for highly complex and expensive equipment. The task has a six-month duration, and requires the purchase of the equipment at the beginning of the task to enable the project team to conduct the activities required to complete the task. The task begins December 1.

8. The chapter describes the problems of budgeting projects with S-shaped and exponential-shaped life-cycle curves. What might be the budget problems if the life cycle of a project was just a straight diagonal line from 0 at project start to 100 percent at project completion?

9. If a firm uses program budgeting for its projects, is an activity budget not needed? If it is, then of what value is the program budget?

10. As a senior manager, you oversee a project with a total estimated cost of 245 engineer-months of effort.

Three months ago, however, the project had fallen behind by about 25 engineer-months so you authorized the hiring of three additional engineers, which you felt should more than make up for the delay in the remaining year of the project (3 × 12 months = 36 engineer-months). You have just received the latest quarterly project status report and are surprised to learn that the project is now 40 engineer-months behind schedule! Your first reaction is to calculate how many more engineers need to be hired to make up for the increased delay. Using Brooks's concept of the

"mythical man month," explain what might be happening here.

11. So what was wrong with the purchasing manager's assistant's solution (outlined in Section 4.3) to the problem of having an inadequate supply of hard-to-obtain parts?

12. Describe what the managers might discuss upon viewing Figure 4-6 to reach a decision about which alternative to pick.

INCIDENTS FOR DISCUSSION

A Budgeting Novice

Alexander Jones was an experienced project manager of a small machine shop. He had always had complete authority when working with the clients on specifications of the projects as well as when working with the project team on the schedule. His boss, however, did not feel comfortable letting Alex determine project budgets. The boss always did that himself.

A client approached Alex about designing a piece of surgical equipment. Alex was excited about this project because his usual job was to design and make parts of factory equipment. He was delighted to have a chance to do something that might directly affect humankind. Alex knew what the surgical tool was intended to do and had figured out what had to be done to design and manufacture it. He had even estimated the labor-hour requirement. He wanted to do all the planning discussions with the client, including discussions on the budget.

Questions: What do you think Alex should show to his boss, so that the boss would feel more comfortable letting Alex determine and monitor the project's budget? What should Alex say to persuade the boss?

Major Dynamic Ground Systems

Major Dynamic Ground Systems has been manufacturing M1A2 Abrams tanks for the United States Army and foreign armies since 1986. The company recently designed a new tank and is preparing to build it. They developed a detailed budget to be used during the construction of the first tank.

The total budget for this first tank is $75 million. The controller, Francis Gunner, believes the initial budget for the new tank is too low. Mr. Gunner feels the planning group underestimated some of the costs. Francis is concerned that there may be major cost overruns on the project. He wants to work closely with the project manager to control the costs and remain within the budget.

Question: How would you monitor the costs of this project?

General Sensor Company

Justin Jordan has been named Project Manager of the General Sensor Company's new sensor manufacturing process project. Sensors are extremely price sensitive. General has done a great deal of quantitative work to be able to accurately forecast changes in sales volume relative to changes in pricing.

The company president, Guy General, has faith in the sensitivity model that the company uses. He insists that all projects affecting the manufacturing costs of sensors be run against the sensitivity model to generate data to calculate the return on investment. The net result is that project managers, like Justin, are under a great deal of pressure to submit realistic budgets so go/no-go project decisions can be made quickly. Guy has canceled several projects that appeared marginal during their feasibility stages and recently fired a project manager for overestimating project costs on a new model sensor. The project was killed very early in the design stages, and six months later a competitor introduced a similar sensor that proved to be highly successful.

Justin's dilemma is how to construct a budget that accurately reflects the costs of the proposed new process. Justin is an experienced executive and feels comfortable with his ability in estimating costs of projects. However, the recent firing of his colleague has made him a little gun-shy. Only one stage of the four-stage sensor manufacturing process is being changed. Justin has detailed cost information about the majority of the process. Unfortunately the costs and tasks involved in the new modified process stage are unclear at this point. Justin also believes that the new modifications will cause some minor changes in the other three stages, but these potential changes have not yet been clearly identified. The stage being addressed by the project represents almost 50 percent of the manufacturing cost.

Question: Under these circumstances, would Justin be wise to pursue a top-down or a bottom-up budgeting approach? Why? What factors are most relevant here?

C A S E

St. Dismas Assisted Living Facility Project Budget Development—2

Fred Splient gave his ALF Project Steering Committee two months to develop an action plan for their area of responsibility in the project. Each member was told to include the tasks, predecessors and successors, resources needed, responsible person, and an estimated cost. He asked that these be presented to the steering team on August 31.

All through July the ALF project team scrambled to identify the steps required to open the facility and to determine what it would cost. Each team member met with his or her departmental staff to get help in identifying what was needed. For example, the COO spoke with the Dietary Department head and asked that she develop a plan to meet all requirements to set up the facility to feed the residents. The COO then asked the Facilities Manager to develop an action plan to prepare the building and maintain it. The COO also met with the Rehab Services Medical Director and his clinical staff to identify the residents' probable medical needs based on the projected population, and to develop an action plan to prepare to meet the residents' health needs. The COO asked the therapy manager to prepare a plan to develop social activities for the residents.

Everyone on the team called the Chief Financial Officer for help in determining the budgets for their action plans. The CFO also had to validate the estimates of cost and revenue from facility operations, and to project earnings and return on the investment. Like any good administrator, when the CFO realized he had no expertise in this area, he hired a consultant to help him determine the project costs and budget. Dr. Sara Sharf was chosen as the consultant—she had over five years' experience in developing business plans for assisted living facilities.

Dr. Sharf recommended that St. Dismas target the middle income geriatric population since there were many up-scale facilities in the area. Dr. Sharf and the market researchers determined what level of rent people in that population could and would pay. They then looked at what needed to be in the facility to meet the needs of their targeted population. After additional site visits of facilities and meetings with the selected construction contractor, they finalized the layout of units and common space areas that would be included in the design. The Construction Project Manager requested and received an action plan and cost estimate from the construction contractor. The contractor had estimated that construction cost would probably run about $70 per square foot with a standard deviation of $3.67. He could not be absolutely sure because of potential change orders.

He emphasized that the estimates assumed that the project would be completed without further changes in its design concept.

While the CFO was haggling with the construction contractor about determining a more accurate cost estimate, he received a phone call from Dr. Zen Link, the Head of Geriatric Medicine at St. Dismas. Dr. Link's secretary had seen men measuring the land behind the parking lot and she wanted to know what was going on; so did Dr. Link. Since Dr. Link was one of the hospital's best referrers, the CFO told him about the potential project. Dr. Link felt that his input was needed up front as he was the only person on staff who would know the health needs of the facility's residents and appropriate equipment needs and staffing models that should be set up. With Dr. Link's input, the CFO estimated the operating costs to run the facility and projected the occupancy rates needed to cover those costs. The Rehab Services Medical Director, who was a member of the original project team, was quite upset when he saw Dr. Link's budget for the medical equipment that was to be purchased for the facility. The Medical Director felt that Dr. Link wanted to purchase too much expensive equipment, which was not necessary to have on site. The hospital had the majority of the equipment that was necessary and there was no need to duplicate it, thus inflating that portion of the budget. The CFO did not want to get in the middle of their argument so he left Link's budget just as Link submitted it and hoped someone would raise the issue at the next Steering Team Meeting. The CFO was quite concerned about the lack of experience of the team in developing such a budget, and he felt that there was far more uncertainty in the budget than the estimates reflected.

With the construction cost estimate and an outline of the services to be provided, the following projected capital expenditure was developed.

Preliminary Project Budget

Apartment Type	Net Sq Ft	Units	Total Sq Ft
Studio units	450	20	9,000
1 BR/bath units	600	80	48,000
		100	57,000
Common space	0.3		17,100
Net to gross	1.3		22,230
Total gross sq ft			96,330
Square feet			96,330
Est cost per sq ft			$70.00

Construction Costs

Building	$ 6,743,000
Contingency	674,300
Land	600,000
Program development & equipment costs	405,000
Furniture	400,000 *(see below)
A&E fees @ 5%	347,000
Financing costs	202,000
Capitalized interest	135,000
Site improvements	125,000
Phone & IS system	30,000
Kitchen equipment	30,000
Total	$ 9,991,300

Organizational costs:

Legal and accounting	25,000
Initial marketing	250,000 $2,500/unit
Project consultant	80,000
Follow-up market survey	20,000
Total organizational costs	375,000
Total	$10,066,300

*	Heavy Asst.	Light Asst.
Studio	5 units $4,160/unit	15 units $3,280/unit
1 BR/bath	20 units $5,460/unit	60 units $3,780/unit

The CFO developed an income statement for the next 20 years. The first three years are shown below.

St. Dismas Assisted Living
Pro Forma

	Year 1	Year 2	Year 3
Service Revenues			
Studios	$ 256,662	$ 414,012	$ 430,572
One bedroom	408,564	1,398,197	2,077,321
Additional person revenue	30,866	72,291	98,841
Ancillary revenue	28,969	67,656	92,417
Total service revenues	725,061	1,952,155	2,699,151
Operating Expenses			
Salaries and wages	376,657	649,606	692,734
Employee benefits	82,865	142,913	152,401

	Year 1	Year 2	Year 3
Supplies	69,571	55,910	73,434
Purchased services	76,177	50,000	50,000
Utilities	217,516	—	—
Insurance	48,000	—	—
Other	29,002	78,086	107,966
Total operating expenses	899,788	976,515	1,076,535
Income (Loss) Before Other Expenses	(174,727)	975,640	1,622,616
Other Expenses (Income)			
Depreciation and amortization	560,200	560,700	561,200
Interest expense	—	—	—
Interest income	(1,226)	11,321	47,451
Total other expenses (income)	558,974	572,021	608,651
Net Income (Loss)	$(733,701)	$ 403,619	$1,013,965
Internal Rate of Return	10.1		
Average Occupied Units			
20 Units	12.3	19.0	19.0
80 Units	19.6	52.6	75.0
	46		
Total	31.9	71.6	94.0
Resident Days			
20 Units	4,488	6,935	6,935
80 Units	7,146	19,191	27,380
Total	11,634	26,126	34,315
Full-time Equivalents	21.8	37.8	38.8
Cash Flow:			
Net income (loss)	$ (733,701)	$ 403,619	$1,013,965
Minus: capital investment	(10,079,000)	(5,000)	(5,500)
Add: depreciation and amortization	560,200	560,700	561,200
Add: working capital change	130,656	82,500	18,638
Net cash flow	$(10,121,845)	$1,041,819	$1,588,302

The CFO, Dr. Sharf, and the Project Steering Team were ready to combine their individual plans and costs into a composite plan and budget.

QUESTIONS:

1. The cost per square foot for the units is given in the text together with its standard deviation. What other areas of cost or revenue are likely to have cost uncertainty? How should these uncertainties be handled?

2. How would you suggest the team handle the issue of Dr. Link's supposedly inflated medical equipment costs?

C A S E

Photstat Inc.

Photstat Inc. is contemplating the formation of a project team to develop a new service. Briefly, the service would allow customers to order customized mouse pads over the Internet based on photographs or other artwork sent electronically to the firm.

The company estimates that the price of the mouse pad will be between $10 and $15 per unit with all prices in this range equally likely. Based on historical data, Photstat estimates that the total market size for these types of products in their first year follows a normal distribution with a mean of 100,000 units and a standard deviation of 10,000. Again, according to historical data, Photstat's market share tends to be normally distributed with a mean of 30 percent and standard deviation of 3 percent. Market growth tends to follow a normal distribu-

tion growing an average of 10 percent per year with a standard deviation of 3 percent. Estimates from the equipment manufacturer selected to design and produce the required equipment indicate that the cost of the equipment is normally distributed with a mean of $500,000 and a standard deviation of 60,000. Historical data indicate there is a 10 percent chance that the equipment will last for only three years. Similarly, there is a 60 percent chance the equipment will last six years, a 20 percent chance it will last eight years, and a 10 percent chance the equipment will last 10 years. The variable costs of similar products were found to be normally distributed with a mean of $3 and a standard deviation of $0.25. Finally, an economic analysis undertaken by the firm suggests that the rate of inflation in any given year is normally distributed with a mean of 3 percent and a standard deviation of 0.5 percent.

QUESTIONS

1. What is the expected value of the project?
2. Simulate this project 100 times and compute the average profit over the 100 replications. Plot a histogram of the outcomes of the 100 replications.

3. How does the average of the simulation compare to the expected value you calculated? What are the managerial implications of this difference?

BIBLIOGRAPHY

1. AMOR, J. P., and C. J. TEPLITZ. "An Efficient Approximation for Project Composite Learning Curves." *Project Management Journal*, September 1998.

2. BADIRU, A. B. "Incorporating Learning Curve Effects into Critical Resource Diagramming." *Project Management Journal*, June 1995.

3. BROOKS, F. P. *The Mythical Man-Month*. Reading, MA: Addison-Wesley, 1975. (Another classic work that had a major impact on managers, particularly in the Information Systems area.)

4. CAMM, J. D., J. R. EVANS, and N. K. WOMER. "The Unit Learning Curve Approximation of Total Cost." *Computers in Industrial Engineering*. Vol. 12, No. 3, 1987.

5. EVANS, J. R., and D. L. OLSON. *Introduction to Simulation and Risk Analysis*. Upper Saddle River, NJ: Prentice Hall, 1998. (An excellent book using Crystal Ball® software.)

6. GAGNON, R. J., and S. J. MANTEL, JR. "Strategies and Performance Improvement for Computer-Assisted

Design." *IEEE Transactions on Engineering Management*, November 1987.

7. HAMBURGER, D. H. "Three Perceptions of Project Cost—Cost is More Than a Four Letter Word." *Project Management Journal*, June 1986. (Recommended reading for any project manager who is not familiar with accounting.)

8. HERTZ, D. B., and H. THOMAS. *Risk Analysis and Its Applications*. New York: Wiley, 1983. (The name "Hertz" is almost synonymous with risk analysis, particularly strong in the area of financial risk.)

9. LAWRENCE, A. O. "Using Automated Estimating Tools to Improve Project Estimating." *PM Network*, December 1994.

10. LIBERATORE, M. J., and G. J. TITUS. "The Practice of Management Science in R & D Project Management." *Management Science*, August 1983.

11. MALLAK, L. M., H. A. KURSTEDT, JR., and G. A. PATZAK. "Planning for Crises in Project Management." *Project Management Journal*, June 1997.

12. MARTIN, J. E. "Selecting an Automated Estimating Tool for IS Development Projects." *PM Network*, December 1994.

13. PMI Standards Committee. *A Guide to the Project Management Body of Knowledge*, Upper Darby, PA: Project Management Institute, 1996.

14. SHAFER, S. M., and J. R. MEREDITH. *Operations Management: A Process Approach with Spreadsheets*. New York: Wiley, 1998.

15. SIMON, H. *The New Science of Management Decisions*, rev. ed. Englewood Cliffs, NJ: Prentice Hall, 1997. (An excellent and readable classic on management science with a particularly good introduction to risk analysis.)

16. TOWNSEND, H. W. R., and G. E. WHITEHOUSE. "We Used Risk Analysis to Move Our Computer." *Industrial Engineering*, May 1977.

5

Scheduling the Project

Consider the job of planning a project, developing a budget for it, and scheduling all of the many tasks involved. It should be obvious that these three activities are not actually separable. Because a budget must include both the amounts and timing of resources received or expended, one cannot prepare a budget without knowing the specifics of each task and the time period(s) during which the task must be undertaken. Similarly, the project action plan implies a schedule just as a schedule implies a plan. It is useful to begin study of these interdependent, partial descriptions of a project with an examination of the planning process because this process is the foundation of all that follows. The decision about whether to turn our attention first to the budget or the schedule is arbitrary. We chose the budget largely because most readers have some familiarity with the subject. The problem is that planning, budgeting, and scheduling are parts of the same basic process. They are considered separately only because we cannot write about all three at the same time.

The project schedule is simply the project plan in an altered format. It is a convenient form for monitoring and controlling project activities. Actually, the schedule itself can be prepared in several formats. In this chapter, we describe the most common formats—Gantt charts and PERT/CPM networks—and demonstrate how to convert an action plan or WBS into these formats. We also note some of the strengths and weaknesses of the different displays. In addition, we reintroduce risk analysis and risk management applied directly to the project schedule. From this analysis we show how to estimate the likelihood that a project can be completed on or before a specific time. (In Chapter 6, we explore what to do if it appears that the project will not be completed on schedule.) In addition to standard analytic methods for risk management, we also demonstrate simulation methods.

We start with simple plans and schedule them manually. After scheduling by hand, we turn to the computer and use MSP to do our scheduling and many other tasks for us. The same approach is used for risk management. First, problems involving risk will be solved by hand. Once the theory is understood, we use the computer to handle the same problems without so much arithmetic.

5.1   PERT AND CPM NETWORKS

In the late 1950s, the Program Evaluation and Review Technique (PERT) and the Critical Path Method (CPM) were independently developed. PERT was developed by the U.S. Navy, Booz-Allen Hamilton (a business consulting firm), and Lockheed Aircraft (now Lockheed Martin Corp.); and CPM was developed by Dupont De Nemours Inc. When they were developed, there were significant differences in the methods. For example, PERT used probabilistic (or uncertain) estimates of activity durations and CPM used deterministic (or certain) estimates but included both time and cost estimates to allow time/cost trade-offs to be used. Both methods employed networks to schedule and display task sequences. (Throughout this chapter, we will use the words "activity" and "task" as synonyms to avoid constant repetition of one or the other.) Both methods identified a *critical path* of tasks that could not be delayed without delaying the project. Both methods identified activities with *slack* (or *float*) that could be somewhat delayed without extending the time required to complete the project. While PERT and CPM used slightly different ways of drawing the network of activities, anything one could do with PERT, one could also do with CPM and vice versa. When writing about the history of project management, differentiating PERT and CPM is important and interesting. When managing projects, the distinction is merely fussy.

The Language of PERT/CPM

Several terms used in discussing PERT/CPM analysis have been adopted from everyday language but have quite different meanings than in common usage. These terms are defined here as used in PERT/CPM.

Activity—A task or set of tasks required by the project. Activities use resources and time.

Event—An identifiable state resulting from the completion of one or more activities. Events consume no resources or time. Before an event can be *achieved* or *realized*, all its predecessor activities must be completed.

Milestones—Identifiable and noteworthy events marking significant progress on the project.

Network—A diagram of nodes (may represent activities or events) connected by directional arcs (may represent activities or simply show technological dependence) that defines the project and illustrates the technological relationships of all activities. Networks are usually drawn with a "Start" node on the left and a "Finish" node on the right. Arcs are always tipped with an arrowhead to show the direction of precedence, that is, from predecessors to successors.

Path—A series of connected activities (or intermediate events) between any two events in a network.

Critical path—The set of activities on a path from the project's start event to its finish event that, if delayed, will delay the completion date of the project.

Critical time—The time required to complete all activities on the critical path.

In Chapter 3, on planning, we noted that tasks may be divided into subtasks and each of the subtasks may be further divided. To carry out this process, it is necessary to know which tasks are immediate predecessors or successors of which others. The predecessor/successor relationship defines technological dependence. (See Chapter 3, Section 3.3.)

Building the Network

There are two ways of displaying a project network. In one we depict the activities as arrows and events as nodes. This gives an activity-on-arrow (AOA) network, usually associated with PERT. Alternatively, we can create an activity-on-node (AON) network by showing each task as a node and linking the nodes with arrows that show their technological relationship. The AON network is often associated with CPM. To understand the distinction, let us assume a small project represented by the tasks and precedences shown in Table 5-1.

Because it is easiest to draw, we start with the AON network. Because tasks **a** and **b** have no predecessors, they follow the **Start** node. We connect them to the starting node with arrows as in Figure 5-1.

Note that task **c** has **a** as a predecessor and that tasks **d** and **e** have **b** as their common predecessor as shown in Figure 5-2.

The network is easily completed. Task **f** has both **c** and **d** as predecessors, while **g** follows **e**. Because there are no more tasks, we can tie all loose ends to a node labeled **Finish** as in Figure 5-3.

The AOA network is generally more difficult to draw, but depicts the technical relationships of the activities quite well. Beginning the same way, we create a **Start** node from which flow all activities that have no predecessors, in this case **a** and **b**. The completion of these activities results in events (nodes, often drawn as circles) numbered **1** and **2** for easy identification as in Figure 5-4.

Table 5-1 A Sample Set of Project Activities and Precedences

Task	Predecessor
a	—
b	—
c	a
d	b
e	b
f	c, d
g	e

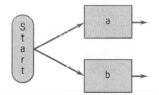

Figure 5-1 Stage 1 of a sample AON network from Table 5-1.

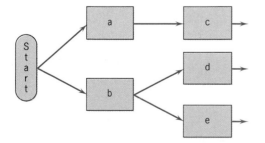

Figure 5-2 Stage 2 of a sample AON network from Table 5-1.

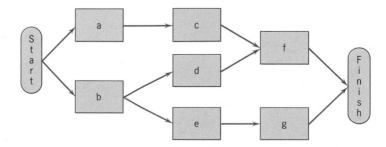

Figure 5-3 A completed sample AON network from Table 5-1.

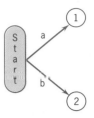

Figure 5-4   Stage 1 of a sample
AOA network from Table 5-1.

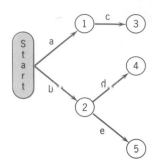

Figure 5-5   Stage 2 of a
sample AOA network
from Table 5-1.

Table 5-1 indicates that task **a** precedes task **c**, and that task **b** precedes both tasks **d** and **e**. Figure 5-5 shows these additions with event nodes **3**, **4**, and **5**, as indicated.

We are left with two activities, **f** and **g**. Task **f** has two predecessors, **c** and **d**. This means that tasks **c** and **d** actually finish at the same node (or event) and that **f** cannot start until this event is achieved, that is until both **c** and **d** are completed. Task **g** is preceded by **e**. Table 5-1 shows no more tasks, and as in the case of the AON network this means that all tasks with no successors should go to a node labeled **Finish**. See Figure 5-6(a) in which the nodes have been renumbered and some combined for viewing simplicity.

We can handle **f** differently by connecting the nodes following **c** and **d** in Figure 5-5 with an arrow drawn with a dashed line, see Figure 5-6(b). This is called a *dummy activity* and merely shows a technological linkage. Generally speaking, dummy tasks are used in situations where two activities have the same starting and finishing nodes or where a single activity connects to two or more nodes. The problem with two activities sharing the same starting and finishing nodes is that it becomes difficult to distinguish the tasks from one another. One solution to this problem is to add an extra ending node for one of the tasks and then draw a dummy task from the new node to the previously shared node. Adding a dummy task in this situation ensures that the tasks have unique identities while at the same time maintaining the correct technological precedence relationships. Dummy tasks require no time and no resources.

With occasional exceptions for clarity, we will use AON networks throughout this book because they are used by most of the popular project management software. An important advantage of AON notation is that the networks are easy to draw. AOA networks, particularly when they have more than 15 or 20 activities, are very difficult to draw by hand. With modern software this is not a serious problem, but the software that

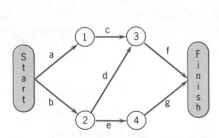

Figure 5-6a   A completed sample
AOA network from Table 5-1.

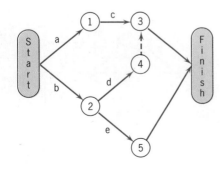

Figure 5-6b   A completed sample
AOA network showing the use of a
dummy task, Table 5-1.

Table 5-2   A Sample Problem for Finding
the Critical Path and Critical Time

Activity	Predecessor	Duration
a	—	5 days
b	—	4
c	a	3
d	a	4
e	a	6
f	b, c	4
g	d	5
h	d, e	6
i	f	6
j	g, h	4

generates AOA networks is quite expensive. AON networks often do not show events, but it is simple enough to add them by showing the event (usually a milestone) exactly as if it were an activity but with zero time duration and no resources. The PM should be familiar with both types of networks.

Finding the Critical Path and Critical Time

Let us now consider a more complicated example. Given the data in Table 5-2, we can start drawing the associated AON network as in Figure 5-7. The activity names and durations are shown in the appropriate nodes.

Note that activity **f** follows both **b** and **c**. If we redraw Figure 5-7 and place the **c** node below the **d** and **e** nodes, we will avoid having several of the arrows crossing one another; see Figure 5-8 for the complete network.

We can add information to the nodes in the network. Just above each node it is common practice to show what is called the *earliest start time* (EST) and *earliest finish time* (EFT) for the associated activity. Just below each node is shown the *latest start time* (LST) and *latest finish time* (LFT) for the activity. The node would appear as in Figure 5-9. The corresponding information for Figure 5-8 is shown in Figure 5-10 and its derivation is described in detail just below.

Activities **a** and **b** may start on Day 0, their ESTs. Their EFTs will be equal to their durations, five and four days, respectively. Tasks **c**, **d**, and **e** cannot start before **a** is completed on Day 5. Adding their respective durations to their ESTs gives us their EFTs, **c** finishing on Day 8, **d** on Day 9, and **e** on Day 11. Task **f** cannot start before *both* **b** and **c**

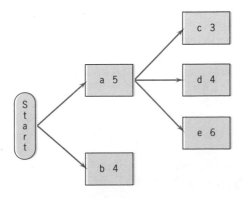

Figure 5-7   Stage 1 of a sample network from Table 5-2.

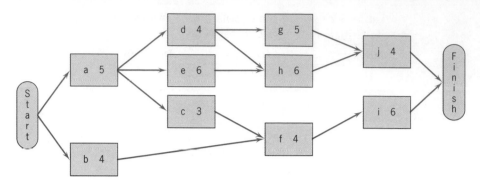

Figure 5-8   A complete network from Table 5-2.

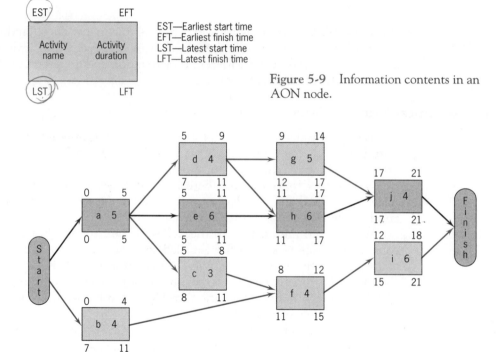

Figure 5-9   Information contents in an AON node.

EST—Earliest start time
EFT—Earliest finish time
LST—Latest start time
LFT—Latest finish time

Figure 5-10   The critical path and time for sample project in Table 5-2.

are finished on Day 8, resulting in the EFT for **f** on Day 12. Similarly, we find EFTs for tasks **g** (9 + 5 = 14) and **h** (11 + 6 = 17). Recall that a successor cannot be started until all predecessors are completed. Thus, **h** cannot start until Day 11 when both **d** and **e** are finished—Days 9 and 11, respectively. The same situation is true for task **j**. It cannot be started until both **g** and **h** are completed on Day 17, giving an EFT of 17 + 4 = 21. Task **i**, following **f**, has an EFT of 12 + 6 = 18. No tasks follow **i** and **j**, completed on Days 18 and 21, respectively. When they are both finished, the project is finished. That event occurs on Day 21.

All activities, and thus all paths, must be completed to finish the project. The shortest time for completion of the network is equal to the longest path through the network, in this case **a-e-h-j**. If any activity on the **a-e-h-j** path is even slightly delayed, the project will be delayed and that identifies **a-e-h-j** as the critical path and 21 days as the critical time. In

Figure 5-10 the critical path is depicted by a bold line—a common practice with PERT/CPM networks. We found the EST and EFT for each activity quite easily by beginning at the start node and moving from left to right through the network, calculating as we go from node to node. This is called a "forward pass" (or "left-to-right pass") and makes it simple to find the critical path and time for PERT/CPM networks.

In a similar fashion, we can perform a "backward pass" (or "right-to-left pass") to calculate the LST and LFT values for each activity. Referring to Figure 5-10, we begin by assuming that we would like to complete the project within the critical time identified in the forward pass, 21 days in our example. Clearly, activities **i** and **j** must be completed no later than day 21 in order not to delay the entire project. Therefore, these activities both have LFTs of 21.

Given a task time of 4 days, **j** must be started no later than day 17 in order to be completed by day 21. Likewise, task **i** can be started as late as day 15 and still finished by day 21 given its 6 day task time. Since task **j** cannot be started any later than day 17, tasks **g** and **h** must be completed by day 17. In a similar fashion, task **f** must be completed by day 15 so as not to delay task **i** beyond its LST. Subtracting the task times from the LFT for each of the tasks yields LSTs of 11, 11, and 12 for tasks **f**, **h**, and **g**, respectively.

Now consider task **d**. Task **d** precedes both tasks **g** (LST = 12) and **h** (LST = 11). The question is, should **d**'s LFT be 11 or 12? The correct answer is 11. The reason being, if task **d** were completed on day 12, task **h** could not start on its LST of day 11. Therefore we note that in situations where a particular activity precedes more than one task, its LFT is equal to the minimum LSTs of all activities it precedes.

The LFTs and LSTs for tasks **b**, **c**, and **e** are easily calculated since each of these tasks precedes a single task. Task **a** precedes tasks **c**, **d**, and **e**. Because task **e** has the lowest EST of five days, the LFT for task **a** is calculated to be five days.

Calculating Activity Slack

If activities on the critical path cannot be delayed without causing the entire project to be delayed, does it follow that activities not on the critical path can be delayed without delaying the project? As a matter of fact, it does—within limits. The amount of time a noncritical task can be delayed without delaying the project is called *slack* or *float*. The slack for any activity is easily calculated as LST − EST = LFT − EFT = slack.

It should be clear that for any task on the critical path, its LFT must be the same as its EFT. It therefore has zero slack. If it finishes later than its EFT, the activity will be late, causing a delay in the project. (Of course, the statement is equally true for its LST and EST.) This rule holds for activities **a**, **e**, **h**, and **j**, all on the critical path. But for activities not on the critical path the LFT and EFT (or the LST and EST) will differ and this difference is the activity slack. Take activity **i**, for example. It could be completed as early as Day 18 because its EST is Day 12 and it has a six-day duration. It must, however, be completed by Day 21 or the project will be delayed. Because **i** has a duration of six days, it cannot be started later than Day 15 (21 − 6). Given an LST of 15 and an EST of 12, task **i** could be delayed up to 3 days (LST − EST or LFT − EFT) without affecting project completion time. Thus, activity **i** has three days of slack.

For another example, consider task **g**. It is a predecessor to task **j** that is on the critical path. Task **j** *must* start on Day 17, which gives task **g** an LFT of 17. It has an EFT of Day 14 and thus has three days of slack. Note also that task **d**, which must be completed by Day 12 so as not to make **g** late, has three days of slack in its role as a predecessor of **g**, but **d** is also a predecessor of critical activity **h**. Task **d** must be completed by Day 11 or **h** will be late to start. Task **d**, therefore, has only two days of slack, not three.

Slack for other tasks are determined in the same way. Task **f** precedes **i**, and the latter has an LST of Day 15. Given an LFT of 15, **f** must start no later than Day 11. Its EST of Day 8 means that **f** has three days of slack. Task **c** is a predecessor of **f** and because the latter's LST is Day 11, **c** must be completed by then. With an LFT of 11 and an EFT of 8, **c** has three days of slack. The only remaining task to be considered is **b**. This task is linked to **f** and, like **c**, must be complete by **f**'s LST, Day 11. With an EFT of Day 4, **b** has seven days of slack.

Throughout this discussion of calculating slack we have made two assumptions that are standard in these analyses. First, when calculating slack for a set of activities on a noncritical path, the calculation for any given activity assumes that no other activity on the path will use any of the slack. Once a project is underway, if a predecessor activity uses some of its slack, its EFT is adjusted accordingly and the ESTs of successor activities must also be corrected. We have also assumed that the critical time for the project is also the project's due date, but it is not uncommon for a project to have "project slack" (or "network slack"). Our 21-day project might be started 23 days before its promised delivery date in which case activities on the "critical path" would have two days of slack and noncritical activities would have an additional two days of slack.

Milestones may be added to the display quite easily: Add the desired milestone event as a node with zero duration. Its EST will equal its EFT, and its LST and LFT will be equal. Milestones should, or course, be immediate successors of the activities that result in the milestone events. Finally, if a starting date has been selected for the project, it is common to show EST, EFT, LST, and LFT as actual dates.

Before continuing, a pause is in order to consider the managerial implications of the critical path and slack. The PM's primary attention must be paid to activities on the critical path. If anything delays one of these activities, the project will be late. At the start of the project, the PM correctly notes that activity **a** is on the critical path and **b** is not. This raises an interesting question. Can any resources reserved for use on **b** be borrowed for a few days to work on **a** and thereby shorten its duration? The nature of **b**'s resources and **a**'s technology will dictate whether or not this is possible. If **a**, for example, could be shortened by a day by using **b**'s resources for four days, the critical path would be shortened by a day. This would cause no problem for **b**, which had seven days of slack. If the delivery date for the project remains the same, the entire project would then have a day of slack. The presence of project slack tends to lower the PM's pulse rate and blood pressure.

Doing It the Easy Way—Microsoft Project (MSP)

As promised, once the reader understands how to build a network by hand, we can introduce tools provided through project management software. The first task is transferring information from the project action plan into the software, MSP in this case. This is not difficult. MSP presents a tab entry table much like the action plan template shown in Table 5-3. It has spaces where the tasks can be identified, plus spaces for activity durations and predecessors. The software automatically numbers each activity that is entered. MSP offers a great number of options for viewing the data once it is entered into the action plan or entry view. If a specific start date or finish date is already determined for an activity, MSP allows you to enter it as well.

Once the action plan data is entered, MSP will automatically draw an AON PERT/CPM network as shown in Figure 5-11. Note that the figure lacks start and finish nodes—because they were not entered on the activity list. Note also that the tasks in the network appear with ID numbers in order, flowing from left to right and from the top to the bottom. In Figure 5-11 several arrows cross, which may be confusing. The

Table 5-3   An MSP Version of Sample Problem in Table 5-2

ID	Task Name	Duration	Predecessors
1	a	5 days	
2	b	4 days	
3	c	3 days	1
4	d	4 days	1
5	e	6 days	1
6	f	4 days	2, 3
7	g	5 days	4
8	h	6 days	4, 5
9	i	6 days	6
10	j	4 days	7, 8

nodes show the activity name, ID number, duration, and start and finish times. These nodes are easily customized to show many different things concerning each specific activity.

It is simple to add Start and Finish nodes as milestones to make the network easier to understand. An activity named "Start" is entered at the top of the list, and an activity named "Finish" at the bottom. We want these activities to appear as milestones, significant events in the life of the project. In MSP a milestone is an activity with a duration of 0. Because we want the Start and Finish milestones to be linked to the beginning and ending activities of the project, all predecessors will have to be changed in light of these additions. For example, **a** and **b** will now have Start as a predecessor, and

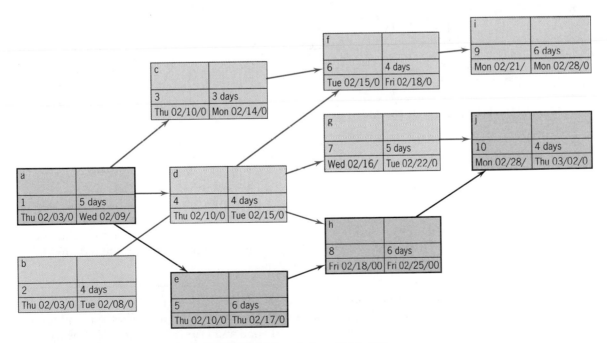

Figure 5-11   An MSP version of PERT/CPM network from Table 5-3.

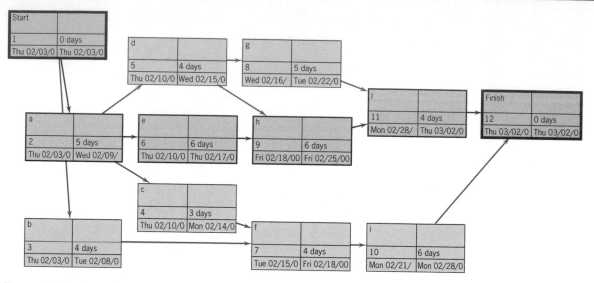

Figure 5-12   A modified version of MSP network from Figure 5-11.

the last two activities, **i** and **j**, are predecessors to Finish. (In MSP, predecessors are indicated by task ID numbers rather than the task names used here for clarity.) Redrawing the network to get rid of the crossing arrows is also simple. As we noted when drawing the network manually, this is corrected by moving the **c**, **f**, and **i** nodes down to the bottom of the network. In MSP that is easily done by simply dragging the nodes to whatever location you wish. See Figure 5-12 for the results of both changes. Notice in Figure 5-12 that because we added Start and Finish to the activity list, the other activities have been renumbered to conform to the changed list.

MSP will also calculate slack. (For details, click on MSP's "**Help**," type "Slack," and follow the directions.) MSP, and some writers, differentiate between "total slack" and "free slack." Total slack is LFT − EFT or LST − EST as we explained in the section just above. Free slack is defined as the time an activity can be delayed without affecting the start time of *any* successor activity. Take activity **b** for example. Its EFT is four days, but it could be finished as late as eight days without affecting task **f** in any way. It is thus said to have four days of free slack. Using **b** as an example, the rule for calculating free slack for an activity is

$$\text{Free slack for } \mathbf{b} = \text{EST of earliest successor} - \mathbf{b}\text{'s EST} - \mathbf{b}\text{'s duration}$$
$$4 = 8 - 0 - 4.$$

The total slack for **b** is seven days as we calculated in the section on finding slack.

These same calculations can be done by using the Solver in Excel®. To see how this is accomplished, refer to [5, Chapters 5 and 6]. Finding the critical path is a fairly straightforward problem in linear programming, but it often takes more time than doing the same problem by hand, and certainly much more time (entering the required information) than letting MSP solve the problem.

Following the definition of some terms commonly used in PERT/CPM analysis, both AON and AOA networks are illustrated. EST and EFT are found for all network activities, and the critical time and critical path are identified by the forward-pass method. LST and LFT are calculated for all activities by the backward-pass method, and slack is defined as either LST − EST or LFT − EFT. The managerial implications of the critical path and of project slack are briefly discussed. The same problem used for illustrating networks is entered into MSP and shown as an output of the software.

5.2   PROJECT UNCERTAINTY AND RISK MANAGEMENT

In Chapter 4, Section 4.4, in the subsection on risk analysis, we mentioned making most likely (or normal), optimistic and pessimistic cost estimates for project tasks. Such estimates were shown in Table 4-5, and we promised to illustrate how to use these and similar estimates on task duration to determine the likelihood that a project can be completed by some predetermined time or cost. It is now time to keep that promise.

Calculating Probabilistic Activity Times

First, it is necessary to define what is meant by the terms "pessimistic," "optimistic," and "most likely" (or "normal"). Assume that all possible durations (or all possible costs) for some task can be represented by a statistical distribution as shown in Figure 5-13. The individual or group making the estimates is asked for a task duration, a, such that the actual duration of the task will be a or lower less than 1 percent of the time. Thus a is an optimistic estimate. The pessimistic estimate, b, is an estimated duration for the same task such that the actual finish time will be b or greater less than 1 percent of the time. (These estimates are often referred to as "at the .99 or the 99 percent level," or at the "almost never" level.) The most likely or normal duration is m, which is the mode of the distribution shown in Figure 5-13.

The mean of this distribution, also referred to as the "expected time," T_E, can easily be found in the following way.*

$$T_E = (a + 4m + b) / 6$$

For the statisticians among our readers, this calculation is an estimate of the true mean of a beta distribution. The beta distribution is used because it is far more flexible than the more common normal distribution and more accurately reflects actual time and cost outcomes [3, 4, 6, and 12].** The calculation itself is merely a weighted average of the three time estimates, a, m, and b using weights of 1-4-1, respectively.

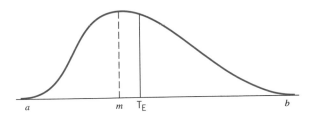

Figure 5-13   The statistical distribution of all possible times for an activity.

*MSP refers to the normal or most likely time as the "expected" time. After one has entered the optimistic, pessimistic, and "expected" times in MSP, it then will calculate the "duration," which is T_E in our notation. In most works on project management, T_E is denoted as the expected time or the mean time.

**For readers who have never studied statistics or who have forgotten what they once learned, there is a brief appendix on statistics and probability at the end of this book.

We can also estimate the standard deviation, σ, of this distribution as

$$\sigma = (b - a) / 6$$

In this case, the "6" is not a weighted average but rather an assumption that the range of the distribution covers six standard deviations (6σ). It follows that the variance of this distribution is estimated as

$$\text{Var} = \sigma^2 = ((b - a) / 6)^2$$

The assumption that the range of the distribution, $b - a$, covers six standard deviations is important. It assumes that the estimator actually attempted to judge a and b so that more than 99 percent of all cases were between these estimates, that is, greater than a and less than b. We have never met a PM who was comfortable with such extreme levels of likelihood. Ninety-nine percent translates to "almost never outside the range," and almost never leads to estimates of a and b that are so small and large, respectively, as to be nearly useless.

Estimators are not, however, so uncomfortable making estimates at the 95 or 90 percent levels. These estimates are within the range of everyday experience. These levels, however, do not cover 6σ, so using the formula given above for finding the standard deviation or the variance will result in a significant underestimation of the uncertainty associated with activity durations and cost estimates. Correcting for such errors is simple. If a and b estimates are made at the 95 percent level, the following should be used to find σ (and squared to find the variance):

$$\sigma = (b - a) / 3.3$$

If estimates of a and b are made at the 90 percent level

$$\sigma = (b - a) / 2.6***$$

The Probabilistic Network, an Example

Table 5-4 shows a set of tasks, their predecessors, and optimistic, most likely, and pessimistic durations for each activity, plus the expected time and activity duration variance.

The expected time for each activity was calculated by using the previously-noted weighted average of the three time-estimates. (The fractional remainders for these calculations are left in sixths for convenience because each T_E will be added to others.) For example, to find T_E for activity **a**, we have

$$\begin{aligned} T_E &= (a + 4m + b) / 6 \\ &= (8 + 4(10) + 16) / 6 \\ &= 64 / 6 \\ &= 10\ 4/6 \text{ days} \end{aligned}$$

The variance for **a** is also easily found as

$$\begin{aligned} \text{Var} &= ((b - a) / 6)^2 \\ &= ((16 - 8) / 6)^2 \\ &= (8 / 6)^2 \\ &= (1.33)^2 \\ &= 1.78 \end{aligned}$$

***A more detailed explanation of this problem and its solution may be found in [8, pp. 325–328]. Other ways of dealing with the estimation problem are also mentioned in the same place.

Table 5-4   A Sample Set of Project Activities with Uncertain Durations

Activity	Pred.	Opt. a	Norm. m	Pess. b	T_E $(a+4m+b)/6$	Var. $((b-a)/6)^2$
a	—	8	10	16	10 4/6	1.78
b	a	11	12	14	12 1/6	.25
c	b	7	12	19	12 2/6	4.00
d	b	6	6	6	6	.00
e	b	10	14	20	14 2/6	2.78
f	c, d	6	10	10	9 2/6	.44
g	d	5	10	17	10 2/6	4.00
h	e, g	4	8	11	7 5/6	1.36

(The traditional $((b - a) / 6)^2$ was used to calculate the variance, solely because it is traditional. A problem at the end of this chapter will ask the reader to recalculate the variance assuming 95 and 90 percent estimations, thereby repeating some of the calculations shown in this section.)

The network associated with the data in Table 5-4 appears in Figure 5-14. Note that the entries inside the nodes are the activity identifier, T_E, and variance, in that order. Some activities are known with certainty (i.e., $a = m = b$), as in task **d** in this example. A 60-day toxicity test of a new drug will be estimated to take 60 days, not more and not less. (Once in a great while the test may get fouled up and the estimate will be wrong, but our drug manufacturing friends tell us this is quite rare.) In some cases, the optimistic and most likely times are the same, $a = m$. We might, for instance, allow a specific time for paint to dry, a time that is usually sufficient, but may not be if the weather is very humid. Occasionally, the most likely and the pessimistic times may be the same, $m = b$, as in **f**. Sometimes the range may be symmetric, $(m - a) = (b - m)$, but more often it is not. Some activities have little uncertainty in duration, which is to say, low variance. Some have high uncertainty, high variance.

The expected time for each activity is used to find the critical path and critical time for the network. A forward pass is made, and the critical path is found to be **a,b,d,g,h**. The critical time is 47 days. Because the mean time (T_E) is used for all activities, there is a 50–50 probability of completing the project in 47 days or less—and also, 47 days or more. Activity slack is calculated by using a backward pass, exactly as we did in the previous section.

There are several problems with conducting the risk analysis in the way that we are demonstrating. For example, given the uncertainty in path durations, we cannot be sure that **a,b,d,g,h** is actually the critical path. One of the other paths, **a,b,c,f**, for example, may turn out to be longer when the project is actually carried out. Remember that a, m, and b are estimates, and remember also that the durations are ranges, not point estimates. We refer to **a-b-d-g-h** as the critical path solely because it is customary to call the path with the longest expected time the "critical path." Again, *only after the fact do we know which path was actually the critical path.* The managerial implication of this caveat is that the PM must carefully manage all paths that have a reasonable chance of being the actual critical path. It is also well to remember that in reality all projects are characterized by uncertainty. Sometimes, with routine maintenance projects, for example, activity variances are quite small, but they are rarely zero.

There are also problems with conducting the same type analysis by use of simulation. We will delay discussions of the assumptions behind these methods and a comparison of the pros and cons of such analyses until we have completed descriptions of both methods. In the meantime, it is helpful to bear in mind that the analysis started above, and continued just below, and the simulation methods we then discuss are simply two different methods of accomplishing essentially the same thing.

Table 5-5   An MSP Version of a Sample Problem from Table 5-4

ID	Task Name	Predecessors	Duration	Optimistic Dur.	Expected Dur.	Pessimistic Dur.
1	Start		0 days	0 days	0 days	0 days
2	a	1	10.67 days	8 days	10 days	16 days
3	b	2	12.17 days	11 days	12 days	14 days
4	c	3	12.33 days	7 days	12 days	19 days
5	d	3	6 days	6 days	6 days	6 days
6	e	3	14.33 days	10 days	14 days	20 days
7	f	4, 5	9.33 days	6 days	10 days	10 days
8	g	5	10.33 days	5 days	10 days	17 days
9	h	6, 8	7.83 days	4 days	8 days	11 days
10	Finish	7, 9	0 days	0 days	0 days	0 days

Once More the Easy Way

Just as it did for the deterministic sample network, MSP can easily handle the probabilistic network, though as we will see, it does not do some of the calculations that we demonstrate. Those can be done easily enough in Excel®. The stochastic (a fancy synonym for "probabilistic," from the Greek word for "conjectural" and pronounced "sta kas′ tic" or "stō kas′ tic") network used for the preceding discussion is shown below as a product of MSP. Table 5-4 becomes MSP Table 5-5, and Figure 5-14 becomes MSP Figure 5-15.

While Figure 5-14 shows the total elapsed time from Day 0 to Day 47 as one proceeds from left to right, the MSP equivalent, Figure 5-15, shows time as start and finish calendar dates. The project starts on Friday, February 4, 2000, and is completed on Monday, April 10, 2000. That is a total elapsed calendar time of 67 days—remember that 2000 is a leap year. The time appears significantly different from the 47 days that we determined above was the expected time for the project. This difference is caused by the fact that MSP assumes (defaults to) a five-day workweek. (It is not difficult to change that to some other assumption about the workweek.) Not counting Saturdays and Sundays, the project has an expected duration of 47 days, as we thought it should.

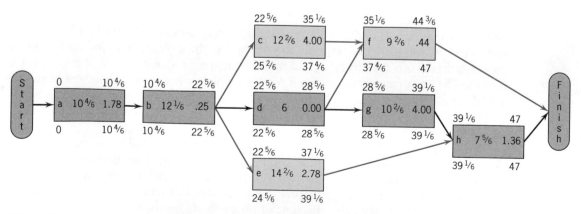

Figure 5-14   An AON network from Table 5-4.

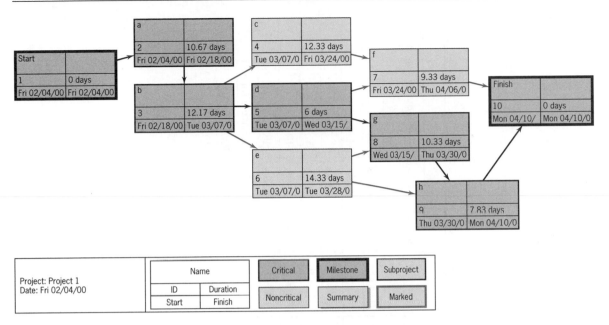

Figure 5-15   An MSP version of a sample problem network in Figure 5-14.

Table 5-6 shows an action plan for development and approval of a project proposal directed to the YMCA for sponsoring a day care service. The action plan covers the process from the investigation of the need for the service through the creation of an implementation plan, given that the YMCA accepts the proposal. In addition to the a, m, and b results, the personnel resource requirements for each activity are shown.

The network for this project appears in Figure 5-16. Note that there is no Start or Finish node, but they are not needed because the start and dates for each activity are

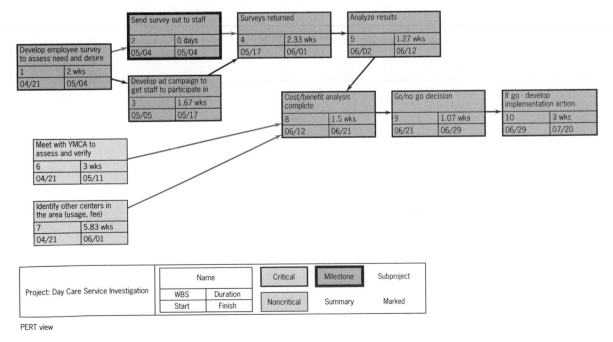

PERT view

Figure 5-16   A PERT/CPM network for the day care project (MSP).

Table 5-6 Three-Time Duration Example for a Day Care Project, with T_E and Resources Shown (MSP)

Day Care Service Investigation Project Plan

ID	Task Name	Predecessors	T_E	a	m	b	Resource Names
1	Develop employee survey to assess need and desire		2 wks	1 wk	2 wks	3 wks	Proj Mgr
2	Send survey out to staff	1	0 days	0 wks	0 wks	0 wks	HR
3	Develop ad campaign to get staff to participate in survey	1	1.67 wks	1 wk	1.5 wks	3 wks	Marketing
4	Surveys returned	2, 3	2.33 wks	2 wks	2 wks	4 wks	
5	Analyze results	4	1.27 wks	4 days	6 days	10 days	Proj Mgr
6	Meet with YMCA to assess and verify proposal for service		3 wks	3 wks	3 wks	2 wks	HR, Proj Mgr
7	Identify other centers in the area (usage, fee structure, etc.)		5.83 wks	4 wks	6 wks	7 wks	HR
8	Cost/Benefit analysis complete	6, 7, 5	1.5 wks	1 wk	1.5 wks	2 wks	Finance, Proj Mgr
9	Go/No Go decision	8	1.07 wks	2 days	1 wk	2 wks	Exec Team
10	If Go, develop implementation action plan	9	3 wks	1 wk	3 wks	5 wks	HR, Proj Mgr, Marketing

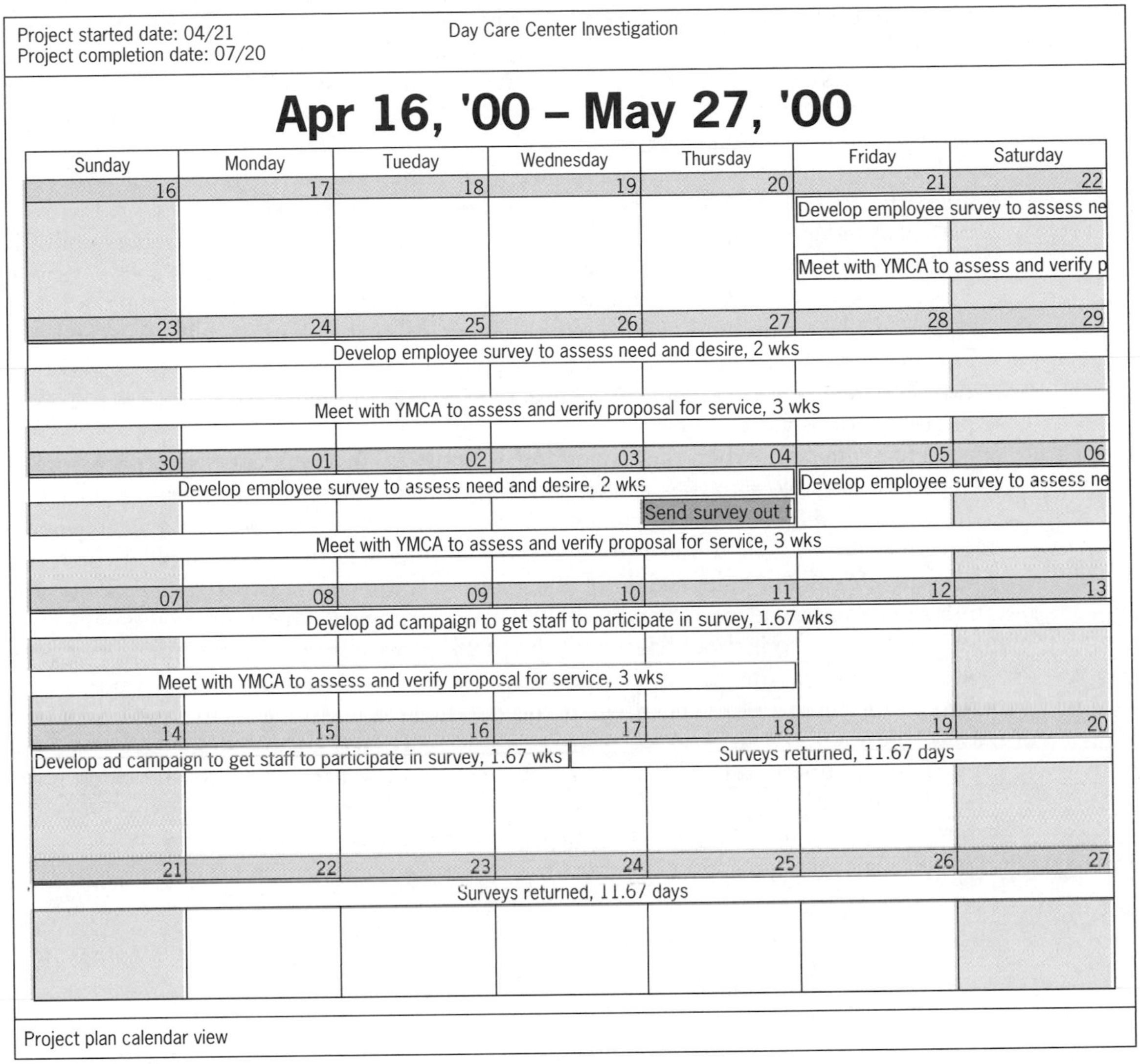

Project started date: 04/21
Project completion date: 07/20

Day Care Center Investigation

Apr 16, '00 – May 27, '00

Sunday	Monday	Tueday	Wednesday	Thursday	Friday	Saturday
16	17	18	19	20	21	22
					Develop employee survey to assess ne	
					Meet with YMCA to assess and verify p	
23	24	25	26	27	28	29

Develop employee survey to assess need and desire, 2 wks

Meet with YMCA to assess and verify proposal for service, 3 wks

30	01	02	03	04	05	06

Develop employee survey to assess need and desire, 2 wks   Develop employee survey to assess ne

Send survey out t

Meet with YMCA to assess and verify proposal for service, 3 wks

07	08	09	10	11	12	13

Develop ad campaign to get staff to participate in survey, 1.67 wks

Meet with YMCA to assess and verify proposal for service, 3 wks

14	15	16	17	18	19	20

Develop ad campaign to get staff to participate in survey, 1.67 wks   Surveys returned, 11.67 days

21	22	23	24	25	26	27

Surveys returned, 11.67 days

Project plan calendar view

Figure 5-17   An MSP project calendar for the day care project, for the period 4/16/00 to 5/27/00.

shown in the activity nodes. In addition to the network, the project calendar for the period from April 16, to May 27, 2000 is also shown, see Figure 5-17. This view simply shows the relevant project activities laid out on a standard calendar.

The Probability of Completing the Project on Time

Let us now return to our sample problem of Table 5-4 and Figure 5-14. Recall that the project has an expected critical time of 47 days. How would you respond if your boss said, "The client just called and wants to know if we can deliver the project on April 30, 51 working days from today. I've checked, and we can start tomorrow morning."

You know the mean project duration is 47 days, but if you promise delivery in 47 days you have a 50 percent chance of being late. That seems to you to be too risky. Tomorrow morning will be 50 working days before April 30, so you wonder: What is the probability that the project will be completed in 50 days or less?

This question can be answered with the information available concerning the level of uncertainty for the various project activities. First, there is an assumption that should be noted. The individual variances of the activities in a series of activities (such as a path through a network) may be summed to find the variance of the set of activities on the path itself, if the various activities in the set are *statistically independent*. In effect, statistical independence means the following in this example: If **a** is a predecessor of **b**, and if **a** is early or late, it will not affect the *duration* of **b**. Note what this does *not* say. It does *not* say that the date when **b** is completed will not be affected. If **a** is late, **b** is also likely to be late, but the time required to accomplish **b**, its duration, will not be affected. This may be a subtle distinction, but it is important because the condition of statistical independence is usually met by project activities, and this allows us to answer the boss's question seriously.

There are times when the assumption of statistical independence is not met. For example, assume two activities require some type of software code to be written. If during the project the code writer originally assigned to the project becomes unavailable and a less experienced code writer is assigned to the tasks, the times to complete these two tasks are clearly not independent of one another. If the lack of experience increases the task time and/or variance of one task, it is likely to impact other tasks in the same fashion. In this case, one should deal with the problem by reestimating the duration of both tasks. In general, this should be done anytime the resources supplied to a project are different from those presumed when the duration of project activities was originally estimated.

The first question is: What are the chances that the path of **a-b-d-g-h**, which is apparently the critical path, will be completed on or before 50 days after the project is started? We can find the answer by finding Z in the following equation:

$$Z = (D - \mu) / \sqrt{\sigma_\mu^2}$$

where:

    D = the desired project completion time.

    μ = the sum of the T_E activities on the path being investigated.

    σ_μ^2 = the variance of the path being considered (the sum of the variances of the activities on the path).

The exact nature of Z will become clear shortly. Using the problem at hand, $\mu = 47$ days, $D = 50$ days, and $\sigma_\mu^2 = 1.78 + .25 + .00 + 4.00 + 1.36 = 7.39$ days. (The square root of 7.39 = 2.719). Using these numbers, we find

$$Z = (50 - 47) / 2.719$$
$$= 1.10$$

Because the square root of the variance of a statistical distribution equals the standard deviation of that distribution, Z is the number of standard deviations separating D and μ. The distribution in question is the distribution of the times required to complete the path **a-b-d-g-h**. Consider all possible combinations of the activity times of the tasks on this path. This would include all possibilities from a combination of all optimistic times to a combination of all pessimistic times and everything in between. And even this does not include the highest and lowest project duration outcomes because the estimates do not cover 100 percent of all possible activity times; they cover only 99+ per-

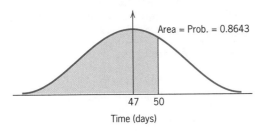

Figure 5-18   The statistical distribution of completion times of the path **a-b-d-g-h** in Table 5-4.

cent. We can illustrate the frequency distribution of the critical path completion times in Figure 5-18. (The Central Limit theorem allows the use of a normal distribution.)

The calculation of Z made above shows the desired date, D, to be approximately 1.1 standard deviations above the expected critical time, μ, for the project. If we define the total area under the curve as 1.0 (100 percent of all times), then the area under the curve to the left of 50 days is equivalent to the probability that the path **a-b-d-g-h** will be completed in 50 days or less.

Table 5-7 shows the probability associated with a wide range of values of Z. For Z = 1.10, the probability is .8643 or about 86 percent that this path will be finished on or before day 50. Again, we remind you that because of uncertainty, other paths may turn out to be critical, possibly delaying the project. Therefore, calculating the probability that the entire project is completed by some specified date requires calculating the probability that all paths that comprise the project are finished by the specified time.

Excel®'s NORMDIST function can be used as an alternative to Table 5-7 for calculating the probability that a path finishes by a specified time, D. The syntax of this function is as follows:

$$=\text{NORMDIST}(D,\mu,\sigma_\mu,\text{TRUE})$$

To illustrate, the probability that path **a-b-d-g-h** is completed on or before 50 days can be calculated with Excel® as $=\text{NORMDIST}(50,47,2.719,\text{TRUE})$.

Selecting Risk and Finding D

We can also work this problem backwards. Assume that a client is very important, very demanding, and will be very upset if the project is late. The client has asked when the project output will be available. The client insists on a firm date. How sure do you wish to be about being on time? (Don't say 100 percent because that implies a time so long that no one will believe you.) Carefully considering the matter, you decide that you want a 95 percent probability of meeting your promised completion date. When should you tell the client to expect delivery?

This is the same problem solved just above, but now D, the desired date, is the unknown while the probability associated with Z is preset at .95. Referring to Table 5-7 we can see that for a .95 probability, Z will have a value of 1.645. Therefore,

$$Z = (D - \mu) / \sqrt{\sigma_\mu^2}$$
$$1.645 = (D - 47 / 2.719$$
$$D = 47 + 1.645(2.719)$$
$$D = 51.5 \text{ days}$$

Say, noon of the 52nd day. Note, this result indicates that there is a 95 percent chance of completing path **a-b-d-g-h** in 51.5 days. Remember that this does not mean that there is a 95 percent chance of completing the entire project in 51.5 days.

Table 5-7 The Cumulative (Single Tail) Probabilities of the Normal Probability Distribution (Areas under the Normal Curve from $-\infty$ to Z).

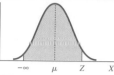

Example: the area to the left of $Z = 1.34$ is found by following the left Z column down to 1.3 and moving right to the .04 column. At the intersection read .9099. The area to the right of $Z = 1.34$ is 1 − .9099 = .0901. The area between the mean (dashed line) and $Z = 1.34 = .9099 − .5 = .4099$.

z	00	.01	.02	.03	.04	.05	.06	.07	.08	.09
.0	.5000	.5040	.5080	.5120	.5160	.5199	.5239	.5279	.5319	.5359
.1	.5398	.5438	.5478	.5517	.5557	.5596	.5636	.5675	.5714	.5753
.2	.5793	.5832	.5871	.5910	.5948	.5987	.6026	.6064	.6103	.6141
.3	.6179	.6217	.6255	.6293	.6331	.6368	.6406	.6443	.6480	.6517
.4	.6554	.6591	.6628	.6664	.6700	.6736	.6772	.6808	.6844	.6879
.5	.6915	.6950	.6985	.7019	.7054	.7088	.7123	.7157	.7190	.7224
.6	.7257	.7291	.7324	.7357	.7389	.7422	.7454	.7486	.7517	.7549
.7	.7580	.7611	.7642	.7673	.7704	.7734	.7764	.7794	.7823	.7852
.8	.7881	.7910	.7939	.7967	.7995	.8023	.8051	.8078	.8106	.8133
.9	.8159	.8186	.8212	.8238	.8264	.8289	.8315	.8340	.8365	.8389
1.0	.8413	.8438	.8461	.8485	.8508	.8531	.8554	.8577	.8599	.8621
1.1	.8643	.8665	.8686	.8708	.8729	.8749	.8770	.8790	.8810	.8880
1.2	.8849	.8869	.8888	.8907	.8925	.8944	.8962	.8980	.8997	.9015
1.3	.9032	.9049	.9066	.9082	.9099	.9115	.9131	.9147	.9162	.9177
1.4	.9192	.9207	.9222	.9236	.9251	.9265	.9276	.9292	.9306	.9319
1.5	.9332	.9345	.9357	.9370	.9382	.9394	.9406	.9418	.9429	.9441
1.6	.9452	.9463	.9474	.9484	.9495	.9505	.9515	.9525	.9535	.9545
1.7	.9554	.9564	.9573	.9582	.9591	.9599	.9608	.9616	.9625	.9633
1.8	.9641	.9649	.9656	.9664	.9671	.9678	.9686	.9693	.9699	.9706
1.9	.9713	.9719	.9726	.9732	.9738	.9744	.9750	.9756	.9761	.9767
2.0	.9772	.9778	.9783	.9788	.9793	.9798	.9803	.9808	.9812	.9817
2.1	.9821	.9826	.9830	.9834	.9838	.9842	.9846	.9850	.9854	.9857
2.2	.9861	.9864	.9868	.9871	.9875	.9878	.9881	.9884	.9887	.9890
2.3	.9893	.9896	.9898	.9901	.9904	.9906	.9909	.9911	.9913	.9916
2.4	.9918	.9920	.9932	.9925	.9927	.9929	.9931	.9932	.9934	.9936
2.5	.9938	.9940	.9941	.9943	.9945	.9946	.9948	.9949	.9951	.9952
2.6	.9953	.9955	.9956	.9957	.9959	.9960	.9961	.9962	.9963	.9964
2.7	.9965	.9966	.9967	.9968	.9969	.9970	.9971	.9972	.9973	.9974
2.8	.9974	.9975	.9976	.9977	.9977	.9978	.9979	.9979	.9980	.9981
2.9	.9981	.9982	.9982	.9983	.9984	.9984	.9985	.9985	.9986	.9986
3.0	.9987	.9987	.9987	.9988	.9988	.9989	.9989	.9989	.9990	.9990
3.1	.9990	.9991	.9991	.9991	.9992	.9992	.9992	.9992	.9993	.9993
3.2	.9993	.9993	.9994	.9994	.9994	.9994	.9994	.9995	.9995	.9995
3.3	.9995	.9995	.9995	.9996	.9996	.9996	.9996	.9996	.9996	.9997
3.4	.9997	.9997	.9997	.9997	.9997	.9997	.9997	.9997	.9997	.9998

We can arrive at the same answer using the Excel® NORMINV function. The syntax of this function is

$$=\text{NORMINV}(\text{probabiity},\mu,\sigma_\mu)$$

In our example, this function would be used as follows:

$$=\text{NORMINV}(.95,47,2.719)$$

The Case of the Unreasonable Boss

What happens if your boss is unreasonable, a "pointy-hair" type who insists that he wants the project we have been discussing delivered in 45 days instead of the later delivery times we have considered thus far? To find the likelihood that you can deliver, we return to Z. In this case,

$$Z = (45 - 47) / \sqrt{7.39}$$
$$= -2 / 2.719$$
$$= -.74$$

Reference to Table 5-7 reveals that there are no negative Zs. This merely indicates that D is less than μ. A glance at Figure 5-18 will show this because $-.74$ is to the left of μ. To find the probability associated with a negative Z, we find the probability of Z as if it were a positive number—for Z = .74. Because Table 5-4 is based on a normal distribution which is symmetric, the negative Z will be as far below μ as the positive Z is above it. Therefore, for a negative number the probability will be 1 minus the probability for the same positive number, $P(-Z) = 1 - P(Z)$. The probability for Z = .74 is .77 and thus the probability of Z = $-.74$ is $(1 - .77) = .23$. (With Excel®'s NORMDIST and NORMINV functions, this transformation is not required.) As the PM—other things being the same—you have between a 1 in 4 and a 1 in 5 chance of completing the project on time, not very good odds. The weasel words "other things being the same" will be removed in the next chapter when we reconsider the problem of the pointy-haired boss.

The Problem with Mergers

We are not, of course, writing of big businesses joining to get bigger, but of paths in a network that merge. When two or more paths through a network join, even at the end of the network, paths that have little slack or high variance may become critical simply by chance. For example, examine path a-b-c-f in Figure 5-14, a path with a duration of 46.5 days and a path variance of 6.47 days. What is the chance that this path will be longer than our expected project completion time of 47 days?

Elementary probability theory (see Appendix B) states that if the probability of event A occurring is P(A) and the probability of event B occurring is P(B), then the probability of *both* events A and B occurring is P(A) × P(B), assuming the events are independent. Tasks **a** and **b** are common to both paths so we ignore them. Tasks **d**, **g**, and **h** have an expected duration of 24.17 days, and their path has a variance of 5.36. Tasks **c** and **f** have an expected duration of 21.67 days, and that path has a 4.44 variance. Because **d**, **g**, and **h** have an expected completion time of 24.17 days, there is .5 chance these activities will take longer than 24.17 days. Therefore, we can ask: What is the probability that the **c-f** path will exceed 24.17 days? Back to Z.

$$Z = (D - \mu) / \sqrt{\sigma_\mu^2}$$
$$= (24.17 - 21.67) / \sqrt{4.44}$$
$$= 2.5 / 2.11$$
$$= 1.18$$

An examination of Table 5-7 shows that for Z equal to 1.18 the probability that the path **c-f** will be 24.17 days or less is .86. (Using Excel® we can write =NORMDIST(24.17,21.67,2.11,TRUE). The probability that both paths will be 24.17 days or less is .5 × .86 = .43.

It is interesting to remember we began by allowing 50 days for this project and found that the apparent critical path had a .86 probability of being completed in 50 days. What is the likelihood that path **a-b-c-f** will take longer than 50 days? You can do the arithmetic, but it is approximately equal to .015. So if we have 50 days for the project, we need not worry too much about **c-f**.

One more problem: both **g** and **e** are predecessors of **h**. Task **g** is on the path with the highest expected time, but **e** is not. What is the chance that **e** will force **h** to start late? Because tasks **d** and **e** both start at the same time, assuming they both use their ESTs, we can ignore their common predecessor, **b**, in answering this question. If **b** is not included, we simply compare **d-g** with **e**. The path **d-g** has an expected duration of 16.3 days and a variance of 4.00. Task **e** has an expected duration of 14.3 days and a variance of 2.78. The question is: What is the probability of **e** $\geq$ 16.3 days? Back to Z once again.

$$Z = (16.3 - 14.3) / \sqrt{2.78}$$
$$= 2 / 1.67$$
$$= 1.20$$

Table 5-4 indicates that **e** will be equal to or less than 16.3 days 88 percent of the time which means that it will force **h** to start late only about 12 percent of the time.

The probability that both **e** and **g** will be completed by the LST for **h** (39 1/6 days) is $.5 \times .88 = .44$. The chance that *all three paths* will be completed in 47 days (T_E for the apparent critical path) is now equal to $.50 \times .86 \times .88 = .38$ or slightly less than 40 percent. The chance that all three will be completed by Day 50, the boss's original due date, is still well above 80 percent. The reason for introducing some slack for the entire project is now clear. It should also be clear that given a large project with considerable uncertainty and many paths from start to finish this manner of dealing with risk is lengthy and probably tedious. More important than tedium, at times the assumption of statistical independence of the paths is not met. There is an alternative way to deal with risk, but it is based firmly on the concepts and issues we have just discussed so they must be understood before tackling the alternative, simulation.

> Uncertainty and risk management are introduced. Optimistic, most likely, and pessimistic estimates of task duration are made and expected activity times are calculated as well as the standard deviation and variance of task time distributions. From this data the mean times for all paths are calculated, and the probability of the apparent critical path completion on or before a predetermined date can be found. In addition, the probability of completion can be set in advance and the path delivery date consistent with that probability can be determined. The problem of merge bias is then investigated.

5.3   SIMULATION

In this section we can take a different approach to managing risk. Specifically, we build on the probabilistic foundation established in the previous section and use simulation to handle the arithmetic as well as help us to understand the consequences of uncertainty. Simulation analysis can provide insight into the range and distribution of project completion times. To illustrate this, we use the project activities listed in Table 5-4 and the corresponding network diagram shown in Figure 5-14.

To begin, the information given in Table 5-4 for activities **a** through **h** was entered in the Excel® spreadsheet shown in Table 5-8. Formulas were then entered in columns

Table 5-8 Data from Table 5-4 Entered into Excel® Spreadsheet

	A	B	C	D	E	F	G
1	Activity	*a*	*m*	*b*	TE	Variance	Std. Dev.
2	a	8	10	16	10.67	1.78	1.33
3	b	11	12	14	12.17	0.25	0.50
4	c	7	12	19	12.33	4.00	2.00
5	d	6	6	6	6.00	0.00	0.00
6	e	10	14	20	14.33	2.78	1.67
7	f	6	10	10	9.33	0.44	0.67
8	g	5	10	17	10.33	4.00	2.00
9	h	4	8	11	7.83	1.36	1.17
10							
11	Formulas:						
12	Cell E2	=(B2+(4*C2)+D2)/6 {copy to E3:E9}					
13	Cell F2	=((D2−B2)/6)∧2 {copy to F3:F9}					
14	Cell G2	=(D2−B2)/6 {copy to G3:G9}					

E–G to calculate the T_E, activity variances, and activity standard deviations based on the optimistic, most likely, and pessimistic time estimates listed in columns B–D. For the purpose of this example, we will make one simplifying assumption. Namely we will assume that the activity times are normally distributed rather than having a beta distribution. To illustrate, referring to Table 5-8 we assume that the distribution of completion times for activity **a** comes from a normal distribution with a mean (T_E) of 10.67 and standard deviation of 1.33. It is worth noting that while generating random activity times from a beta distribution is relatively straightforward in Excel®*, the process is complicated from a statistical point of view. Specifically, generating random activity times from a beta distribution requires the specification of two shape parameters which requires an understanding of advanced statistical topics beyond our scope. Therefore, we note that our emphasis here is on the process of simulating project completion times rather than the proper determination of the statistical distribution used to model activity completion times. Clearly, this later topic is most appropriately addressed in a formal probability and statistics course.

To simulate the completion of this project, the spreadsheet shown in Table 5-9 was developed. Completing the project is simulated by generating random activity times for the eight activities and then adding up the activity times that make up each path to determine how long the paths take to complete. Obviously, the longest path determines the project completion time. The spreadsheet shown in Table 5-9 was created to simulate 50 replications of the project (rows 3–52).

In the spreadsheet, columns A–H are used to store the randomly generated activity times for activities **a** to **h**, respectively. In column I the time to complete path **a-b-c-f** is calculated on the basis of the activity times generated in columns A–H. For example, in cell I3, the formula =A3+B3+C3+F3 was entered. Columns J, K, and L were used in a

*For readers with a background in statistics, random activity times from a beta distribution can be generated in Excel® as follows: =BETAINV(RAND0, shape parameter 1, shape parameter 2, optimistic time, pessimistic time).

Table 5-9 Simulating Project Completion Times in Excel®

	A	B	C	D	E	F	G	H	I	J	K	L	M
1	Activity	Activity	Activity	Activity	Activity	Activity	Activity	Activity	Path 1	Path 2	Path 3	Path 4	Project
2	A	B	C	D	E	F	G	H	abcf	abdf	abdgh	abeh	Finish Time
3									0	0	0	0	0
4									0	0	0	0	0
5									0	0	0	0	0
6									0	0	0	0	0
7									0	0	0	0	0
8									0	0	0	0	0
9									0	0	0	0	0
10									0	0	0	0	0
11									0	0	0	0	0
12									0	0	0	0	0
13									0	0	0	0	0
14									0	0	0	0	0
15									0	0	0	0	0
16									0	0	0	0	0
17									0	0	0	0	0
18									0	0	0	0	0
19									0	0	0	0	0
20									0	0	0	0	0
21									0	0	0	0	0
22									0	0	0	0	0
23									0	0	0	0	0
24									0	0	0	0	0
25									0	0	0	0	0
26									0	0	0	0	0
27									0	0	0	0	0
28									0	0	0	0	0
29									0	0	0	0	0
30									0	0	0	0	0
31									0	0	0	0	0
32									0	0	0	0	0
33									0	0	0	0	0
34									0	0	0	0	0
35									0	0	0	0	0
36									0	0	0	0	0
37									0	0	0	0	0
38									0	0	0	0	0
39									0	0	0	0	0
40									0	0	0	0	0
41									0	0	0	0	0
42									0	0	0	0	0
43									0	0	0	0	0
44									0	0	0	0	0
45									0	0	0	0	0
46									0	0	0	0	0
47									0	0	0	0	0
48									0	0	0	0	0
49									0	0	0	0	0
50									0	0	0	0	0
51									0	0	0	0	0
52									0	0	0	0	0
53								Minimum	0	0	0	0	0
54								Maximum	0	0	0	0	0
55								Average	0	0	0	0	0

similar fashion to calculate the time to complete paths 2–4, respectively. Once entered, the formulas in cells I3:L3 can be easily copied to cells I4:L52.

Column M keeps track of when the project is actually completed on a given replication. Since the longest path determines the time when the project is completed, =MAX(I3:L3) was entered in cell M3 and then copied to cells M4:M52.

To generate random activity times for activities **a–h**, first select **Tools** from Excel®'s menu bar. Next select **Data Analysis**, and then select **Random Number Generation** in the Data Analysis box.

After selecting **Random Number Generation**, the Random Number Generation dialog box is displayed as shown in Figure 5-19. First, we will generate 50 random activity times for activity **a** (cells A3:A52). Recall that for the purpose of this example we are assuming that activity **a** is approximately normally distributed, with a mean of 10.67 and standard deviation of 1.33.

To generate 50 random numbers of activity **a**, we specify 1 for the Number of Variables and 50 for the Number of Random Numbers. (In Excel® the Number of Variables field specifies how many columns of random numbers to generate while the Number of Random Numbers field specifies how many random numbers to generate in each column.) Then, we tell Excel® that the random numbers should be generated from a normal distribution. Next, the mean and standard deviation are entered in their respective fields. Finally, we tell Excel® to place the random numbers in cells A3:A52 by specifying this range in the Output Range box. After entering this information, the Random Number Generation box appears as shown in Figure 5-19.

After selecting the **OK** button in the Random Number Generation dialog box, 50 random activity times from a normal distribution with a mean of 10.67 and standard deviation of 1.33 are automatically entered in cells A3:A52, as shown in Table 5-10.

This procedure is repeated to generate activity times for activities **b–h**. Table 5-11 shows the spreadsheet after generating random activity times for the remaining seven activities.

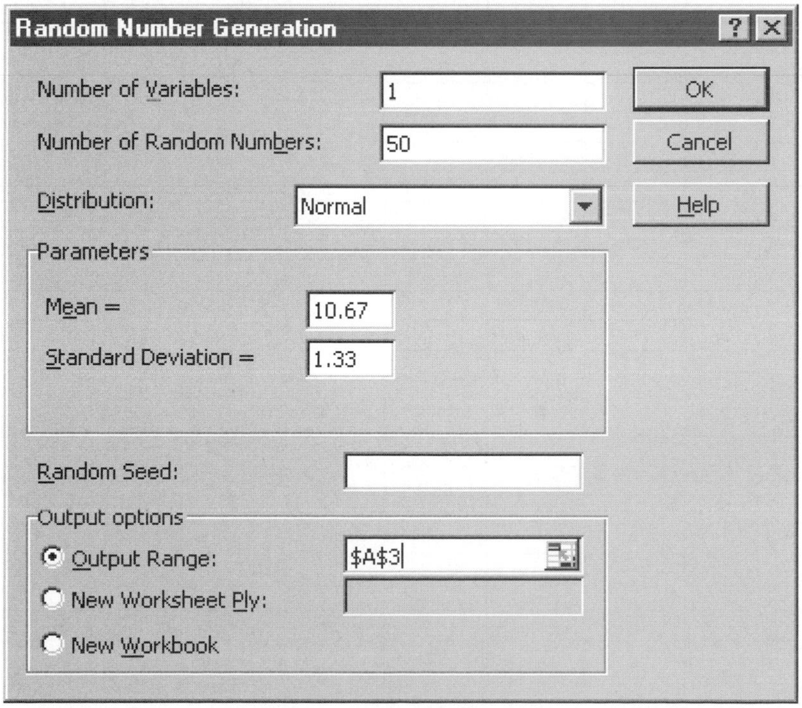

Figure 5-19 Random Number Generation dialog box in Excel®.

Table 5-10 Random Activity Times Generated for Activity **a** (Excel®)

	A	B	C	D	E	F	G	H	I	J	K	L	M
1	Activity	Activity	Activity	Activity	Activity	Activity	Activity	Activity	Path 1	Path 2	Path 3	Path 4	Project
2	A	B	C	D	E	F	G	H	abcf	abdf	abdgh	abeh	Finish Time
3	10.3								10.3	10.3	10.3	10.3	10.3
4	9.0								9.0	9.0	9.0	9.0	9.0
5	11.0								11.0	11.0	11.0	11.0	11.0
6	12.4								12.4	12.4	12.4	12.4	12.4
7	12.3								12.3	12.3	12.3	12.3	12.3
8	13.0								13.0	13.0	13.0	13.0	13.0
9	7.8								7.8	7.8	7.8	7.8	7.8
10	10.4								10.4	10.4	10.4	10.4	10.4
11	12.1								12.1	12.1	12.1	12.1	12.1
12	9.2								9.2	9.2	9.2	9.2	9.2
13	9.8								9.8	9.8	9.8	9.8	9.8
14	8.4								8.4	8.4	8.4	8.4	8.4
15	8.2								8.2	8.2	8.2	8.2	8.2
16	9.4								9.4	9.4	9.4	9.4	9.4
17	9.6								9.6	9.6	9.6	9.6	9.6
18	7.9								7.9	7.9	7.9	7.9	7.9
19	9.9								9.9	9.9	9.9	9.9	9.9
20	10.1								10.1	10.1	10.1	10.1	10.1
21	10.8								10.8	10.8	10.8	10.8	10.8
22	10.2								10.2	10.2	10.2	10.2	10.2
23	10.2								10.2	10.2	10.2	10.2	10.2
24	10.2								10.2	10.2	10.2	10.2	10.2
25	12.5								12.5	12.5	12.5	12.5	12.5
26	10.6								10.6	10.6	10.6	10.6	10.6
27	10.4								10.4	10.4	10.4	10.4	10.4
28	10.0								10.0	10.0	10.0	10.0	10.0
29	13.3								13.3	13.3	13.3	13.3	13.3
30	11.8								11.8	11.8	11.8	11.8	11.8
31	13.8								13.8	13.8	13.8	13.8	13.8
32	9.8								9.8	9.8	9.8	9.8	9.8
33	12.9								12.9	12.9	12.9	12.9	12.9
34	8.5								8.5	8.5	8.5	8.5	8.5
35	11.4								11.4	11.4	11.4	11.4	11.4
36	11.9								11.9	11.9	11.9	11.9	11.9
37	13.2								13.2	13.2	13.2	13.2	13.2
38	10.6								10.6	10.6	10.6	10.6	10.6
39	10.0								10.0	10.0	10.0	10.0	10.0
40	11.6								11.6	11.6	11.6	11.6	11.6
41	10.2								10.2	10.2	10.2	10.2	10.2
42	11.7								11.7	11.7	11.7	11.7	11.7
43	8.7								8.7	8.7	8.7	8.7	8.7
44	9.5								9.5	9.5	9.5	9.5	9.5
45	8.6								8.6	8.6	8.6	8.6	8.6
46	10.2								10.2	10.2	10.2	10.2	10.2
47	10.6								10.6	10.6	10.6	10.6	10.6
48	10.7								10.7	10.7	10.7	10.7	10.7
49	10.2								10.2	10.2	10.2	10.2	10.2
50	13.6								13.6	13.6	13.6	13.6	13.6
51	8.4								8.4	8.4	8.4	8.4	8.4
52	9.7								9.7	9.7	9.7	9.7	9.7
53								Minimum	7.8	7.8	7.8	7.8	7.8
54								Maximum	13.8	13.8	13.8	13.8	13.8
55								Average	10.5	10.5	10.5	10.5	10.5

Table 5-11 The Final Spreadsheet Simulating the Completion of the Project 50 Times (Excel®)

	A	B	C	D	E	F	G	H	I	J	K	L	M
1	Activity	Activity	Activity	Activity	Activity	Activity	Activity	Activity	Path 1	Path 2	Path 3	Path 4	Project
2	A	B	C	D	E	F	G	H	abcf	abdf	abdgh	abeh	Finish Time
3	10.3	13.4	11.3	6.0	15.1	9.9	10.0	10.3	44.9	39.6	50.0	49.1	50.0
4	9.0	12.2	8.7	6.0	14.6	8.3	8.6	8.4	38.2	35.5	44.2	44.2	44.2
5	11.0	11.7	13.6	6.0	15.1	10.2	11.4	8.5	46.5	38.9	48.7	46.4	48.7
6	12.4	11.8	17.6	6.0	16.6	10.4	7.4	6.9	52.1	40.5	44.4	47.6	52.1
7	12.3	11.8	15.2	6.0	12.2	10.0	11.6	5.3	49.3	40.0	48.9	41.5	49.3
8	13.0	12.2	21.1	6.0	13.3	9.4	10.8	5.9	55.7	40.6	47.9	44.5	55.7
9	7.8	12.3	15.1	6.0	16.1	7.9	11.3	6.8	43.0	33.9	44.2	43.0	44.2
10	10.4	11.3	8.9	6.0	14.0	9.8	9.1	8.4	40.4	37.5	45.1	44.1	45.1
11	12.1	11.9	7.1	6.0	14.4	8.2	6.5	9.1	39.3	38.3	45.8	47.5	47.5
12	9.2	12.2	15.7	6.0	12.1	9.8	10.2	7.4	46.9	37.2	45.1	40.9	48.9
13	9.8	11.8	14.2	6.0	15.2	7.9	11.2	5.9	43.7	35.5	44.7	42.6	44.7
14	8.4	12.2	19.1	6.0	16.7	10.5	10.9	8.7	50.2	37.1	46.2	46.1	50.2
15	8.2	12.3	8.9	6.0	13.3	9.8	9.5	6.7	39.2	36.3	42.8	40.6	42.8
16	0.4	13.3	12.0	6.0	11.9	9.4	11.5	9.0	44.1	38.1	49.2	43.6	49.2
17	9.6	11.2	13.3	6.0	15.8	8.7	10.4	7.7	42.8	35.5	44.9	44.4	44.9
18	7.9	12.2	4.4	6.0	14.9	9.6	11.8	8.1	34.1	35.6	45.9	43.1	45.9
19	9.9	13.1	15.4	6.0	10.0	9.7	10.9	6.3	48.1	38.7	46.2	39.3	48.1
20	10.1	12.4	12.9	6.0	17.0	8.9	9.8	7.9	44.3	37.4	46.1	47.4	47.4
21	10.8	12.3	8.1	6.0	16.5	7.9	8.3	7.7	39.3	37.1	45.2	47.3	47.3
22	10.2	11.7	17.4	6.0	14.1	9.3	12.7	8.3	48.6	37.2	48.9	44.3	48.9
23	10.2	11.8	13.5	6.0	15.4	9.0	12.4	8.4	44.6	37.0	48.8	43.8	48.8
24	10.2	12.3	12.6	6.0	12.4	8.9	10.4	7.8	43.9	37.3	46.6	42.6	46.6
25	12.5	12.9	7.3	6.0	15.4	10.0	10.8	5.8	42.7	41.4	47.8	46.4	47.8
26	10.6	12.5	10.3	6.0	14.3	9.8	10.6	8.3	43.2	38.8	47.9	45.6	47.9
27	10.4	13.0	16.4	6.0	12.9	8.0	9.7	10.0	47.8	37.4	49.1	46.3	49.1
28	10.0	11.8	12.3	6.0	14.2	9.1	9.3	8.9	43.1	36.8	45.9	44.9	45.9
29	13.3	12.1	8.7	6.0	10.9	9.0	7.4	10.7	43.0	40.4	49.5	47.0	49.5
30	11.8	12.4	11.8	6.0	12.9	9.1	9.9	7.4	45.0	39.3	47.5	44.4	47.5
31	13.8	12.5	12.1	6.0	16.2	8.5	8.3	7.2	47.0	40.8	47.8	49.8	49.8
32	9.8	11.7	8.4	6.0	15.6	9.3	11.7	7.6	39.3	36.9	46.8	44.8	46.8
33	12.9	12.7	11.1	6.0	11.9	9.2	11.5	8.0	46.0	40.8	51.2	45.5	51.2
34	8.5	13.1	11.8	6.0	17.6	9.9	9.9	5.2	43.3	37.5	42.6	44.3	44.3
35	11.4	12.2	21.6	6.0	17.1	8.9	8.7	7.1	54.1	38.5	45.4	47.8	54.1
36	11.9	12.9	17.4	6.0	14.7	9.0	11.8	8.2	51.2	39.8	50.7	47.7	51.2
37	13.2	11.9	16.5	6.0	14.7	9.7	8.8	10.4	51.3	40.8	50.3	50.1	51.3
38	10.6	12.4	13.7	6.0	14.2	9.2	7.2	8.0	45.9	38.2	44.2	45.2	45.9
39	10.0	12.4	16.5	6.0	15.9	9.6	12.0	8.6	48.5	38.0	49.0	46.9	49.0
40	11.6	11.9	13.2	6.0	13.0	8.8	10.7	5.7	45.4	38.2	45.8	42.1	45.8
41	10.2	12.2	12.4	6.0	14.4	7.9	10.2	7.2	42.7	36.2	45.8	44.0	45.8
42	11.7	12.2	5.5	6.0	14.4	9.8	7.5	9.4	39.2	39.7	46.7	47.6	47.6
43	8.7	11.8	17.9	6.0	13.8	9.2	12.2	10.1	47.6	35.8	48.8	44.4	48.8
44	9.5	12.6	8.2	6.0	15.0	9.5	12.8	9.3	39.9	37.7	50.3	46.5	50.3
45	8.6	11.8	12.6	6.0	14.4	9.9	10.3	7.3	43.0	36.3	44.1	42.2	44.1
46	10.2	12.6	15.0	6.0	14.8	9.4	10.7	8.0	47.2	38.2	47.5	45.5	47.5
47	10.6	12.1	14.4	6.0	14.3	10.5	8.9	7.3	47.7	39.3	44.9	44.4	47.7
48	10.7	12.1	11.5	6.0	14.2	9.4	10.2	6.5	43.7	38.2	45.5	43.5	45.5
49	10.2	12.1	19.1	6.0	14.8	8.2	12.2	8.2	49.7	36.6	48.8	45.4	49.7
50	13.6	12.5	13.6	6.0	13.0	9.3	7.6	8.1	48.9	41.3	47.8	47.2	48.9
51	8.4	13.0	8.4	6.0	13.7	10.3	8.3	8.5	40.1	37.7	44.3	43.6	44.3
52	9.7	12.4	9.8	6.0	16.3	9.8	8.8	9.5	41.4	37.8	46.4	47.9	47.9
53								Minimum	34.1	33.9	42.6	39.3	42.8
54								Maximum	55.7	41.4	51.2	50.1	55.7
55								Average	44.9	38.1	46.8	45.1	47.9

Several insights emerge as a result of this simulation analysis. First, in the preceding 50 replications of the project, the fastest project completion time was 42.8 days and the longest was 55.7 days. Furthermore, 60 percent (30/50) of the time path 3 was the critical path. Path 1 was the critical path 26 percent (13/50) of the time, and path 4 was the critical path 16 percent (8/50) of the time. (The astute reader will note that the number of cases sums to 51 and the percentages add to 102 percent. This is because paths 3 and 4 tied on the second trial.) This clearly demonstrates the problem of trying to determine which path will be the critical path when the activity times are uncertain. In the example presented here, we observe that three of the four paths have the potential to become the critical path. Of course, the more times the project is replicated, the more confidence we have in the results.

We can take this analysis a step further and investigate the actual distribution of project completion times. To do this, the Histogram tool in Excel® was used to create the histogram based on the values contained in cells M3:M52, as shown in Figure 5-20.

As the histogram shows, the project completion times appear to be approximately normally distributed.* The average and standard deviation of the project completion times can be easily calculated as 47.9 and 2.63, respectively. This suggests that in this case the time to complete this project follows a normal distribution with a mean of 47.9 days and standard deviation of 2.63. We can use this information in a fashion similar to the way the information was used about individual paths to calculate the probability that the project is completed by some specified time. For example, the probability that the project is completed within 50 days can be calculated using Excel® as

$$=NORMDIST(50,47.9,2.63,TRUE)$$

which equals .7877. Therefore there is a 79 percent chance of completing this project in 50 days or less. We can also flip the question around and determine what project completion date has a 95 percent chance of being completed as follows:

$$=NORMINV(.95,47.9,2.63)$$

which equals 52.23. Therefore, there is a 95 percent chance that this project can be completed in $52\frac{1}{4}$ days or less.

Traditional Statistics vs. Simulation

At a recent conference on the literature of project management, there was a session devoted to risk management. The participants, all highly experienced PMs from several different industrial sectors, were not of a single mind about the optimum way to handle

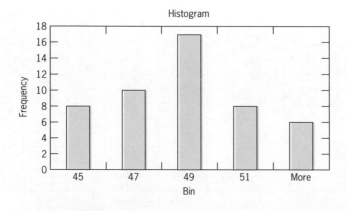

Figure 5-20 The distribution of project completion times based on 50 simulations (Excel®).

---

*The reader with a background in statistics may wish to verify this with the Chi-Square Goodness-of-Fit test or with a normal probability plot.

the problems we have discussed in this chapter. Some favored the traditional statistical approach, some favored simulation, and some favored adding sizable contingency allowances in both the budget and the schedule, and then ignoring uncertainty. A decade ago, the group that ignored uncertainty would have been in the majority, but they were the smallest of the three groups at this discussion. Dealing with risk is no longer the esoteric interest of a few statisticians, but is now an everyday problem for the PM.

The major difficulty is making sure that the risk analyst understands risk analysis. Irrespective of how the arithmetic is performed, by human or machine, the analyst must understand the nature of the calculations, what they mean and what they do not mean. Conducting a risk analysis by examining the many paths through a large network, and finding those that may turn out to be critical or near-critical, can be an overwhelming task. There may be hundreds or thousands of activities and dozens of paths to be examined. Simply identifying the paths is a daunting job.

There are a number of issues associated with either the statistical approach or simulation. With an important exception we note just below, both procedures assume that task durations are statistically independent. As we noted above, this might not be the case when resources are shared across the tasks, but the problem can be handled by reestimating task durations based on the altered resource. Second, with the same exception, both procedures assume that the paths are independent of one another. Even when paths have tasks in common, the common task durations (and variances) are the same for every path in which they are an element during any given estimate of path duration by whatever procedure. It is as if a constant is being added to each path.

The exception we mention is that simulation has a direct way of circumventing the assumption of statistical independence if the assumption is not realistic. With simulation, one simply includes the activity or path dependencies as a part of the model. The dependencies are modeled by expressing the functional relationship between the activities or paths along with its distribution, mean, and variance so that it may become a variable in the simulation. While this can be done in the statistical approach also, it is much more difficult to handle.

Both approaches require the analyst to enumerate alternate paths and to calculate the T_E and variance for each activity. Using the statistical process, the analyst must find the T_E and variance for each path. Using simulation, the machine selects a sample from the distribution of activity times for each activity and then calculates the path duration for each path enumerated.

On the other hand, no matter which method is used, it is rarely necessary to evaluate every path carefully. In a large network many paths will have both short duration and low variance when compared to high duration paths. Even when it is technically possible for one of the short paths to be critical, it is often very unlikely. For example, consider the path **a-b-d-f** in our example. It shares activities **a**, **b**, and **d** with **a-b-d-g-h**, the path with the longest T_E. Activity **f** has a pessimistic time of 10 days. Activities **g** and **h** have optimistic times of $5 + 4 = 9$ days. What is the probability that **f** will take on its maximum value at the same time that both **g** and **h** take on their minimum values so that **a-b-d-f** will be longer than **a-b-d-g-h**, not to mention simultaneously longer than the remaining two paths? Given that these estimates were made at the $\pm 3\sigma$ limit, the probability of **g** or **h** being at or below their optimistic estimates is $(1 - .9987) = .0013$ for each. It is the same for **f** being at or above its pessimistic estimate. These three things must happen at the same time for **a-b-d-f** to be longer than **a-b-d-g-h**. The probability is $.0013^3 = .000000002$. That probability is not zero, but most PMs will not spend time and effort worrying about it. Even when estimates of the optimistic and pessimistic times, a and b, are made at the 90 percent level, the chance that the activities on these particular paths will simultaneously take on their high or low extreme values is about one in a thousand.

The PM will discover the duration of each activity when, and only when, the activity is completed, which is to say after the fact, regardless of the method used to estimate and calculate project duration. Dealing with activity duration as certain does not make it so. We cannot know which of the paths will take the longest time to complete until the project is actually completed. And because we cannot determine before the start of the project which path will be critical, we cannot determine how much slack the other paths will have. We can, however, often make reasonable estimates. We can put our managerial efforts on the activities and paths most likely to require our efforts.

Because of the calculational exertion required by the statistical method, we recommend simulation as the preferred tool for risk analysis—after, and only after, the analyst understands the underlying theory of the analysis.

In addition to Excel®, there are other excellent tools for simulating project networks. For example, Crystal Ball®, an excellent Excel® add-in, can be used to facilitate and enhance the simulation of the project networks. More specifically, Crystal Ball® can automatically select the best distributions to be used to model alternative activities if historical data are available for these activities. Likewise, Crystal Ball® can determine the best distribution to use to model the project completion times and other outputs of the simulation analysis. Furthermore, Crystal Ball® has a comprehensive set of probability distributions available and the selection of these distributions is facilitated by graphically showing the analyst the shape of the distribution based on the parameters specified. This capability allows the user to interact with the software when specifying the parameters of a distribution. The analyst can immediately assess the impact that alternative parameter settings have on the shape of the distribution. Another powerful feature of Crystal Ball® is its ability to quickly calculate the probability associated with various outcomes such as the probability that the project can be completed by a specified time. In addition, Crystal Ball® can display the results in a variety of formats including frequency charts, cumulative frequency charts, and reverse cumulative frequency charts. It also provides all relevant descriptive statistics. The CD accompanying this book contains a copy of Crystal Ball®, and a brief discussion of using this package to simulate project networks is contained in Appendix C.

We would be remiss, however, not to warn the PM that even slight variations in the formulation of the simulation tool can lead to (usually) small differences in the results of the simulation. One popular formulation for Excel® added nine-tenths of a day to the expected time of our example, based on a run of 4,000 simulations, and about the same amount to the 95 percent probability estimate. The difference is less than 2 percent, but different tools rarely produce precisely the same results.

> Using the sample problem, risk analysis is carried out by a simulation program built into Excel®. Each step in the process is described. Conclusions similar to those reached in the statistical procedure of Section 5.2 are reached through simulation. The two procedures are compared by examining the assumptions on which they are based as well as the problems encountered in using them. The computational effort and assumptions required by the traditional statistical approach lead us to the conclusion that simulation is the preferred technique for carrying out risk analysis.

5.4 THE GANTT CHART

Henry Gantt, a major figure in the "scientific management" movement of the early twentieth century, developed the Gantt chart around 1917. A Gantt chart is a type of bar chart that displays project activities as bars measured against a horizontal time scale. It is the most popular way of exhibiting sets of related activities in the form of schedules.

WBS	Task	Duration	Predecessors	Month 1	Month 2	Month 3
1	a	10.67 days		a ▭		
2	b	12.17 days	1	. b ▭		
3	c	12.33 days	2		c ▭	
4	d	6 days	2		d ▭	
5	e	14.33 days	2		e ▭	
6	f	9.33 days	3, 4		f ▭	
7	g	10.33 days	4		g ▭	
8	h	7.83 days	5, 7			h ▭

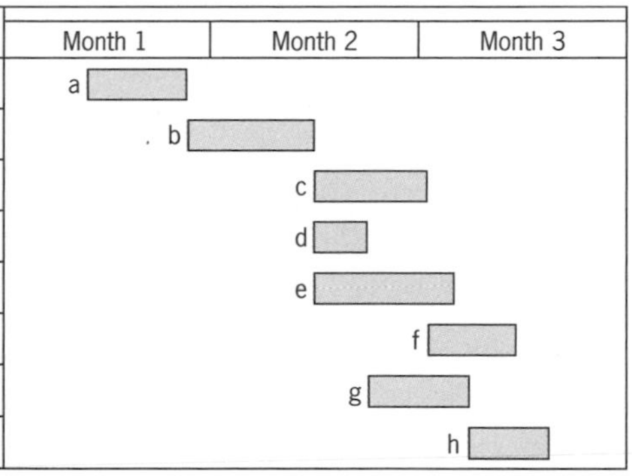

Figure 5-21
A Gantt chart of a sample project in Table 5-4 (MSP).

The Chart

Figure 5-21 shows a Gantt chart of the sample project in Table 5-4. The expected times are used in this illustration. Clearly, Gantt charts are easy to draw. Because task names are usually descriptive, each task shows its name, WBS number, or ID number in order to identify predecessors. Any activity that has no predecessors starts at the beginning of Day 1 and extends to its duration (as in task **a**). An activity with predecessors begins when its latest predecessor has been completed (as in task **f** or **h**).

Problems in understanding the chart can arise, however, when several tasks begin at the same time and have the same duration. If one such task is on the critical path and the others are not, it may be difficult to find the critical path on a Gantt chart. For instance, had **c** and **d** both been the same duration, it would not have been possible to tell which was predecessor to **f** and which to **g**, just by looking at the chart. This is only a problem when the Gantt chart is prepared manually. Most software, MSP included, will use arrows, bolded bar outlines, colored boxes, or some other visible means of marking the critical path on a Gantt chart as in Figure 5-22.

Even with software aid, the technical dependencies are harder to see on a Gantt chart than on a PERT/CPM network. On the network, technical dependencies are the focus of the model. As can be seen in Figure 5-22, information can easily be added to the chart to show such things as EST, EFT, LST, LFT, and slack.

Selecting another example for illustration purposes, it is simple to show resource requirements as in the Day Care project (see Table 5-6). The three-time estimates can be shown in Figure 5-23 as well as in Table 5-6, but Figure 5-23 shows only T_E to save space. Time and resource requirements may also be automatically transferred to the Gantt chart if desired.

It is also easy to show the current status of a project that is partially complete, as in Figure 5-24. This project was started on April 21, and its progress is being measured as of June 6. (The calendar dates shown as column titles above the bars indicate the first day of the period, in this case, four one-week periods.) Note that Activity 4 starts $1\frac{1}{2}$ days late. It was scheduled to start at midday on May 17, but did not begin until May 19. Activity 4 finishes a week late. If nothing is done to correct the matter, and if nothing happens to increase the lateness, the project will finish about a week late.

Software such as MSP makes it easy to use a Gantt chart or network to view critical tasks and paths of a project. One can even experiment with adjustments to the project—play "what if" with the project schedule, immediately observing results of the experiments on the screen. At times the PM may question an estimate of task duration, or of the a, m, and b time estimates, submitted by a member of the project team. It is simple to enter alternate time estimates and instantly see the impact on project duration.

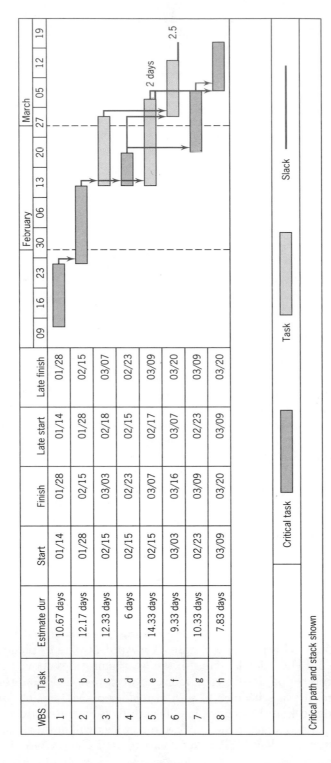

WBS	Task	Estimate dur	Start	Finish	Late start	Late finish
1	a	10.67 days	01/14	01/28	01/14	01/28
2	b	12.17 days	01/28	02/15	01/28	02/15
3	c	12.33 days	02/15	03/03	02/18	03/07
4	d	6 days	02/15	02/23	02/15	02/23
5	e	14.33 days	02/15	03/07	02/17	03/09
6	f	9.33 days	03/03	03/16	03/07	03/20
7	g	10.33 days	02/23	03/09	02/23	03/09
8	h	7.83 days	03/09	03/20	03/09	03/20

Critical path and stack shown

Critical task

Task

Slack

Figure 5-22   A Gantt chart of the sample project in Table 5-4 showing critical path, path connections, slack, EST, LST, EFT, and LFT (MSP).

Figure 5-23 A Gantt chart of a day care project showing expected durations, critical path, milestone, and resource requirements (MSP).

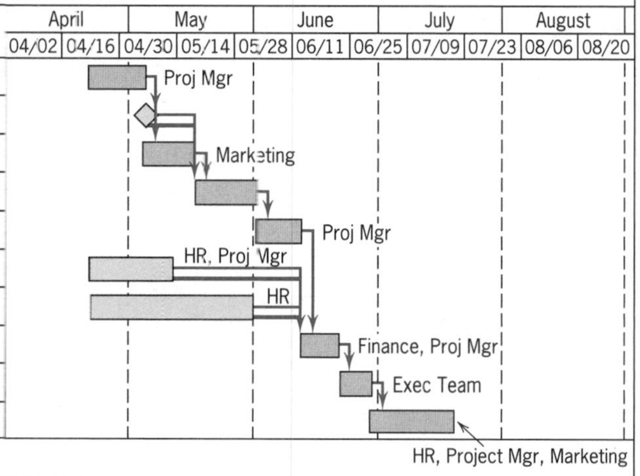

143

Day Care Investigation

ID	Task Name	Actual Dur.	Baseline Dur.	Start	Finish	Baseline Start	Baseline Finish
1	Develop employee survey to assess need and desire	2 wks	2 wks	04/21	05/04	04/21	05/04
2	Send survey out to staff	0 days	0 days	05/04	05/04	05/04	05/04
3	Develop ad campaign to get staff to participate in survey	1.67 wks	1.67 wks	05/05	05/17	05/05	05/17
4	Surveys returned	2.33 wks	2.33 wks	05/19	06/05	05/17	06/01
5	Analyze results	0.2 wks	1.27 wks	06/09	06/19	06/02	06/12
6	Meet with YMCA to assess and verify proposal for service	2 wks	3 wks	04/21	05/04	04/21	05/11
7	Identify other centers in the area (usage, fee structure, etc.)	5.83 wks	5.83 wks	04/21	06/01	04/21	06/01
8	Cost/Benefit analysis	0 days	1.5 days	06/19	06/28	06/12	06/21
9	Go/No Go decision	0 wks	1.07 wks	06/28	07/06	06/21	06/29
10	If Go, develop implementation action plan	0 wks	3 wks	07/06	07/27	06/29	07/20

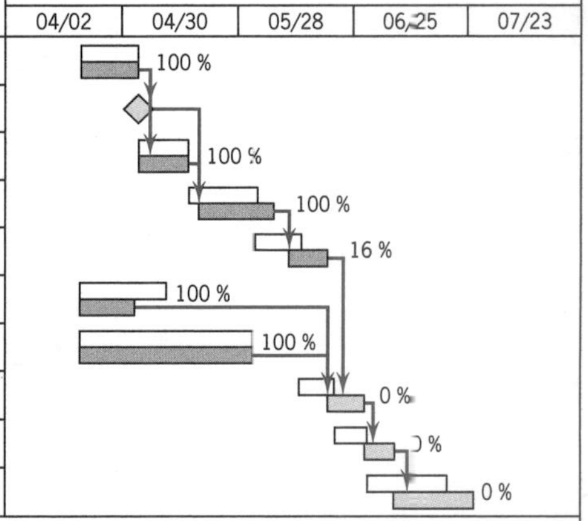

Timeline: 04/02 | 04/30 | 05/28 | 06/25 | 07/23

Legend: Task | Progress | Baseline task | Completed milestone | Milestone

Project start date: 04/21
Project current date: 10/04

Progress shown

Figure 5-24   A progress report on a day care project showing actual progress vs. baseline (MSP).

144

A great deal of information can be added to Gantt charts without making them difficult to read. A construction firm of our acquaintance added the following symbol to activities that were slowed or stopped because of stormy weather 🐝 . They used other symbols to indicate late deliveries from vendors, the failure of local government to issue building permits promptly, and other reasons why tasks might be delayed. Milestone symbols—diamonds, ◇, in MSP—are added to the charts, with different shading or color to differentiate between "scheduled" and "completed" milestones. MSP is limited only by the PM's imagination in what can be shown on a network, Gantt chart, or in a project plan.

The major advantage of the Gantt chart is that it is easy to read. Such charts commonly decorate the walls of the project office (or "war room"). They can be updated easily. This is both the strength and the weakness of the Gantt chart. Anyone interested in the project can read a Gantt chart with little or no training—and with little or no technical knowledge of the project. This is the chart's strength. Its weakness is that to interpret beyond a simplistic level what appears on the chart or to alter the project's course may require an intimate knowledge of the project's technology—not necessarily visible on the chart, but available on the network or the project's action plan. Not uncommonly, the Gantt chart is deceptive in its apparent simplicity.

We should add that one must be cautious about publicly displaying Gantt charts that include activity slack, or LSTs and LFTs. Some members of the project team may be tempted to procrastinate and tackle the work based on the LST or LFT. If done, this makes a critical path out of a noncritical path and becomes an immediate source of headaches for the PM who, among other things, loses the ability to reschedule the resources used by tasks that once had slack. Senior managers have even been known to view activity slack as an invitation to shorten an entire project's due date. We recommend caution and careful education of the boss.

At base, the Gantt chart is an excellent device to aid in monitoring a project or in communicating information on its current state to others. Gantt charts, however, are not adequate replacements for networks. They are complementary scheduling and control devices.

> The Gantt chart is a useful complement to a project network. It is easily constructed and read. It can contain a considerable amount of information and is an excellent communication device about the state of a project. Its major weakness is that it does not easily expose the project's technology, that is, the technical relationships between a project's many activities. Even with predecessors marked on a Gantt chart, it is difficult to see the project technology and, thus, to use the Gantt chart alone to manage a complex project. PERT/CPM networks are often used as complements to Gantt charts.

5.5 EXTENSIONS TO PERT/CPM

There have been several extensions to both network and chart forms of project scheduling. At times these extensions are quite sophisticated, for example, the application of fuzzy set theory to aid in estimating activity durations in cases where activity durations are difficult to estimate because project activities cannot be well defined [7]. In this section we briefly discuss two extensions of traditional scheduling methods, precedence diagramming and GERT. (Elihu Goldratt's critical chain [1] is a scheduling method using networks that combines project scheduling with resource allocation. It is discussed in Chapter 6 on resource allocation.) We then comment on some of the managerial implications of the two fundamental approaches to risk management taken in this chapter, statistical analysis and simulation.

Precedence Diagramming

One problem with PERT/CPM networks is that it is difficult to show lead/lag relationships between activities. If one were building a sidewalk from the back door to a patio, for example, there would be a task named "Pour concrete," and the next task would have to be "Wait for concrete to harden." "Remove concrete forms" or "Score concrete joints" might follow this. The "wait" activity requires no resource except time, say one day if the weather is pleasant. Rather than create an activity called "Wait," precedence diagramming allows the planner to build in an equivalent lag. The "Remove forms" task cannot start until one day after the "Pour concrete" task has ended.

With precedence diagramming, activities may be linked in the following ways:

1. **Finish-to-start linkage.** This is the most common linkage and applies to situations when the preceding task must be completed before the successive task can be started. An example is given in Figure 5-25 where in constructing a new house, the lot must be surveyed before the foundation can be staked out.

2. **Start-to-start linkage.** The start-to-start linkage is commonly used to start two or more activities at the same time. Thus this linkage is used in cases where the start of one activity depends on the start of its preceding activity. In Figure 5-25 this is exemplified in the situation where the start of the moving van loading activity can begin shortly after the start of the pack household contents activity. Clearly, loading the moving van can be started before the final box of household contents is packed.

3. **Finish-to-finish linkage.** The finish-to-finish linkage is used in situations where it is desirable for two or more activities to finish at the same time. In Figure 5-25 this is illustrated by the activities priming the walls and purchasing the wallpaper. Since it is desirable to hang the wallpaper right after the walls are primed, it is appropriate to complete priming the walls and purchasing the wallpaper at the same time.

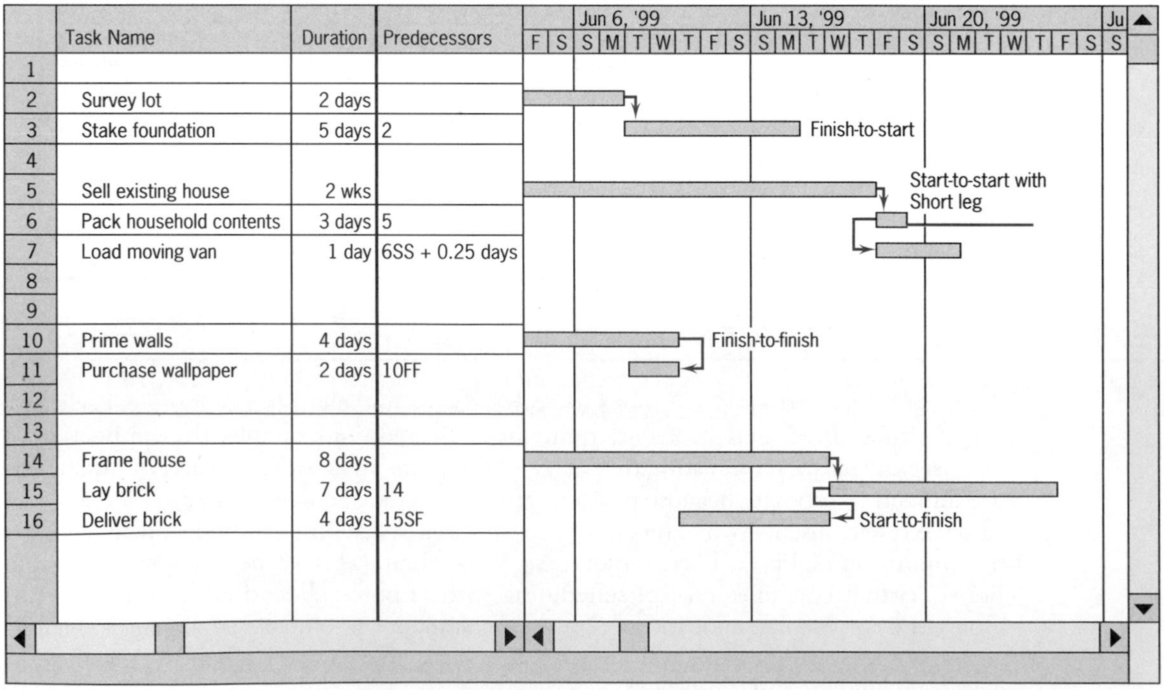

Figure 5-25   Precedence diagramming conventions.

4. **Start-to-finish linkage**. The start-to-finish linkage is used to ensure that a particular activity finishes based on the preceding activity's start time. This type of relationship is common in the delivery of materials. Referring to Figure 5-25, the delivery of bricks is scheduled to coincide with the start of the brick-laying task. By using the start-to-finish linkage, the brick-laying operation drives the brick-delivery task. Had a finish-to-start linkage been used from deliver brick to lay brick, then the delivery of the bricks would have controlled the brick-laying task and not vice versa.

The nomenclature for these linkages is straightforward in the language of MSP. By default, MSP assumes a finish-to-start linkage. Therefore, nothing special was required to specify a finish-to-start relationship between survey lot and stake foundation in Figure 5-25. In the predecessor column in row 7, "6SS+0.25" was entered which indicates that activity 6 is the predecessor of this activity and the relationship is start to start (SS). Also note that the "+0.25" was added to reflect the small delay in beginning loading the moving van. In row 11, "10FF" indicates that activity 10 is the predecessor and that the linkage is finish to finish (FF). Finally, the "15SF" in row 16 indicates that task 15 precedes task 16 and the linkage is start to finish (SF). Similarly, if the precedence had read "2.3SS+4" it would indicate that the activity in question should start four days after activity 2.3 has started.

MSP allows the PM great flexibility in responding to constraints placed on the project. Rather than using leads or lags, a PM might specify a date on which a task should be started or finished. Similar relationships can be shown in PERT/CPM networks, but to do so effectively and easily we must be able to split tasks. For instance, we could split the "Wait for concrete to harden" into two tasks. "Wait one day for concrete to harden" would precede the "Remove forms" task, and another "Wait for concrete to harden a second day" which might precede a task that requires the use of a heavy wheelbarrow on the sidewalk. A simpler and more efficient way to deal with leads and lags between activities is to incorporate the time into the predecessor and successor activities. One can display such activities on a Gantt chart. Fortunately, MSP and most other project management software make it easy to incorporate leads and lags through precedence diagramming.

The activities involved can be probabilistic and even the leads and lags (when they are programmed as "activities" in a network) may be uncertain using their own a, m, and b estimates—but usually they are not. As with projects without need of lead/lag activities, unless the projects are quite small, simulation is usually faster and easier than the more formal statistical procedures. Precedence diagramming is widely used—even by people who are unfamiliar with the technique's proper name.

Other Methods

There are several other variations on PERT/CPM and Gantt charts. For the most part, they are proprietary products and must be individually purchased or leased. Of these, most represent little significant improvement on the standard methods covered above. One exception is the Graphical Evaluation and Review Technique (GERT). GERT combines flowgraphs, probabilistic networks, and decision trees. The result is a complex but powerful scheduling method. The major difference between traditional PERT/CPM and GERT is that GERT can allow a wide range of statistical distributions for estimates of activity duration—but so can most of the readily available simulation packages. GERT also allows loops back to earlier events, as in the case of rework on manufactured parts, whereas loops are not allowed in PERT/CPM. Further, GERT allows probabilistic branching from a node. This is applicable, for example, when quality control rejects some percent of output, accepts some percent for rework, and unconditionally accepts the rest. GERT is a valuable addition when it is required, but there is often a simpler and cheaper, if somewhat less effective, way to deal with such problems.

There are also variations of GERT. Q-GERT, for one, simulates queues or waiting lines in networks and has application in job shops. The solution techniques for these networks are complex and require extensive calculation, but they may be quite cost effective in the right applications. (See [9] for further discussion.)

Final Thoughts on the Use of These Tools

A decade ago it was common to hear, "No one uses PERT or CPM." It was not true. One heard, "No one uses that probability stuff." It was not true. We even heard, "No one used _____ computer package," which was also untrue. These statements were not true a decade ago—and they are even less true (if that is semantically possible) today. Current software makes it easy to use networks and Gantt charts. Current software handles three-time estimates of duration and can do all the calculations almost instantly. Current software makes simulation a straightforward procedure.

Excel® or many other popular spreadsheets can calculate variances and find expected times. MSP can do some of these calculations, but not others. MSP does not find the standard deviation or variance of three-time duration estimates and cannot find the probability of completing a task or the entire project within a given time limit. These calculations are, however, easily handled by simulation on Crystal Ball® or Excel®. The analyst, of course, must examine the paths, and select those for further analysis. The software can do the arithmetic, but the analyst must enter the appropriate numbers and ask for the appropriate calculations for each path to be analyzed, and then find the probabilities. With large networks, this will probably be a massive and tedious task. On the other hand, it is almost never required to enumerate and evaluate all paths in a simulation—even if simulation could do so rapidly.

As we have noted several times, the same arguments and methods are appropriate for managing uncertainty in resource usage and preparing project budgets. The calculations and simulations are the same as those used with task and project duration.

When struggling with risk analysis and management, it is well to remember why the PM must engage the struggle. The PM is responsible for keeping the project within its budget and on time. This chapter is devoted to developing the information the PM requires to meet these responsibilities. The PM does not manage the project as a totality; rather he or she manages the specific tasks and subtasks that make up the project. The methods introduced above are intended to help the PM understand precisely where management effort is needed.

As we noted briefly above, it is relevant to point out that identifying one or more paths as critical might actually be detrimental to project performance—if the PM is not managing the project team as well as the project. If the PM is not alert to the possibility, activity slack may lead to neglect of noncritical activities. As Parkinson teaches us, work tends to fill the time allowed, and activities lose their slacks. For example, noncritical paths may slip far enough behind schedule that they become critical—simply because the project team perceives them to be of low priority. At the same time, the apparently critical path may finish ahead of schedule because of the extra management attention it receives.

Goldratt [1, Ch. 13] refers to other causes of project delay resulting from "human nature." There is, for instance, the "student syndrome." Given the deadline for a homework assignment, students often plead for more time. Given more time, many simply postpone starting the assignment. Goldratt also reminds us that if a task is finished early, its successor tasks are still started when they were originally scheduled. The result is that delays resulting from tasks finishing late are not offset by the potential gains from those that finish early. There is also the fact that "five plus five equals thirteen." If one team member estimates that one task will require five days and a second team member estimates that a successor task will require five days, the boss then estimates that the pair will require 13 days—just to be safe. The work, of course, will expand to require at least 13 days.

If the PM becomes entranced with the technology of the project and fails to manage the project team, the team itself can become confused and frustrated as the reality of the project unfolds. Today's path-slack disappears and a new critical path is born—only to change tomorrow when some other path becomes critical. In such cases, and they are common in reality, it is not easy to remind oneself that *recognizing and analyzing uncertainty does not cause uncertainty—nor does it cause uncertainty to disappear.* The PM's job includes teaching project team members enough about risk that they can understand its nature and, thereby, cooperate in developing ways in which the team can deal with it.

At this point, it is helpful to remember that there are problems for which risk analysis, by whatever method, is probably not required. Routine maintenance and routine construction projects are among such cases—unless the projects are quite large or have not been performed recently. In most such projects the routine character of the work means that the variances of task durations are quite small and the cost of carrying out a careful risk analysis is rarely justified.

> The section discusses extensions of Gantt charts and PERT/CPM. Precedence diagramming, developed as a convenient way to include leads and lags between activities, is explained. GERT is a network technique that allows probabilistic branching, loops, and other conditions not allowed by PERT/CPM. Finally, we consider some of the managerial problems often associated with risk analysis.

In the next chapter, we turn our attention to resource allocation and the problems of controlling the use and flow of resources. We also deal with the issue of integrating schedule and budget by examining the nature of time-resource trade-offs.

REVIEW QUESTIONS

1. How would a PM manage critical path tasks differently than non-critical path tasks?

2. How is slack determined?

3. How do you determine the EST for an activity with two predecessors? How do you determine the LFT for an activity with two successors?

4. Will all the activities on a non-critical path have the same slack? Why or why not?

5. For the following project,

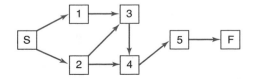

(a) List all predecessors of task 5.

(b) List all predecessors of task 4.

(c) List all predecessors of the network finish (F).

6. What is a "dummy" activity?

7. Consider Figure 5-14. Paths **a-b-c** and **a-b-d** converge at activity **f**, but we ignored this potential merge problem in the text. Why?

8. What is meant by "project slack?"

9. When using AON networks, how does one indicate an event such as a project milestone?

10. A probabilistic network has a critical path of 21 days and a .95 probability of completing this path in 24 days. Therefore, the project has a .95 chance of being finished by the end of the 24th day. True or False? Briefly explain your answer.

11. "Not uncommonly, the Gantt chart is deceptive in its apparent simplicity." Briefly explain.

12. When activity times are known with certainty, the critical path is defined as the set of activities on a path from the project's start event to its finish event that, if delayed, will delay the completion date of the project. Why must this definition be modified in situations where the activity times are not known with certainty? Are there any dangers associated with not modifying the definition?

DISCUSSION QUESTIONS

13. How might you use the network approach to help prepare cost estimates?

14. When would it be accurate to determine the probability of project completion by multiplying the probabilities of all the paths through the network together? When would it not be accurate?

15. Reconcile Question 14. If this approach is *not* accurate, would the probability of completion considering the critical path alone be more accurate? How might you estimate the correct probability without resorting to simulation?

16. Why do you think most PMs use MSP's Gantt chart format (see Figure 5-20) more commonly than the network format?

17. Which of the linkages in precedence diagramming do you think is most commonly used? Why?

18. In the calculation of variance for optimistic and pessimistic activity duration estimates made at the 95 or 90 percent level, the denominator of the fraction that approximates the standard deviation of the time distribution changes from the traditional $(b - a) / 6$ to $(b - a) / 3.3$ for 95 percent and to $(b - a) / 2.6$ for 90 percent. Where did the 3.3 and the 2.6 come from?

19. Given all the estimating done to determine the duration of project activities, what does it mean to say that "only after the fact do we know which path was actually the critical path?"

20. It was noted that "the PM must manage the project team as well as the project." Explain why.

PROBLEMS

21. Refer to the network in Figure 5-14. What is the probability that path **a-b-c-f** will interfere with the promised project completion of 50 days? Recall that the critical path, **a-b-d-g-h**, had a probability of .86 for a 50-day completion. What is the probability that both paths will be complete in 50 days?

22. Refer to Table 5-4 and Figure 5-14. Recalculate the variance for each activity on the assumption that the optimistic and pessimistic estimates were made with a 95 percent probability. Recalculate the probability that the critical path will be completed in 50 days.

23. Refer to Table 5-4 and Figure 5-14. Recalculate the variance for each activity on the assumption that the optimistic and pessimistic estimates were made with a 90 percent probability. Again, recalculate the likelihood that the critical path will be finished in 50 days.

24. Given the information in the following table, draw the AOA network. Using the same information, enter the data into MSP assuming a seven-day workweek. (To change the calendar in MSP from its five-day week default click "**Help**, type "calendar change," and follow directions.) Develop the appropriate AON network and Gantt chart. Using any method you wish, find the critical path and critical time for the network. Then find the slack for all activities.

Activity	Predecessor	Duration
a	—	5 days
b	—	7
c	—	4
d	a	6
e	b	9
f	b	6
g	c	4
h	d, e	6
i	d, e	8
j	f, g, h	9
k	i	10
l	j	9

25. In the following table, task durations are given in weeks. The estimates were made at the 95 percent level (see Section 5.2, Calculating Probabilistic Activity Times subsection).

Activity	Predec.	Opt.	Normal	Pess.
a	—	2	4	6
b	—	3	5	9
c	a	4	5	7
d	a	4	6	10
e	b, c	4	5	7
f	d	3	4	8
g	e	3	5	8

a. Find the expected time and variance for each task.
b. Draw the network (either AOA or AON) and find the critical path and time.
c. Find the probability that the critical path will be completed in 23 weeks.
d. Find the probability that the other main path will be completed in 23 weeks.
e. What is the probability that the entire network will be completed in 23 weeks?

26. Enter the following information into an Excel® spreadsheet. The time estimates were made at the 90 percent level (see Section 5.2, Calculating Probabilistic Activity Times subsection). All activity times are in days.

Activity	Predec.	Opt.	Normal	Pess.
a	—	5	6	9
b	—	4	4	6
c	—	7	9	15
d	a	6	6	6
e	b	4	5	7
f	b	12	16	17
g	c	8	12	20
h	c	7	9	16
i	d, e	10	14	18
j	f, g	6	12	20
k	h	7	9	14

a. Draw the network. (You may use MSP, or draw an AOA or AON network by hand.)
b. Using Excel®, calculate the expected time (T_E) and variance for each activity.
c. Using the expected times, find the critical path and critical time.
d. Find the probability that the critical path will be completed in 38 days or less.
e. Are there any serious sources of merge bias? What are they? Calculate the probability of finishing the project on or before day 38 when merge bias is included.
f. Assume that the times in the table were made on the 99+ percent level. Recalculate the activity variances with this assumption and find the probability that the critical path will be complete in 38 days. (Note, the altered assumption will change activity variance, but not the expected activity durations.) Briefly explain the difference in probabilities.
g. How many days are required for the critical path to have a .9 probability of completion?

27. Given the project in Problem 25, simulate the completion of the project 150 times, assuming that the activity times follow a normal distribution and that the time estimates are made at the 95 percent level.
(a) Determine the probability of each path becoming the critical path.
(b) What is the probability that the project is completed in 23 weeks?
(c) How do your answers compare with your answers in Problem 25?

28. The project referred to in Problem 27 has been partially completed. Task **a** required four weeks, task **b** nine weeks, task **c** four weeks, and task **d** five weeks. Update the simulation model you developed for Problem 27 and calculate the probability that the project will be finished in 23 weeks. Explain why the probability of completing the project in 23 weeks has changed.

DISCUSSION PROBLEM

29. The following activities were listed during a brainstorming session on product development. Find the appropriate predecessor-successor relationships and then construct an AON network to reflect the project using the activity duration times given in the information table. Assume a five-day workweek. Find the critical path and time for the project. Find the slack for all activities.

1. **Organize the sales office:** Hire sales manager. (6 weeks)
2. **Hire sales personnel:** The sales manager will recruit and hire the salespeople needed. (4 weeks)
3. **Train sales personnel:** Train the salespeople hired to sell the product to the distributors. (7 weeks)

4. **Select advertising agency:** The sales manager will select the agency best suited to promote the new product. (2 weeks)

5. **Plan advertising campaign:** The sales office and advertising agency will jointly plan the advertising campaign to introduce the product to the public. (4 weeks)

6. **Conduct advertising campaign:** The advertising agency will conduct a "watch for" campaign for potential customers. (10 weeks)

7. **Design package:** Have packaging engineer design the package most likely to "sell." (2 weeks)

8. **Set up packaging facility:** Prepare to package the products when they are received from the manufacturer. (10 weeks)

9. **Package initial stocks:** Package stocks received from the manufacturer. (6 weeks)

10. **Order and receive stock from the manufacturer:** Order the stock from the manufacturer. The time given includes the time for delivery. (13 weeks)

11. **Select distributors:** The sales manager will select the distributors whom the salespeople will contact to make sales. (9 weeks)

12. **Sell to distributors:** Take orders from the distributors for the new product, with delivery promised for the product-introduction date. If orders exceed stock, assign stock on a quota basis. (6 weeks)

13. **Ship stock to distributors:** Ship the packaged stock to distributors in accord with their orders or quota. (6 weeks)

What managerial problems and opportunities do you see as a result of your work?

INCIDENT FOR DISCUSSION

Springville Fire Department

The city of Springville is building a new fire station in their city. The city is expanding and is in need of a second fire station closer to the newer areas of the city to ensure shorter response times. The project manager and the project team have been selected for the project. The team is very interested in selecting the scheduling technique that will be used to follow the project through to completion.

The project manager, city manager, and chief of the fire department have set the following criteria for the

process of selecting the scheduling technique: easy to use, shows durations of tasks, shows milestones, can see the flow of work, can see the sequence of events, can depict which tasks can be undertaken at the same time, and can tell how far tasks are from completion. The city manager favors the Gantt chart, the chief likes PERT, and the project manager prefers CPM.

Questions: If you were the project manager, which method would you use, and why?

CASE

St. Dismas Assisted Living Facility Project Action Plan—3

The steering team meeting held August 31 went quite well. Fred felt that his team members had worked well together at determining the steps and the associated costs of the project. The CFO presented the project budget first, and then project team members presented their draft action plans.

The COO presented the following action plan:

ID	Task Name	Duration	Predecessors	Resource Names
55	**Operational Implementation Plan**			
56	Management/Organization structure	87 days		CFO, Legal, VP Mktg
57	Recruit & hire Executive Director	17.4 wks		Splient
58	Interior design issues decided (furnishings, etc.)	20 days		COO
59	Determine what was provided with lease and what was furnished in some units	2 wks		

ID	Task Name	Duration	Predecessors	Resource Names
60	Determine budget for interior	10 days		
61	Carpet and wall finish determined	2 wks	59	
62	Furniture and room layout	2 wks	59	
63	Facility and equipment needs defined	4 wks		COO
64	Staffing determined	2 wks		COO, Dr. Link
65	Office space for physicians	4 wks		Dr. Link
66	Medical staffing needs determined & Director appointed	4 wks		Dr. Link
67	Food service	45 days		
68	Menu's selected	8 wks		
69	Waiting and service staffing needs determined	4 wks		
70	Additional equipment needs	4 wks	68FS–3 wks	
71	Telecommunications services	45 days		
72	Investigate phone service options	45 days		Chief Engineer
73	Certification/Accreditation requirements	42 days		
74	Investigate requirements & timing of applicants with Dept. of Health to open facility	0 days		Legal
75	Develop clinical and operational quality monitoring systems	0 days		
76	Develop financial systems (billing, etc.)	6 wks		CFO
77	Human resources	79 days		HR Director
78	Work force management recommendations	6 wks		HR Director
79	Action plan for recruitment developed	2 wks	78	
80	Policies and procedures developed	60 days		
81	Obtain 'samples' of assisted living policies & procedures from other institutions	4 wks		Legal
82	Investigate assisted living laws proposed in other states/federal	12 wks		Legal
83	Technology & information systems	344 days		CIO
84	Develop plan for technology access for residents (TV, Cable, PC's)	3 wks		
85	Investigate software/technology options for residents	12 wks		CIO

The Chief Legal Counsel for the medical center presented his project plan. Fred had asked him to join the team when it became apparent that there were significant compliance and legal issues associated with this project.

ID	Task Name	Duration	Predecessors	Resource Names
36	**Legal and Licensing Requirements**	154 days		
37	Research licensing requirements for residential care facility	38 days		Legal
38	Uniform accessibility standard compliance (# hndcp accessible beds)	2 wks		
39	Investigate law firm and outline services	4 wks		
40	Prepare action plan for license	2 wks	39	
41	File license - by opening date	0 days	40	
42	Curb-cut approval from county (access to County Rd.)	53 days		Legal

ID	Task Name	Duration	Predecessors	Resource Names
43	Investigate corporate structure for assisted living	115 days		Legal, CFO
44	Determine Board of Trustee membership	3 wks		
45	Appoint Board of Trustees	4 wks	44	
46	Prepare draft Code of Regulation	4 wks	45	
47	Prepare document and filing of governance structure	12 wks	46	
48	Draft service agreement with St. Dismas for services provided	4 wks	47	Legal
49	Lease issues	110 days	48	Legal
50	Research Long Term Care insurance requirements	12 wks		
51	Facility "rules" defined (i.e., smoking, firearms, pets, financial planning)	4 wks	50	
52	Spell out changes for residents in moving from "light" to "heavy" assisted	6 wks		
53	Lease template prepared	6 wks	52, 50, 51	
54	Review all marketing materials for compliance	154 days		Legal

The Vice President of Marketing presented her action plan and stated that she and her staff were responsible for every step in the plan. She was still working with her staff to determine who does what. The Marketing VP made it clear to the team that she needed five months for the marketing plan implementation to be able to meet the occupancy requirements at start up. She restated that her team must have this lead time to the completion of the construction and furnishing phase of the project.

ID	Task Name	Duration	Predecessors
86	**Marketing**	270 days	
87	Community mailing about construction project	0 days	
88	Initial informational meetings	16 days	
89	St. Dismas volunteers	1 day	
90	Community groups	4 days	
91	St. Dismas staff (all shifts)	3 days	
92	Presentation prepared for Speaker's Bureau	0 days	88
93	Provide updates to community	0 days	92
94	Inquiry log established	0 days	88
95	Groundbreaking ceremony - during National Hospital Week	0 days	
96	Marketing plan developed and implemented	180 days	
97	PR firm contracted	4 wks	
98	Marketing plan developed	8 wks	97
99	Determine name and signage for facility	0 days	98
100	Hire Marketing Director	4 wks	98
101	Marketing plan ready to implement	0 days	98, 100
102	Implementation of marketing plan - 5 months before facility ready then ongoing	20 wks	101

As Fred was explaining that the next job of the group was to complete a final version of all action plans and firm up the schedule of the project, the Construction Project Manager stated that it was his turn to present his broad action plan for construction of the facility. He also added that he had a major scheduling issue to bring to the team. The Construction Project Manager presented the following broad action plan for facility construction.

ID	Task Name	Duration	Predecessors
1	**Construction & Furnishing**	369 days	
2	Facility construction	329 days	
3	Phase 1 - Foundation & excavation (basement/1st floor slab)	95 days	
4	Phase 2 - Structure (steel/framing)	113 days	3FS–60 days
5	Phase 3 - Enclosure (masonry/windows/roof)	134 days	3
6	Phase 4 - Interiors (drywall/ceiling/flooring/casegoods)	234 days	3
7	First 45 (light assisted) units ready to prepare for occupancy	0 days	6FS–5 wks
8	First 45 units ready for residents	8 wks	7
9	Remaining 57 units (light & heavy) ready to prepare for occupancy	0 days	6
10	Construction complete	0 days	9
11	Building ready for residents	8 wks	10

The construction PM proceeded to explain that the scheduling constraints that the Board of Trustees gave the team were not feasible. The Board wanted construction to begin immediately after the elections in November and to be ready for occupants by June. The contractor did not want to begin the project at the beginning of winter. The first phases of the action plan detailed work that needed to be completed outside. If the weather was bad, the construction PM knew the schedule would be affected. The construction project manager also pointed out that the schedule created by the contractor was designed around a 40-hour, five-day workweek. If the building project began in November, the estimated project duration would be increased by one to two months, during which time some construction crewmen would have to be paid, thereby increasing the building cost.

The PM recommended that construction begin in February or March of the following year, which would give the facility a shorter build time and a lower cost. The budget and project duration submitted were based on a March 1 start date. He stated that the construction phase of the project did not need to hold up the other members of the project team, they could begin their work on the project anytime.

QUESTIONS

1. Draw a Gantt chart for the construction phase of the project. What is the completion date if construction starts in March? What is the completion date of the project if construction is started in November?

2. Why is it not possible to meet the scheduling constraints set by the Board? What is your recommendation to handle the scheduling problem?

3. When will the project be completed based on your recommendation?

4. Develop a Gantt Chart of the Marketing Plan and Implementation Phase of the Project. Determine the start date of the Marketing Plan phase of the project in order to meet your recommended facility ready for occupancy date.

5. What is the next step the team members must take in order to complete their action plans?

C A S E

NutriStar

NutriStar produces a line of vitamins and nutritional supplements. It recently introduced its Nutri-Sports Energy Bar, which is based on new scientific findings about the proper balance of macronutrients. The energy bar has become extremely popular among elite athletes and other people who follow the diet. One distinguishing feature of the Nutri-Sports Energy Bar is that each bar contains 50 milligrams of eicosapentaenoic acid (EPA), a substance strongly linked to reducing the risk of cancer but found in only a few foods, such as salmon. NutriStar was able to include EPA in its sports bars because it had previously developed and patented a process to refine EPA for its line of fish-oil capsules.

Because of the success of the Nutri-Sports Energy Bar in the United States, NutriStar is considering offering it in Latin America. With its domestic facility currently operating at capacity, the President of NutriStar has decided to investigate the option of adding approximately 10,000 square feet of production space to its facility in Latin America at a cost of $5 million.

The project to expand the Latin American facility involves four major phases: (1) concept development, (2) definition of the plan, (3) design and construction, and (4) start-up and turnover. During the concept development phase, a program manager is chosen to oversee all four phases of the project and the manager is given a budget to develop a plan. The outcome of the concept development phase is a rough plan, feasibility estimates for the project, and a rough schedule. Also, a justification for the project and a budget for the next phase are developed.

In the plan definition phase, the program manager selects a project manager to oversee the activities associated with this phase. Plan definition consists of four major activities that are completed more or less concurrently: (1) defining the project scope, (2) developing a broad schedule of activities, (3) developing detailed cost estimates, and (4) developing a plan for staffing. The outputs of this phase are combined into a detailed plan and proposal for management specifying how much the project will cost, how long it will take, and what the deliverables are.

If the project gets management's approval and management provides the appropriations, the project progresses to the third phase, design and construction. This phase consists of four major activities: (1) detailed engineering, (2) mobilization of the construction employees, (3) procurement of production equipment, and (4) construction of the facility. Typically, the detailed engineering and the mobilization of the construction employees are done concurrently. Once these activities are completed, construction of the facility and procurement of the production equipment are done concurrently. The outcome of this phase is the physical construction of the facility.

The final phase, start-up and turnover, consists of four major activities: pre-start-up inspection of the facility, recruiting and training the workforce, solving start-up problems, and determining optimal operating parameters (called centerlining). Once the pre-start-up inspection is completed, the workforce is recruited and trained at the same time that start-up problems are solved. Centerlining is initiated upon the completion of these activities. The desired outcome of this phase is a facility operating at design requirements.

The following table provides optimistic, most likely, and pessimistic time estimates for the major activities.

Activity	Optimistic Time (months)	Most Likely Time (months)	Pessimistic Time (months)
Concept Development	3	12	24
Plan Definition			
Define project scope	1	2	12
Develop broad schedule	0.25	0.5	1
Detailed cost estimates	0.2	0.3	0.5
Develop staffing plan	0.2	0.3	0.6
Design and Construction			
Detailed engineering	2	3	6
Facility construction	8	12	24
Mobilization of employees	0.5	2	4
Procurement of equipment	1	3	12
Start-up and Turnover			
Pre-start-up inspection	0.25	0.5	1
Recruiting and training	0.25	0.5	1
Solving start-up problems	0	1	2
Centerlining	0	1	4

QUESTIONS

1. Draw a network diagram for this project. Identify all the paths through the network diagram.

2. Simulate the completion of this project 100 times assuming that activity times follow a normal distribution. Estimate the mean and standard deviation of the project completion time.

3. Develop a histogram to summarize the results of your simulation.

4. Calculate the probability that the project can be completed within 30 months. What is the probability that the project will take longer than 40 months? What is the probability that the project will take between 30 and 40 months?

BIBLIOGRAPHY

1. GOLDRATT, E. M., *Critical Chain*, Great Barrington, MA, North River, 1997.

2. HULETT, D. T., "Project Schedule Risk: Monte Carlo Simulation or PERT?" *PM Network*, February 2000. (Hulett comes to the same general conclusion that we do. Simulation is superior to the statistical methods of PERT for complex problems. In stating his case, however, he fails to note that for a PM to use simulation effectively, the PM should understand the statistics of simulation.)

3. KAMBUROWSKI, J., "New Validations of PERT Times." *Omega, International Journal of Management Science*, Vol. 25, No. 3, 1997.

4. KEEFER, D. L., and W. A. VERDINI, "Better Estimation of PERT Activity Time Parameter." *Management Science*, September 1993.

5. LAWRENCE, J. A., JR., and B. A. PASTERNAK, *Applied Management Science*, New York: Wiley, 1998. (This book has solution techniques for finding the critical path and time for a network using Excel's® Solver.)

6. LITTLEFIELD, T. K. JR., and P. H. RANDOLPH, "An Answer to Sasieni's Question on PERT Times." *Management Science*, October 1987.

7. MCMAHON, C. S., "Using PERT as an Approximation of the Fuzzy-Project Network Analysis." *IEEE Transactions on Engineering Management*, May 1993.

8. MEREDITH, J. R., and S. J. MANTEL, JR., *Project Management: A Managerial Approach*, 4th ed., New York, John Wiley, 2000.

9. PRITSKER, A. A. B., "GERT Networks." *The Production Engineer*, October 1968. (This paper marks the introduction of GERT. While not widely adopted as a scheduling technique, GERT and GERT derivatives are powerful methods when applied appropriately.)

10. PYRON, T., *Using Microsoft Project 98*, Que Corporation, Indianapolis, IN, 1997. (T. Pyron has also written *Special Edition Using Microsoft Project 2000*, which is to be published by Que in the fall of 2000.)

11. RUSKIN, A. M. "Using *Unders* to Offset *Overs*." *PM Network*, February 2000.

12. SASIENI, M. W., "A Note on PERT Times." *Management Science*, December 1986.

CHAPTER

6

Allocating Resources to the Project

In this chapter we consider the problem of allocating physical and human resources to projects.* The physical and human resources are granted to and used by the project in order to meet the project's performance objectives. The amount of resources that can be allocated, of course, depends on the timing of the allocation as well as on the total supply of resources available for allocation. Mainly, resource allocation concerns how we allocate specific, limited resources to specific activities (or projects) when there are competing demands for the same limited resources.

Projects compete with each other for the same resources in two different ways. First, consider a resource that is limited but is not consumed when used, the services of a specific technical specialist for instance. The problem here is which project gets to use the resource first and which must wait. Second, consider a resource that is limited and is consumed when used, a specific chemical reagent for instance. In this case, the second project may have to wait until more of the reagent can be purchased and delivered. In both cases, the project that must wait may suffer a schedule delay that makes it late. Just as projects may compete for resources, different activities of the same project may compete. Two or more concurrent activities might require the same personnel, or equipment, or even work space. One activity will be given priority, and the other(s) must wait.

In order to manage resources in such a way as to optimize the use of a limited supply, trade-offs must be made. The interaction of project scheduling and resource scheduling is clear, but we will examine several different solutions to the allocation problem. Those include the Critical Path Method (CPM), Goldratt's "critical chain" [4], and

---

*With a few exceptions, we will not make a distinction between human and nonhuman resources in this chapter. We need not distinguish between them in order to consider the allocation problem. The tasks of administering the human and nonhuman resources are quite different, of course.

158

many different priority rules for allocating scarce resources. The primary cause of concern is resource scarcity. If some resources (including time) were not scarce, the resource allocation problem would be concerned solely with profit maximization—a relatively easy problem.

In Chapter 5, we evaluated project durations solely in terms of time. A project was either on time or not. Now we must also consider when and for what purposes scarce people, equipment, material, and facilities are used. The PM's performance is judged by the skill with which the trade-offs of time, resources, and performance are managed so the PM must make constant use of cost/benefit analysis. There are countless questions to be answered. "If we come in late on this project, we face a $1,000 per day penalty. How much project slack do we need and what resources at what costs are required to get it?" "If I hire Cheatem Engineering Associates as design consultants, can I improve project performance by 3 percent, without extending the project's due date?" "Adding project slack and hiring a consultant require monetary resources that could be used for other things. Are these the best uses for the dollars?"

At times, the PM is asked to take on a project in which there are the usual time, budget, and performance goals, but which also constrain the trade-offs that the PM may wish to make if required to help the project meet its most important goals. For example, some projects are *time constrained* and must be completed by a fixed time. In such cases, resources (and possibly performance) are variable. Some projects are *resource constrained* and cannot go over budget or use more than a fixed amount of a specific resource. In these cases, time (and possibly performance) is variable. Occasionally, a senior manager suffers from a case of the micromanagement virus and fixes time, cost, and performance, thereby leaving the PM with no flexibility whatsoever. Such projects are certain to fail unless the micromanager has been profligate with the firm's resources, which is highly unlikely for micromanagers. The fault actually lies with the PM who accepts command of such a project. (For those who are thinking that such a PM may find him or herself without a job following a refusal of an assignment, we would note the senior manager in question is insuring that the PM will fail. Do you want to work for someone who will not allow you to succeed?)

We will start our tour through the wilds of resource allocation by reconsidering the problem of dealing with a pointy-haired boss who insists that a project be completed in much less than its expected duration.

6.1 EXPEDITING A PROJECT

The unreasonable boss problem in Chapter 5, Section 5.2 could be used as our example here, but a smaller problem will help avoid unnecessary arithmetic. Our problem is set in a deterministic world rather than in a probabilistic one, for the same reason. (Please remember that in reality all projects are carried out under conditions of uncertainty.) Finally, we must also take note of an assumption usually adopted when activities are scheduled, as we did in Chapter 5. That assumption is that all estimates of task duration, whether deterministic or probabilistic, are based on normal or standard resource loadings.

The Critical Path Method

In traditional CPM, the rules of "standard practice" apply and the *normal* task duration estimate is made with the normal or standard-practice resource usage. Then a second estimate, referred to as the *crash* duration, is made based on the resources required to expedite the task. More resources of the type already used might be added, more workers and shovels if there is a ditch to be dug. On the other hand, the technology used to dig the ditch might be totally altered, utilizing a backhoe or a Ditch Witch®, for example. When making estimates for crashing, it is important to make sure that the resources required to crash the project are, in fact, available. Using a machine to dig the ditch in three hours instead of the three days required for a worker with a shovel is dependent on the fact that the machine is available and can be on site when needed. (Of course, the warning about resource availability applies equally to normal resource requirements as well as to crash requirements.) It is also important to note that some tasks *cannot* be crashed. One must not assume that because it takes one woman nine months to carry and bear a child that nine women can accomplish the same result in one month.

Consider the project described in Table 6-1. There is a set of activities, predecessors, normal task duration estimates, crash duration estimates, and columns that shows estimates for normal cost and crash cost. One crash duration is marked with an asterisk. For this activity, the task may be carried out in normal time or in crash time, but the duration must be one or the other; it cannot be broken down to one-day segments. Activities without the asterisk may be split into one-day segments charged at the "cost per day" increments shown in the last column. Figure 6-1(*a*) shows the project as a Gantt chart, and Figure 6-1(*b*) shows it as a PERT/CPM network. All task durations (and costs) are normal. The network is included because it shows the various activity paths more clearly.

As can easily be seen, the critical path is **a-c-f**, and the critical time is 21 days. The total cost of the project is $400, the sum of the normal costs of all activities. If the client wants the project completed in 20 days, additional resources will be needed. What to do?

Two things are self-evident. First, it is good management to crash the least cost activities before more costly ones; and second, there is no point in crashing activities not on the critical path because the project's duration would not be shortened.

While **e** has the lowest cost per crash day, it does not lie on the critical path so it should be ignored. Activities **a**, **c**, and **f** are on the critical path and of these, **a** is the least-cost choice. Therefore, we crash **a** as shown in Figure 6-2. We lower **a**'s normal time by one day. It now equals the crash time and cannot be shortened further. The critical path is unchanged, the critical time has been lowered to 20 days, and the cost of the project is $400 + 30 (**a**) = $430. ($30 is the *additional* cost above normal for crashing **a** one day. The (**a**) is simply a notation to remind us which activity was

Table 6-1   Sample Problem for Crashing a Project

Activity	Predecessor(s)	Normal Duration	Crash Duration	Normal Cost	Crash Cost	Cost per Day
a	—	6 days	5 days	$ 60	$ 90	$30/d.
b	—	7	4	50	150	33/d.
c	a	6	4*	100	160	N.A.
d	a	7	7	30	30	N.A.
e	b	5	4	70	85	15/d.
f	c	9	7	40	120	40/d.
g	d, e	7	4	50	230	60/d.

*This task can be carried out in six or four days only.

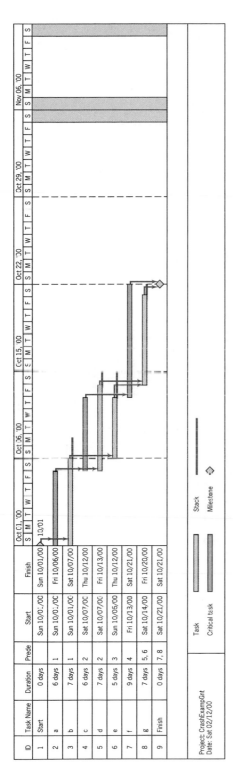

Figure 6-1(a) Gantt chart of sample crash problem—21-day project (MSP).

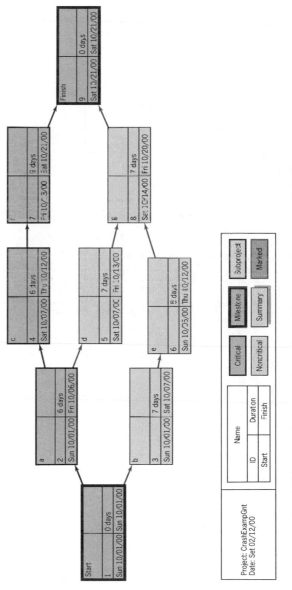

Figure 6-1(b) AON network for sample crash problem—21-day project (MSP).

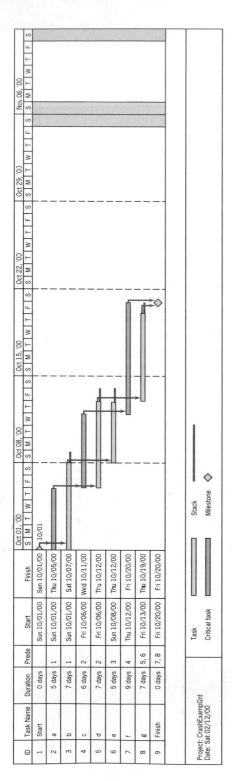

Figure 6-2   Gantt chart for 20-day solution to crash problem (MSP).

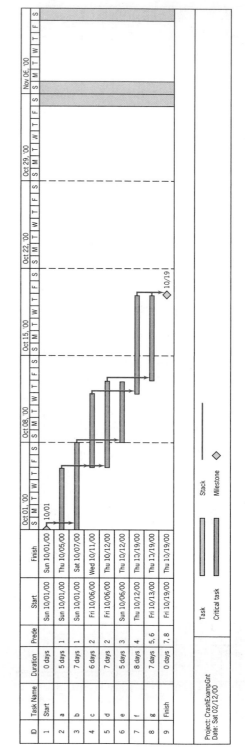

Figure 6-3   Gantt chart for 19-day solution to crash problem (MSP).

crashed and contributed to the additional cost.) Before stopping our investigation, we check all other paths through the network to make sure that they do not limit our ability to shorten project duration to 20 days. The path **a-d-g** is 19 days and thus allows our 20-day solution.

We report the 20-day solution to the client who decides that this is not sufficient. He wants the project sooner. Returning to Table 6-1, we consider the problem of shortening the project from its original 21-day duration to 19 days. We know that **a** is available for crashing, and **f** costs $40 more than normal cost and that is the next lowest cost for path **a-c-f**. On the other hand, rather than crashing **a** and **f** at a cost of $70, we could crash **c** alone. That will cut the duration of **a-c-f** by two days for an incremental cost of only $60. That would be an excellent idea were it not for the fact that not crashing **a** means that no matter what we do with other activities on **a-c-f**, the path **a-d-g** which requires 20 days will limit us to a one-day improvement in project duration. The result is that we crash **a** and **f** for one day each, **a** now has a 5-day duration and **f** is 8 days (see Figure 6-3). Project duration has been lowered to 19 days, and the cost is $400 + 30 (**a**) + 40 (**f**) = $470. The entire network is now critical, all paths being 19 days.

An examination of Figure 6-3 reveals another interesting feature of the problem. There are two paths leading to **g**: **a-d** and **b-e**. The two activities on the latter path are inexpensive to crash, but it does not matter. If we wish to crash the project further, crashing either **b** or **e** will not help. The path to **g** cannot be shortened beyond its current 12-day duration. Activity **a** has been crashed to its limit, and **d** is not crashable. The **a-d** path merges with the **b-e** path at **g**, thus, no matter what is done to **b** and **e**, the start time of **g** cannot be reduced to less than 12 days. We will ignore path **b-e** from now on.

The client examines the plan for a 19-day duration and appreciates our effort but asks, "What about 18 days?" We have two critical paths and if project duration is to be shortened, *both* paths must be shortened. Activity **g** is the only element of path **a-d-g** (or of path **b-e-g**) that can be crashed so we cut **g** by one day at an incremental cost of $60. Activity **f** could be shortened by another day at a cost of another $40—crashing **f** by two days raises the project cost by $80. It is less expensive not to crash **f** at all, but to crash **c** instead. We now have an 18-day project, see Figure 6-4. All activities are critical, and the total cost of the project is $400 + 30 (**a**) + 60 (**c**) + 60 (**g**) = $550.

We can even shorten the project to 17 days by crashing both **f** and **g** one more day, and to 16 days by crashing them still another day. Activities **a**, **c**, **f**, and **g** have been crashed to their limits, see Figure 6-5. No further crashing will help so **b**, **d**, and **e** remain at their normal times and costs. The total project cost of the 16-day project is now $50 (**b**) + 30 (**d**) + 70 (**e**) + 90 (**a**) + 160 (**c**) + 120 (**f**) + 230 (**g**) = $750. Because we crashed the project by taking the least cost options first, no matter how many days the project was crashed, it was shortened at the least cost. Figure 6-6 shows cost as a function of project duration.

One final note on CPM. The same method is used when the task durations are probabilistic, that is, using three time estimates. In this case, optimistic, most likely, and pessimistic activity duration estimates are made for the "normal" resource loading and new optimistic, most likely, and pessimistic duration estimates must be made for crash resource loading. The PM should remember that the variance of both the normal and crash activity times largely depends on the technology used to accomplish the activity in question. Thus the variance of the normal activity time may be quite different from the variance of the crash time. The project budget can be determined in exactly the same way. The solution to project duration and resource cost levels can be made by using the standard analytical method used in the last chapter, or by simulation, also described in Chapter 5.

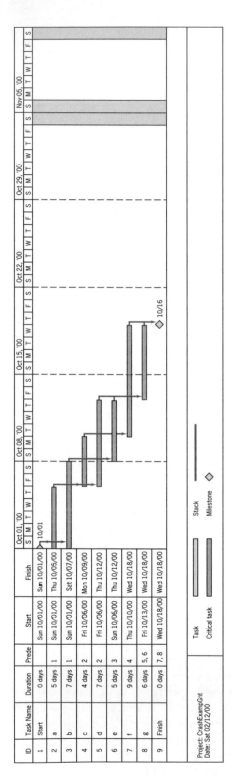

ID	Task Name	Duration	Prede	Start	Finish
1	Start	0 days		Sun 10/01/00	Sun 10/01/00
2	a	5 days	1	Sun 10/01/00	Thu 10/05/00
3	b	7 days	1	Sun 10/01/00	Sat 10/07/00
4	c	4 days	2	Fri 10/06/00	Mon 10/09/00
5	d	7 days	2	Fri 10/06/00	Thu 10/12/00
6	e	5 days	3	Sun 10/06/00	Thu 10/12/00
7	f	9 days	4	Thu 10/10/00	Wed 10/18/00
8	g	6 days	5, 6	Fri 10/13/00	Wed 10/18/00
9	Finish	0 days	7, 8	Wed 10/18/00	Wed 10/18/00

Project: CrashExampGnt
Date: Sat 02/12/00

Task   Stack

Critical task   Milestone

Figure 6-4   Gantt chart for 18-day solution to crash problem (MSP).

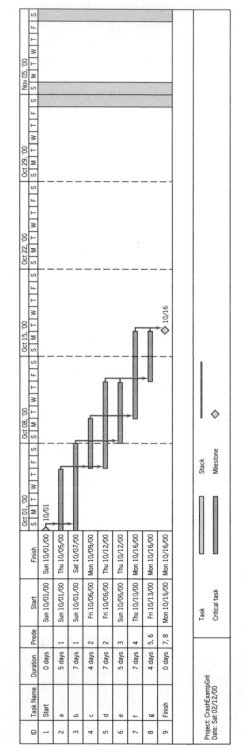

ID	Task Name	Duration	Prede	Start	Finish
1	Start	0 days		Sun 10/01/00	Sun 10/01/00
2	a	5 days	1	Sun 10/01/00	Thu 10/05/00
3	b	7 days	1	Sun 10/01/00	Sat 10/07/00
4	c	4 days	2	Fri 10/06/00	Mon 10/09/00
5	d	7 days	2	Fri 10/06/00	Thu 10/12/00
6	e	5 days	3	Sun 10/06/00	Thu 10/12/00
7	f	7 days	4	Thu 10/10/00	Mon 10/16/00
8	g	4 days	5, 6	Fri 10/13/00	Mon 10/16/00
9	Finish	0 days	7, 8	Mon 10/15/00	Mon 10/16/00

Project: CrashExampGnt
Date: Sat 02/12/00

Task   Stack

Critical task   Milestone

Figure 6-5   Gantt chart for 16-day solution to crash problem (MSP).

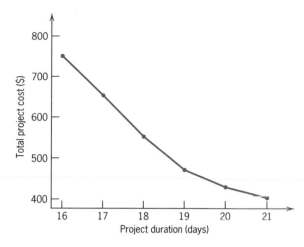

Figure 6-6   Project cost vs. project duration for sample crash problem.

Using Excel® to Crash a Project

As you read the preceding material, you might have wondered whether spreadsheets or other computerized approaches could be used to facilitate the task of crashing a project. While it is typical in real-world projects to find that only a few of the many paths are involved in crashing, occasionally many are involved. In such cases, the manual approach discussed earlier can become quite tedious. In this section, we demonstrate how use of Excel® spreadsheets can greatly facilitate the task of choosing the activities to crash so that a project is completed by a specified deadline at minimum cost.

To illustrate this, the data from Table 6-1 were entered into the spreadsheet shown in Table 6-2. Figure 6-7 shows the network diagram for this project based on the activity-on-the-arrow (arc) convention or AOA. As you will see, the AOA convention is particularly well suited for this type of analysis since we need to keep track of both the duration of each activity and the time of occurrence of each event. In this example we do make one change to the data in Table 6-1. Namely, we assume that activity **c** may be crashed one day at a time. While the spreadsheet approach discussed here can handle the situation where activities must be crashed completely or not at all, we make this change to simplify our ensuing discussion.

At the top of the spreadsheet the specified deadline is entered in cell B1 and the total cost of completing the project including both normal cost and crash cost is calculated in cell B2. Below this, columns A to G contain the information given in Table 6-1. Note that in column G the crash cost per day is calculated by dividing the incremental cost of crashing the activity as much as possible by the maximum number of days the activity can be shortened.

In column H the maximum amount each activity can be crashed is calculated by subtracting the crash duration from the normal duration. Column I corresponds to our decision, namely, how much to crash each activity. Then based on the values entered in column I, the cost of crashing each activity is calculated in column J. Finally, in column K the actual time to complete the activity is calculated by subtracting the amount the activity is crashed (column I) from the activity's normal duration (column C).

In cells A15:B21 another table was created to keep track of the event times of each node in the network diagram shown in Figure 6-7. Node 1 is excluded because we assume that this node occurs at time zero. As you will see, we need to keep track of the time each event occurs to ensure that the precedence relationships in the network dia-

Table 6.2   Sample "Crash" Problem in Table 6-1 Transferred to an Excel® Spreadsheet

	A	B	C	D	E	F	G	H	I	J	K
1	Deadline:	21									
2	Total Cost:	$400									
3											
4			Normal	Crash	Normal	Crash	Cost per	Maximum	Amount	Crashing	Actual
5	Activity	Preced.	Duration	Duration	Cost	Cost	Day	Crash Amt.	to Crash	Cost	Time
6	a	—	6	5	$60	$90	$30.00	1		$0.00	6
7	b	—	7	4	$50	$150	$33.33	3		$0.00	7
8	c	a	6	4	$100	$160	$30.00	2		$0.00	6
9	d	a	7	7	$30	$30	N.A.	0		N.A.	7
10	e	b	5	4	$70	$85	$15.00	1		$0.00	5
11	f	c	9	7	$40	$120	$40.00	2		$0.00	9
12	g	d, e	7	4	$50	$230	$60.00	3		$0.00	7
13	Total				$400					$0.00	
14											
15		Event									
16	Node	Time									
17	2										
18	3										
19	4										
20	5										
21	6										
22											
23	*Key Formulas:*										
24	Cell B2	=E13+J13									
25	Cell G6	=(F6-E6)/(C6-D6) {copy to cells G7:G12}									
26	Cell H6	=C6-D6 {copy to cells H7:H12}									
27	Cell J6	=I6*G6 {copy to cells J7:J12}									
28	Cell K6	=C6-I6 {copy to cells K7:K12}									

gram are not violated. For example, we need to make sure that node 4 does not occur until after node 2 occurs, plus the time it takes to complete activity **c**.

We now demonstrate how Excel's® Solver can be used to help determine which activities to crash so that the entire project is completed within 20 days at the minimum costs. To begin, select **Tools** from the menu bar and then **Solver** from the next menu that appears. The Solver Parameters dialog box is now displayed (see Figure 6-8). The

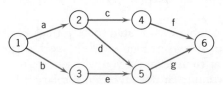

Figure 6-7   AOA network of sample "crash" problem.

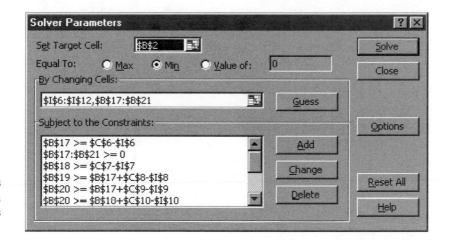

Figure 6-8 Excel's Solver® loaded with data and constraints from crash problem.

Target Cell field refers to the cell in the spreadsheet that we would like to either minimize or maximize. In our case, we would like to minimize the total cost of completing the project, which is calculated in cell B2. To specify this, we enter B2 in the **Target Cell** field and then select the **Min** radio button.

Next we tell Excel® what cells it can change in order to find the solution with the minimum total project completion cost. In the spreadsheet shown in Table 6-2, the values or cells that can be changed are the amount of time each activity is crashed (cells I6:I12) and the time when each event occurs (cells B17:B21). Thus as is shown in Figure 6-8, these ranges were entered in the **By Changing Cells** field.

The final type of information we need to enter is the limitations or constraints associated with this situation. Perhaps the most obvious constraint is that we want to complete the project within 20 days (cell B1). Since node 6 (cell B21) corresponds to the event of the project being completed, we can specify this constraint as follows:

$$B21 \le B1$$

Another important set of constraints is needed to make sure we don't crash an activity more than the maximum number of days that it can be crashed. Constraints to ensure this could be entered as follows:

$$I6 \le H6 \text{ (activity } \mathbf{a})$$
$$I7 \le H7 \text{ (activity } \mathbf{b})$$
$$I8 \le H8 \text{ (activity } \mathbf{c})$$
$$I9 \le H9 \text{ (activity } \mathbf{d})$$
$$I10 \le H10 \text{ (activity } \mathbf{e})$$
$$I11 \le H11 \text{ (activity } \mathbf{f})$$
$$I12 \le H12 \text{ (activity } \mathbf{g})$$

Alternatively, by employing a shorthand approach that capitalizes on a spreadsheet's ability to deal with ranges, these seven constraints could be entered as a single constraint as

$$I6:I12 \le H6:H12$$

Another set of constraints is needed to make sure that the precedence relationships specified in the network diagram are not violated. We do this by keeping track of the event times of the nodes. For example, the event time of node 2 cannot occur until after activity **a** has been completed (assuming that the project begins at time zero). The time to complete activity **a** is its normal time less the amount of time it is crashed. Since cell B17 corresponds to the event time for node 2, mathematically we could enter this constraint as follows:

$$B17 \geq C6 - I6$$

This constraint says that the event corresponding to node 2 cannot occur until after activity **a** has been completed.

Constraints for the other nodes could be created in a similar fashion. For example, the constraints for nodes 3 and 4 would be

$$B18 \geq C7 - I7$$
$$B19 \geq B17 + C8 - I8$$

The constraint for node 4 says in effect that the event corresponding to node 4 cannot occur until after the event corresponding to node 2 (cell B17) occurs plus the time it takes to complete activity **c**.

Moving on to node 5, note that this node has two arrows pointing to it. A node with more than one arrow pointing to it will need a separate constraint for each arrow. Thus we need the following two constraints for node 5.

$$B20 \geq B17 + C9 - I9$$
$$B20 \geq B18 + C10 - I10$$

This first constraint says that node 5 (cell B20) cannot occur until after node 2 has occurred (cell B17) plus the amount of time it takes to complete activity **d**. The second constraint says that node 5 cannot occur until after node 3 (cell B18) has occurred plus the amount of time it takes to complete activity **e**.

Node 6 is handled in a similar way to node 5 as follows:

$$B21 \geq B19 + C11 - I11$$
$$B21 \geq B20 + C12 - I12$$

Finally, since it does not make sense to crash an activity a negative amount of time, nor does it make sense for a node to occur at a time less than time zero, we add constraints to ensure these outcomes are not generated. Using Excel's® shorthand approach, these constraints can be specified as follows:

$$I6:I12 \geq 0$$
$$B17:B21 \geq 0$$

In this example we assume that the activities can be crashed a fraction of a day. If we preferred to assume that the activities had to be crashed either a whole day or nor at all, we could easily add additional constraints to the model to reflect this preference.

To enter these constraints, select the **Add** button in the **Subject to the Constraints** section of the Solver Parameters dialog box. The entire set of constraints needed is as follows:

$$B21 \leq B1$$
$$I6:I12 \leq H6:H12$$
$$B17 \geq C6 - I6$$
$$B18 \geq C7 - I7$$
$$B19 \geq B17 + C8 - I8$$

$$B20 \geq B17 + C9 - I9$$
$$B20 \geq B18 + C10 - I10$$
$$B21 \geq B19 + C11 - I11$$
$$B21 \geq B20 + C12 - I12$$
$$I6:I12 \geq 0$$
$$B17:B21 \geq 0$$

After entering these constraints, the Solver Parameters dialog box appears as shown in Figure 6-8. Before finding the least costly way to crash the project down to 20 days, select the **Options . . .** button and click on the **Assume Linear Model** check box and then click **OK**. Now to find the least cost solution, select the **Solve** button in the Solver Parameters dialog box. As is shown in Table 6-3, Excel® identified the same solution

Table 6-3   Excel® Spreadsheet for Crash Problem, 20-Day Solution and Cost

	A	B	C	D	E	F	G	H	I	J	K
1	Deadline:	20									
2	Total Cost:	$430									
3											
4			Normal	Crash	Normal	Crash	Cost per	Maximum	Amount	Crashing	Actual
5	Activity	Preced.	Duration	Duration	Cost	Cost	Day	Crash Amt.	to Crash	Cost	Time
6	a	—	6	5	$60	$90	$30.00	1	1	$30.00	5
7	b	—	7	4	$50	$150	$33.33	3	0	$0.00	7
8	c	a	6	4	$100	$160	$30.00	2	0	$0.00	6
9	d	a	7	7	$30	$30	N.A.	0	0	N.A.	7
10	e	b	5	4	$70	$85	$15.00	1	0	$0.00	5
11	f	c	9	7	$40	$120	$40.00	2	0	$0.00	9
12	g	d, e	7	4	$50	$230	$60.00	3	0	$0.00	7
13	Total				$400					$30.00	
14											
15		Event									
16	Node	Time									
17	2	5									
18	3	8									
19	4	11									
20	5	13									
21	6	20									
22											
23	Key Formulas:										
24	Cell B2	=E13+J13									
25	Cell G6	=(F6-E6)/(C6-D6) {copy to cells G7:G12}									
26	Cell H6	=C6-D6 {copy to cells H7:H12}									
27	Cell J6	=I6*G6 {copy to cells J7:J12}									
28	Cell K6	=C6-I6 {copy to cells K7:K12}									

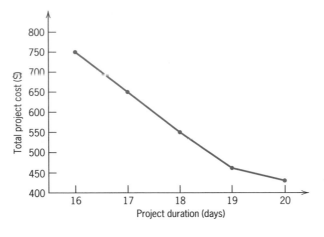

Figure 6-9   Cost/duration graph for sample crashing project (Excel®).

that we obtained earlier using the manual approach. Specifically, the solution suggests crashing activity **a** by one day (cell I6). This results in completing the project by day 20 (cell B21) at a total project cost of $430 (cell B2).

Having set up the spreadsheet, we can now quickly and easily evaluate the cost of incrementally increasing the amount the project is crashed. Doing this simply requires changing the deadline entered in cell B1 and then clicking on the **Solve** button. A summary of this analysis is provided in Figure 6-9.

Fast-Tracking a Project

In addition to crashing a project in order to expedite it, a project may also be *fast-tracked*. Used primarily in the construction industry, the term refers to an expediting technique in which the design and planning phases of a project are not actually completed before the building phase is started. Usually design and plan are finished before the building is started, so letting them overlap reduces project duration—if the fact that design and planning are incomplete does not result in a significant amount of rework and change orders during the building phase.

For many projects in construction, maintenance, and similar areas, a large proportion of the work is routine. In these cases, fast-tracking rarely causes serious problems. The number of change orders in fast-tracked construction projects is not significantly different from that for similar projects that were not fast-tracked [6].

> When task durations are estimated, an assumption is made that task resources are set at "normal" levels. This is the "standard practice" assumption. Traditionally, CPM project duration estimates also include a "crash" estimate together with estimates of the crash time and the resources required to shorten the duration of project activities. By selectively choosing which activities to crash by how much, we can determine the minimum cost for all possible project completion times. Both manual and spreadsheet methods are illustrated.

6.2   RESOURCE LOADING

From the first day on the job, the PM is concerned with *resource loading*. Resource loading refers to the amounts of specific resources that are scheduled for use on specific activities or projects at specific times. It usually takes the form of a list or table. Figure 6-10 is an MSP generated action plan and Gantt chart of a project aimed at producing a

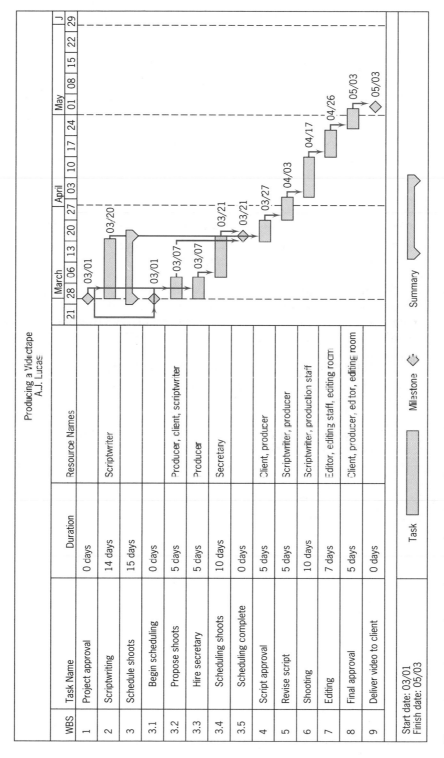

Figure 6-10   Action plan and Gantt chart for production of a videotape (MSP).

videotape. Task names, WBS numbers, durations, finish dates, and the resource requirements for each step in the process are shown. (Precedences are not listed in the action plan, but they are illustrated on the Gantt chart.)

After the project plan was developed, the PM confirmed the availability of each required resource, and obtained schedules for each. MSP allows the PM to create an individual availability calendar for each resource on the project. From these calendars, resource schedules are automatically generated, and Table 6-4 shows the schedules for several of the required resources. (Any resource not shown in Table 6-4 works a five-day week, 8:00 AM to 5:00 PM with an hour off for lunch, usually 12–1 PM, without exceptions during the period of the project.) Among other things, the PM noted the following:

- The scriptwriter is available to work six days per week, and nine hours per day.
- The editing room has limited availability, 9:30 AM to 3:00 PM each day.
- The client, whose input is required for several activities, will be on vacation between March 13 and March 26.

When the calendars for each resource were entered into MSP's database for the project, the project schedule was recalculated. The revised plan is shown in Figure 6-11. Note that the project completion date has been extended from May 3 to May 17. The client's vacation and the availability of the editing room are major contributors to the extension.

From the project plan, the new schedule, and the list of resources required, a resource-loading table was derived by MSP, see Table 6-5. As we noted earlier, a project's resource loading is a list of the amounts of various specific resources that are scheduled for use on specific activities at specific times during the life of the project. A brief study of the data in Table 6-5 reveals that in the first few days of the project [Wednesday through Saturday (March 1–4)] the scriptwriter is slightly overallocated. During the four days of the project this person is scheduled to work 72 hours. That seems a bit much allowing only six hours per day for eating, sleeping, and all of life's other activities. The scriptwriter's first full week is also overallocated at 58 hours. The producer's first three days are also overallocated at 48 hours. Something must be done, and it will be discussed in the next section.

An examination of this table reveals an interesting anomaly in MSP and most other project management software. Unless specified otherwise, MSP assumes that any resource assigned to an activity will work on that activity 100 percent of the time available on the resource calendar. For example, Figure 6-10, WBS 3.2, "Propose shoots" lists the client as a resource (in addition to the producer and scriptwriter). The activity is scheduled to take five days. The PM is aware that in all likelihood the client will only be needed to attend one or two meetings (an hour or two each) to approve or amend the shoots proposed by the producer and scriptwriter. Nonetheless, the resource-loading table (Table 6-5) indicates that the client will spend 40 hours (5 days at 8 hours/day) on the activity.

Were this a large project with a large number and variety of resources it might be necessary to correct this "error." MSP and other software packages have several ways to do this. The PM could allocate a specific percentage of a resource's time for work on the project, or could restrict the availability of the resource on the calendar, for example. In this case, however, because the client has no cost per hour, and because everyone involved in the project, including the client, understands the nature of the client's work, the matter can be ignored.

Quite apart from problems in scheduling the activities, there are other resource-loading issues that may face the PM. For instance, there are cost and management issues

Table 6-4   Resource Availability Calendars for Selected Resources for Videotape Production (MSP)

Project: *Producing a Videotape*	*Resource Availability Calendars*		
Name	*Standard Rate*	*Overtime Rate*	*Work*

Scriptwriter

	$25.00/hr (modified Standard)	$40.00/hr	192 hrs
RESOURCE CALENDAR			
Day	Hours		
Monday	8:00 AM - 12:00 PM, 1:00 PM - 6:00 PM		
Tuesday	8:00 AM - 12:00 PM, 1:00 PM - 6:00 PM		
Wednesday	8:00 AM - 12:00 PM, 1:00 PM - 6:00 PM		
Thursday	8:00 AM - 12:00 PM, 1:00 PM - 6:00 PM		
Friday	8:00 AM - 12:00 PM, 1:00 PM - 6:00 PM		
Saturday	8:00 AM - 12:00 PM, 1:00 PM - 6:00 PM		
Sunday	Nonworking		
Exceptions:	None		

Producer

	$45.00/hr (unmodified Standard)	$60.00/hr	200 hrs
RESOURCE CALENDAR			
Day	Hours		
Monday	8:00 AM - 12:00 PM, 1:00 PM - 5:00 PM		
Tuesday	8:00 AM - 12:00 PM, 1:00 PM - 5:00 PM		
Wednesday	8:00 AM - 12:00 PM, 1:00 PM - 5:00 PM		
Thursday	8:00 AM - 12:00 PM, 1:00 PM - 5:00 PM		
Friday	8:00 AM - 12:00 PM, 1:00 PM - 5:00 PM		
Saturday	Nonworking		
Sunday	Nonworking		
Exceptions:	None		

Client

	$0.00/hr (modified Standard)	$0.00/hr	120 hrs
RESOURCE CALENDAR			
Day	Hours		
Monday	8:00 AM - 12:00 PM, 1:00 PM - 5:00 PM		
Tuesday	8:00 AM - 12:00 PM, 1:00 PM - 5:00 PM		
Wednesday	8:00 AM - 12:00 PM, 1:00 PM - 5:00 PM		
Thursday	8:00 AM - 12:00 PM, 1:00 PM - 5:00 PM		
Friday	8:00 AM - 12:00 PM, 1:00 PM - 5:00 PM		
Saturday	Nonworking		
Sunday	Nonworking		
Exceptions:			
Date	Hours		
03/13 - 03/26	Nonworking		

Editing room

	$0.00/hr (modified Standard)	$0.00/hr	96 hrs
RESOURCE CALENDAR			
Day	Hours		
Monday	9:30 AM - 3:00 PM		
Tuesday	9:30 AM - 3:00 PM		
Wednesday	9:30 AM - 3:00 PM		
Thursday	9:30 AM - 3:00 PM		
Friday	9:30 AM - 3:00 PM		
Saturday	Nonworking		
Sunday	Nonworking		
Exceptions:	None		

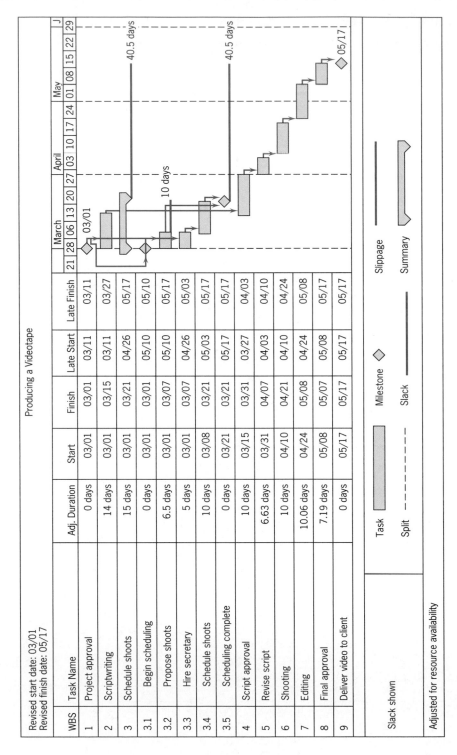

Figure 6-11 Gantt chart for videotape project, adjusted for client availability (MSP).

Table 6-5   Resource Loading Chart for Videotape Production (MSP)

**Producing a Videotape
Resource Loading**

Resource Name	Standard Rate	Overtime Rate	Work	March				April					May		
				02/28	03/06	03/13	03/20	03/27	04/03	04/10	04/17	04/24	05/01	05/08	05/15
Scriptwriter	$25.00/hr	$40.00/hr	192 hrs	72h	58h	22h		10h	30h						
Scriptwriting			112 hrs	36h	54h	22h									
Propose shoots			40 hrs	36h	4h										
Revise script			40 hrs					10h	30h						
Producer	$45.00/hr	$60.00/hr	200 hrs	48h	32h	20h		0h	40h					37.5h	2.5h
Propose shoots			40 hrs	24h	16h										
Hire secretary			40 hrs	24h	16h										
Script approval			40 hrs			20h	20h								
Revise script			40 hrs					0h	40h						
Final approval			40 hrs											37.5h	2.5h
Client	$0.00/hr	$0.00/hr	120 hrs	24h	16h			40h						37.5h	2.5h
Propose shoots			40 hrs	24h	16h										
Script approval			40 hrs					40h							
Final approval			40 hrs											37.5h	2.5h
Secretary	$10.00/hr	$20.00/hr	80 hrs	24h		40h	16h								
Schedule shoots			80 hrs	24h		40h	16h								
Editor	$25.00/hr	$45.00/hr	176 hrs							40h	40h	40h	16h	37.5h	2.5h
Shooting			80 hrs							40h	40h				
Editing			56 hrs									40h	16h		
Final approval			40 hrs											37.5h	2.5h
Production staff	$20.00/hr	$35.00/hr	80 hrs							40h	40h				
Shooting			80 hrs							40h	40h				
Editing staff	$20.00/hr	$35.00/hr	56 hrs									40h	16h		
Editing			56 hrs									40h	16h		
Editing room	$0.00/hr	$0.00/hr	96 hrs									27.5h	27.5h	27.5h	13.5h
Editing			56 hrs									27.5h	27.5h	1h	
Final approval			40 hrs											26.5h	13.5h

Overallocated resources bolded

that must be considered. It is easy to overutilize resources, particularly human resources; note the hours required of the scriptwriter and producer during the first days of the project. For hourly workers, overtime work is usually quite expensive. In the case of the scriptwriter, overtime hours are not sufficient, and another writer may be needed for the first one or two weeks. On the other hand, it is common to find middle managers consistently working 45–60 hours per week—if they have a desire for upward mobility. In the software industry or in architecture, to pick two typical examples, individuals often work 60–80 hours per week or more in order to complete specific projects on time. Because we usually overload our best people, they are the ones most apt to quit and go elsewhere—and they rarely tell us why in their exit interviews. For most senior executives, the workloads are often very heavy—consistently 65–70 or more hours per week. These are the people who are overstressed at the very times they must make momentous decisions.

Such resource-loading documents as Figure 6-5 are among management's most frequent requests of the PM, precisely so they can monitor such situations. As we will see in the section on resource leveling, managers sometimes make incorrect assumptions about the capacity of work groups, and the PM must take on an educational role.

The Charismatic VP

The Vice-President and Manager of a division of a large chemical company became aware that a number of projects he had assigned to his subordinates were not being completed on time. Some were finished late, and others were simply unfinished. The VP was tireless, spending 60–80 hours per week at work. He was very well liked, and his people tried hard to please him. If he asked a subordinate if a task could be handled, invariably the answer was "Yes."

The VP began to suspect that he was overcommitting his subordinates. He suggested this to his people, but most of them insisted that they could handle the work. Not entirely convinced, the VP installed a project-oriented management system and initiated resource-loading reports for all personnel doing project work. The reports showed clearly that the division had an urgent need for additional staff engineers.

As is typical of such cases, the individuals most overworked were the most experienced and most skilled people. Those engineers with spare time were the least skilled and, for the most part, recent hires. The untrained remained untrained. The Vice-President, however, altered work assignments and ordered that additional engineers be hired. Overscheduling was limited to 125 percent (50 hours per week), and at that level for a limited time only. A policy of partnering new engineers with experienced cohorts was instituted. Within six months, division projects were progressing reasonably on time.

> Resource loading is usually displayed as a list of the amounts of specific resources assigned for use on specific project activities at specific times, or as a graph showing the level of a resource's capacity required against the project calendar. To be useful for scheduling, the resource must have a calendar showing the resource's availability. The calendar should include hours—and days—worked each week, any holidays on which the resource will not be available, and any other information affecting the availability of the resource. Resource cost per unit of usage should be included on the calendar, plus any additional cost for overtime or overuse. Overscheduling a resource may cause serious problems for the PM.

6.3 RESOURCE LEVELING

Look once again at Figure 6-11. Tasks 2, 3.2, and 3.3 are all scheduled to start on March 1. The scriptwriter is required for the first two of the three items and the producer for the last two. The scriptwriter's calendar (Table 6-4) indicates that the scriptwriter can work a 54-hour week—six days per week at nine hours per day. The producer is available for a standard 40-hour week. The resource-loading table (Table 6-5) shows the above-mentioned tasks assigned to the scriptwriter and producer. Apparently both are expected to do two different jobs at the same time.

The scriptwriter's conflict must be reduced. Figures 6-12 and 6-13 illustrate the problem clearly. Both illustrations are MSP outputs. Figure 6-12 lists all tasks for which the scriptwriter is scheduled. Figure 6-13 indicates that the scriptwriter is overallocated by a factor of two during the period from March 1 to March 4.* (Recall that the project begins on March 1, not February 28, and so the scriptwriter works only four days—36 hours—during the first week of March.)

Figure 6-12 also shows considerable slack in WBS 3.2. If we ask MSP to level resources, the software will move activities so that resources do not exceed their capacities—and will do so by using available slack first, *where possible*, rather than extending the project duration. (Clearly, the PM could do the same thing manually, but the job becomes complex and time-consuming on all but small projects.) Figures 6-14 and 6-15 show the effect of resource leveling on the scriptwriter's workload. In this case the project duration was not affected because there was sufficient slack in WBS 3.2, and the leveling operation used it.

Project start date: 03/01 Project finish date: 05/17					Resource Overallocated: Scriptwriter									
					March					April				May
WBS	Task Name	Duration	Sch. Start	Sch. Finish	28	06	13	20	27	03	10	17	24	01	08	15
2	Scriptwriting	14 days	03/01	03/15	Scriptwriter									
3.2	Propose shoots	6.5 days	03/01	03/07	Producer, client, scriptwriter									
5	Revise script	6.63 days	03/31	04/07	Scriptwriter, producer									

Prior to resource leveling		
Preleveled task	Preleveled milestone	◇
Preleveled split	Milestone	◆
Task	Delay	
Split	Slack	
Progress	Summary	

Figure 6-12   Resource overallocation report for scriptwriter showing all activities (MSP).

---

*If MSP's Gantt chart view is set to show weekly intervals, it indicates resource usage for an entire week even if the resource is actually used for only a day during that week. To see resource usage with more precision, set the MSP calendar to show daily or hourly intervals.

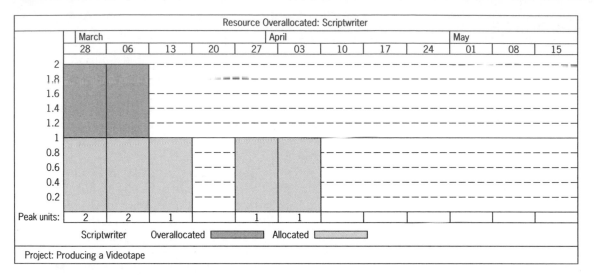

Figure 6-13   Graphic resource overallocation report for scriptwriter (MSP).

To understand Figure 6-14 correctly requires an understanding of MSP. The figure appears to report that the scriptwriter is still working overtime on Tasks 2 and 3.2. This would also mean that there was an error in Figure 6-15 that shows no such thing. The scriptwriter's efforts are, in fact, solely devoted to scriptwriting (Task 2), but the producer and the client are working on Task 3.2, so the task is shown as being underway. MSP has split Task 3.2, and the scriptwriter begins work on the task on Wednesday, March 15 after work on Task 2 has been completed. The second part of Task 3.2 does not begin until all work on Task 2 is complete. It is easy to verify that this has happened. Figure 6-16 shows the resource allocation, after leveling the scriptwriter's workload, using a daily calendar. The scriptwriter is not assigned more than nine hours per day. On March 15 work transfers from Task 2 to Task 3.2.

The problem of the still overallocated producer is another matter. This is the same problem we discussed above concerning the client's need to attend some meetings. The fact that the producer is overscheduled is not really a problem. Neither of the conflicting tasks (WBS task 3.2 and 3.3) requires eight hours per day of work by the producer. The duration of five days for Task 3.2 (Propose shoots), for example, indicates that the producer will be spending some time during a five-day period on the job of proposing locations and settings for videotaping. Similarly, Task 3.3 (Hire secretary) will require the producer to interview some candidates for the secretarial position during the same five-day period, but this will not be a full-time job either. The five-day durations are an indication of when the tasks are expected to be complete. *Task duration is not necessarily dictated by the amount of labor required to complete the task, but by the calendar time required to complete it.* Sometimes, of course, the amount of labor may be the determinant of calendar time, but often it is not.

At this point a short digression is appropriate. As a student of project management reading this book, you probably know little of the reality of the projects used here as examples of this or that project management problem. As a PM working on a real-world project, you know a great deal more about the reality of your project than could possibly be explained in this book on the subject. The PM of the videotape project knows that there will be no problem raised by the apparent conflict in the allocation of the producer's time. The PM could have used one of the methods we noted in the discussion of

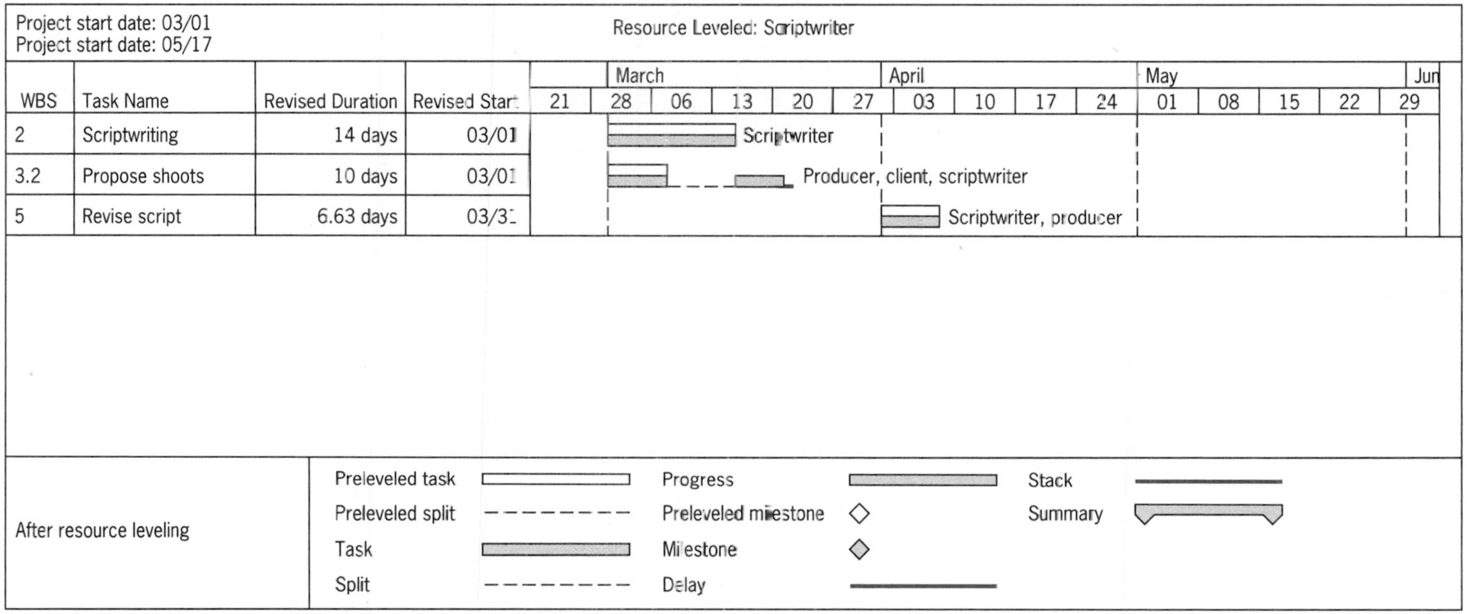

Project start date: 03/01
Project start date: 05/17
Resource Leveled: Scriptwriter
WBS
Task Name
Revised Duration
Revised Start
March
April
May
Jun
21
28
06
13
20
27
03
10
17
24
01
08
15
22
29
2
Scriptwriting
14 days
03/01
Scriptwriter
3.2
Propose shoots
10 days
03/01
Producer, client, scriptwriter
5
Revise script
6.63 days
Scriptwriter, producer
After resource leveling
Preleveled task
Preleveled split
Task
Split
Progress
Preleveled milestone
Milestone
Delay
Stack
Summary

Figure 6-14 Resource leveled report for scriptwriter showing all activities (MSP).

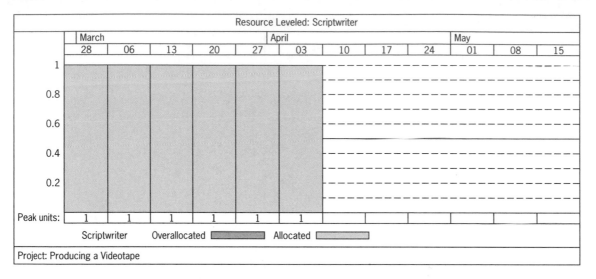

Figure 6-15   Graphic resource leveled report for scriptwriter (MSP).

resource loading to handle the matter, but elected not to take the time and effort. This, then, is another of the trade-offs the PM must make. Not every facet of a project requires equal managerial care. The PM must decide where to expend his or her managerial efforts—and then take responsibility for the decision.

A resource allocation decision may be intended to avoid future problems rather than to cure a present problem. While the scriptwriter is not overallocated, the PM decided to add a second scriptwriter to WBS 2. The PM also leveled the producer's apparent overallocation just to add some slack to the producer's schedule. Both of these additions were made to insure that the project was not made late by a glitch in the producer's work or in the scriptwriting activity, which is on the project's critical path. (See Section 6.5 for additional information about the advisability of having some excess capacity in projects.) The result of all these moves is seen in Figure 6-17. The project can be finished five days earlier than indicated in Figure 6-11.

When resources are added to a project, the PM may be asked to explain just how the project budget came to be underestimated. To answer such a question, the PM would be well advised to contact the administration of any large city that has recently built a sports stadium.

A more or less steady state demand for human resources is highly desirable—if it is not seriously inconsistent with the technological demands of the project. The cost of adding, laying-off, or permanently releasing human beings is very high for both hourly and salaried personnel. If the parent organization is quite large and is operating many projects that have reasonably high commonality in their demand for certain skills, it is often possible to set up "pools" for such skills as clerical, machine operation, and similar types of workers. When pools are used to supply resources for projects, careful records must be kept to ensure fast determination of skill availability and that the proper charges are made to all projects.

Pools of like resources from which labor can be added temporarily to projects tend to cut costs for the firm as a whole. Pools also cut the cost of managing the project. The PM's job is made easier, and the cash flows of the project are less volatile. The PM will spend far less time trying to find and recruit personnel. Such pools, however, are useful only if the labor is not subdivided into highly specialized subtasks. Secretarial skills are

Producing a Videotape
Resource Work Hours
Scriptwriter Leveled

Resource Name	Work	W	T	F	S	S	Mar 06, '00 M	T	W	T	F	S	S	Mar 13, '00 M	T	W	T	F	S
Scriptwriter	192 hrs	9h	9h	9h	9h	9h	9h	9h	9h	9h	9h	9h	9h	9h	9h	9h	9h	9h	9h
Scriptwriting	112 hrs	9h	9h	9h	9h	9h	9h	9h	9h	9h	9h	9h	9h	9h	9h	4h			
Propose shoots	40 hrs	0h	0h	0h	0h	0h	0h	0h	0h	0h	0h			0h	0h	5h			
Revise script	40 hrs																		
Producer	200 hrs	16h	16h	16h			16h	16h	3h					16h	16h	4h		8h	8h
Propose shoots	40 hrs	8h	8h	8h			8h	8h											
Hire secretary	40 hrs	3h	3h	3h			8h	8h	3h										
Script approval	40 hrs													8h	8h	4h			
Revise script	40 hrs																	8h	8h
Final approval	40 hrs																		
Client	120 hrs	8h	8h	8h			8h	8h						8h	8h				
Propose shoots	40 hrs	8h	8h	8h			8h	8h											
Script approval	40 hrs													8h	8h				
Final approval	40 hrs																		
Secretary	80 hrs						8h	8h	8h	8h	8h			8h	8h	8h	8h	8h	8h
Schedule shoot	80 hrs						8h	8h	8h	8h	8h			8h	8h	8h	8h	8h	8h
Editor	176 hrs																		
Shooting	80 hrs																		
Editing	56 hrs																		
Final approval	40 hrs																		
Production staff	80 hrs																		
Shooting	80 hrs																		
Editing staff	56 hrs																		
Editing	56 hrs																		
Editing room	96 hrs																		
Editing	56 hrs																		
Final approval	40 hrs																		

Figure 6-16 Daily resource loading chart for videotape project, scriptwriter leveled (MSP).

Producing a Videotape
A.J. Lucas

WBS	Task Name	Resource Names	Duration	Start	Finish
1	Project approval		0 days	03/01	03/01
2	Scriptwriting	Scriptwriter [2]	7 days	03/01	03/08
3	Schedule shoots		15 days	03/01	03/21
3.1	Begin scheduling		0 days	03/01	03/01
3.2	Propose shoots	Producer, client, scripwriter	15 days	03/01	03/20
3.3	Hire secretary	Producer	5 days	03/01	03/07
3.4	Schedule shoots	Secretary	10 days	03/08	03/21
3.5	Scheduling complete		0 days	03/21	03/21
4	Script approval	Client, producer	7.25 days	03/08	03/29
5	Revise script	Scriptwriter, producer	6.5 days	03/29	04/05
6	Shooting	Editor, production staff	10 days	04/05	04/19
7	Editing	Editor, editing staff, editing room	10.06 days	04/19	05/03
8	Final approval	Client, producer, editor, editing room	7.19 days	05/03	05/12
9	Deliver video to client		0 days	05/12	05/12

Start date: 03/01
Finish date: 05/12

Additional scriptwriter added to activity 2

Task		Milestone ◇	Summary ◇

Figure 6-17 Final videotape project Gantt chart schedule, with two scriptwriters and producer leveled (MSP).

less specialized than, say, the skills required to design, generate, or test computer software. The conclusion is that secretarial pools are feasible, but that software design, generation, and testing should be done by "teams" in which the required specialists are available.

Resource Loading/Leveling and Uncertainty

Figure 6-18 is a resource-loading chart for a software engineering group in a large firm. The chart depicts the total number of hours required of a resource group (all members from one department assigned to the firm's projects) displayed against the group's capacity. (MSP resource-loading information was exported to an Excel® spreadsheet and displayed graphically. The process of producing such displays is quick and not difficult.) There are 21 members of the group. They are scheduled for 40 hours per five-day week by the firm. Figure 6-18 covers a 34-week period. The graph shows estimated workhours (28,282) committed by this team for projects that are currently on the company's books. The delivery-date commitments are such that group workloads exceed the group's capacity through much of March and April, for a brief period in the middle of May, and again in the latter part of June. (The total of these overloads is 1,747 hours, or a bit more than 83 hours per person.)

A rough estimate of group capacity is

$$21 \text{ (people)} \times 40 \text{ (hours per week)} \times 34 \text{ (weeks)} = 28,560 \text{ labor-hours.}$$

But a few corrections are in order. There are three national holidays in the period, Memorial Day, the Fourth of July, and Labor Day. The time lost for the holidays is:

$$21 \times 3 \text{ (days)} \times 8 \text{ (hours)} = 504 \text{ labor-hours,}$$

which lowers capacity to 28,056 labor-hours. Assume further that 11 people take a two-week vacation during the 34-week period, a conservative assumption given the fact that the period includes May through September. The time for 11 vacations is an additional capacity loss of

$$11 \times 2 \text{ (weeks)} \times 40 = 880 \text{ labor-hours}$$

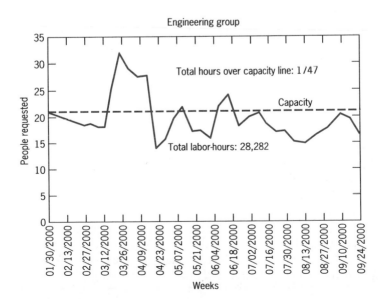

Figure 6-18
Thirty-four-week resource loading chart for a software engineering group (MSP and Excel®).

There are now 28,056 − 880 = 27,176 labor-hours available and even if the group's work were evenly distributed across the 34-week period, the team's capacity is about 1,100 less than the scheduled demand for work. The workload is 28,282 / 27,176 = 1.04 or 104 percent of capacity.

A 4 percent shortage of capacity does not seem like much. Why not increase the hours worked per week for these salaried software engineers to 41.6 hours per week? The added capacity will (roughly) equal the estimated workload. While such a move might help, it would not begin to solve the problem. For instance, is it likely that no engineers in the group will be ill and absent on any of the 170 workdays? Is it likely . . . no; is it possible that every task the group is scheduled to perform will be ready for the group's work exactly on schedule? Is it possible that all required facilities and equipment will be available when needed? Is it possible that there will be no change orders extending the time required for any phase of the work the group is committed to complete? In reality, the probability that any of the above conditions will be met is, as mathematicians are wont to say, vanishingly small. But even if they were met, what about that large bulge of work required in March and April?

For many years, the study of Operations Management has included the subject of "line balancing." (See [10], pp. 230 ff.) The purpose of line balancing is to construct a manufacturing production line such that the individual production units on the line can generate the required amount of product with as little excess capacity as possible. Minimizing excess capacity in the elements of a production line is one test of production line efficiency. This concept, when applied to the resources used by projects—as it often is—is a precursor to disaster. Even in production lines, some excess capacity is required to deal with minor problems and variations that arise during the production process. In projects, the level of uncertainty surrounding the "production process" is so much greater that the amount of excess capacity in the work force needs to be much larger. If this flies in the face of managerial instinct, it is because that instinct is sometimes in error. We will revisit this problem in the following section.

The result of the situation displayed in Figure 6-18 is that all the projects to which this team of engineers is devoted are going to be late and over budget unless some drastic steps are taken to prevent it. The firm in question is known for high-quality work, and it is assumed that the projects will be completed more or less on time with a reasonable percent of the promised specifications in place and working. How this comes about is quite simple. Engineers in this firm are scheduled to work a 40-hour week. They do not, however, work 40-hour weeks. They average between 50 and 60 hours per week. At a 55 hour week, for example, the capacity of the group is approximately 37,500 labor-hours. Given the 28,282 labor-hour workload, the system would operate, on average, at about 75 percent of capacity—which explains the engineering group's ability to meet most of its delivery-date commitments.

> Most project management software will, when asked politely, level out the loads (usage) for individual resources and warn the PM when a resource is scheduled for greater-than-capacity workloads. Whenever possible, the leveling will utilize any available activity slack rather than extend the duration of the project. When a resource is assigned to an activity, it is assigned for 100 percent of its availability unless the PM specifies otherwise.
>
> It is often necessary to have significant excess resource capacity on projects because of the uncertainty that exists in all projects.

ALLOCATING SCARCE RESOURCES TO PROJECTS

When we leveled resources in the case of the overworked scriptwriter, MSP simply used the available activity slack to reschedule WBS item 2. The project completion date was not altered because the WBS 2's slack was large enough to swallow the added time. Often, that is not possible and the software needs instruction about what priority to use when allocating scarce resources to several tasks—which tasks should get the resources immediately and go first, and which may be delayed. In order to select a suitable method for assigning priorities, we need to understand how the problem is solved.

Most solutions start with the PERT/CPM schedule. Given this initial solution, each activity is examined period by period and resource by resource. If the demand for a resource exceeds its supply, the software considers the tasks one by one and assigns resources to the tasks according to some priority rule chosen by the PM. Tasks that receive resources under this rule proceed as originally scheduled. Tasks that do not get resources are delayed until ongoing tasks are completed and the required resources are freed-up for use. If this increases the project duration, the change will be visible on the project's Gantt chart or network as it was when the videotape project client was not available while on vacation. (See Figures 6-10, 6-11, and 6-17.) No matter what priority rule is used, the project's technology always takes precedence.

Some Comments about Constrained Resources

Every time a project falls behind schedule, the PM is apt to plead for more resources. In spite of the PM's complaints about the scarcity of resources, serious cases of resource scarcity rarely apply to resources in general, but rather to one or two very specific resources. We call such resources "Walts." The term was derived from the name of an individual, Walter A., who is employed by a large insurance company. Walt is a specialist in the rules and laws affecting insurance policies for certain types of casualty losses in the firm's commercial lines of business. He has an excellent analytical mind and many years of experience. His knowledge is required when designing new policies in this area of risk. The firm has only one Walt, and while the firm is training others, such training takes years. Walt is a true scarce resource. Projects requiring Walt's input are scheduled around his availability.

There are many other examples. Military combat missions may be scheduled around the availability of attack aircraft. Construction projects may be scheduled around the availability of a large crane. A Broadway opening may be scheduled around the availability of a star actress. The key problem to be solved is deciding which activities get the scarce resource and in what order.

Some Priority Rules

There are many possible rules for assigning preference to some activities over others when allocating scarce resources. Most popular project management software packages have a limited number of rules that can be automatically applied to level overallocated resources so many of the priority rules for assigning scarce resources to activities may have to be applied manually. Fortunately, as we will see, this is not as difficult as it might seem. Several of the most commonly used rules are as follows:

As soon as possible—This is the standard rule in scheduling. Activities are scheduled to start on their ESTs, and resources are made available with that in mind.

As late as possible—With this rule, resources are made available so that activities start on their LSTs whenever possible without increasing the project's duration. This may seem irrational, but it preserves the firm's resources and delays cash outflows as long as possible. (This rule is also compatible with Eliyahu Goldratt's contention that the "student syndrome" leads workers to delay starting an activity until the last possible moment [4, Ch. 13].)

Shortest task duration first—Always consistent with technological precedences, shorter tasks are given priority over longer tasks. This rule maximizes the number of tasks that can be completed by a system in a given time period.

Minimum slack first—Tasks are supplied with resources in inverse order of their slacks. This rule usually minimizes the number of late activities.

Most critical followers—The number of successors on the critical path(s) for each activity is counted. Activities with a higher number of critical successors take precedence. The rationale here is that such activities would cause the greatest damage to project performance if they are late.

Most successors—The same as the previous rule except that all successors are counted. This rule has the same rationale as the preceding rule.

Most resources first—With this rule, the greater the use of a specific resource on a task, the higher the task's priority for the resource. This rule is based on the assumption that more important activities have a greater demand for scarce resources.

In addition to these rules, there are many others. For example, it may be company policy to put favored customers' projects at the head of the resource line—or to reserve special resources for such clients by withholding them from the available supply. The same type of favoritism is sometimes shown to specific projects of high value to the parent firm. (Some firms show favoritism to specific high-value *activities*, but this rule makes little sense because *all* activities of an individual project must be completed to finish the project.) Application of a value measure for allocating scarce resources across several projects is both rational and common.

There are many other priority rules that might be used, but most project management software packages recognize only a few; however, assigning scarce resources manually is not difficult. From our earlier example, recall Figure 6-12, in which all tasks requiring the scriptwriter were listed alone on a Gantt chart showing the task duration, scheduled start, scheduled finish, activity slack, and other needed information. The scheduled start dates would allow us to apply either the early or late start rules. Information on activity slack allows us to use the minimum slack rule. Task duration is the necessary input to apply the Shortest Task Duration rule. The project network, Gantt chart, and the task list all allow a simple count of followers, critical or not. MSP and most other project management software allow verbal or numeric priorities to be assigned easily. This allows the use of any priority system required.

Considerable research has been done on these rules [2, 8, and 9], and the minimum slack rule is usually best or second best. It rarely performs poorly. If a high-slack task is not given resources in one period, its slack is automatically decreased and in the next period it has a better chance of receiving resources. The resource allocation is repeated periodically (hourly, daily, weekly, or monthly, etc.), depending on the time frame of the project's activities. If a task becomes critical, that is, all the slack is used up before the activity receives resources, the project will be delayed. We will consider borrowing resources from ongoing tasks when we discuss the allocation of scarce resources among several projects.

> When a resource is overallocated, MSP can level resource usage by adopting a variety of priority rules, including available activity slack. If there is insufficient slack, other priority rules may be used to allocate the scarce resource. Most of the priority rules originated as job shop scheduling rules. The minimum slack rule usually works best. Only a few critical resources are actually scarce in the sense that project schedules must be adjusted to resource availability.

6.5 ALLOCATING SCARCE RESOURCES TO SEVERAL PROJECTS

When the problem of allocating scarce resources is extended to the case when several projects are being carried out concurrently, the size and complexity of the problem increase but the nature of the underlying problem remains the same. The projects might be independent or members of one large superproject. In any case, there is a decided advantage if several projects are joined as a set.

Consider a single project for a moment. It is composed of a set of first-level tasks connected in a technological relationship of predecessors and successors. Each first-level task is composed of a set of second-level tasks, also arranged in technologically determined ways. The second-level tasks are divided into third-level tasks, and so on, much like the fleas in Jonathon Swift's famous verse:

> So, naturalists observe, a flea
> Hath smaller fleas that on him prey;
> And these have smaller still to bite 'em;
> And so proceed *ad infinitum*.

If we take several projects, we can link them together with *pseudoactivities*, here defined as activities that have duration but do not require any resources. The set of projects linked in such a way becomes a sort of superproject and can be "managed" like any other. We can use the pseudoactivities to establish precedences between the projects they connect, and thus we can separate the projects in time. This is simplest to illustrate as an AOA network (see Figure 6-19), but a Gantt chart could be used by displaying the projects with leads and lags. Each node in Figure 6-19 represents a project, and the arrows connecting them are pseudoactivities. The temporal relationships of the projects are altered by varying the duration of the pseudoactivities.

The individual projects are interrelated by specifying predecessor/successor relationships in MSP. Thus they appear (to MSP) to be parts of one project. If the original project calendars are put on the same time base (exactly as we did with individual activities when scarce resources were allocated among several activities in a single project), we can use the single-project resource-allocation methods for several projects at a time. (MSP's ability to handle projects with a very large number of activities on multiple levels is not limited by the software but by the size of the computer's memory.) MSP can also easily link many large projects, treated as separate and independent, but they share

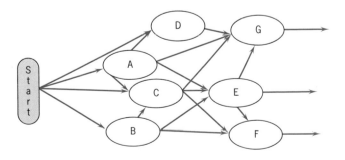

Figure 6-19   Multiple projects connected with pseudoactivities shown on a time line.

the same set of resources. The pseudoactivities may represent technological relationships among the projects—which will often be the case when individual projects are parts of an overall program. Pseudoactivities may separate projects according to planned delivery dates, or the separations may be completely arbitrary.

Putting a set of projects into a format that deals with them as a single project allows us to use MSP's resource loading and leveling charts and tables. Remembering that the calendars of all projects should be adjusted to the same time-base, we can examine the status of resource allocation—or overallocation—for all activities in all projects over any time period. By using the leveling routines, we can also examine the consequences of adopting different resource allocation priority rules. Further, we can examine the implications of adding more resources by comparing the costs of additional resources with the costs that might accrue from late deliveries or delays if the resources are not added. The assignment and handling of various priority rules are, of course, the same as in the single project case. The number of cases to be investigated will be larger in the multi-project case, but few genuine Walts are involved. Extending or contracting the pseudoactivities is the mechanism by which we change the start or finish dates of projects in order to avoid overallocation of Walts.

Whatever the priority rule, the PM faces the problem of choosing between the alternative outcomes that result from different priority rules, as well as different arrangements and durations of the pseudoactivities. There are many measurable criteria available to help us choose a priority rule. The most common are *schedule slippage, resource utilization*, and *in-process inventory*.

Schedule slippage simply measures the amount by which a project, or a set of projects, is delayed by application of a leveling rule (or by extending a pseudoactivity so that a project finishes later because it starts later). As we noted above, the PM (and senior management) must trade off penalty costs or the possible displeasure of clients against the cost of adding resources, if that is possible, or by reducing the overallocation of Walts. Just as serious is the ripple effect that often occurs when a delay in one project causes a delay in others. Indeed, expediting one project typically causes disturbances in the schedules of others.

Resource utilization is important because it is expensive to make resources available. It is helpful to smooth out the peaks and valleys in resource usage thereby minimizing the amount of resources needed. This is particularly important for expensive machine and human resources. On the other hand, as we have written before, efforts to control resource costs by setting system capacity as close as possible to the demand on the system is seriously counterproductive when there is uncertainty in the system and the demand made on it.

The level of in-process inventory is a measure of how much unfinished work is in the system. Clients have little desire to pay for things they have not yet received—though partial prepayment is sometimes arranged by contract—and the organization carrying out projects may have large quantities of human and material resources invested in projects that have little value until they are complete. Minimizing this measure of effectiveness is a major function of the shortest-task-first rule for assigning resources.

The minimum slack rule is probably the best overall priority rule according to research on the subject. It gives the best combination of minimum project slippage, minimum resource idle-time, and minimum in-process inventory [2]. While first-come-first-served may be the client's idea of "fair," it is a poor priority rule when measured against almost any of the others. If the minimum slack rule produces ties among two or more projects (or activities), the shortest task rule seems to be the best tie-breaker.

The Basic Approach

It is now appropriate to stop for a moment and consider a matter. The basic approach taken here to solve project loading and leveling problems is borrowed from a manufacturing model that has widespread application and works equally well for software and hardware. While the model does not apply to continuous processes, it fits projects neatly. It is called the "job shop" model.

Our problem is that there exists a set of activities belonging to one or more projects all eager for processing by a limited set of facilities or other resources. Not all activities require the same subset of facilities or resources, and some activities are more in need of immediate attention than others. To make matters worse, some activities need more work than others, and some insist (for technological reasons, of course, rather than natural cussedness) on being dealt with before others.

As if this were not enough, the activities do not have access to the facility or resources at precise, predetermined times so the PM or facility manager does not know—with any great precision—when to expect specific activities to be ready for processing. Finally, even when an activity does arrive, and when the facility is ready to begin, there may still be considerable uncertainty about exactly how much time it requires to do the processing. Remember that we are discussing the unfinished outputs of some projects. They have completed a previous activity and are now waiting for resources to engage in the next activity for which they are scheduled. All of these activities involve the use of a scarce resource (or two) that we must allocate to the waiting activities.

In this setting, a scarce facility (resource) is like a bottleneck. A line or queue of activities waiting to be processed forms in front of the processor. Assume that jobs arriving to join the queue arrive randomly at an average or expected rate of λ jobs per unit of time. Also assume that the time required for the processor to service the activities is random and has an average or expected rate of μ jobs per unit of time. The behavior of queues has been studied for many years and under our assumptions, not unreasonable for the constrained resource, multiproject problem, the average number of jobs in the waiting line is given by $J = (\lambda/\mu) / (1 - \lambda/\mu)$. Note what happens when the arrival rate of tasks approaches the system's capacity, for example, λ approaches μ. J, the number of jobs in the queue, heads toward infinity. This supports our earlier contention that production or servicing systems must have excess capacity unless they are tightly controlled assembly-line type operations—and even these need a small amount of excess capacity to handle the normal, small variations in arrival or service rates.

Other Priority Rules

As we noted, many of the priority rules we have discussed predate PERT/CPM having been derived from the well-known rules for job shop scheduling. There are, however, a few priority rules that depend directly on PERT/CPM scheduling methods. For example, there is a rule that allocates scarce resources to activities in such a way as to minimize project duration—or minimize the total duration of a set of projects. Another rule gives precedence to activities on the basis of activity finish times, the earliest late-finish times go first. Still another schedules so that the largest number of activities is finished in some given time period. There are many others (see [7], for instance), and most are available on commercial software.

Resource Allocation and the Project Life Cycle

Whatever the scheduling rule, the scheduling method assigns scarce resources to activities on the basis of the degree to which the activity meets some priority conditions. Once the most urgent cases (as measured by the priority rule) have been given resources, the next most urgent cases receive their resources. The process continues until there are no more activities qualified under the rule.

If all critical activities demanding scarce resources are supplied, but the remaining stock of scarce resources is depleted before all noncritical activities are resource loaded, the less urgent activities go unsupplied. When this happens, the less urgent activities become more urgent as period after period passes until they rise far enough up the priority rank list and receive their resources. But what happens if the stock of scarce resources is depleted before all the critical activities receive resources? For example, when using the minimum slack rule, what happens if we run out of our scarce resource before we run out of critical (zero slack) activities?

When this condition occurs, it is often possible to borrow resources from another (ongoing) activity that is lower on the priority list, that is, has some slack in the case of the minimum slack rule. Perhaps we could even deschedule such an activity and take all the scarce resource being used, restoring the scarce resource later when the descheduled activity has risen higher on the priority list. The decision about whether to borrow some resources from a high-slack ongoing task or whether to stop the task and use all its resources is made by looking at the implication of either action on the project. Borrowing the scarce resource may only slow down progress on an activity or it may stop the activity altogether. If borrowing does the latter, it would make sense to borrow all other resources at the same time.

We can also use our knowledge of the project's life cycle to help make the decision. Figure 6-20 shows both types of project life cycle that were discussed in Chapter 1, Section 1.4. The Type 1 life cycle shows decreasing returns to additional resources toward the end of the project. If we borrow from or deschedule activities late in the life of a Type 1 project, we lose proportionately little from the project. If we borrow from or deschedule activities late in the life of a Type 2 project, we may destroy it completely. On the other hand, if the borrowing or descheduling is done near the middle of the life of the project, our conclusion might be exactly the opposite. We need to understand the general shape of the project's life cycle curve in order to assess the implications of slowing or stopping it.

> Allocating scarce resources among multiple projects is more complicated than the single project case, but is not different in its basic logic. The several projects are linked with pseudoactivities and treated as if they were the individual activities of a single project. Schedule slippage, resource utilization, and in-process inventory are measures of the goodness of any priority rule.
>
> Much of the allocation problem results because project facilities/resources have insufficient excess capacity to handle the uncertainties associated with projects. The shape of the project's life cycle helps determine whether or not resources can be borrowed from ongoing activities to supply stalled activities with critical resource needs.

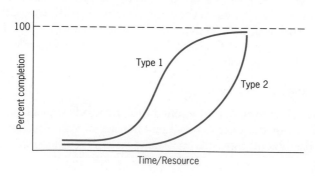

Figure 6-20   Project or task life cycles.

6.6   GOLDRATT'S *CRITICAL CHAIN*

Much research has been done on scheduling with constrained resources, and the findings verify what was expected—projects are completed faster when there are fewer of them struggling for attention from a limited set of facilities [1]. More recently, in the book *Critical Chain* [4] Eliyahu Goldratt applies his Theory of Constraints—so brilliantly developed in his famous book, *The Goal* [5]—to the constrained resource problem. While Goldratt's focus in the *Critical Chain* is on a single project with multiple demands on a scarce resource, the logic extends to the multiproject case without alteration.

To begin our discussion of Goldratt's approach, imagine for the moment that you are sitting in a room full of people with extensive experience as both project team members and project managers. Now imagine the responses you would hear if the group were asked the question: "What things troubled you most about the projects you have been involved with?" Our experience suggests that the following are typical of the responses that would be offered:

- Project due dates are too often unrealistic.
- There are too many changes made in the project's scope.
- Key resources and data are often unavailable when needed.
- The budget is frequently unrealistic and therefore often exceeded.
- It seems like my project is always in competition for resources with other projects.

One interesting observation is that these same issues tend to be raised regardless of the organizational context. Thus we tend to hear strikingly similar complaints regardless of whether the group is referring to a construction project, a software development project, a project to develop an advertising campaign, or an R&D project.

Based on this, is it all that farfetched to conclude that the causes of problems are generic across all types of projects? In our opinion, this is not unlikely. As we have discussed throughout this book, project management is fundamentally concerned with effectively trading off performance, cost, and time. Referring back to the earlier list of complaints, it can be seen that each issue deals with one or more of the three primary project objectives.

Given our conclusion that the problems encountered when managing projects tend to be strongly related to the need to trade off one project objective for another, a natural question arises concerning the extent to which the need to make these trade-offs are caused by human decisions and practices. In other words, can more effective project management minimize the occurrence of these problems? To investigate this issue, let's examine the first complaint regarding unrealistic due dates in more detail.

One way to investigate this issue is to see if we can identify any generally accepted practices that would tend to cause the shared perception of many project workers that project due dates are often set too optimistically. To make our discussion more concrete, consider the three AOA network diagrams shown in Figure 6-21. The primary difference between the three diagrams is the degree of interdependence across the paths. In scenario 1, there is only a single path. In scenario 2, the path B-C-D-E is preceded by three activities A1, A2, and A3. Therefore, the completion of path B-C-D-E depends on which of its three preceding tasks takes the longest. In scenario 3 there are two completely independent paths each consisting of five tasks.

Assume that as project manager you are told that all of the tasks in the three network diagrams require ten days to complete. What completion time would you calculate for each project? If you assume that the activity times are known with certainty, then

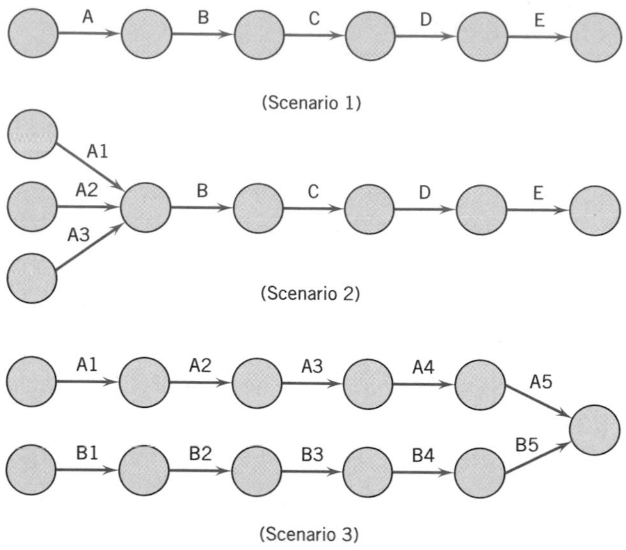

Figure 6-21 Three project scenarios.

what we learned in Chapter 5 indicates that all three projects would have the same duration of 50 days. If you find this result somewhat unsettling, you are in good company. Thinking about it intuitively, how can a simple project like scenario 1 with a single path and only five activities have the same duration as scenario 2 with three paths and seven activities, or with scenario 3 with two paths and ten activities?

Perhaps part of the problem is our assumption that the activity times are known with certainty. To investigate this further, let's assume that all activity times are normally distributed with a mean of ten days and standard deviation of three. The results of simulating the completion of the three projects 200 times each are summarized in Table 6-6.

As you can see from Table 6-6, removing the assumption that the activity times are known with certainty leads to quite different results. Scenario 1's average duration was slightly higher than the 50 we calculated earlier under the assumption of deterministic time estimates. To a large extent with this linear structure, activities that take less than the expected time tend to cancel out the variability of activities that take more than the expected time, resulting in an overall average completion time that is close to the expected completion time for the project. (Remember, in Chapter 5 we discovered that this canceling out rarely happens in the real world, because activities may start late or on time, but rarely start early because resources are usually not available before the activity's EST.) Also observe that the more interdependent scenarios 2 and 3, on average, take even longer than scenario 1 and that their minimum times are significantly longer than scenario 1's minimum time.

Table 6-6 Project Completion Time Statistics
Based on Simulating Three Projects 200 Times

	Scenario 1	Scenario 2	Scenario 3
Average	50.4	51.9	53.4
Std. Dev.	7.1	6.3	5.3
Max.	69.4	72.7	69.3
Min.	30.1	36.1	39.3
Median	50.0	51.8	53.1

Perhaps most important, note that while the average completion times of the projects are still close to 50, this is simply the average project completion time after simulating the execution of each project 200 times. That is, approximately 50 percent of the time the projects will be completed in less than 50 days and 50 percent of the time the projects will be completed in more than 50 days under the reasonable assumption that the distribution of project completion times follows a symmetrical distribution. (Note that here we are referring to the distribution of project completion times as being symmetrical, not the project activity times). In other words, had we determined the project duration based on the assumption that the activity times are known with certainty (when they were actually probabilistic), we would incur a greater than 50 percent chance that the actual project duration would exceed this estimate. How would you like to have responsibility for a project that has less than a 50 percent chance of being completed on time? *This example clearly demonstrates how the commonly made assumption of known activity times in practice can lead to quite unrealistic project deadlines.*

It is important to point out that the results would have been even more dramatic had the activities required some common resources. Similarly, the results would have been more dramatic and realistic had a nonsymmetrical distribution been used to model the activity times. Why, you might ask, would a nonsymmetrical distribution more realistically model the activity times? Suppose you scheduled a status meeting to last 20 minutes. Is there *any* chance the meeting will last 40 minutes longer than expected, or 60 minutes? What about 40 minutes less, or −20 minutes?

Based on the discussion to this point and assuming that project workers have a general desire to be recognized for good performance, what do you imagine project workers do when they are asked to provide time estimates for tasks if they will be held responsible for actual task duration? Do you think they give an estimate that they believe provides them with only a 50 percent chance of being met? Or, more likely, do you imagine they inflate or *pad* their estimate to increase the likelihood of successfully completing the task on time? What would you do?

If you are like most of the people, you would inflate your time estimate. Unfortunately, inflated time estimates tend to create even more problems. First, inflating the time estimate has no impact on the actual probability distribution of completing the activity. Second, what do you imagine happens in cases when a project team member finishes early? More than likely, the team member believes that it is in his or her best interest to remain silent about completing activities in less than the allotted time so that future time estimates are not automatically discounted by management based on a track record of early task completions. Moreover, there are sometimes penalties for completing early, such as storage of materials. Third, just as things tend to fill available closet and storage space in your home, work tends to fill available time. Thus, the scope of the task may be expanded to fill the available time, as Parkinson's Law dictates.

Perhaps even more dangerous than the inflated estimate becoming a self-fulfilling prophecy is that, after receiving approval for a task based on an inflated time estimate, workers may perceive that they now have plenty of time to complete the task and therefore *delay starting the task*, as we noted in Chapter 5. Goldratt refers to this as the *student syndrome*, likening it to the way students often delay writing a term paper until the last minute. The problem of delaying the start of a task is that obstacles are frequently not discovered until the task has been underway for some time. By delaying the start of the task, the opportunity to cope with these obstacles and complete the task on time is greatly diminished.

In summary, we observe that the common practice of simply adding up task durations often leads to unrealistic project due dates. This is primarily the result of assuming the task times are known with certainty, and that we ignore path mergers and

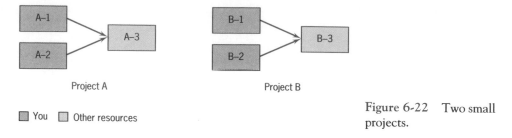

You   Other resources

Figure 6-22   Two small projects.

assume that the paths are independent. A natural consequence of this is that project team members will tend to inflate their time estimates. Inflated time estimates further compound the problem, particularly in cases where the student syndrome comes into play.

In our discussion we used computer simulation to investigate the impact that increasing interdependencies in a project network has on the distribution of project completion times. In Chapter 5, we elaborated on the benefits of using Crystal Ball® to carry out simulation analyses. This discussion is applicable to the current discussion as well because Crystal Ball® can be used to investigate a variety of issues related to resource allocation. To illustrate this, the impact of not reporting early completion times is simulated using Crystal Ball® in Appendix C.

Multitasking

Up to this point, our perspective has been a single project. We now investigate another problem created by conventional practice—the practice of assigning people concurrently to multiple projects.

When project team members are assigned to multiple projects, they have to allocate their time across these projects or *multitask*. Multitasking involves switching from a task associated with one project to another task associated with a different project. To illustrate this, consider the two small projects shown in Figure 6-22. The completion of each of the projects' three tasks requires you and one additional resource. Further, the completion of each task requires five days.

In Figures 6-23(a) and 6-23(b), Gantt charts have been developed for two alternative ways of completing the tasks. In Gantt chart 6-23(a), you switch between projects

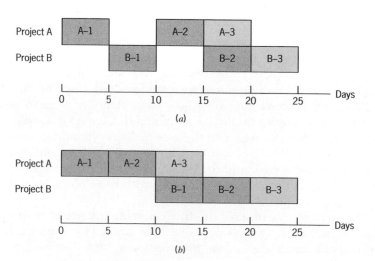

Figure 6-23   Alternative Gantt charts for projects A and B.

after each task is completed, while in Gantt chart 6-23(*b*) you complete all of your assigned tasks for Project A before beginning any work on Project B. In both of these cases the two projects are finished in 25 days; therefore aren't both sequences equally desirable? The answer is absolutely not. First, while it is true that in both cases Project B is finished by time 25, in the first sequence Project A finishes in 20 days, while in the second sequence Project A finishes five days earlier. Therefore the sequence shown in the second Gantt chart is preferable because it results in Project A finishing five days earlier with no penalty to Project B.

Perhaps even more important, our analysis overlooks another significant factor. Specifically, there is typically a penalty or cost associated with switching from working on one project to another. In your own experience as a student, is it more efficient to complete the assignment for one course and then move on to another course or is it more efficient to complete one project management homework problem, then move on to an accounting problem, then on to a statistics problem, then back to a project management problem, and so on? Obviously each time you switch to a different course you have to retrieve the appropriate textbook, find the right page, recall where you left off, and (perhaps most significantly) get into the proper frame of mind. As this example demonstrates, switching attention from project to project is likely to extend activity times. Eliminating such switching costs further increases the benefits associated with the Gantt chart shown in Figure 6-23(*b*).

Common Chain of Events

According to Goldratt, the activities discussed above lead to the following chain of events:

1. Assuming that activity times are known and that the paths are independent leads to underestimating the actual amount of time needed to complete the project.
2. Because the time needed to complete the project is underestimated, project team members tend to inflate their time estimates.
3. Inflated time estimates lead to work filling available time, workers not reporting that a task has been completed early, and perhaps most importantly, the student syndrome.
4. An important caveat then becomes that safety time is usually visible to project workers and is often misused.
5. Misused safety time results in missed deadlines and milestones.
6. Hidden safety time further complicates the task of prioritizing project activities.
7. The lack of clear priorities likely results in poor multitasking.
8. Task durations increase as a result of poor multitasking.
9. Uneven demand on resources—some overloaded and others underloaded—may also occur as a result of poor multitasking.
10. In an effort to utilize all resources fully, more projects will be undertaken to make sure that no resources are underutilized. (Recall the impact of this policy from our discussion of waiting lines in Section 6.5.)
11. Adding more projects further increases poor multitasking.

According to Goldratt, this chain of events leads to a vicious cycle. Specifically, as work continues to pile up, team members are pressured to do more poor multitasking. Increasing the amount of poor multitasking leads to longer activity times. Longer activity times lead to longer project completion times, which ultimately lead to more projects in the waiting line.

It might have occurred to you that one way to reverse this cycle would be to add more resources. According to Goldratt, however, the appropriate response is to reduce the number of projects assigned to each person in an effort to reduce the amount of bad multitasking. Incidentally, a simple way to measure the amount of bad multitasking is to calculate the difference between the time required to do the work for a task and the elapsed time actually required to complete the task.

Determining when to release projects into the system is the primary mechanism for ensuring that the right amount of work is assigned to each person. If projects are started too early they simply add to the chaos and contribute to poor multitasking. On the other hand, if projects are started too late, key resources may go underutilized and projects will be inevitably delayed.

Consistent with his Theory of Constraints, Goldratt suggests that the key to resolving this trade-off is to schedule the start of new projects based on the availability of bottleneck resources or Walts. Goldratt further suggests that time buffers be created between resources that feed bottleneck resources and the bottleneck resources.

While properly scheduling the start of new projects does much to address the problems associated with poor multitasking, it does little to address the problem of setting unrealistic project deadlines and the accompanying response of inflated time estimates. Relying on elementary statistics, it can be easily shown that the amount of safety time needed to protect a particular path is less than the sum of the safety times required to protect the individual activities making up the path. The same approach is commonly used in inventory management where it can be shown that less safety stock is needed at a central warehouse to provide a certain service level than the amount of safety stock that would be required to provide this same service level if carried at multiple distributed locations.

Based on this intuition, Goldratt suggests reducing the amount of safety time added to individual tasks and then adding some fraction of the safety time reduced back into the system as safety buffer for the entire project, called the *project buffer*. The amount of time each task is reduced depends on how much of a reduction is needed to get project team members to change their behavior. For example, the allotted time for tasks should be reduced to the point that the student syndrome is eliminated. Indeed, Goldratt suggests using activity durations where in fact there is a high probability that the task will not be finished on time.

The Critical Chain

Another limitation associated with traditional approaches to project management is that the dependency between resources and tasks is often ignored. To illustrate this, consider the network diagram shown in Figure 6-24. According to the figure, the activities emanating from node 1 require resource **A**, while the activities emanating from nodes 2 and 3 require resources **C** and **B**, respectively. Using traditional approaches to project management, two paths would be identified: **A1-C1** with a duration of 17 days and **A2-B1** with a duration of 11 days. Taking this approach a step further we would conclude that path **A1-C1** is the critical path.

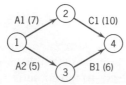

Figure 6-24   Sample network diagram.

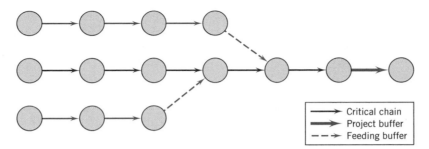

Figure 6-25   Project and feeder buffers.

The problem with this logic is that activities **A1** and **A2** are not truly independent as the diagram would seem to indicate since their completion requires the same resource. Based on this new insight, we see that if resource **A** completes activity **A1** first, thereby delaying the start of **A2** for 7 days, then path **A1-C1**'s duration remains 17 days while path **A2-B1**'s duration increases from 11 to 18 days. Likewise, if resource **A** completes activity **A2** first then path **A1-C1**'s duration increases from 17 to 22 days while path **A2-B1**'s duration remains 11 days. (This is precisely what was considered when we examined the process of resource leveling.)

To address the need to consider both precedence relationships and resource dependencies, Goldratt proposes thinking in terms of the longest chain of consecutively dependent tasks where such dependencies can arise from a variety of sources including precedence relationships among the tasks and resource dependencies. Goldratt coined the term *critical chain* to refer to the longest chain of consecutively dependent activities.

Based on this definition of the critical chain, there are two potential sources that can delay the completion of a project. One source of delay is in the tasks that make up the critical chain. The project buffer discussed earlier is used to protect against these delays (see Figure 6-25). The second source of delay is in the tasks external to the critical chain. These tasks can also delay the completion of the project if delays in these "feeder" paths end up delaying one or more of the tasks on the critical chain. As shown in Figure 6-25, safety time can be added to these paths as well to ensure that they do not delay tasks on the critical chain. The safety time added to chains other than the critical chain is called a *feeding buffer* since these paths often feed into or merge with the critical chain. Thus, the objective of feeding buffers is to ensure that noncritical chains are completed so that they do not delay tasks on the critical chain.

Clearly activities on the critical chain should be given the highest priority. Likewise, to ensure that resources are available when needed, they should be contracted at the start of the project. It is also wise to keep these resources updated on the status of the project and to remind them periodically of when their input will be needed. Goldratt suggests reminding these resources two weeks before the start of their work, then three days prior to their start, and finally the day before they start. Since any delay of an activity on the critical chain can cause a delay of the entire project, it is important that a resource immediately switch to the task on the critical chain when needed.

The critical chain concept identifies the facts that activity times are unknown and independent, that workers will inflate their time estimates to protect themselves, early completion tasks will not be reported, the work will expand to fill the time, tasks will not be started until the last minute, multitasking will be misapplied, resource demands will be uneven and result in task delays, and more projects and tasks will be undertaken to increase resource utilization. All these contribute to project delays and inefficiencies. To correct these problems, feeder time buffers are cut severely to change behavior, a project buffer is added at the end of a project, the release of projects and tasks is based on the availability of bottleneck resources, and time buffers are added to resources that feed bottleneck resources.

The last three chapters on budgeting, scheduling, and allocating resources are the outcome of the planning process we described in Chapter 3. These subjects, taken together, are a description of what to do. Now we turn to two allied subjects: how to report what is going on and how to control it.

REVIEW QUESTIONS

1. Given the fact that a project's resource requirements are clearly spelled out in the project's action plan, why are PMs so concerned with resource allocation?

2. Explain the difference between a project that has a fixed delivery day and one that has a fixed limit on resource usage. Why might a PM be interested in this difference?

3. What does it mean to "fast-track" a project?

4. List as many things as you can think of that should be entered into a specific resource's calendar.

5. Explain why project-oriented firms require excess resource capacity.

6. The arrival and departure times of commercial aircraft are carefully scheduled. Why, then, is it so important to have excess capacity in the airport control tower?

7. Explain the difference in the problems faced by a PM who is short of secretarial resources and one who is short of a "Walt."

8. When allocating scarce resources to several different projects at the same time, why is it important to make sure that all resource calendars are on the same time base (i.e., hourly, daily, weekly . . .)?

9. List and describe the three most common criteria by which to evaluate different resource allocation priority rules.

10. Why is the problem of allocating scarce resources to a set of projects similar to the problem of scheduling a job shop?

11. What is meant by the "student syndrome"?

DISCUSSION QUESTIONS

12. Describe the fundamental trade-offs made when deciding whether or not to crash a project. If the decision is made to crash, what additional trade-offs must be made?

13. Discuss the advantages of "labor pools" in a project-oriented company. Are there any potential disadvantages with the use of pools?

14. What purpose(s) might be served by using each of the following priority rules for allocating scarce resources?
   a. As late as possible
   b. Shortest task duration time first
   c. Minimum slack first

15. Linking a group of projects together with pseudoactivities creates a sort of superproject. What does this mean, and why would anyone want to do it?

16. Describe in your own words what is meant by Goldratt's critical chain. How does it work?

17. Projects A and B are both nearing completion. You are managing a superimportant project C that requires an immediate input of a resource being used by both projects A and B, but is otherwise unavailable. Project A has a Type 1 life cycle. Project B's life cycle is Type 2. From which (or both or neither) do you borrow the resource? Why?

18. Goldratt suggested that to avoid the "student syndrome," it is a good idea to set activity durations so short that there is a high probability that the task will not be finished on time. On the other hand, it has long been known that setting people up for failure is strongly demotivating. What should the PM do?

PROBLEMS

19. Given the following project to landscape a new building site:

Activity	Immediate Predecessor	Activity Duration (days)	Resource Used
A	—	2	X, Y
B	A	2	X
C	A	3	X
D	B, C	4	X, Y
E	D	3	W, X
F	D	1	W, X, Y
G	E, F	2	X, Y

(a) Draw a Gantt chart using MSP.
(b) Assuming a five-day week, find the critical path and project duration in days.
(c) Given that each resource is assigned 100 percent to each task, identify the resource constraints.
(d) Using the MSP default, level the resources and determine the new project duration and critical path.
(e) Identify what alternative solutions can be used to shorten the project duration without overallocating the resources.

20. Given the following project (all times are in days):

Activity	Predecessor	Normal Time	Normal Cost	Crash Time	Crash Cost
a	—	5	$50	3	$150
b	—	4	40	2	200
c	b	7	70	6	160
d	a, c	2	20	1	50
e	a, c	3	30	—	—
f	b	8	80	5	290
g	d	5	50	4	100
h	e, f	6	60	3	180

(a) Draw the network (AOA or AON) and find the critical path, time, and cost for an all-normal level of project activity.
(b) Calculate the crash cost-per-day (all activities may be partially crashed).
(c) Find the optimal way of getting an 18-day delivery time. What is the project cost?
(d) Find the optimal way of getting a 16-day delivery time. What is the project cost?
(e) Calculate the shortest delivery time for the project. What is the cost?
(f) Repeat questions (c), (d), and (e) using Excel®.

21. Given the following AOA network, determine the first activity to be given extra resources by the following priority rules:

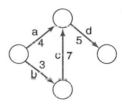

a. Shortest task first
b. Minimum slack first
c. Most critical followers
d. Most successors

22. Given the project shown in Figure 5-10 of Chapter 5, assume that a facility used by activities **c** and **d** is scarce. To which activity would you assign the facility first, given the following rules:
a. Minimum slack rule
b. Most followers
c. Most critical followers
d. Shortest task first
e. As late as possible

INCIDENTS FOR DISCUSSION

PenquinNet Software Engineering Company

Elizabeth Tertle is a senior programmer for PenquinNet, a midsize software engineering company. Elizabeth has been selected to manage the project of designing the next version of their Web-searching tool. The current tool has been a great success for the business. The President of PenquinNet wants to move very quickly in launching this new version. Elizabeth did an action plan for the project and estimated it would take about five months to complete, using one experienced programmer who helped create the previous version and two junior programmers allocated full-time to the project. The President wants the project completed in four months.

Elizabeth thinks she can cut time off the project, but at an increased cost. She decides to use the resource allocation version of CPM.

Questions

1. What information must Elizabeth gather to use this method properly? How should she use this version of CPM to reduce the project time?

2. Discuss how the different types of resources (experienced programmer and junior programmer) and their experience affect the project's completion time and the project's cost?

Southern Kentucky University Bookstore

Southern Kentucky University (SKU) bookstore is beginning a major project of automating their inventory system. The bookstore is organized into four business units: Textbooks, General Merchandise—insignia merchandise (sweatshirts, coffee mugs, etc.), General Books, and Convenience (candy, soft drinks, etc.). Lisa O'Brien, the Bookstore Manager has decided to name each business unit supervisor as the PM of his or her area's automation project. Each department has its own information systems person assigned so Lisa feels that each area can work independently and then all meet her deadline of completion. The project is scheduled for completion right before school starts in the fall, with staggered "Go Live" dates for each of the business units. Each unit will do its own data entry and then work with the others on testing and implementation.

Missy Motz is the supervisor of the Textbook division of the bookstore. Missy is concerned that her department will not have enough resources to complete the automation project. The textbook department is always swamped with book orders from professors right before school starts. Missy thinks she has enough staff to handle the data entry, but is concerned about supplying personnel at the times and quantities required as the implementation is phased in over each of the business units.

Missy knows a little bit about resource allocation techniques. She remembers that one of the most effective allocation techniques is to work first on the activity with minimum slack, so she instructed her staff to approach any tasks they are assigned as members of the project team on that basis.

Questions

1. Is the minimum slack rule a reasonable way to schedule resources of the Textbook division? Why or why not?

2. What complication is added by making this project four separate projects?

C A S E

St. Dismas Assisted Living Facility Resource Usage—4

The project team for the Assisted Living Facility (ALF) project was working to prepare in-depth action plans, complete with the resource requirements for their projects' tasks.

Marc Alison, MD, the Medical Director of Rehabilitation Services for St. Dismas Medical Center was responsible for developing an action plan with the objective of identifying the scope and associated costs of health services to offer residents. The Medical Director included in the action plan the development of an assessment tool that would be used to determine the required level and cost of care for prospective residents. This tool would also be used to ensure that the appropriate population was housed at the facility. It was important to have a way to distinguish a person who was too sick and needed a more intense level of care than that offered by the Assisted Living Facility. Once the assessment of a potential resident was completed, the facility staff could determine if the person assessed was a good candidate for the facility. This phase of the project plan was critical to the success of the project.

Dr. Alison's approach was to develop the assessment tool and test it on individuals that matched the marketing department's target population of the assisted living facility. He felt he had a great opportunity to find his test population by using some of the current St. Dismas patients who were almost ready for discharge from the hospital. He could also use some of the older volunteers who currently worked at the hospital. Dr. Alison felt strongly that a physician should assess potential residents but he also knew that it might be cost prohibitive to have such an expensive resource conducting pre-admission assessments. He thought that if a physician developed and tested the tool first, then additional testing could be conducted using less costly health care professionals to conduct the evaluations.

Dr. Alison knew he would have to work with Dr. Zen Link, Head of Geriatric Medicine on developing the tool. Dr. Link was familiar with the elderly population that the marketers were targeting and could offer valuable insights on how to assess the health status of potential residents. Dr. Link also had an extensive practice at St. Dismas and would have some patients who might agree to help test the assessment tool. Dr. Alison would also need the services of the CFO and his staff to determine the cost of the health services the residents would need. Dr. Alison prepared and presented the following action plan to the project steering team:

ID	Task Name	Duration	Predecessors	Resource Names
1	**Medical/Health services determined**	48.25 days		
2	Physical health assessment tool for residents developed	25.75 days		Alison, Link
3	Develop tool	2 wks		Alison, Link
4	Test of assessment tool conducted by physicians (12 patients)	6 hrs	3	Alison, Link
5	Revise tool as necessary	1 wk	4	
6	Test of tool conducted by other health professionals (i.e., phys. asst., RN, therapist)	2 wks	5	
7	Admission & Discharge criteria finalized	1.5 wks	6	Alison, Splient
8	Investigate copyrighting assessment tool	3 wks	4	Legal
9	Assessment tool finalized	0 days	7	
10	Copyright tool	0 days	8, 9	
11	Financial impact of health services determined	15 days		
12	Costs determined	1 wk	9	Alison, CFO
13	Scope of health services determined to include in base rate	2 wks	12	Proj. Steering Team
14	Scope of services to provide on a fee for service basis	2 wks	12	Proj. Steering Team
15	Finalize services and programs to be offered	0 days	13, 14	

The project team was impressed with the thought that went into Dr. Alison's action plan. They were delighted with the prospect of copyrighting an admission and discharge assessment tool, but they raised some questions about Dr. Alison's resource assignments. The COO asked how Drs. Alison and Link were going to assess a sufficient sample of people in six hours' time given their busy clinical schedules. Dr. Alison replied that he and Dr. Link would be doing all of the other steps in the action plan during their normal 8 AM to 5 PM workday. The step to test the tool on real patients, however, would take some scheduling. Dr. Alison added that his colleague intended to conduct evaluations of current patients, with their permission, during their regular office visits. Dr. Alison admitted he had not figured out how he was going to see his share of the test group. He knew he could see some inpatients ready for discharge from the hospital during the time he did his rounds. He also wanted to test the tool on at least a dozen people from the volunteer staff who matched the prospective resident population. He informed the team that his secretary had agreed to phone the volunteers and see if any of them were interested. She said she could do this during her normal workday, so he had not included her time in the action plan.

Dr. Alison sat silently thinking about how long this step in his action plan would take, given his current workload. He knew that he would only be available to do the assessments during the time that he allocated for administrative hospital work, Wednesday from 8:00 AM to noon. He did not want to give up any of his clinical time, because his patients had been scheduled months in advance. Dr. Alison wanted to personally test the tool on at least 12 people. He estimated each assessment would take no more than a half hour (that is why he said that step would take six hours to complete).

Dr. Alison was not sure what to do next. He told the project team he would get back to them.

QUESTIONS

1. Prepare a Gantt chart with resources for the action plan Dr. Alison submitted. Begin this project on January 3. Prepare a resource calendar for Dr. Alison.

2. How would you handle Dr. Alison's resource problem?

3. Given Dr. Alison's availability, how long will it take to complete testing of the assessment tool?

4. Prepare a Gantt chart for Dr. Alison's plan incorporating any changes you recommend.

C A S E

Charter Financial Bank

Charter Financial Bank operates three branches in a southeastern city. Ray Copper, Vice-President of Information Technology at the bank, has recently been charged by the bank's president to develop a Website to promote bank services, to provide access to customer account information, and to allow individuals to apply online for loans and credit cards.

Ray decided to assign this project to Rachel Smith, one of two directors in the information technology group. Since Charter Financial did not currently have a presence on the Web, Ray and Rachel agreed that an appropriate starting point for the project would be for the project team to benchmark existing Websites in order to gain a better understanding of the state-of-the-art in this area. At the conclusion of their first meeting, Ray asked Rachel to prepare a rough estimate of how long this project would take and how much it would cost if it were pursued at a normal pace. Noting that the president appeared particularly anxious to launch the Website, Ray also requested that Rachel prepare a time and budget estimate related to launching the Website as quickly as possible.

During the first project team meeting, the team identified seven major tasks associated with the project. The first task was to benchmark existing Websites. The team estimated that completing this task at normal pace would likely require 10 days at a cost of $15,000. However, the team estimated that this task could be completed in as few as seven days at a cost of $18,750 if the maximum allowable amount of overtime was used.

Once the benchmark study was completed, a project plan and project definition document would need to be prepared for top management approval. The team estimated that this task could be completed in five days at a cost of $3,750 working at a normal pace or in three days at a cost of $4,500.

When the project received the approval of top management, the Website design could begin. The team estimated that Website design would require 15 days at a cost of $45,000 using no overtime or 10 days at a cost of $58,500 using all allowable overtime.

After the Website design was complete, three tasks could be carried out simultaneously: (1) developing the Website's database, (2) developing and coding the actual Web pages, and (3) developing and coding the Website's forms. The team estimated that database development would require 10 days and cost $9,000 using no overtime, but could be completed in seven days at a cost of $11,250 using overtime. Likewise, the team estimated that developing and coding the Web pages would require 10 days and cost $15,000 using no overtime or could be reduced by two days at a total cost of $19,500. Developing the forms was to be subcontracted out and would take seven days at a cost of $8,400. The organization that was to be used to create the forms does not provide an option for paying more for rush jobs.

Finally, once the database was developed, the Web pages coded, and the forms created, the entire Website would need to be tested and debugged. The team estimated that this would require three days at a cost of $4,500. Using overtime, the team estimated that the testing and debugging task could be reduced by a day at a total cost of $6,750.

QUESTIONS

1. What is the cost of completing this project if no overtime is used? How long will it take to complete the project?
2. What is the shortest amount of time in which the project can be completed? What is the cost of completing the project in the shortest amount of time?
3. Suppose that the benchmarking study actually required 13 days as opposed to the 10 days originally estimated. What actions would you take to keep the project on a normal schedule?
4. Suppose the President wanted the Website launched in 35 days. What actions would you take to meet this deadline? How much extra would it cost to complete the project in 35 days?

BIBLIOGRAPHY

1. ADLER, P. S., A. MANDELBAUM, V. NGUYEN, and E. SCHWERER. "Getting the Most Out of Your Product Development Process." *Harvard Business Review*, March–April 1996.

2. FENDLEY, L. G. "Towards the Development of a Complete Multiproject Scheduling System." *Journal of Industrial Engineering*, October 1968. (This is an early, but excellent paper on evaluating various scarce resource priority rules.)

3. GOLDRATT, ELIYAHU M., *Project Management the TOC Way* (uncorrected proofs), The North River Press: Great Barrington, MA, 1998.

4. GOLDRATT, E. M., *Critical Chain*. Great Barrington, MA: North River, 1997.

5. GOLDRATT, E. M., and J. COX. *The Goal*. 2nd rev. ed., Great Barrington, MA: North River, 1992.

6. IBBS, C. W., S. A. LEE, and J. I. LI, "Fast-Tracking's Impact on Project Change." *Project Management Journal*, December 1998.

7. JOHNSON, R. V. "Resource Constrained Scheduling Capabilities of Commercial Project Management Software." *Project Management Journal*, December 1992. (An out-of-date work, but an excellent guide to the analysis of software capabilities in this area.)

8. KURTULUS, I., and E. W. DAVIS. "Multi-Project Scheduling Categorization of Heuristic Rules Performance." *Management Science*, February 1982. (Another early classic on resource priority rule evaluation.)

9. KURTULUS, I., and S. C. NARULA. "Multi-Project Scheduling: Analysis of Project Performance." *IEEE Transactions on Engineering Management*, March 1985.

10. SHAFER, S. M., and J. R. MEREDITH. *Operations Management: A Process Approach with Spreadsheets*. New York: John Wiley, 1998.

C · H · A · P · T · E · R

7

Monitoring and Controlling the Project

Project monitoring and control are, in some ways, simply the opposite sides of project selection and planning. The bases for selection dictate what to monitor and the details of planning identify the elements to be controlled. *Monitoring* is the collection, recording, and reporting of project information that is of importance to the project manager and other relevant stakeholders. *Control* uses the monitored data and information to bring actual performance into agreement with the plan. Clearly, the need to exert proper control mandates the need to monitor the proper activities and elements of the project. Frequently, the distinction between monitoring and control is blurred, and their interaction often makes us think we are working on a single task, but they are highly distinct and serve significantly different purposes.

Although the data gathered from monitoring often serve many objectives—auditing, keeping management informed, learning from mistakes—these are all secondary compared to the purpose of control. The purpose of monitoring is to ensure that all interested parties have available, when needed, the information required to exercise control over the project. Thus, the key issue in designing an effective monitoring and control system is to create an information system that gives the project manager and others the information they need to make informed, timely decisions that will keep project performance as close as possible to the plan.

7.1   THE PLAN-MONITOR-CONTROL CYCLE

Managing a project involves continually planning what to do, checking on progress, comparing progress to plan, taking corrective action to bring progress into agreement with the plan if it is not, replanning, and so on. As noted previously, the fundamental items to be planned, monitored, and controlled are time, cost, and performance so that the project stays on schedule, does not exceed its budget, and meets its specifications.

This plan-monitor-control cycle constitutes a "closed-loop" process that continues until the project is completed. Figure 7-1 illustrates the information and authority flows for such a cycle in an engineering project. Note that the information flows up the organization and the authority flows down.

Unfortunately, it is often the case that when particularly complex, challenging, or uncertain projects are initiated, the planning-monitoring-controlling effort is minimized so that "the real work" can be done. It is a great temptation to focus on doing something, anything, rather than to spend time on planning, monitoring, and controlling, especially if the stakes are high and the project is a difficult one. It is precisely such projects, however, that most desperately need the maturity of a project manager who realizes the importance of creating an effective planning-monitoring-controlling process.

We are familiar with many firms that incurred tremendous expense and large losses because the planning process was inadequate for the project tasks undertaken. For example, a retailer won a bid to supply a regional office of a national firm with a computer, terminals, and software. Due to insufficient planning, the installation was completed far beyond the due date with very inadequate performance. The project failure disqualified the retailer from bidding on an additional 20 installations planned by the national firm. Another firm in the construction industry ran 63 percent over budget and 48 percent over schedule on a major project because the PM had managed similar projects several times before and "knew what to do without going into all that detail that no one looks at anyway."

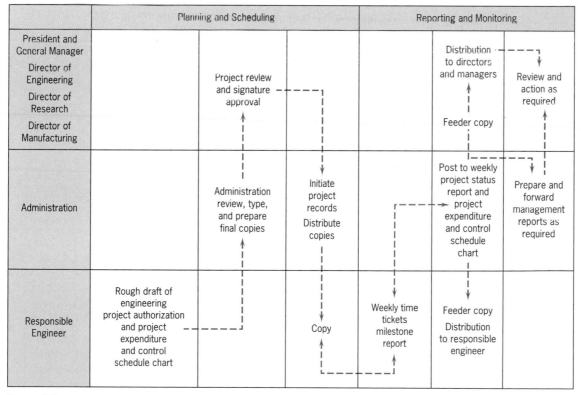

Source [6]

Figure 7-1 Project authorization and expenditure control system information flow.

Designing the Monitoring System

The key to setting up a monitoring system is to identify the special characteristics of performance, cost, and time that need to be controlled in order to achieve the project goals stated in the action plan. Also, the exact boundaries within which these characteristics should be controlled must be determined. Moreover, performance characteristics should be specified for each level of detail in the project: subtasks, tasks, and so on all the way up to the project itself. In order to manage for overall project success, control must be exercised at the detailed work level for each aspect of project performance or no significant change will occur.

It is the action plan that identifies what is being done, when, and the planned level of resource usage for each task and subtask in the project. Real-time data must then be identified by which to measure achievement against these plans. The mechanisms to gather and store such data must be designed. In addition to data collection systems for hard data, the monitoring system should include telephone logs, change tracking/control systems, documentation processes for both formal (e.g., meetings) and informal communications, and other such softer data collection systems. The monitoring system is the direct connection between project planning and control.

An example of one way of achieving this planning/control connection is to monitor project progress on the MSP Gantt chart, as shown in Figure 5-24 of Chapter 5. The original Gantt chart provides the baseline, and every time there is a change the "tracking Gantt" chart is updated to reflect the change. The software automatically adjusts all information to reflect the change. Another way illustrated later in this chapter is to use an "earned value" chart with its preestablished baseline. A third method is to monitor the critical chain buffers described in Chapter 6. Critical chain software packages such as ProChain® include buffer reports in their output which can direct the managers to problem areas where attention needs to be focused. The PM should remember to number and save each version of all monitoring documents to ensure a timely and accurate record for the project history that is discussed in Chapter 8.

It is temptingly easy to focus monitoring activities on data that are easily gathered rather than those that are important for control purposes. For example, too often it is the hard, "objective" measures that are monitored when soft, "subjective" data revealed in phone calls and water-cooler or happy-hour conversations are what are needed for proper control.

Too often, intensity of activity is measured instead of results. Because the measurement of project performance may be difficult, there is a strong tendency to let project inputs serve as surrogate measures of output, such as assuming that if 50 percent of the budget has been spent then 50 percent of the tasks must be completed. Probably the most common error is monitoring data generally related to project performance but that virtually never changes from one collection period to the next—with no significant change, there will be no significant control activity.

It is essential to spend time up front designing the planning-monitoring-controlling process, especially for more challenging projects. The action plan is the primary document to guide the design of the monitoring system in terms of the detailed tasks and resources that need to be controlled in order for the project to achieve its time, cost, and performance goals. Common errors in setting up monitoring systems are monitoring easy measures instead of relevant measures, monitoring activity in place of results, monitoring inputs as surrogates for outputs, and monitoring measures that don't change from one period to the next.

7.2   DATA COLLECTION AND REPORTING

Once we have decided on the type of data we want to monitor, the next question is how to collect this data and turn them into information useful for controlling the project. This is the activity of data collection and reporting. In this section we cover the physical collection of data and the analysis of that data, if necessary, to transform them into information. Once transformed, however, there are many ways to present the information and these are covered under the topic of *reporting*, including a discussion of the three main types of reports. A very special means of both collecting and disseminating data, and even sometimes information, is the proverbial "meeting," and we offer some advice for this often painful phenomenon—both in-person and virtual meetings are included. The use of electronic means for distributing information or reports is briefly examined.

At some point we have to decide what data we need to collect and precisely how to go about collecting them. A number of questions are raised. Should we design and use special forms? Should data be collected just before or after an important milestone? Should time and cost data always be collected at the same time each month? There are many such issues that arise when considering the data collection process and most of them can only be answered in the context of a specific project. There are a few generalizations that can be made concerning the information needed to control projects; these are described in the next section.

Data Collecting

The majority of data to be collected will eventually exist in one of the following five formats.

1. **Frequency counts**   A simple tally of the occurrence of an event is common—for example, days without an accident. Often a count of events per time period or as a fraction of some standard number is used, such as complaints per month, defects per thousand products, and fraction of luggage lost.

2. **Raw numbers**   Actual amounts are used, usually in comparison to some expected or planned amount, such as dollars spent, hours required, and pounds consumed. The comparison to plan may take the form of variances, that is, differences between planned and actual, or ratios of one to the other. The ratio format is particularly appealing for reporting on a control chart with predetermined limits, as is described later in the chapter. When collecting raw amounts it is important that the basis, time period, and collection process always be the same.

3. **Subjective numeric ratings**   These are usually subjective estimates of some quality offered by specialists in the topic, such as ordinal "rankings" of performance. They can be reported in the same ways as raw numbers, but they often cannot be mathematically processed in the same ways raw numbers can.

4. **Indicators and surrogates**   When it is especially difficult to find a direct measure of a variable, indicators or surrogates are frequently used instead. If this approach is taken, it is important that the indicator or surrogate be as directly related to the variable as possible. For example, body temperature is an indicator of infection and years of experience can be a surrogate for expertise. The number of salespersons, however, would be a poor, and clearly indirect, measure for level of customer service.

5. **Verbal characterizations**   Other variables that are difficult to measure, such as team spirit or client-supplier cooperation, may take the form of verbal characterizations. These forms of data are acceptable and useful as long as the terminology is limited and is uniformly understood by all parties.

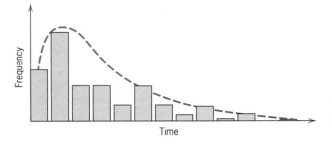

Figure 7-2　Number of bugs per unit of test time during test of Datamix software program.

Data Analysis

Following the collection of the data through the monitoring system, it will frequently be necessary to analyze or process the data in some manner before reporting it for control purposes. This may take the form of simple aggregation of the data, such as averaging the values, or something as complex as fitting statistical distribution functions to the data to ascertain relationships, effects, and trends. Crystal Ball® can do this with ease. Some of the quality management techniques for the presentation and analysis of data are often useful here [e.g., see 11, p. 64]. As an example, a common graph used in quality management shows the range of sample values taken on a periodic basis, such as daily. If the samples' range—the largest minus the smallest value—appears to be increasing over time, this may indicate that a machine is wearing out or needs maintenance.

Figures 7-2 and 7-3 illustrate curve fitting where charts are updated on a regular basis and curves are fit to the data in order to help the PM estimate the cost and time required to achieve the performance goals for the project. Figure 7-4 shows the trend in the ratio of actual material cost to planned cost so the PM can step in should the values indicate a likely problem.

In general, significant differences from plan should be highlighted or "flagged" in some way so the PM or other person exercising control cannot overlook the potential problem. The many techniques of statistical quality control [see 11, Ch. 3] are helpful for determining what size variances are "significant," and may even help in determining causes and effects. These formal approaches, however, are often "after the fact" techniques for correcting (controlling) problems—variances occur, are reported, investigated, and then some action is taken. The astute PM, however, is much more interested in *preventing* fires rather than putting them out, thus the value of timely data collection and reporting.

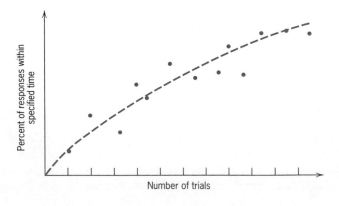

Figure 7-3　Percent of specified performance met during successive repeated trials.

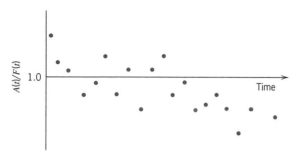

Figure 7-4   Ratio of actual material cost to estimated material cost for aircraft parts company.

Last, it should be noted that data analysis is sometimes used for the assignment of blame. The PM will not find this a helpful endeavor in managing the project. The goal is to achieve the project objectives through correcting deviations from plan, not to find scapegoats or assign guilt. The PM needs all team members performing at the top of their capabilities. Frequent blame placing strongly encourages team members to avoid taking the risks necessary to achieve a project's goals.

Reporting and Report Types

After the data have been collected and analyzed, they need to be reported in some form. There are many possible report formats, but the most popular are project status reports, time/cost reports, variance reports, update presentations, and similar documents. All tables, charts (such as PERT/CPM and Gantt), and especially action plans should be updated to reflect current reality. In addition to alerting team members to potential problems, such updates help maintain team morale. Where known, some form of "comparables" should also be reported such as distributions of previous data, perhaps from earlier but similar projects, so that the PM and others can better interpret the data. As we have noted before, any time project reports, plans, or other documents are updated, great care should be taken to preserve all documents from earlier stages of the project's life. When the project is completed, a project "history" should be prepared and these materials will be invaluable.

Although everyone concerned with the project should be tied into the reporting system in some fashion, not everyone needs to receive the same information. In addition to, say, aggregating the data for senior managers with many other such projects under their authority, reports may vary in terms of the frequency of distribution and detail as well as the particular measures being reported. The client may wish to have reports on cost or schedule while functional management may wish to see reports on technical performance, for example. In following the nature of the WBS, the team members may need data or information at the task or subtask level on a frequent, perhaps daily, basis.

In general, it is a good idea to avoid *periodic* reports except in those cases in which the flow of data is periodic, for example, accounting data. Let the project's milestones, scope changes, problems, and the project team's needs for information dictate the timing of reports. It is our feeling that reports issued routinely every day, week, month, or quarter do not get read. An exception to this rule against periodic reporting is made for reports mandated by senior management who must examine the status of many projects and may need to compare the performance of many projects against the same time frame.

The explosion of electronic media for both collecting and disseminating data and information, including project management software such as MSP, makes it possible to customize a wide range of information for different audiences. This means that more data are available for collection, and more frequent updating is possible. Clearly, this can lead to an overload of reporting that is just as dangerous as underreporting. Important events, problems, and trends tend to be hidden in a mountain of detail. Thus, it is crucial that the reporting system be well designed to make use of such modern technological marvels without abusing the recipient of their capabilities. More is said about this later in this section.

The reports delivered to those engaged in carrying out or managing the project should be timed to allow control to be exercised before completion of the task in question. The project action plan, again, identifies the level of tasks and responsibilities according to the level of management, and this provides guidance for both the level of detail and the timing of reports. For example, drug efficacy tests require a long time to conduct so frequent reports would not be appropriate. In contrast, performance verification tests on new silicone chips can result in hundreds of discrepancies within a matter of hours, so daily or even more frequent reports are necessary.

In addition to WBS-determined data and information, individual managers may wish to see specific types of information in their reports and these should be included as well. Moreover, they may even have preferences on the timing of reports, which should also be followed when they are within reason. The PM, however, must make sure that the relevant (for their level) information about project progress is included in their reports, and in such a way that it cannot be overlooked. Similarly, it is of no value reporting information or data to those who cannot use it for purposes of control, such as reporting overhead costs to the project chemist.

For projects, there are primarily three distinct types of reports: *routine*, which we have been describing so far, *exception*, and *special analysis*. Exception reports are primarily intended for special decisions or unexpected situations where affected team members and outside managers need to be made aware of a change, and the change itself needs to be documented. Special analysis reports are prepared to disseminate the results of a special study in a project concerning a particular opportunity or problem for the project. They may be distributed to top management, other project managers who would benefit from the knowledge, functional managers, or anyone who might be affected or interested. Typical subjects might include studies of new materials, capabilities of new software, and descriptions of the impact of new government regulations.

In addition to the benefits of reports for the purposes of control, they offer other benefits as well. For one thing, they provide the mutual understanding between stakeholders in a project regarding the goals, progress, difficulties, successes, and other on-going events of importance to the project. They also help in communicating the need for coordination among those working on the tasks and subtasks of the project. In addition, there are often changes to the goals and functioning of projects. Reports can communicate this information in a timely and appropriate fashion, thus minimizing the confusion often encountered during such changes. They help maintain the visibility of the project, and the project team, to top management, functional managers, colleagues, and clients. Finally, unless the project is a disaster, status reports help keep the project team motivated.

A special problem often encountered in designing project monitoring and reporting systems is the relationship between the project's information system and the overall organization's information system. The PM is, understandably, not free to define costs and other measures in ways that differ from the organization's definition of such measures as documented in the overall information system. Thus, the PM is advised to use the regular information system as the definitional prototype for project monitoring and reporting, making adjustments and additions as necessary for the special circumstances and measures needed for the project at hand. The PM should be aware, however, of another danger— using modules of the organizational information system for the project monitoring and reporting system because the fit may not correspond well. For example, an accounting module to track costs in a shop operation will not be adequate for tracking project costs.

Software packages such as MSP offer extensive and varied reporting mechanisms. Gantt charts show the current status of a project (see Chapter 5, Figure 5-24), and reports show the availability of various resources (see Chapter 6, Table 6-4) or the demands for work from individuals or groups (see Table 6-5 or Figure 6-12), just to name a few. MSP not only allows the PM to distribute the information anywhere that has electronic communication capability, but also allows easy customization of the reports limited only by the PM's imagination. A PM can highlight tasks that are running late (or running early if such exist), and add large red **X**s to mark cost overages. The level of detail reported on Gantt charts is also completely controllable, so the PM can send only first-level tasks to senior management, and the highest level of detail to project team members.

Meetings

For many project workers and managers, meetings are about as welcome as Herpes diseases or a call from the IRS. So far in our discussion, we have talked about reports as if they were going to be delivered by hand, snail mail, or e-mail. Often, however, they (or their substance) are delivered through face-to-face meetings. These meetings can range from regular, highly formalized and structured presentation/question/answer sessions to informal, off-the-cuff get-togethers. Project review meetings, regardless of the format, are always important.

Although such meetings are usually dreaded because of their length, lack of actionable conclusions, and general waste of time, this need not be the case. The following guidelines should help avoid the problems with such meetings.

- Some meetings, such as the Weekly Progress Report (also known as "show and tell"), should rarely be held at all. Although not always possible, try to hold meetings only for making group decisions or generating input among meeting members for dealing with important problems or opportunities. That is, hold meetings to take advantage of face-to-face interaction when no other approach or technology can substitute.

- Distribute a written agenda in advance of the meetings. The lead time for distributing the agenda should be sufficient to allow attendees to prepare to deal with agenda items. In addition to a list of the issues that will come before the group, the agenda should announce the meeting's pre-set starting and stopping times. Stick with both. Don't wander off the agenda, don't let the meeting run into overtime, and especially do not penalize those who show up on time by making them wait for those who are late.

- If homework needs to be done before the meeting by the attendees, check to be sure they will be prepared, and above all make sure you are prepared.

- If you chair the meeting, you should take your own minutes. The minutes should contain a final set of action items including what is to be done, by whom, and by when. The minutes are a critically important piece of documentation for a project, documenting important decisions and responsibilities. Do not delegate this responsibility. Microsoft Word® has a template for creating an agenda and for taking minutes that focus on action items.

- Avoid attributing remarks to individuals in the minutes. Remarks are meant to foster group process, not to be documented for eternity and for all to see. (Obviously this doesn't apply to designated or volunteered responsibilities.) As well, do not record and report votes taken in the meeting. It seems inappropriate to report that the motion to send a get-well card to the boss was passed—four yea and three nay. When the group has made a decision, by whatever means, that decision becomes the unanimous position of the group. Disagreement and debate are appropriate during the meeting, not after the decision is made.

- Although courtesy is always in order, excessive formality at project meetings is not. Thus, Robert's Rules of Order can safely be left at the door.

- If a crisis arises and a meeting is deemed necessary to deal with it, make sure the meeting is restricted to that issue alone. If a stopping time cannot be predetermined, an acceptable alternative is "When the crisis is resolved."

Virtual Reports, Meetings, and Project Management

In this chapter on monitoring, reporting, and control, it is important to note that PMs can and do effectively utilize what has come to be called the "information revolution." Using the Internet, communicating and reporting about the project's status is now easily accomplished whether project team members are in the next cubicle or across the world. One large high technology company uses secure Web pages on the Internet to collect, store, and disseminate information on various projects. They have several Web pages that are specifically designed to communicate project information to and from clients. Others are designed for the sole use of members of the project team. Still others are created to communicate with the firm's senior management.

A senior project manager in the software firm mentioned above offered the following comments on project communication:

> In today's entrepreneurial corporate environment, it is necessary to communicate project information at varying levels of detail. Users run the gamut from software engineers to Business Unit (BU) general managers. Many of these users may not know or need to know how to use the project manager's planning tools. In addition, management may not want users from other BUs to have the same level of access as users doing and managing most of the work. It is important to have tools capable of limiting the detail if the user is not interested in it or is not permitted to see it, and providing detail where and when the user needs it. There are third-party software tools that claim to do at least some of this.

Web pages can hold any information that the project manager wants to share, such as progress-to-date on a project, resources assigned to a task, status of a particular task, and expenses to date. The amount of information that can be shared is limited only by the planning and monitoring processes that are put into place and the project manager's imagination.

Software programs such as MSP let you utilize the organization's local area network or intranet, as well as the Internet, to help with project communication and monitoring. A project manager can electronically check the status of a task or any resource on the team and have updated information automatically entered into a project plan. Electronic work groups can be set up to monitor task completion, resource usage, and to provide reports to a group of individuals who have an interest in the project's status. For example, milestone reports can be sent to a senior management work group, and up-to-date personnel usage reports can be sent to the Human Resources department.

Using Microsoft Project 2000® (MP2000), including Project Central®, the converse is also true. With MP 2000 and an appropriate computer network, anyone with authorized access can update his or her section of a project plan and submit it back to the PM for inclusion. Project teams and management at any site across the world will greatly benefit from these features. Microsoft says that users of the Project Central® feature do not need access to a "resident" copy of the software. Valuable real-time reports can be prepared without lengthy phone conversations, or costly on-site meetings. The technological progress of the current "turn of the century" only means more effective and timely use of project information for planning, monitoring, and communicating. Utilizing video conferencing, virtual presentations, Web posting, email, etc. greatly enhance the PM's ability to manage a project.

Thus *virtual project teams* are created, perhaps spread across continents, with members contributing their own pieces of the project and being monitored and controlled by the PM at another location [2]. In addition to its use for helping with the planning, monitoring, and control of projects, the Internet can also be a rich source of information. The project team can find building codes, technical aid, databases, patent information, expert contacts, and almost anything else on the Internet.

> For the monitoring system, data in various forms have to be collected, analyzed, and reported. Data also need to be aggregated, manipulated in various ways, and compared with planned values in order to allow effective control. The monitoring system helps PMs prevent problems instead of having to solve them. Project reports vary in content and frequency, depending on who the reports are targeted to and what controls they will exert. A special consideration is the relationship between the organization's information system and the project's system. In addition to printed reports, reports may also have to be given orally at meetings but steps can be taken to maximize the effectiveness of such meetings. The Internet and the organization's local area network (intranet) have enhanced project communication and meetings as well as facilitated the management of geographically dispersed virtual projects.

7.3 EARNED VALUE

So far, we have discussed monitoring segments of a project—individual tasks, subtasks, and such. Of primary importance, however, is deriving some measure of overall project progress in terms of performance, budget, and schedule. Such a measure exists and goes by the name of "earned value."

The common problem with comparing actual expenditures against plan (a.k.a. baseline or budget) for any given time period is that the comparison fails to consider the actual progress made on the project. Thus, if expenditures are lower than expected for a given period it may be either good or bad, depending on whether progress is in line with that amount of expenditure. Similarly, if expenditures are higher than expected, this may be acceptable if progress is sufficiently greater than planned for that period.

The earned value of a project is calculated by multiplying the budgeted cost of each task by the percentage of completion of that task and summing over all tasks for the project. This process is more difficult than it might sound. The percent of an activity's budget actually spent by a given date is not, in general, a good indicator of the percent of that activity's completion. For example, the major cost for a task might be for obtaining the machinery to do the task, a cost that will be incurred before any progress is made on that task. Or perhaps the major cost will not be charged until completion of the task. *To the best of our knowledge, there is no satisfactory way to measure accurately the percent of completion of most tasks, let alone to measure accurately the percent of completion of an entire project.*

As a result, three conventions have been adopted for estimating progress on tasks, but they must not be confused with reality. The most popular is 50-50: the task is listed as 50 percent complete when work on it is initiated, and the other 50 percent is added when the task is completed. This approach avoids the difficult problem of trying to estimate progress while the task is being executed. Another convention is 100 percent when the task is complete and zero percent before that. The last approach is trying to estimate percentage completion by using the ratio of cost expended to the total cost budgeted for a task. Similarly, one could use the ratio of the actual time elapsed relative to the total scheduled task time.

These conventions are meant for application only to individual tasks on a project, not to the project as a whole. In fact, applying these conventions to the project as a whole may result in a seriously misleading number because none of the conventions noted has much semblance of reality. If one must estimate the percent complete for an activity—and as we shall see, one must—the best guess of a knowledgeable person is probably the best that can be done for most tasks.

As the earned value of a project is calculated, a graph such as that shown in Figure 7-5 can be constructed. Given the limitations of the input data, such a figure provides a basis for evaluating cost, schedule, and performance to date. The earned value completed to date tells the manager whether progress is up to expectation, the "baseline" planned for this point in time. Any difference is called the "schedule variance," which shows how much the project is ahead of or behind schedule. As seen in the figure, the value completed to date is less than the baseline estimate for this point in the project's life and represents about a ten-day delay, resulting in a negative schedule variance (delay is negative). The actual cost, however, is considerably above the amount of value completed, resulting again in a negative (bad) "spending variance," and even exceeds the baseline cost for this point. Thus, this figure represents a difficult situation—a project significantly behind schedule and considerably over budget at this time in the project's life.

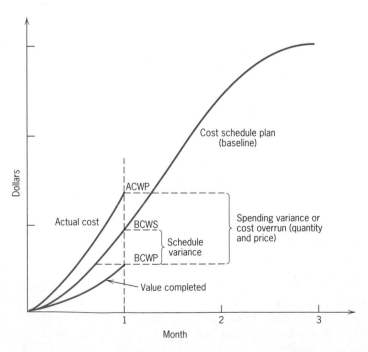

Figure 7-5 Earned value chart.

The variances on the earned value chart are calculated based on two simple rules:* (1) A negative variance is "bad" and a positive variance is "good" and, (2) the spending and schedule variances are calculated as the earned value minus some other measure. In particular, the cost or spending variance is the earned value, more formally known as the *budgeted cost of work performed* (BCWP), less the *actual cost of work performed* (ACWP). The schedule variance is the earned value (BCWP) less the *budgeted cost of work scheduled* (BCWS) to have been performed to date as determined from the baseline plan. All measures are made as of the same date. For a variety of examples of different possible scenarios, see Figures 7-6(a), (b), and (c).

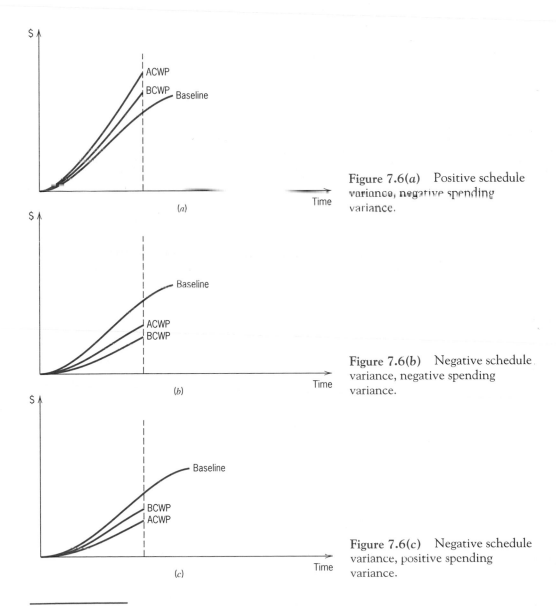

Figure 7.6(a) Positive schedule variance, negative spending variance.

Figure 7.6(b) Negative schedule variance, negative spending variance.

Figure 7.6(c) Negative schedule variance, positive spending variance.

---

*Here we adopt the standard Project Management Institute convention that a negative variance is undesirable. While this convention is most common, it is not universal either in the literature or in practice. For example, MSP does not always follow this convention.

Although the above method of calculating variances is relatively standard, another way of handling the data is more useful for making comparisons at different points in time, or across different projects, or among different project managers. This procedure is simply to take the ratios of the measures rather than their differences. Thus, the spending or cost variance becomes the *Cost Performance Index* (CPI) = BCWP/ACWP, and the schedule variance becomes the *Schedule Performance Index* (SPI) = BCWP/BCWS. Values less than 1.0 are undesirable.

We illustrate the above with a simple example. Suppose that work on a project task was expected to cost $1500 to complete the task and the workers were originally scheduled to have finished today. As of today, however, the workers have actually expended $1350, and our best estimate is that they are about 2/3 finished. Our calculations follow:

$$\text{Cost/spending variance} = \text{BCWP} - \text{ACWP} = 1500(2/3) - 1350 = -350$$
$$\text{Schedule variance} \qquad = \text{BCWP} - \text{BCWS} = 1500(2/3) - 1500 = -500$$
$$\text{CPI} \qquad\qquad = \text{BCWP/ACWP} \quad = 1500(2/3)/1350 \quad = .74$$
$$\text{SPI} \qquad\qquad = \text{BCWP/BCWS} \quad = 1500(2/3)/1500 \quad = .67$$

Thus, we are spending more than the baseline plan indicates and, given what we have spent, we have not made as much progress as we should have.

We can use these calculations to determine some additional items of interest as well, such as the *estimated (remaining cost) to completion* (ETC) and the projected (*total cost) estimated at completion* (EAC) if nothing is done to correct the problem. Given that the *budget at completion* (BAC) is 1500 and the BCWP is 1500(2/3) = 1000,

$$\text{ETC} = (\text{BAC} - \text{BCWP})/\text{CPI} = (1500 - 1000)/.74 = 676$$

Note that this assumes that the work will be completed at the same level of efficiency or inefficiency as conducted thus far. The total cost to complete the task is

$$\text{EAC} = \text{ETC} + \text{ACWP} = 676 + 1350 = 2026$$

That is, the projected additional cost to complete this task is $676 which, when added to the cost accrued to date of $1350 gives a total task cost to completion of $2026 rather than the original estimate of $1500. (See [3 and 7].)

Tables 7-1 and 7-2, illustrate the application of some of these variance calculations for a project to produce a videotape. Tables 7-1 and 7-2 were generated by MSP.

Table 7-1 depicts a status report for the videotape project outlined in Chapter 6. (Figure 6-17 shows the final plan for this project. Shortly after the project started, several small change orders were approved and the reader will note a few minor differences between the activity start/finish times in Figure 6-17 and those in Table 7-1.) Table 7-1 is an overview of the actual information on the project steps compared to the baselines for duration, start dates, finish dates, cost, and hours worked. The project began 3/1/00 and is scheduled to be completed by 5/26/00. The project baseline or budgeted task and cost information is compared to what actually happened.

At any point during the project the action plan can easily be updated. MSP uses earned value analysis as a tool to compare the actual to the baseline action plan. Table 7-1 shows the project updated as of 4/14/00. Task 2.0 has a baseline (budgeted) duration of 14 days. It actually took 22 days to complete. Task 3.3 took only 3 days instead of the baseline of 5 days. Since we hired the secretary earlier, we could start task 3.4 for scheduling the shoots earlier than expected. Because task 2.0 took longer, however, task 4.0 was delayed in starting. (MSP makes these adjustments automatically once actual information is entered.) All other tasks were on schedule. Step 6 is underway and not yet completed. Steps 7 to 9 have not yet begun.

Table 7-1 MSP Project Status Report for Videotape Project, 4/14/00

Project Status as of: 04/14/2000

Producing a Videotape

WBS	Task Name	Act. Start	Baseline Start	Actual Finish	Baseline Finish	Act. Dur.	Baseline Duration	Act. Cost	Baseline Cost	Act. Work	Baseline Work
1	Project approval	03/01/2000	03/01/2000	03/01/2000	03/01/2000	0 days	0 days	$0.00	$0.00	0 hrs	0 hrs
2	Script writing	03/01/2000	03/01/2000	03/23/2000	03/15/2000	22 days	14 days	$4,400.00	$2,800.00	176 hrs	112 hrs
3	Schedule shoots	03/01/2000	03/01/2000	03/20/2000	03/22/2000	13.69 days	15.69 days	$4,680.00	$5,400.00	224 hrs	240 hrs
3.1	Begin scheduling	03/01/2000	03/01/2000	03/01/2000	03/01/2000	0 days	0 days	$0.00	$0.00	0 hrs	0 hrs
3.2	Propose shoots	03/01/2000	03/01/2000	03/07/2000	03/07/2000	6.5 days	6.5 days	$2,800.00	$2,800.00	120 hrs	120 hrs
3.3	Hire secretary	03/01/2000	03/01/2000	03/03/2000	03/07/2300	3 days	5 days	$1,080.00	$1,800.00	.240 hrs	40 hrs
3.4	Schedule shoots	03/06/2000	03/08/2000	03/20/2000	03/22/2000	10 days	10 days	$800.00	$800.00	80 hrs	80 hrs
3.5	Scheduling complete	03/20/2000	03/22/2000	03/20/2000	03/22/2000	0 days	0 days	$0.00	$0.00	0 hrs	0 hrs
4	Script approval	03/23/2000	03/15/2000	03/31/2000	03/31/2000	6.38 days	10 days	$1,800.00	$1,800.00	80 hrs	80 hrs
5	Revise script	03/31/2000	03/31/2000	04/10/2000	04/10/2000	6.63 days	6.63 days	$2,800.00	$2,800.00	80 hrs	80 hrs
6	Shooting	04/10/2000	04/10/2000	NA	04/24/2000	4.5 days	10 days	$1,620.00	$3,600.00	72 hrs	160 hrs
7	Editing	NA	04/24/2000	NA	05/12/2000	0 days	10.5 days	$0.00	$2,520.00	0 hrs	168 hrs
8	Final approval	NA	05/12/2000	NA	05/26/2000	0 days	7.5 days	$0.00	$2,800.00	0 hrs	1600 hrs
9	Deliver video to client	NA	05/26/2000	NA	5/26/2000	0 days	0 days	$0.00	$0.00	0 hrs	0 hrs

Table 7-2 MSP Earned Value Report for Videotape Project, 4/14/00

Project Status as of: 04/14/2000   **Producing a Videotape**
Earned Value Chart

WBS	Task Name	BCWS	BCWP	ACWP	SV	CV	EAC	BAC	VAC
1	Project approval	$0.00	$0.00	$0.00	$0.00	$0.00	$0.00	$0.00	$0.00
2	Script writing	$2,800.00	$2,800.00	$4,400.00	$0.00	($1,600.00)	$4,40.00	$2,800.00	($1,600.00)
3	Schedule shoots	$0.00	$2,800.00	$4,680.00	$2,800.00	($8,80.00)	$4,680.00	$5,400.00	$720.00
3.1	Begin scheduling	$0.00	$0.00	$0.00	$0.00	$0.00	$0.00	$0.00	$0.00
3.2	Propose shoots	$2,800.00	$2,800.00	$2,800.00	$0.00	$0.00	$2,800.00	$2,800.00	$0.00
3.3	Hire secretary	$0.00	$0.00	$1,080.00	$0.00	($1,080.00)	$1,080.00	$1,800.00	$720.00
3.4	Schedule shoots	$0.00	$0.00	$800.00	$0.00	($800.00)	$800.00	$800.00	$0.00
3.5	Scheduling complete	$0.00	$0.00	$0.00	$0.00	$0.00	$0.00	$0.00	$0.00
4	Script approval	$1,800.00	$1,800.00	$1,800.00	$0.00	$0.00	$1,800.00	$1,800.00	$0.00
5	Revise script	$2,800.00	$2,800.00	$2,800.00	$0.00	$0.00	$2,800.00	$2,800.00	$0.00
6	Shooting	$1,620.00	$1,620.00	$1,620.00	$0.00	$0.00	$3,600.00	$3,600.00	$0.00
7	Editing	$0.00	$0.00	$0.00	$0.00	$0.00	$2,520.00	$2,520.00	$0.00
8	Final approval	$0.00	$0.00	$0.00	$0.00	$0.00	$2,800.00	$2,800.00	$0.00
9	Deliver video to client	$0.00	$0.00	$0.00	$0.00	$0.00	$0.00	$0.00	$0.00

Table 7-2 is the earned value table prepared by MSP once the project information is updated. Note that only completed stand-alone tasks or subtasks have final cost variances calculated for them. Summary tasks show the roll-up variances for their subtasks. The columns titled EAC, BAC, and VAC show "estimate at completion," "budget at completion," and "variance at completion," respectively. MSP does not adjust the estimate to complete by the CPI of the project to date as we did above. (In Microsoft Project 2000® the adjustment can be made manually.)

The data in Table 7-2 were not corrected to reflect the PMI Project Management Body of Knowledge (PMBOK) definitions. As noted above, Microsoft Project does not always calculate the variances as recommended by the PMI. The definitions of the calculations used in the earned value analysis in MSP are very similar to those in this book that are, in turn, those recommended by the PMI. Some of the actual calculations performed by the software, however, are not the same as those described in the MSP HELP files. For example, MSP defines the CV as follows:

The difference between how much it should have cost to achieve the current level of completion (BCWP) and how much it has actually cost (ACWP), up to the status date or today's date. If the CV is positive, the cost is currently under the budgeted (or baseline) amount; if the CV is negative, the task is currently over budget. CV = Budgeted Cost of Work Performed − Actual Cost of Work Performed.

This is in agreement with the generally accepted definition.

The VAC is defined as follows by MSP, "*Variance At Completion = Estimated At Completion − Budgeted At Completion.*" As displayed in Table 7-2, the CV is calculated accurately and the VAC is calculated backwards. For the VAC, when MSP shows a negative number it is good, and a positive number is bad. We find this to be confusing. (The HELP files in MSP also differ on these calculations.) In any event, faced with this minor problem in a management report, we suggest the PM should simply alter the signs on VAC to conform with the PMI definition.

Our detailed calculations above were for a particular project task, but the approach can sensibly be extended to an entire project if and only if a reasonable estimate can be made about the percent completion of the project. The conventional 0/100, 50/50, or percent of budget (time) expended are too ham-handed. The calculations made for individual tasks, however, can be aggregated. Taken with the overall CPI and SPI for the project to date, one can estimate the CPI and SPI, and the cost or schedule at completion for the project.

If the earned value calculations indicate a cost or schedule deficiency, the PM must still figure out what to do (control) to get the project back on budget or schedule. Options include borrowing resources from other tasks, holding a brainstorming meeting with the project team, requesting extra resources from senior management, or informing the client and/or senior management of the projected deficiency. Unfortunately, research on 700 projects indicated that the chances of correcting a poorly performing project more than 15–20 percent complete were effectively nil [5].

An interesting exception to this situation is that of ViewStar Corporation, under contract to design an Accounts Receivable imaging system for Texas Instruments. As the project progressed, although costs were under control, earned value progress fell behind. To catch up, ViewStar directed the project team to meet only *key* project requirements at the least cost and time [10]. Earned value thereafter rapidly increased back to the planned schedule.

> Earned value represents a way to capture both in-process performance and cost on a certain date as measured against budget or schedule. Including the planned costs and actual costs allows the calculation of spending and schedule variances, where negative values are undesirable. Using these figures, a projection can be made of costs to completion and total cost for the task or project under consideration. Although percentage completion makes limited sense for individual tasks and work elements, it has little meaning for the project as a whole. Nonetheless, one can aggregate the individual task earned values and variances to make reasonable estimates of project completion costs.

7.4 PROJECT CONTROL

Control, the act of reducing differences between plan and actuality, is the final element in the planning-monitoring-controlling cycle. Monitoring and comparing activities with plan, and reporting these findings is to no avail if actions are not taken when reality deviates significantly from what was planned. This is not to say that the act of noting and reporting discrepancies may not by itself correct the deviations. Simply bringing discrepancies to light may be all that is needed to correct some problems. When it is not, however, active control is needed to bring performance, schedule, cost, or perhaps all three, back in line with plan. Particularly in large projects with a wealth of detail and constant hubbub, it is all too easy to lose sight of these three fundamental targets. Large projects develop their own momentum and tend slowly to move out of hand, going their own way regardless of the wishes of the PM, top management, and even the client. In large projects early control is crucial!

Control is one of the PM's most difficult tasks, invariably involving both mechanistic and human elements. Sometimes humans, through action or inaction, set in motion a chain of events that eventually results in a discrepancy between actuality and plan. Sometimes events occur that affect people in a negative way leading to undesirable discrepancies. Anger, frustration, irritation, helplessness, apathy, despair, and many other emotions arise during the course of a normal project and affect the activities of the project team members who experience them. It is over this welter of confusion, emotion, inertia, fallibility, and general cussedness that the PM tries to intervene and exert control.

Control is difficult for a number of reasons, perhaps the most important of which is that it involves human behavior. The problem that the human element poses for control by the PM is that it invariably involves the project team, a "we" group rather than a "they" group—a group we perceive as our friends. Yet it is difficult to criticize friends, which is exactly what control does. Control means interceding in an activity that someone has been doing and "correcting" it, thereby implying that someone was at fault and doing something wrong.

Another reason that control is difficult is that problems are rarely clear cut, so the need for change and redirection is also fuzzy. In fact, most discrepancies uncovered by a monitoring system turn out to be "messes," in the terminology of Ackoff [1]. As we have said elsewhere, a "mess" is a general condition of a system that, when viewed by a manager, leads to a statement that begins, "%#∧@*&+#!!!" and goes downhill from there. The discovery of a mess leads the PM to suspect that there is a cluster of problems affecting the project; and in situations as complex as a project, identification of the real problems is difficult. Determining what to control raises further difficulties. Indeed, it is rarely clear if someone took an incorrect action, and thus needs to be corrected, or if the discrepancy (mess) was simply the work of an unkind Mother Nature.

Purposes of Control

There are two primary purposes of control: the stewardship of organizational assets and the regulation of results through the alteration of activities. So far in this chapter we have primarily discussed the latter in terms of the plan-monitor-control cycle, and we will spend the majority of the rest of the chapter on this purpose also. Thus, we take a moment to discuss the first purpose, conserving the organization's three primary assets: physical, human, and financial.

Physical asset control is concerned with the maintenance and use of the project's physical assets. This includes the timing as well as quality of maintenance being conducted on the assets. For example, it is important to conduct preventive maintenance prior to that last stage of the project life cycle known as the *Last Minute Panic* (LMP), even though the precise timing of the LMP is usually unknown. And, of course, physical inventory must be received, inspected, certified for payment to suppliers, and perhaps stored prior to use. All project assets, even the project coffeepot, project team's couch, and project library, must be controlled. Most important, however, is the set of physical equipment that was charged to the client that must be delivered to the client at the end of the project.

The stewardship of human resources primarily involves controlling and maintaining the growth and development of the project team. Fortunately, projects provide a particularly fertile environment for cultivating humans, given that each project typically offers a unique professional experience over a short duration. These experiences, more than performance appraisals and reports, foster growth and development of project team members.

Last, financial control involves stewardship of the organization's expenditures on the project, including both conservation of financial resources and regulation of resource use. Most accounting tools used for projects are excellent in this area of control: current asset controls, project budgets, capital investment controls, audits, and even representation on the project team through the project accountant. We cannot overemphasize the importance of proper conformance to both the organization's and the client's financial control and record-keeping standards.

Nevertheless, the PM is invariably more inclined toward the *use* of project assets than to their conservation. Although most PMs view the conservationist mindset as that of the fabled librarian who is happiest when all the library's books have been collected from readers and are neatly sorted in their proper places on the bookshelves, PMs must realize the dual, albeit conflicting, roles they have assumed. These antithetical attitudes must, however, be merged and compromised in the PM as best they can.

An example of the use of extensive controls to help produce a successful project was the Metro Turnback project for San Francisco [16]. This massive, high-risk, 11-year underground construction project was conducted in the high-traffic, downtown region of the city. To keep the project on schedule and within budget, an extensive and complex Management Plan and Control System was devised. To illustrate the depth of this monitoring and control system, its subsystems are listed here: Project Code of Accounts, Cost Code of Accounts, Control Budget, Trend Program, Scope Change Log, Monthly Contract Cash Flow Schedule, Contractual Milestone Summary Schedule, Construction Schedule, Three-Week Rolling Construction Schedule, Quality Control and Quality Assurance Program, Contractor's Nonconformance Report, and Corrective Action Report.

For an example of what happens when control is inadequate, we turn to Cincinnati, Ohio, to quote from *The Cincinnati Enquirer* of January 21, 2000:

> Guesswork, management neglect and possible criminal conduct allowed city engineers to report as completed $15 million in street repairs that were never done, a city audit says.
>
> . . . . In annual reports between 1991 and 1997, the city's Engineering Division reported that a total of 818 lane miles [of street repairs] has been completed at a cost of about $65 million.
>
> The internal audit found that only 460 lane miles have been completed, costing $50.5 million. [*Cincinnati Enquirer*, January 21, 2000, p. 1]

At this writing, the issue is still in a frantic "blame someone else" state (and displays certain aspects of low comedy) with the city's Engineering Division, City Council, and City Manager all involved in the matter. There is little doubt that inadequate and unaudited reporting coupled with incompetent control by managers on several levels over a period of 7 years all contributed to the fiasco.

Project control, the final activity in the planning-monitoring-control cycle, involves taking action when reality deviates from plan. It includes both mechanistic and human elements, and because it is closely concerned with human behavior, is one of the most difficult tasks of the PM. It includes two seemingly antithetical purposes: (1) stewardship of the organization's and the client's, physical, human, and financial assets, and (2) the use of these assets to bring project actuality into conformance with the plan. Somehow, the PM must meld these two purposes into a uniform focus of activity.

7.5 DESIGNING THE CONTROL SYSTEM

When designing the control system, there are certain helpful guidelines to keep in mind. For instance, the primary purpose of the control system is to correct error, not to identify and punish the guilty. Managers must realize that the past cannot be changed, no matter how loudly they yell. Moreover, investment in control is subject to sharply diminishing returns. The cost of control increases faster and faster while the degree of control—and its value—increases more and more slowly.

We could, if we wished, control the quality of "hardware store" type wooden yardsticks, so that they were accurate to 1/10,000th of an inch. But who cares? Moreover, who would be willing to invest the increased cost in a product that is usually given away as a gift? Thus, there is some optimum amount of resources worth investing in the control process. The control system should exert control only to the degree required to achieve its objectives; additional control will not help and may be cost-inefficient.

In the same vein, as the degree of control increases beyond some difficult-to-define point, innovation and creativity are discouraged until they are finally shut off completely. In general, the control system should employ the lowest degree of hassle consistent with accomplishing its goals. It is best to avoid annoying those people whose cooperation is needed to reach project goals. To summarize, the control system should be cost-effective and should operate with the minimum force required to achieve the desired end results.

There are three primary mechanisms by which the PM exerts control: *process reviews, personnel assignment,* and *resource allocation.* The process review is directed to an analysis of the process of reaching the project objectives rather than on the results, per se. Because results are largely dependent on the process used to achieve them, the process can be subjected to control even if the results cannot. On R&D projects, for example, project team members usually cannot be held responsible for research or technological outcomes, but they can certainly be held responsible for adherence to the proposal, the budget, and the schedule. Care must be taken, however, not to overstress method as opposed to results; although methods are controllable, it is still the results that count.

As an example of the effective use of process controls, Australia's 7-year Parliament House construction project matched the inherent construction complexity with an equally sophisticated set of schedule, cost, and time controls. The time controls, for instance, included four levels of increasing detail that could be accessed during progress review and coordination meetings [12].

Control can also be exercised through personnel assignments based on past project productivity. Although it is relatively easy to separate workers in the top and bottom quartiles by measuring performance or productivity, separating the middle two quartiles is much more difficult so this approach should be used carefully. Moreover, reassignment can have drawbacks in terms of creating elite groups of top producers but demotivating everyone else on the team.

Controlling resource allocation can be a powerful motivator—and demotivator. Resources are usually allocated to the more productive or important tasks and this can significantly influence the attainment of project results. (Remember that all tasks in a project must be completed to complete the project.) As in the use of other control techniques, the PM needs to exercise care when making decisions about which tasks need the resources in the future, regardless of past efficiencies.

There are some common mistakes PMs and other organizational managers make when trying to control projects. For example, when controlling processes, there is the danger of emphasizing short-run results at the expense of long-run objectives. Excessive control directed to specific objectives can result in sacrificing other project objectives. Across-the-board cuts in resource allocations tend to reward those who have already overspent or overhired while penalizing the frugal and efficient. Finally, focusing on certain items for control can distract the attention of team members from other, equally important items: "What isn't counted, doesn't count." There is hardly a community in the United States that has not adopted a set of standardized tests to measure the learning of school children. The salaries of teachers are affected by these test results. It should, therefore, hardly come as a shock to the public that teachers spend considerable time and effort "teaching to the test."

Types of Control Systems

The process of controlling a project, or any other system, is more complex than might be expected. Decisions must be made concerning where in the project we will try to exert control, what is to be controlled, how it will be measured, and how much deviation from plan will be tolerated before we intercede. It is helpful in making these decisions first to understand thoroughly the primary types of control systems used by project managers: *go/no-go controls* and *post-control.*

Before discussing the nature and use of these control systems, it is important to note that every control system must contain certain elements if it is to be useful. Any project (or production system) can be described in terms of its inputs, the process by which it works on the inputs, and the outputs that result. To control a project (or any production system) requires the following components:

1. Each control must have a *sensor*, the duty of which is to measure any aspect of the project's output that one wishes to control. For instance, it must be able to measure the length of the yardstick we mentioned earlier.

2. The control system must have a *standard* for each thing measured. For the yardstick, the standard is 36 inches.

3. Next, the control system needs a *comparator*, a mechanism that compares the output of the sensor with the standard.

4. Given the results of the comparison, the control system needs a *decision maker* to decide if the difference between what the sensor measured and the standard is large enough to warrant attention. For the yardstick, a group of 23 engineers attending a project management seminar did not expect (or require) accuracy greater than plus or minus $\frac{1}{4}$ inch. For more precise measurement they would insist on a steel tape measure.

5. The final piece required in a control system is an *effector*. If the decision maker decides that some action is required to reduce the difference between what the sensor measures and the standard requires, the effector must take some action. It may operate on the input or the process (or both), to fix the problem.

Some control systems use all five of these elements automatically, for example, the mechanisms that control the ph (level of acidity) of the blood, the temperature of a home, the speed of an automobile operating on cruise control, or the speed with which a sheet of steel moves through a rolling mill. Such systems are called "cybernetic control systems" (kybernet is Greek for helmsman or steersman) or "negative feedback loops" or "steering controls." All of the parts listed above must be present and operative to control any process. It is the PM's responsibility to ensure that such control elements are available and operating in project control. The process will not be automatic during project control. It must be operated by the PM or the PM's deputy.

The go/no-go control takes the form of tests (sensors) to determine if some specific precondition (standard and comparator) has been met before permission is granted to continue (decision maker and effector). This type of control can be used on almost every aspect of a project. The project plan, budget, schedule, earned value charts, and other such information can all operate as control documents so the PM has prespecified milestones (standards) as control checkpoints. The PM can intercede at any level of the project tasks and subtasks for which detail is available in these control documents.

It is worth repeating that the primary aim of the PM is to intercept problems before they arise—at least before they get serious—so it is worthwhile for the PM to include an early warning system with the control system. In this way, potential problems can be exposed and dealt with before they turn into full-blown disasters. Because any project early warning system will include people, it is important for the PM to make it known that the messenger who brings bad news will not be shot, but anyone who sweeps bad news or problems under the rug will be!

An example of a status report used by the agricultural products division of a large chemical company for go/no-go control is illustrated in Figure 7-7. As can be seen, some of the tasks are completed, some are in progress, and some have not yet started. Details from the PM or additional reports about those tasks completed and in progress are used to make the go/no-go decisions.

Post-controls, also known as postperformance reviews, are applied after the project has been completed. Although it might appear that this is the legendary situation of

Task	Project #1	Project #2	Project #3
Priorities set	C	C	C
PM selected	C	C	C
Key members briefed on RFP	C	C	C
Proposal sent	C	C	C
Proposal accepted as negotiated	C	C	C
Preliminary design developed	C	W/10	C
Design accepted	C	W/12	C
Software developed	C	NS/NR	N/A
Product test design	C	W/30	W/15
Manufacturing scheduled	C	NS/NR	W/8
Tools, jigs, fixtures designed	W/1	NS/NR	W/2
Tools, jigs, fixtures delivered	W/2	NS/NR	W/8
Production complete	NS/HR	NS/HR	NS/HR
Product test complete	NS/HR	NS/HR	NS/HR
Marketing sign-off on product	NS/HR	NS/HR	NS/HR

Notes:

N/A—Not applicable
C—Completed
W—Work in progress (number refers to month required)
NS—Not started
NR—Need resources
HR—Have resources

Figure 7-7 Sample project milestone status report.

locking the barn door after the horse has been stolen, it is not. The purpose here is not to control the already completed project, but to allow future projects to learn and profit from past project experience. Such lessons might include information about certain suppliers, cost-estimating procedures, or even ways of improving the process of managing projects. Certain managerial methods, organizational procedures, or processes might be altered for future projects, resulting in greater predictability and control and, one hopes, better performance, cost, or schedule results.

The earlier the PM can intercede in a problem, the more likely the project team will be able to correct its activities, but humans respond to these controls in different ways. Response to go/no-go controls tends to be neutral. Because there is no gradation between excellent and barely acceptable, or between terrible and just unacceptable, the fine line of acceptability thus becomes a very sharp knife, subject to complaint and irritation. In a project, however, any criticism tends to be leveled toward the team instead of the individual so the response is often less severe than it might have been otherwise.

Tools for Control

We have already described some of the tools that can help the PM in designing and applying the control system: variance analysis, trend projections, and earned value analysis. With trend projection, for instance, the PM can plot a budget, plan, or growth curve as shown in Figure 7-8 and then, as actual values come in with project progress, plot these as a dashed line on the same chart. Using the dashed line, the PM can forecast on a continuing basis what the projected completion will be. Based on the projection, the PM can decide if there is a problem, what alternatives exist for control, what they will cost and require, and what they will achieve.

Another useful tool for a PM is the *critical ratio*. A critical ratio indicates to a manager when a task or process is becoming unacceptable, typically when the ratio drops below 1. By tracking the ratio, the manager can anticipate when a problem may be brewing. The calculation of the critical ratio for project tasks is the product of a *schedule*

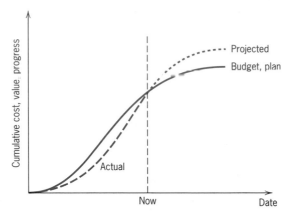

Figure 7-8 Trend projection.

ratio and a *cost ratio*. The schedule ratio is actual progress divided by scheduled progress, as measured by some common standard such as earned value: BCWP/BCWS. Clearly, ratios greater than one are desirable. The cost ratio is budgeted cost divided by actual cost, or in earned value nomenclature, BCWP/ACWP. Again, values greater than one are most desirable. Taking the product of these two ratios thus gives us an overall measure that includes performance, cost, and schedule.

$$CR = (\text{actual progress/scheduled progress}) \times (\text{budgeted cost/actual cost})$$

Note that the two ratios are equally important in the calculation of the critical ratio. If one ratio is bad, it can be offset by the other ratio if it is equally good. For example, if the actual progress is 2 and the scheduled progress is 3, resulting in a schedule ratio of 2/3, and the budgeted cost is 6 and the actual cost is 4, resulting in a cost ratio of 3/2, their product, $2/3 \times 3/2 = 1$. Thus, although the project is behind schedule, the cost is correspondingly below budget so everything is fine if lateness is no problem for this activity. This may not really be acceptable to the PM so a wise PM will evaluate the components of a critical ratio as well as the overall value. Remember that the measurement of progress is subject to the same warnings we noted in the discussion of earned value.

Similar calculations are given in Table 7-3 where the above example is an illustration of Task Number 1. Task 2 is on budget but progress is lacking so too much money was spent than should have been spent; when the project is completed, it will probably go over budget. Similarly, Task 3 is on schedule but is over budget, creating another probable cost overrun. The critical ratios for Tasks 4 and 5 both exceed 1.0, and none of the subratios is a problem. Task 4 is ahead of schedule and on budget, and Task 5 is on schedule and below budget. The PM may want to look further into these happy events to see what is going on, or if the monitoring system is reporting accurately.

Table 7-3 (actual progress/scheduled progress) × (budgeted cost/actual cost)

Task Number	Actual Progess		Scheduled Progress		Budgeted Cost		Actual Cost		Critical Ratio
1	(2	/	3)	×	(6	/	4)	=	1.0
2	(2	/	3)	×	(6	/	6)	=	.67
3	(3	/	3)	×	(4	/	6)	=	.67
4	(3	/	2)	×	(6	/	6)	=	1.5
5	(3	/	3)	×	(6	/	4)	=	1.5

Table 7-4 Monitoring the Critical Ratio

Day	Actual Project Progess		Scheduled Project Progress		Budgeted Project Cost		Actual Project Cost		Critical Ratio
July 17	(13	/	14)	×	(28	/	26)	=	1.00
18	(18	/	17)	×	(34	/	26)	=	1.15
⋮		⋮			⋮		⋮		

Beyond evaluating each of the activities of a project, a critical ratio for the project as a whole can be calculated as well, as illustrated in Table 7-4. Here, the project is assumed to consist of the five tasks in Table 7-3 and the values of each element of the critical ratio are summed on a daily basis with the critical ratio calculated for each day. This ratio can then be itself tracked in a table (see Table 7-4 where the first day is from Table 7-3) and plotted on a *control chart*. The PM can also set some "control limits" for the critical ratio so that if they are exceeded on the upside or downside, an investigation is in order, as shown in Figure 7-9. Different tasks, of course, may warrant different control limits. Further, the upside limits may be different, probably larger, than the downside (problem) limits.

Dealing with such differences is the purpose of another tool, the *control chart*. Any measure—the volume of raw material being used, the cost of contract labor in the project, the hours of computer time—can be plotted and tracked on a control chart such as that shown in Figure 7-10. As illustrated, control limits for intervention can be set by the PM and shown on the chart so that when a measure exceeds one of these limits, action is instigated.

Another recent development, *benchmarking*, can be a useful tool for a PM when designing a monitoring and control system [4, 8, 9, 14, 15]. The process here is to make

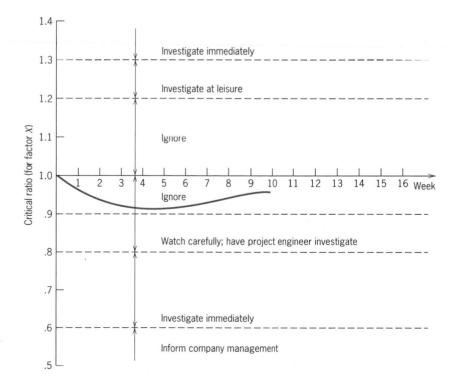

Figure 7-9 Critical ratios with control limits.

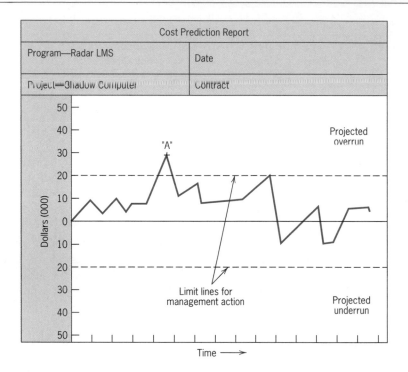

Figure 7-10 Cost control chart.

comparisons to "best in class" practices across organizations, or divisions, or even departments within an organization. An example is a recent benchmarking study [9] to generate data for a Project Management Maturity Model. The model measures project processes, tools, techniques, and practices across a range of industries, the various life-cycle phases, and the eight knowledge areas of *PMBOK*.

An example of an internal benchmarking study was Johnson Control's benchmarking the project management procedures of their own highly successful product development project managers, to be used by less successful project managers. They identified four common sets of procedures these successful PMs all used. These procedures are now used to train new employees, standardize practices, create a common language, tie together company functions, and create a positive project management culture [13].

> Designing the project control system entails many issues but the major guiding objective should be to create a balanced system where the benefits obtained exceed the cost of control. The primary means to active control by the PM are process reviews, personnel reassignment, and resource allocation. Two types of control systems are useful for projects: go/no-go and post-controls. Tools to aid the PM in control are variance analysis, trend projections, earned value analysis, critical ratios, control charts, and benchmarking.

7.6 SCOPE CREEP AND CHANGE CONTROL

If midcourse changes in the project specifications are not controlled, the following are typical results: a newspaper front-page headline reading "**Stadium costs soaring;**" an article on a inner page stating that "Change orders . . . are one of the most common sources of waste and fraud during projects, experts say;" and a quote from a County Commissioner, "The project is in trouble, but it's absolutely recoverable. . . . We can work out responsibility for those payments at a later time. Now is not the time to start pointing fingers." An auditor appointed to look into the matter "found that there is not sufficient oversight to properly monitor the change orders, check if they were necessary and determine who is responsible" (see *Cincinnati Enquirer*, February 15, 2000, pages A-1 and A-4).

Input from over 500 project managers regarding the most important single problem facing the PM indicates that coping with changes is at the top of their list. The most common source of changes is the natural tendency of the client, as well as the project team members, to try to improve the project's output as the project progresses—a phenomenon so frequently encountered a name for it has been coined, "scope creep." The most common result of scope creep is an upset client who was not (or claims not to have been) told how long the change would delay the project and how much it would raise the project's cost.

New technologies and materials become available, new requirements and needs become apparent, and these lead to changed projects. The later these changes are made in the project, the more difficult and costly they become. The one absolutely certain thing about a project—even though virtually nothing in a project is ever certain—is that there will definitely be concerted attempts to change it. PMs must expect these attempts and be prepared to deal with them. Fighting change is not appropriate. The best approach is for the PM to set up a well-controlled, formal process whereby such changes can be introduced and accomplished with as little distress as possible.

This process is known as the *change control system*. The purpose of this system is to:

- review all requested changes (either content or procedural changes)
- identify all impacts the change may have on other project tasks
- translate these impacts into alterations of project performance, schedule, and cost
- evaluate the benefits and disadvantages of the requested changes
- identify and evaluate alternative changes that might accomplish the same ends with greater benefits and/or fewer disadvantages
- install a process so that individuals with appropriate authority may accept or reject the proposed changes
- communicate accepted changes to all concerned parties
- ensure that the changes are implemented properly
- prepare reports that summarize all changes to date and their impacts

Avoiding scope creep is not possible. Controlling it, and thereby reducing some of the pain, is possible—if the PM follows a few rules.

1. Every project contract must include a *change control system* by which requests for changes in the project's plan, processes, budget, schedule, or deliverables are evaluated.

2. Every project change must be introduced by a *change order* that includes a description of the agreed-upon change together with any resulting changes in the plan, processes, budget, schedule, or deliverables.

3. Changes must be approved in writing by the client's agent as well as by a representative of senior management of the firm conducting the project.

4. The project manager must be consulted on all proposed changes prior to the preparation and approval of the change order. (The PM's approval is not required.)

5. Once the change order has been approved, the project master plan must be amended to reflect the change and the change order becomes a part of that plan.

The process of controlling change is not complicated. For large projects, a change control board consisting of all interested parties is recommended for handling change requests. For smaller projects, a smaller group may be designated. The main source of trouble with requested changes is typically that the PM, in an attempt to avoid bureaucracy, adopts an informal process of handling requests for change. Such a process leads to misunderstanding on the part of the party requesting the change and before the PM can undo the damage, the organization is committed to extending the scope of the project but without the additional resources and time to do it.

> Scope creep arises quite naturally from both the client as well as the project team as new capabilities and needs surface during the course of the project. Rather than trying to handle change requests on an informal basis, the PM must anticipate that they will inevitably arise and institute a formal *change control system* to handle them. The purpose of the system is to evaluate each change formally to determine its benefits as well as its costs and other impacts on the project, and to make arrangements for obtaining the resources and altering the project specifications as needed to implement the change, if it is eventually approved.

REVIEW QUESTIONS

1. Why can't the PM use the organization's current information system for project monitoring and reporting?

2. What does it mean to say that project monitoring and control are on the opposite sides of project selection and planning?

3. The monitoring system is the direct connection between project planning and control. Why is this true?

4. Why is it probably a good idea to avoid periodic reports, except in specific cases such as reports tied to the organization's account system?

5. Aside from the obvious benefits for project control, what other benefits might result from a good project reporting system?

6. If the calendar should not dictate reporting frequency, what should?

7. Using earned value analysis, explain how the total cost of a partially completed project can be estimated.

DISCUSSION QUESTIONS

8. When making an estimate for the time and cost to execute a project, should the time and cost required to develop the planning, monitoring, and controlling systems be included as well? Should the actions required to monitor and control a project be included in the project's action plan or WBS?

9. The chapter included an example of a firm where the PM dispensed with all the planning formality because no one ever looked at it anyway. What did the PM think the purpose of such planning was in this firm? What should the firm do in the future to correct this problem?

10. In fields such as psychology and sociology, verbal characterizations are frequently used to show the amount of some factor. How might one set up such a measure for a project management characteristic such as the "energy" of the project team?

11. How might one measure team morale?

12. How can the PM circumvent the problem that the monitoring system can only report on activities that have passed, thus telling the PM what has already gone wrong but not what will go wrong in the future?

13. How might using electronic media to report project information lead to problems with control?

14. Explain how the earned value chart captures all three objectives of a project: performance, cost, and schedule.

15. Why isn't there an earned value reporting convention that allows progress on a task to be credited when the task is half completed? Wouldn't this be more accurate than giving credit only when the task is finally completed?

16. When would spending and schedule variances be more informative than ratios? When would ratios be better?

17. How should a PM reconcile the dual purposes of control: conserving resources and regulating results through the use of resources?

18. Identify situations where each of the following control tools might be useful: earned value charts, benchmarking, critical ratios, control charts, variance analysis, trend projections.

19. How might the existence of a change control system affect the behavior of a client, or a project team member, who desires to make a change in the project?

20. "In order to manage for overall project success, control must be exercised at the detailed work level for each aspect of project performance or no significant change

will occur." Does this mean that the PM should micromanage the project? If not, what does it mean?

21. Select a hypothetical project (e.g., designing and building a Web site, installing a new machine in an assembly line, or conducting a major inspection and repair of a passenger aircraft), and briefly describe an example of how each of the following types of control data might be used for project control:

   (a) Frequency counts
   (b) Raw numbers
   (c) Subjective numeric ratings
   (d) Indicator and surrogate measures

22. Of all the rules for conducting meetings, the most difficult to enforce is the injunction against the weekly (or daily) standard project progress report (the "show and tell" meeting). Why is this, and under what circumstances do you think that such meetings are justified?

23. If your project management software calculates earned value, or any other standard item to be reported, differently than the Project Management Institute suggests, should you deal with this matter in management reports? If so, how?

PROBLEMS

24. A project in its 26th week has an actual cost of $270,000. It was scheduled to have spent $261,000. For the work performed to date, the budgeted value is $272,000. What are the cost and schedule variances for the project? What are the SPI and CPI?

25. A project has just completed the 87th item in its action plan. It was scheduled to have spent $168,000 at this point in the plan, but has actually spent only $156,000. The foreman estimates that the value of the work actually finished is about $162,000. What are the spending and schedule variances for the project? What are the SPI and CPI?

26. The following project is at the end of its sixth week. Find the cost and schedule variances. Also find the CPI and SPI. Then find the critical ratio of the pro-

ject using earned value calculations. Finally, calculate the ETC and EAC for the project.

Activity	Predecessors	Duration (wks)	Budget ($)	Actual Cost ($)	% Complete
a	—	2	300	400	100
b	—	3	200	180	100
c	a	2	250	300	100
d	a	5	600	400	20
e	b, c	4	400	200	20

27. Repeat Problem 26 using MSP (omit calculation of CPI and SPI).

INCIDENTS FOR DISCUSSION

St. Margaret's Hospital

Mary Lynn DeCold is the Quality Improvement Director at St. Margaret's Hospital, a large acute care facility. She is responsible for monitoring all of the performance improvement projects that take place in the hospital. At any given time numerous projects can

be underway, some departmental and some enterprise-wide efforts.

The Joint Commission on Accreditation of Healthcare Organizations is scheduled to conduct a survey of St. Margaret's in 9 months. It is a requirement of the accrediting agency that three performance improvement projects be spotlighted during the survey. Mary Lynn wants to be sure that she picks three projects that will be finished within the next month or two so that they have at least 6 months' worth of data to show that the project improved performance.

Mary Lynn is having trouble getting information on the status of the three projects she chose. Communication between the project managers and the Quality Improvement Department is not always timely. She wants to be sure that all three are completed in plenty of time before the survey is scheduled. Mary Lynn also wants to be able to tell where the projects are in relation to each other, as they all need to be completed by a certain date. She wonders how she can tell if they are behind or ahead of schedule.

Question: What would you recommend Mary Lynn do?

Stoneworth Paving Company

Stoneworth Paving Company specializes in highway paving jobs for the State of Virginia. When the state first awarded Stoneworth the contract, they stipulated a 1 percent penalty for each week Stoneworth was late on a completion date. Preston Flintrock, the project coordinator for Stoneworth, began to notice that the last two jobs were three weeks late, and the paving job that was due to be completed in the next two weeks was behind schedule. When Preston went in the field to investigate, he found the job to be understaffed, supplier delays, and a high work rejection rate/repaving needed. As a result, Preston decided to establish a better system of project control and present it to his boss.

Question: If you were Preston, what characteristics would you be looking for in a new control system? Will a new control system be adequate for the problem? Explain.

Carver Insurance Company

Alex Franks joined Carver Insurance Company eight months ago. He is an experienced management information systems executive who has been given the task of improving the responsiveness of Carver's information systems group to the end user. After several months of investigation, Alex felt he understood the current situation clearly enough to proceed. First, approximately 90 percent of end-user requests came to Information Services (IS) in the form of a project, or, more commonly, one step of a project. Accordingly, Alex felt he should initially direct his efforts toward integrating IS's approach to projects with the company's formal project management system.

It has been Alex's experience that most problems associated with IS projects suffer from poor project definition and inadequate participation by the end user during the system design phase. Typically, the end user does not become heavily involved in the project until the new system is ready to install. At that point, a great deal of work is required to adapt the system to meet end-user requirements. Alex decided to institute a procedure that put end-user cooperation and participation on the front end of the project. The idea was to define the objective and design of the system carefully, making it consistent with the end user's need. If that was done, system implementation would be reasonably simple, rather than the always disturbing initial introduction to the end user of "his or her new system."

Alex also recognized that something had to be done to control the programming quality of IS's output. A more effective front-end approach to IS projects would subject IS managers to more intense pressure to produce results within user's needs, including time constraints. Alex was concerned that the quality of the IS output would deteriorate under those conditions, especially given the lack of technical expertise on the part of the end users and outside project managers. To solve this problem, Alex recommended creation of an IS quality assurance (QA) manager who would approve the initial steps of the projects and review each additional step. The QA manager would have the authority to declare any step or portion of the output inadequate and to send it back to be reworked.

Questions: Is this a good control system for IS? Why or why not? Does it represent a good control point for company projects using IS to accomplish one portion of the project objective? What would be your answer if you were a non–IS project manager?

Cable Tech, Inc.

Cable Tech is a contract cable wiring company. It provides support to local cable companies in seven states in the midwest. Cable Tech has one operation in each state, and they vary in size from 60 to 250 employees. A disturbing trend has been developing for the last couple of years that Cable Tech management wishes to stop. Incidences of tardiness and absenteeism are on the increase. Both are extremely disruptive in a contract wiring operation. Cable Tech is non-union in all seven locations, and since management wants to keep this situation, it wants a careful, low-key approach to the problem. Assistant Personnel Manager Jean Alister has been appointed project manager to recommend a solution. All seven operations managers have been assigned to work with her on this problem.

Jean has had no problem interfacing with the operations managers. They quickly agreed that three steps must be taken to solve the problem:

1. Institute a uniform daily attendance report that is summarized weekly and forwarded to the main office. (Current practice varies from location to location,

but comments on attendance are normally included in monthly operations reports.)

2. Institute a uniform disciplinary policy, enforced in a uniform manner.

3. Initiate an intensive employee education program to emphasize the importance of good attendance.

In addition, the team decided that the three-point program should be tested before a final recommendation is presented. They thought it would be best to test the program at one location for two months. Jean wants to control and evaluate the test by having a daily attendance report transmitted to her directly at headquarters, from which she will make the final decision on whether or not to present the program in its current format.

Questions: Does this monitoring and control method seem adequate? What are the potential problems?

C A S E

St. Dismas Assisted Living Facility Case—5

It is now just 4 months until the Assisted Living Facility project is scheduled to be completed. The project team is excited because they can watch the construction of the facility and feel they are moving toward the end of this project.

Every week since construction began, the construction project manager, Kyle Nanno, has been holding a meeting of his project team. At the meetings he invites representatives of the construction company, the facilities manager from St. Dismas, the Director of Security, and other key people as he deems necessary. The meetings are scheduled every Friday at 1:00 PM and last not more than one hour. No matter who is or is not there, Kyle starts the meetings exactly at 1:00 PM. Kyle developed the following standing agenda:

1. Review schedule and budget as of today's date

2. Review schedule and budget for next two weeks

3. Issues impacting schedule or budget

4. Next Steps and Action items to be completed

The construction project update presented at the April 11, 2001 meeting is shown below.

After each meeting the construction project manager emails the minutes of the meeting and the action item list generated to each member of the Construction Project team. He also sends the information to Fred Splient, the president of St. Dismas, as well as to each member of the ALF Project Steering Team.

Following the update is the most recent copy of the action items generated at the 4/11/01 construction project meeting.

Upon reading the minutes and action items from the week's meeting, Fred got quite angry. Fred read the minutes every week and would immediately phone Kyle to ask why certain decisions still had not been made. This week he wanted to know why the location of the security panel had not been picked out yet, and what the hair salon issue was about. Kyle decided that these matters would be better discussed face to face. He went to Fred's office.

Kyle proceeded to explain to Fred that the Director of Security, Frank Geagy had not attended the construction project update meeting in weeks. Kyle said that Frank informed him that in light of the cost cutting going on in the hospital, he is short staffed and cannot hire a new security guard. Frank states that he personally has to cover shifts during the time when the update meetings take place. Kyle told Fred that he was not comfortable making the security panel decision without the head of security's input, and that Frank has not returned his phone calls or answered his emails. Fred Splient proceeded to tell Kyle in a very loud and angry voice, "That guy is not short staffed and is not busy covering anyone's shift. Who does he think he is?" Fred instructed Kyle to tell Frank to answer the contractor's questions immediately or the decisions would be made for him.

Kyle said he would do so and then changed the subject. He told Fred that they were still waiting for the city officials to approve the parking lot construction permit. St. Dismas's legal officer estimated that it would take 8–10 weeks to hear back on approval. Kyle allocated that amount of time in the schedule.

Kyle received notice from Fred to proceed with the parking lot project on January 11, 2001. On February 9, he submitted the application for a permit, complete with appropriate plans and descriptions of the proposed lot, and allocated 10 weeks to wait for the county to notify him. He expected approval on or before April 19 and scheduled construction to begin April 20. Privately, he doubted he would hear from the county by his target date.

The lot would take three weeks to build, two weeks to install the lighting and add landscaping, and one week to pave and stripe. The plot had to be completed by the end of June so that parking spaces would be available when Marketing wanted to begin showing the facility to potential residents. This was a tight schedule, but the market-

Assisted Living Facility
Construction Project Update
As of 4/11/01

ID	Task Name	Baseline Start	Actual Start	Baseline Finish	Actual Finish	Baseline Duration	Actual Duration	Remaining Variance	Dur. Variance	Finish Variance
1	Construction & furnishings	03/01/00	03/01/00	07/30/01	NA	369 days	278.76 days	104.24 days	14 days	14 days
2	Facility construction	03/01/00	03/01/00	06/04/01	NA	329 days	285.12 days	57.88 days	14 days	14 days
3	Phase 1 - Foundation & Excavation	03/01/00	03/01/00	07/11/00	08/01/00	95 days	110 days	0 days	15 days	15 days
4	Phase 2 - Structure	04/19/00	05/24/00	09/22/00	10/09/00	113 days	99 days	0 days	−14 days	11 days
5	Phase 3 - Enclosure	07/12/00	08/01/00	01/15/01	01/15/01	134 days	120 days	0 days	−14 days	0 days
6	Phase 4 - Interiors	07/12/20	08/01/00	06/04/01	NA	234 days	139 days	95 days	0 days	14 days
7	First 45 (light-assisted) units ready to prepare for occupancy	05/01/01	NA	05/01/01	NA	0 days	0 days	0 days	0 days	14 days
8	First 45 units ready for residents	05/01/01	NA	06/25/01	NA	8 wks	0 wks	8 wks	0 wks	14 days
9	Remaining 57 units (light & heavy) ready to prepare for occupancy	06/04/01	NA	06/04/01	NA	0 days	0 days	0 days	0 days	14 days
10	Construction complete	06/04/01	NA	06/04/01	NA	0 days	0 days	0 days	0 days	14 days
11	Building ready for residents	06/05/01	NA	07/30/01	NA	8 wks	0 wks	8 wks	0 wks	14 days

Project Manager: K. Nanno

St. Dismas—Assisted Living Facility
Construction coordination meeting 4/11/01
ACTION ITEM LIST

Item	Date Initiated	Date Required	Date Resolved	Required From	Comments
Provide notice to proceed on parking lots	01/10/2001	ASAP	02/11/2001	St. Dismas	Proposal to St. Dismas 1/18/00
Provide P.S. # for designer to purchase accessories	11/9/2000	12/1/2000	02/8/2001	St. Dismas	
What are the security requirements? There are fire doors, and they do not have locks. We have rough-in for card readers, but no electric hardware.	11/9/2000	12/1/2000		St. Dismas Security	Cost proposal to St. Dismas 1/13/00
Lighting review—will exterior lighting in addition to the building mounted lights be required?	12/14/2000	03/15/2001	03/15/2001	St. Dismas lighting consultant & electrician	
Location of security panel	09/28/2000	ASAP		St. Dismas security	
Room number style and placement	01/18/2000	01/27/2001	02/11/2001	St. Dismas designer	Part of signage discussion
Parking lot permit	02/9/2001	ASAP		Contractor	Permit application 2/9/2001, waiting for City to approve
Fire alarm connection to hospital panel	02/11/2001	ASAP		St. Dismas electrician	Conduit required
Hair salon decision	02/11/2001	ASAP		St. Dismas	
Updated fire alarm drawings	02/7/2001	07/1/01		Contractor & electrician	

ing people insisted that residents had to begin preparing for this kind of move at least a month before they took residence. Potential residents needed to see the facility, get familiar with apartment layouts, and they needed a place to park. Also, Marketing insisted on having some occupancy by the opening date.

Kyle told Fred that Legal was calling the county weekly to follow up. Fred wanted to know why the parking lot construction was not outlined on the action plan for facility construction. Fred asked Kyle to add it to the Gantt chart and to do a what-if analysis on the assumption that the county did not respond until May 1. Fred also wanted to know the latest date that they could be notified and still meet a June 15 deadline for completion of the lot.

As Kyle was leaving Fred's office, Fred asked him about the hair salon. Kyle explained that the COO and VP of Marketing had come up with an idea to build and operate a hair salon in the facility for the residents. They thought this might be a great selling point that could generate revenue. They came to Kyle just 2 months ago and asked him to include a hair salon on the first floor of the facility. Kyle explained that he did not have enough information to be able to determine the impact this would have on the construction schedule or the cost of this addition. Fred listened and then wondered if the members of his team had done any analysis to determine if this was a good idea or not. Fred told Kyle he would get back to him on that one. He then made a phone call to the COO and VP of Marketing.

QUESTIONS

1. What do you think the construction project manager should have done when the Director of Security stopped attending the project meetings?

2. Do you think it is an effective communications tool to send the construction project meeting minutes to the ALF steering team and the President? Support your answer.

3. How much time has to be made up for the original, baseline schedule to be met?

4. Develop an action plan and draw a Gantt chart for the Parking Lot phase of the project as originally planned by Kyle. Answer Fred's questions.

5. What information does Fred need to make a decision about building a hair salon?

C A S E

Palmstar Enterprises, Inc.

Palmstar Enterprises, a leading manufacturer of handheld computers, is currently in the process of developing its next generation device, the model 2000c. A key feature of the 2000c is its color display. According to the original project schedule, the 2000c is to be released 1 month from now. Because the amount of time required to convert the existing software to capitalize on the color display was significantly underestimated, the project has fallen behind schedule. The project manager estimates that without additional resources, the development project will be 3 months late. He has also estimated that in-creasing the project's budget of $3 million by 30 percent would permit the project to be completed on schedule. The added budget would be used primarily to staff the project with additional software engineers.

If released on schedule, first quarter demand for the 2000c is forecast to be 200,000 units at an initial price of $450. Demand data for similar products suggest that unit sales will increase 5 percent per quarter over the product's 3-year life. Despite pricing pressures in the market, accounting data indicate that Palmstar is able to maintain a 20 percent contribution margin to profit and overhead through continuous process improvements and efficiencies accruing from producing in larger volumes.

QUESTIONS:

1. What has a larger impact on Palmstar's profits, delaying the 2000c's introduction by 3 months or increasing the project's budget by 30 percent?

2. Are there other factors you would consider in addition to profit?

3. What should Palmstar do? Why?

4. How generalizable do you think the results of your analysis in this particular case are to other situations?

BIBLIOGRAPHY

1. ACKOFF, R. L. "Beyond Problem Solving." *Decision Sciences*, April 1974. (This is a delightful after-lunch speech to a mixed business/academic audience. In this speech Ackoff draws a useful distinction between detecting and describing a "mess" (the task of business), and translating the mess into a set of "structured problems" (the task of the analyst-academic).

2. ADAMS, J. R., and L. L. ADAMS. "The Virtual Project: Managing Tomorrow's Team Today." *PM Network*, January 1997. (An excellent brief discussion that covers the nature of virtual projects and some of the communication methods allowing their proliferation.)

3. BARR, Z. "Earned Value Analysis: A Case Study." *PM Network*, December 1996.

4. BYRNE, J. "Project Management: How Much is Enough? *PM Network*, February 1999.

5. CHRISTENSEN, D. S. "A Review of Cost/Schedule Control Systems Criterion Literature." *Project Man-*

agement Journal, September 1994. (This study of military projects notes that after a project is 15–20 percent complete, its total CPI changes by less than 10 percent and overruns worsen. This article is briefly noted in [7].)

6. DEAN, B. V. *Evaluating, Selecting, and Controlling R&D Projects*. New York: American Management Association Research Study 89, 1968. (A classic work in the field that proposed that the criteria employed to select projects be the criteria used to evaluate those same projects.)

7. FLEMMING, Q. W., and J. M. KOPPLEMAN. "Forecasting the Final Cost and Schedule Results." *PM Network*, January 1996. (This is one of five excellent, instructional articles on earned value by these authors. They appeared in *PM Network* between January 1994 and May 1996.)

8. GUPTA, V. K., and D. J. GRAHAM. "A Customer Driven Quality Improvement and Management Project at Diamond Offshore Drilling." *Project Management Journal*, September 1997.

9. IBBS, C. W., and Y.-H. KWAK. "Benchmarking Project Management Organizations." *PM Network*, February 1998. (This article discusses the development of a tool for finding and assessing the "best" managerial tools for project management.)

10. INGRAM, T. "Client/Server, Imaging and Earned Value: A Success Story." *PM Network*, December 1995.

11. MEREDITH, J. R., and S. M. SHAFER. *Operations Management for MBAs*. New York: John Wiley, 1999.

12. NIXON, T. R. "Project Management at the New Parliament House, Canberra." *Project Management Journal*, September 1987.

13. REITH, W. D., and D. B. KANDT. "Project Management at a Major Automotive Seating Supplier." *Project Management Journal*, September 1991.

14. THAMHAIN, H. J. "Best Practices for Controlling Technology-Based Projects." *Project Management Journal*, December 1996. (A fine analytical study of finding and assessing the "best practices" for controlling high technology projects. It not only finds the "best" control practices, but also generates a "benchmark" to which any firm can compare its practices.)

15. TONEY, F. "What the Fortune 500 Know about PM Best Practices." *PM Network*, February 1997.

16. WU, C., and G. HARWELL. "The MUNI Metro Turnback Project." *PM Network*, May 1998.

8

Evaluating and Terminating the Project

We now come to the final stage in any project—evaluating the result and shutting down the project. As we will see, there are many ways to do both, some relatively formal, some quick and dirty, and some rather casual. We discuss evaluation first, in the generic sense, and then discuss a very specific and often formal type of evaluation known as the project audit. Following this we discuss termination of the project.

8.1 EVALUATION

The term "evaluate" means to set the value of or appraise. A *project evaluation* appraises the progress and performance relative to the project's initial or revised plan. The evaluation also appraises the project against the goals and objectives set for it during the selection process—amended, of course, by any changes in the goals and objectives made during the project's life. In addition, evaluations are sometimes made relative to other similar projects.

The project evaluation, however, should not be limited simply to an after-the-fact analysis. Rather, it is useful to conduct an evaluation at a number of crucial points during the project life cycle. Because the primary purpose of a project evaluation is to give feedback to senior management for decision and control purposes, it is important for the evaluation to have credibility in the eyes of both senior management and the project team. The control purpose of evaluation is meant to improve the process of carrying out projects. The decision purpose is intended to improve the selection process. Thus an evaluation should be as carefully planned and executed as the project itself.

The use of postproject evaluation to help the organization improve its project-management skills on future projects means that considerable attention must be given to managing the process of project management. This is best accomplished and most effective if there is already a project-management guide or manual detailing standardized project-management practices for the organization. Such manuals commonly cover best practices for planning, monitoring, and controlling projects and may include advice on both selecting and terminating projects. An example of such a manual was that developed by Johnson Controls, described in Chapter 7, where internal benchmarking of their most successful project managers identified four sets of detailed project management procedures. These procedures are updated with each new project experience so that the learning that has occurred is captured and made available for future projects.

Evaluation Criteria

There are many different measures that may be applied in a project evaluation. As indicated, senior management may have particular areas they want evaluated for future planning and decisions, and these should be indicated in the charge to the evaluation committee. Beyond that, the original criteria for selecting and funding the project should be considered—for example, profitability, acquiring new competencies for the organization, or getting a foothold in a new market segment. Any special reasons for selection should also play a role. Was this project someone's sacred cow? Did a scoring model identify particularly important quantitative or qualitative reasons to select this project? Was the project a competitive necessity? How the project is progressing on such criteria should be an important part of the evaluation as well.

Certainly, one of the major evaluation criteria would be the project's apparent "success" to date. One study [7] identified four important dimensions of project success. The first dimension is simply the project's *efficiency* in meeting the budget and schedule. Of course, efficiency does not necessarily translate into performance, or effectiveness, so the second (and most complex) dimension is *customer impact/satisfaction*. This dimension includes not only meeting the formal technical and operational specifications of the project but also the less tangible aspects of fulfilling the customer's needs, whether the customer actually uses the project results—that perennial challenge of customer "satisfaction."

The third dimension is *business/direct success* meaning, for external projects, factors such as the level of commercial success and market share and for internal projects, the achievement of the project's goals such as improved yields or reduced throughput time. The final dimension, more difficult to assess, is *future potential* which includes establishing a presence in a new market, developing a new technology, and such.

Two other criteria should also be considered: the project's contribution to the organization's goals, including the unstated objectives of the organization, and the project's contributions to the objectives of project team members. To recognize the project's contributions, all facets of the project must be considered to identify and understand the project's strengths and weaknesses. The evaluation report should include the findings regarding these two criteria, as well as some recommendations concerning the items in Table 8-1.

Table 8-1   Items to Consider for Project Evaluation Report Recommendations

- Communication with the client and senior management
- Locating opportunities for technological advances
- Reduction of indirect costs and direct costs
- Improving the project-management process
- Identification of risks in the organization's use of projects
- Utilization of the skills resulting from project members' work on projects
- Employment of general management experience gained by project managers
- Improving the organization's use of projects
- Increasing the speed of obtaining results in projects

Measurement

Measuring the project's performance against a planned budget and schedule is relatively straightforward, and it is not too difficult to determine if individual milestones have been reached. As we have noted several times, there are complications regarding measurement of actual expenditures and earned values, as well as with reporting on difficult technical issues that may have been deferred while progress was being made along other fronts.

If the project selection process focuses on profits, the evaluation usually includes determination of profits and costs and often assigns these among the several groups working on the project. Conflict typically results. Each group wants credit for revenues. Each group wants costs assigned elsewhere. Although there are no "theoretically correct" solutions to this problem, there are politically acceptable solutions. As with budget and schedule, these are most easily addressed if they have been anticipated and decided when the project was initiated rather than at the end. If allocations are made by a predetermined formula, major conflicts tend to be avoided—or at least lessened.

When a multivariate model (e.g., a scoring model, such as Table C in the scoring model example in Chapter 1) has been used for project selection, measurements may raise more difficult problems. Some measures may be objective and easily measured. Others, however, are typically subjective and may require careful, standardized measurement techniques to attain reliable and valid evaluation results. Interview and questionnaire methods for gathering data must be carefully constructed and executed if their results are to be taken seriously.

> A project evaluation is an appraisal for use by top management. Its criteria should include the needs of management; the organization's stated and unstated goals; the original selection basis for the project; and its success to date in terms of its efficiency, customer impact/satisfaction, business success, and future potential. Measuring the project's success on budget, schedule, and performance is easier than measuring revenues or qualitative, subjective factors. Establishing the measures at project formation is helpful, as well as using carefully standardized measurement techniques for the subjective factors.

8.2 PROJECT AUDITING

A very special type of evaluation is the formal audit. The project audit is a thorough examination of the management of a project, its methodology and procedures, its records, properties, budgets, expenditures, progress, and so on. The project audit is not a financial audit but is far broader in scope and may deal with the whole or any part of the project. For a comparison of the two, refer to Table 8-2. It can also be very flexible, and can focus on any issues of interest to senior management. The project audit is also broader than the traditional management audit that focuses its attention on the organization's management systems and operation. Next we discuss the audit process itself and its result, the audit report.

The Audit Process

The timing of the audit depends on the purpose of the audit, as shown in Table 8-3. Because early problem identification leads to easier solutions, it is often helpful to have an

Table 8-2   Comparison of Financial Audits with Project Audits

	Financial Audits	Project Audits
Status	Confirms status of business in relation to accepted standard	Must create basis for, and confirm, status on each project
Predictions	Company's state of economic well-being	Future status of project
Measurement	Mostly in financial terms	Financial terms plus schedule, progress, resource usage, status of ancillary goals
Record-keeping system	Format dictated by legal regulations and professional standards	No standard system, uses any system desired by individual organization or dictated by contract
Existence of information system	Minimal records needed to start audit	No records exist, data bank must be designed and used to start audit
Recommendations	Usually few or none, often restricted to management of accounting system	Often required, and may cover any aspect of the project or its management
Qualifications	Customary to qualify statements if conditions dictate, but strong managerial pressure not to do so	Qualifications focus on shortcomings of audit process (e.g., lack of technical expertise, lack of funds or time)

audit early in the project's life. Such audits are usually focused on technical issues. Later audits tend to focus more on budget and schedule because most of the technical issues are resolved by this time. Thus, these later audits are typically of less value to the project team and of more interest to general management. An obvious case here is the *post-project audit*, often contractually required by the customer as well as a common ingredient in the Final Project Report.

While audits can be performed at any level of depth, three levels are common. The first is the *general audit*, usually constrained by time and cost and limited to a brief investigation of project essentials. The second is the *detailed audit*, often initiated if the general audit finds something that needs further investigation. The third is the *technical audit*, usually performed by a person or team with special technical skills.

Table 8-3   Timing and Value of Project Audits

Project State	Value
Initiation	Very useful, significant value of audit takes place early—prior to 25 percent completion of initial planning stage
Feasibility study	Very useful, particularly the technical audit
Preliminary plan/ schedule budget	Very useful, particularly for setting measurement standards to ensure conformance with standards
Master schedule	Less useful, plan frozen, flexibility of team limited
Evaluation of data by project team	Marginally useful, team defensive about findings
Implementation	More or less useful depending on importance of project methodology to successful implementation
Postproject	More or less useful depending on applicability of findings to future projects

Typical steps in a project audit are:

1. Familiarize the audit team with the requirements of the project, including its basis for selection and any special charges by upper management
2. Audit the project on-site
3. Write up the audit report in the required format (discussed in the next subsection)
4. Distribute the report

Collecting the necessary data can be expedited by developing forms and procedures ahead of time such as that shown in Figure 8-1. To be effective, the audit team must have free access to all information relevant to the project. Most of the information will come from the project team's records or from various departments such as accounting, human resources, and purchasing. Other valuable information will come from documents that predate the project such as the *Request for Proposal* (RFP), minutes of the project selection committee, and minutes of senior management committees that initiated the project.

DATA COLLECTION FORM

Date: _____   *Auditor:* _____

MANAGERIAL DATA:

Project: _____

Project manager: _____

Start date: _____

Due date: _____

-
-
-

FINANCIAL DATA:

Allocated budget, $: _____

Spent to date, $: _____

-
-
-

TECHNICAL DATA:

% User involvement in design: _____

User training, hours:
    -Planned: _____
    -Completed to date: _____

Software complexity:
    -Lines of code: _____
    -# Modules: _____

Organizational complexity:
    -# Departments involved: _____

-
-
-

Figure 8-1 Form to audit a software installation project.

Special attention needs to be given to the behavioral aspects of the audit. While the audit team must have free access to anyone with knowledge of the project, except the customer, the audit team's primary source of information should be the project team—but project team members rarely trust auditors. Even if the auditor is a member of the project team, his or her motives will be distrusted and thus the information needed by the auditor will be difficult to obtain. Worry about the outcome of the audit produces self-protective activity, which also distracts the project team from activity devoted to the project. Audits are always distracting and uncomfortable to those being audited, much like having a police car in one's rear view mirror while trying to drive.

Trust-building is a slow and delicate process that can be easily stymied. The audit team needs to understand the politics of the project team, the interpersonal relationships of the team members, and must deal with this confidential knowledge respectfully. Regardless, the audit team will undoubtedly encounter political opposition during its work, either to rebuff the team's investigation or to co-opt them. As much as possible, the audit team should attempt to remain neutral and not become involved. If information is given to the audit team in confidence, discreet attempts should be made to confirm such information through nonconfidential sources. *If it cannot be so confirmed, it should not be used.* The audit team must beware of becoming a conduit for unverifiable sources of criticism of the project.

There are other rules the audit team should follow as well. First, project personnel should always be made aware of the in-progress audit. Care must be taken to avoid misunderstandings between the audit team members and project personnel. Critical comments should always be avoided. This is especially true of on-the-spot, offhand opinions and remarks. No judgmental comment should be made in any circumstance that does not represent the consensus opinion of the audit team, and even consensus judgments should be avoided except in official hearings or reports.

The Audit Report

If the audit is to be taken seriously, all the information must be credibly presented. The data should be carefully checked, and all calculations verified. Deciding what to include and what to exclude is also important. The audit report should also be written with a "constructive" tone or project morale may suffer to the point of endangering the project. Bear in mind, however, that constructive criticism never feels that constructive to the criticizee. An example audit report is shown in Figure 8-2.

The report information should be arranged so as to facilitate the comparison between planned and actual results. Significant deviations should be highlighted and explained in a set of footnotes or comments. This eases the reader's work and tends to keep questions focused on important issues rather than trivia. Negative comments about individuals or groups associated with the project should be avoided. The report should be written in a clear, professional, unemotional style and its content restricted to information and issues relevant to the project.

At a minimum, the following information should be contained in the report.

1. *Introduction*: A brief description of the project that includes the project's direct goals and objectives.

2. *Current status*: This compares the work actually completed to the project plan along several measures of performance. The actual *direct* charges made to the project should be compared to the planned budget. If *total* costs must be reported, including allocated overhead charges, total costs should be presented in addition to the direct

AUDIT REPORT

Auditor: <u>Fred Williams</u>
Audit Team: <u>Sarah Smith, Mustafa Tudesco</u>
Date of Audit: <u>March 5-12, 2001</u>
Project Audited: <u>Software Installation Project</u>
Project Manager: <u>Craig Stoutheart</u>

•

•

•

INTRODUCTION

The aim of this project was to install a limited-version ERP system in our corporate office, Greenville production plant, and our southeastern field offices. This included testing of functionality, training of user personnel, and hand-off to the users.

CURRENT STATUS

Direct charges on the project are slightly in excess of the planned budget, as shown in the attached Gantt charts (*not included here*). The planned milestones have been achieved to date but task 451, Interface to Warehouse Inventory System, is experiencing difficulty and is both behind schedule and over budget, as seen in the earned value charts (*not included*). . . .

FUTURE PROJECT STATUS

At this time, it would appear that the project is progressing satisfactorily. Attention is currently being given to task 451 but it appears that a new approach is needed for interfacing the vendor's system with our current system. However, this appears to be a normal and temporary dilemma; progress is expected to catch up to plan within six–seven weeks, and the budget may also. At this time, no recommendations for changes in schedule, scope, or budget appear to be necessary. . . .

CRITICAL MANAGEMENT ISSUES

Interfacing with our existing systems seems to be more difficult than we anticipated. Although the vendor's software is reputed to be one of the easiest to tie in with a firm's existing systems, the difficulties were greater than expected. It is recommended that all upcoming interfacing tasks be examined in greater detail in advance so that these kinds of difficulties do not take us by surprise again. . . .

RISK ANALYSIS AND RISK MANAGEMENT

There does not seem to be any reason at this point to expect either project failure at this stage of the program or serious monetary loss. (The next stage, Implementation, is a separate and higher risk project, however.) As noted above, the major risks in the project do not seem to be equipment compatibility, as we had assumed, but rather software interfacing. If more serious interface issues arise, this could delay the project and/or substantially increase the cost of the project. As noted, it is recommended that future projects with significant software interfaces be examined much more carefully before decisions are made. . . .

FINAL COMMENTS

This report has assumed that the software interface issue will in fact be resolved without significant further delay or cost. If this assumption proves to be incorrect, it could have a major effect on the success of the project, and future projects, not only with this software system but other systems as well. . . .

Figure 8-2   Software installation audit report.

charges, not in place of them. The completed portions of the project, especially planned events and milestones, should be clearly noted. The percent completion of unfinished tasks should also be noted if estimates are available. A comparison of work completed with resources expended should be offered—for example, using MSP earned value reports. The need here is for information that can help pinpoint specific problems. Based on this information, projections can be made concerning the timing and amounts of remaining expenditures required for success. Finally, if there are detailed quality specifications for the project, a full review of quality control procedures and the results of quality tests conducted to date must be reported.

3. *Future project status*: The auditor's conclusions regarding project progress and recommendations for changes in technical approach, schedule, or budget should be made in this section. It is not appropriate, however, to try to rewrite the project proposal. The audit report should consider only work that has already been completed or is well under way; no assumptions should be made about technical problems under investigation at the time of the audit.

4. *Critical management issues*: Any issues that the auditor feels senior management should monitor should be identified here. The relationship between these issues and the project objectives should be briefly described.

5. *Risk analysis and risk management*: This section addresses the potential for project failure or monetary loss. The major risks associated with the project and their projected impact on project schedule/cost/performance should be identified. If alternative courses of action exist that may significantly change future risks, they should be noted at this point.

6. *Final comments*: This section contains caveats, assumptions, limitations, and information applicable to other projects. Any assumptions or limitations that affect the data, accuracy, or validity of the audit report should be noted here. In addition, lessons learned from this audit that may apply to other projects in the organization should also be reported.

The project audit is a thorough examination of the entire project at any level of depth. Early audits tend to focus on more technical aspects of the project while later audits focus on schedule and cost. The audit team must have full access to project data and staff familiar with the project, including the project team. Working with the project team is a delicate behavioral process. The final audit report should be written with a professional and constructive tone and should include the following sections: introduction, current status, future status, critical management issues, risk analysis and risk management, plus final comments.

8.3 PROJECT TERMINATION

Eventually the project is terminated, either quickly or slowly, but the manner in which it is closed out will have a major impact on the quality of life in the organization. Occasionally, the way project termination is managed can have an impact on the success of the project. Invariably, however, it has a major effect on the residual attitudes toward the project held by senior management, the client, the project team, and even others in the organization. It also has a major effect on the organization's successful use of projects in the future.

In some project-organized industries (e.g., construction), project termination is a less serious problem because the team remains relatively intact, moving on to the next project. In other industries, however, the termination of a project, particularly a long and difficult one, is akin to the breakup of a family and may well be stressful, even to the point of grieving. Therefore, the skill and management of the termination process—a project in itself—can have a major impact on the working environment of the larger organization.

When to Terminate a Project

If one adopts the position that sunk costs are irrelevant to current investment decisions, the primary criterion for project continuance or termination should be whether or not the organization is willing to invest the time and cost required to complete the project, given its current status and expected outcome. Although this criterion can be applied to any project, not everyone agrees that sunk costs are irrelevant, nor does everyone agree that this is the best criterion. The criteria commonly applied for deciding whether to terminate a project fall into two general categories: (1) the degree to which the project has met its goals and objectives, and (2) the degree to which the project qualifies against a set of factors generally associated with success or failure. Table 8-4 identifies the most important factors in terminating R&D projects at 36 different companies.

In terms of the first category, if a project has met its goals, the time has come to shut it down. The most important reason for the early termination of a project is the likelihood it will be a technical or commercial failure [1, 2]. The factors associated with project failure, however, vary for different industries, different project types (e.g., R&D versus construction), and different definitions of failure [6].

As we have already noted, there appear to be four generic factors associated with project success [7]: efficiency of project execution, customer satisfaction and use, impact on the firm conducting the project, and contribution to the project firm's future. Success on these dimensions appears to be directly related to the effectiveness of the pro-

Table 8-4   Rank-Ordered Factors Considered in Terminating R&D Projects

Factors	No. of Companies Reporting the Factor as Being Important
Technical	
Low probability of achieving technical objectives or commercializing results	34
Technical or manufacturing problems cannot be solved with available R&D skills	11
Higher priority of other projects requiring R&D labor or funds	10
Economic	
Low profitability or return on investment	23
Too costly to develop as individual product	18
Market	
Low market potential	16
Change in competitive factors or market needs	10
Others	
Too long a time required to achieve commercial results	6
Negative effects on other projects or products	3
Patent problems	1

Source: [2]

ject's management [3]. There also appear to be four fundamental reasons for project failure: (1) a project was not required for this task in the first place; (2) insufficient support from senior management (especially for unanticipated resources); (3) naming the wrong project manager (often a person with excellent technical skills but weak managerial skills); and (4) poor up-front planning.

Types of Project Termination

There are several fundamentally different ways to close out a project: extinction, addition, integration, and starvation. *Project extinction* occurs when the project activity suddenly stops, although there is still property, equipment, materials, and personnel to disburse or reassign. The project was terminated either because it was successfully completed or because the expectation of failure was high. Successful projects are completed and delivered to the client. Failures occur when the project no longer meets cost/benefit criteria, or when its goals have been achieved by another project, often in another firm. An example of the former cause of failure is the cancellation of the *superconducting super collider* (SSC). The SSC project's tremendous costs relative to the lack of clear benefits doomed the project, and it was cancelled during President Clinton's term in office. Other examples of projects facing extinction are when a project's process yield may have been too low, or a drug failed its efficacy tests, or other firms have discovered better alternatives.

One special type of termination that should be noted is termination by "murder," characterized by its unexpected suddenness, and initiated by events such as the forced retirement of the project's champion or the merger of the firm conducting the project with another firm.

Termination-by-addition occurs when an "in-house" project is successfully completed, and institutionalized as a new, formal part of the organization. This may take the form of an added department, division, subsidiary, or other such organizational entity, depending on the magnitude and importance of the project. 3M Corporation often uses this technique to reward successful innovation projects, such as the invention of Post-It Notes®, and Nucor uses its own construction management teams to staff new steel minimills.

Sometimes, project team members become the managers of the new entity, though some team members may request a transfer to new projects within the organization—project life is exciting. Although the new entity will often have a "protected species" status for the first year or so of its life, it eventually has to learn to live with the same burden of overhead charges, policies, procedures, and bureaucracy that the rest of the organization enjoys. Exceptional project status does not carryover to permanent entities. This shift may be a difficult one for the project team to make.

With termination-by-addition, the project property often is simply transferred to the new organizational entity. With *termination-by-integration*, the output of the project becomes a standard part of the operating systems of the sponsoring firm, or the client. The new software becomes the new standard, and the new machine becomes a normal part of the production line. Project property, equipment, material, personnel, and even functions are distributed among the existing elements of the parent or client organization. Whether the personnel return to their functional homes in the organization or become a part of the integrated system, all the following functions of the project need consideration in the transition from project to integrated operations: human resources, manufacturing, accounting/finance, engineering, information systems/software, marketing, purchasing, distribution, legal, and so on.

Termination-by-starvation often occurs when it is impolitic to terminate a project but its budget can be squeezed, as budgets always are, until it is a project in name only. The project may have been suggested by a special client, or a senior executive (e.g., a sacred cow), or perhaps terminating the project would be an embarrassing acknowledgment of managerial failure. Usually a few project personnel members remain with a clerk whose duty it is to issue a "no-progress" report once each quarter. It is considered bad manners for anyone to inquire about such projects.

The Termination Process

It is best for a broadly based committee of reasonably senior executives to make the termination decision in order to diffuse and withstand the political pressures that often accompany such decisions. In general, projects do not take kindly to being shut down. To the extent possible, it is best to detail the criteria used and explain the rationale for the committee's decision, but do not expect sweet reason to quell opposition or to stifle the cries of pain. Again, the PM will need the power of persuasion. In any case, shutting down an ongoing project is not a mechanistic process and should not be treated as such. There are times when hunches and beliefs about the project's ultimate outcomes should be followed. The termination committee that treats the decision as mechanistic is sure to make some costly errors.

The activities required to ensure a smooth and successful project termination will have, hopefully, been included in the initial project plan. The termination process will have much better results for all concerned if it is planned and managed with care—even treating it as a project in itself, as illustrated in Figure 8-3. Usually, the project manager is asked to close out the project but this can raise a variety of problems because the PM is not a disinterested bystander in the project. We believe it is better to appoint a specialist in the process, a *termination manager*, to complete the long and involved process of shutting down a project, preferably someone with some experience in terminating projects. The primary duties of the termination manager are given in Table 8-5.

Many of these tasks will be handled, or at least initiated, by the project manager. Some will have been provided for in the project proposal or contract. One of the more difficult jobs is the reassignment of project personnel. In a functional organization, it usually entails a simple transfer back to duty in the individual's parent department; but at those times when a large project is shut down, many team members may be laid off. In a pure project organization there may be more projects to which project personnel can be transferred but no "holding area" such as a home functional department. As a result, layoffs are more common. The matrix organization, having both aspects, may be the least problematic in terms of personnel reassignments.

It is expected that the termination manager and the organization's Human Resources department will aid loyal project workers in finding new employment. This is

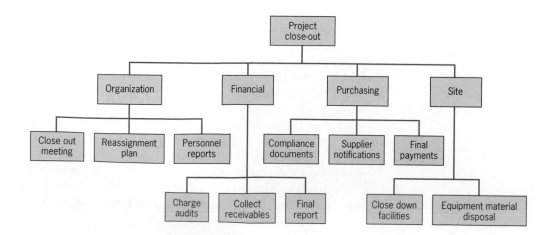

Figure 8-3
A termination project.

Table 8-5   Main Duties of the Termination Manager

- Ensure completion of the work, including that of subcontractors.
- Notify the client of project completion and ensure that delivery and installation are accomplished. Acceptance of the project must be acknowledged by the client.
- Ensure that documentation is complete, including the project final report.
- Clear all accounts and documentation for final billings and client invoicing.
- Redistribute personnel, materials, equipment, and other project resources to appropriate places, including the return of client-provided resources.
- Clear the project with legal counsel, including filings for patents and recording and archiving all nondisclosure documents.
- Determine what records to keep and deliver them to safe and responsible people, such as the organization's archivist, or store them in the organization's archives.
- Ascertain any product support requirements (e.g., spares, service manuals) and ensure that such support will be delivered.
- Oversee the closing of the project's books.

not merely an act of charity. It may prevent the tendency of some team members to seek employment on their own and leave a project early, which can compromise the successful completion of the project. If such people are unsuccessful in finding new jobs, they may drag out the final tasks to give themselves more time—also detrimental to the project. The PM also needs to make it clear at this time that midproject resignations as well as tenure-for-life are both unacceptable. Facing the termination decision in a timely and straightforward manner will pay dividends to the PM, as well as the termination manager, in a smooth project transition.

Clearly, the termination process can be handled well or poorly. An example of the former is Nucor's termination-by-addition strategy where the termination of its Crawfordsville, Indiana, steel plant construction project was planned in detail months ahead of time [4]. An example of poor termination is that which resulted when Atlantic States Chemical Laboratories suddenly saw its contract with Ortec canceled, throwing the project, and its close-out, into disarray [5].

The Project Final Report

The project final report is not another evaluation, though the audits and evaluations have a role in it. The project final report is a history of the project. It is a chronicle, typically written by the PM, of what went right and what went wrong, who served the project in what capacity, what was done, how it was managed, and the lessons learned. The report should also indicate where the source materials can be found—the project proposal, action plan, budget, schedule, earned value charts, audit reports, scope-change documents, all updates of any of the above documents, and so on.

How the report is written, and in what style, is a matter of taste and preference. In any case, the following items should be addressed.

- *Project performance*—perhaps the most important information is what the project attempted to achieve, what it did achieve, and the reasons for the resulting performance. Since this is not a formal evaluation of the project, these items can be the PM's personal opinion on the matter. The lessons learned in the project should also be included here.

- *Administrative performance*—administrative practices that worked particularly well, or poorly, should be identified and the reasons given. If some modification to administrative practices would help future projects, this should be noted and explained.

- *Organizational structure*—projects may have different structures, and the way the project is organized may either aid or hinder the project. Modifications that would help future projects should be identified.

- *Project teamwork*—a confidential section of the final report should identify team members who worked particularly well, and *possibly* those who worked poorly with others. The PM may also recommend that individuals or groups who were particularly effective when operating as a team be kept together on future assignments.

- *Project management techniques*—project success is so dependent on the skill and techniques for forecasting, planning, budgeting, scheduling, resource allocation, control, risk management, and so on that procedures that worked well or badly should be noted and commented upon. Recommendations for improvements in future projects should be made and explained.

The fundamental purpose of the final report is to improve future projects. Thus, recommendations for improvements are especially appropriate and valued by the organization. Of course, none of the recommendations for improvement of future projects will be of any help whatsoever if the recommendations are not circulated among other project managers as well as the appropriate senior managers. The PM should follow up on any recommendations made to make sure that they are accepted and installed, or rejected for cause.

Since most of the information and recollections come from the PM, it is suggested that the PM keep a project "diary." This is not an official project document but an informal collection of thoughts, reflections, and commentaries on project happenings. Not only will the diary help the PM construct the final report, but also it can be a superior source of wisdom for new, aspiring project managers. Above all, it keeps good ideas from getting lost amid the welter of project activities and crises.

Projects are usually terminated either based on (1) the degree to which they are meeting their goals or (2) the degree to which they qualify on factors shown to be linked to success or failure in other projects. The most common reason for early termination is the probability of a technical or commercial failure. The four types of project termination are extinction, addition, integration, and starvation. The termination decision should be decided by a management committee, run by a termination manager, and executed as a project in itself. Placing the project team members in new assignments is a particularly important aspect of termination. The PM should prepare a project final report that makes recommendations for improving the organization's future project-management practices.

REVIEW QUESTIONS

1. If the actual termination of a project is a project in itself, how is it different from other projects?

2. What are some reasons that a failing project might still not be terminated?

3. What might make a project unsuccessful during the termination process?

4. Who would make the best auditors: outside unbiased auditors or inside auditors who are more familiar with the organization, its procedures, and the project? Why?

5. Under what circumstances would you change your answer to the previous question?

6. Would frequent brief evaluations be best, or would less frequent major evaluations be preferred?

7. Should the results of an evaluation or audit be shared with the project team?

8. What are the major purposes served by an after-the-fact project evaluation?

9. Under what circumstances is a detailed audit apt to be useful?

DISCUSSION QUESTIONS

10. How should an audit team handle an audit where it is explicitly restricted from accessing certain materials and/or personnel?

11. What might be some characteristics of a good termination manager?

12. How should a committee decide which termination method to use?

13. What steps might be taken to reduce the anxiety of project team members facing an audit?

14. What are the dangers in evaluating a project based on the reason(s) it was selected (such as its being a competitive necessity), rather than the goals and objectives in the project proposal or contract?

15. It is frequently suggested that items that will become potential problems later in the project life be decided up front, such as how to allocate revenues or dispose of project assets. How can this wisdom be used for project problems that cannot be foreseen?

16. Can you think of any acceptable ways of assigning credit for profits (or responsibility for costs) resulting from a project on which several departments worked?

17. How might an audit team deal with an attempt to co-opt the team?

18. In Section 8.2, subsection *The Audit Report*, six elements are listed that should be included in every audit report. For each element, explain why its inclusion is important.

INCIDENTS FOR DISCUSSION

General Construction Company

General Construction Company has a contract to build three lower-income apartment buildings for the city of Santa Fe, New Mexico. During construction of the first building, the Project Manager formed an auditing team to audit the construction process for each building. He asked the team to develop a list of minimum requirements for the projects and use this as a baseline in the audit. While reviewing the contract documents, one of the audit team members found a discrepancy between the contract minimum requirements and the City's minimum requirements. Based on his findings, he has told the project manager that he has decided to contact the city administrator and discuss the problem.

Question: If you were the project manager, how would you handle this situation? How can a customer be assured of satisfactory project completion?

Lexi Electronics

Lexi Electronics is nearing completion of a two-year project to develop and produce a new digital phone. The phone is no bigger than a Popsicle stick but has all the features of a standard digital cellular phone. The assembly line and all the production facilities will be completed in 5 months. The first units will be produced in 8 months. The plant manager believes it is time to begin winding down the project. He has three methods in mind for terminating the project; extinction, addition, and integration. He is not sure which method is best.

Question: Which of the three methods would you recommend, and why?

C A S E

St. Dismas Assisted Living Facility Case—6

It was a beautiful day in mid-May 2001. The St. Dismas hospital Assisted Living Facility project was nearing completion. As usual, the construction project manager, Kyle

Nanno, was thinking about the project's schedule. It seemed to him that work on finishing the interior of the building was slowing down a bit. He knew that the final weeks of a project always seemed to take forever, but he also knew that the project was running almost two weeks late as a result of a problem encountered during the excavation phase of the construction project.

During March and April, it appeared that they were catching up. Kyle had discussed with the construction contractor that St. Dismas would pay overtime to catch up, but the speed-up was temporary, and the job continued to be late. Kyle was not quite sure why. Progress just seemed to be in slow motion. He decided to meet with Fred Splient, the President and CEO of St. Dismas, to discuss the problems.

Fred suggested that Kyle call in someone to audit the project, in particular to examine the project schedule carefully. Fred also wanted the auditor to look at the project expenses to date. Fred had just received a crude spreadsheet from the CFO, and it did not reflect the progress he thought should have been made as this project was coming to an end.

Fred asked Kyle to find out if anyone in the hospital's accounting department had experience with projects and project-management software. Kyle knew instantly who to call. Caroline Stevens had once helped him on other hospital projects. Kyle trusted her to act impartially and to be able to figure out what was happening.

Caroline agreed to function as the Project Auditor. She began by examining the most recent project schedule from the construction company. She then created a progress-to-date report with MSP. She also did a complete analysis of the CFO's report.

The expense report she reviewed and updated is found below.

Using MSP, Caroline created a graphical progress report on the project as of May 24. She marked the actual progress of each unfinished activity by placing a diamond embedded in a circle on the project's Gantt chart. If the symbol was to the left of the May 24 line that activity was late, the amount of lateness was indicated by the distance of the symbol to the May 24 line. The symbol for on-time activities rested on the May 24 line. If there had been early activities, their symbols would have been to the right of the May 24 line. Caroline's chart is shown below.

Caroline then scheduled a meeting with Kyle and Fred Splient. She reported that she did see a work slowdown. She conducted interviews with the construction team, and it appeared that they were concerned about their next work assignment. They told her that in the past as projects were coming to a close they were told of their next scheduled job. They had not heard anything yet, and they were worried. She also reported that the interior designer had added seven extra days to complete the interiors (Task #6 of the project) because the carpet and wall coverings might arrive a week late from the manufacturer. They actually arrived on schedule. The estimated remaining duration for the interiors to be completed was 34.6 days. The designer did tell her that the furniture had not all arrived so they were withholding about 30 percent of the payment until it all arrived.

Caroline also reported to Fred that it appeared that the expenses that were allocated to pay back St. Dismas for such things as preliminary marketing efforts, legal support, etc. had not yet been expensed to the project bud-

Project Expenses as of 5/24/01

	Budgeted	Actual as of 5/24/01	Remaining $
Construction Costs:			
Building	$6,743,000.00	$6,743,000.00	$0.00
Contingency	674,300.00	453,277.00	221,023.00
Land	600,000.00	600,000.00	0.00
Program development & equipment costs	405,000.00	354,332.00	50,668.00
Furniture	400,000.00	249,679.00	150,321.00
A&E Fees @ 5%	347,000.00	347,000.00	0.00
Financing costs	202,000.00	202,000.00	0.00
Capitalized interest	135,000.00	135,000.00	0.00
Site improvements	125,000.00	147,655.00	−22,655.00
Phone & IS system	30,000.00	22,438.00	7,562.00
Kitchen equipment	30,000.00	23,776.00	6,224.00
Total	$9,691,300.00	$9,278,157.00	$413,143.00
Organizational Costs:			
Legal and accounting	$25,000.00	$0.00	$25,000.00
Initial marketing	250,000.00	0.00	250,000.00
Project consultant	80,000.00	0.00	80,000.00
Follow-up market survey	20,000.00	0.00	20,000.00
Total	$375,000.00	$0.00	$375,000.00
Total	$10,066,300.00	$9,278,157.00	$788,143.00

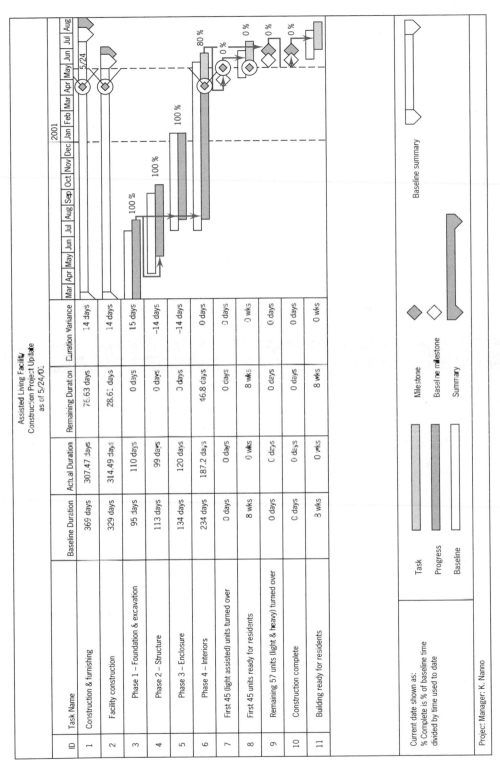

Assisted Living Facility
Construction Project Update
as of 5/24/01

ID	Task Name	Baseline Duration	Actual Duration	Remaining Duration	Duration Variance
1	Construction & furnishing	369 days	307.47 days	76.63 days	14 days
2	Facility construction	329 days	314.49 days	28.61 days	14 days
3	Phase 1 – Foundation & excavation	95 days	110 days	0 days	15 days
4	Phase 2 – Structure	113 days	99 days	0 days	-14 days
5	Phase 3 – Enclosure	134 days	120 days	0 days	-14 days
6	Phase 4 – Interiors	234 days	187.2 days	46.8 days	0 days
7	First 45 (light assisted) units turned over	0 days	0 days	0 days	0 days
8	First 45 units ready for residents	8 wks	0 wks	8 wks	0 wks
9	Remaining 57 units (light & heavy) turned over	0 days	0 days	0 days	0 days
10	Construction complete	0 days	0 days	0 days	0 days
11	Building ready for residents	3 wks	0 wks	8 wks	0 wks

Current date shown as:
% Complete is % of baseline time
divided by time used to date

Task
Progress
Baseline

Milestone
Baseline milestone
Summary

Baseline summary

Project Manager: K. Nanno

*Please note Microsoft Project 98® calculates the duration variance for each step of the action plan by subtracting the actual from the baseline. The summary task baseline and actual duration are then rolled up to the summary tasks' baseline and actual duration figures. The summary tasks' duration variance is then calculated by adding the summary task actual duration plus the remaining duration and then subtracting that sum from the baseline duration.

253

get. The only thing that was expensed was the original project construction budget. That budget seemed to be right on track. Kyle reported that he intended to spend the rest of the contingency budget for overtime work by the construction crews. He also intended to use the rest of the IS budget to purchase computers for the common areas of the facility and to wire those areas for access to the Internet. In addition, he was waiting for bills from some of the companies that supplied the required medical equipment. He was planning to spend all that was allocated for that budgeted item. He was over budget on the site improvements and under budget for the kitchen equipment.

Caroline and Fred praised Kyle for his management of the Construction budget.

As soon as Caroline and Kyle left Fred's office, Fred called his CFO to find out why the other items were still not reflected in the project budget.

QUESTIONS

1. Estimate the final construction budget.
2. What should they do about the work slowdown?
3. Create a Gantt chart with the revisions to the duration of the interiors step. When will the project be completed?
4. What is the importance of the fact that the Hospital staff expenses were not reported under the project budget?

C A S E

Datatech's Audit

Steve Bawnson joined Datatech's engineering department upon obtaining his B.S. in Electrical Engineering almost six years ago. He soon established himself as an expert in analog signal processing and was promoted to Senior Design Engineer just two years after joining the firm. After serving as a Senior Design Engineer for two years, he was promoted to Project Manager and asked to oversee a product development project involving a relatively minor product line extension.

As Steve was clearing his desk to make room for a cup of coffee, his computer dinged indicating the arrival of yet another email message. Steve usually paid little attention to the arrival of new email messages, but for some reason this message caught his attention. Swiveling in his chair to face the computer on the credenza behind his desk, he read the subject line of the message: Notebook Computer Development Project Audit Report. Steve then noticed that the message was addressed to the Vice-President of Product Development and was cc: to him. He immediately opened and read the message.

Datatech had recently adopted a policy requiring that all ongoing projects be periodically audited. Last week this policy was implemented and Steve was informed that his project would be the first one audited by a team consisting of internal and external experts.

Datatech Inc. is a full-line producer of desktop and notebook computers that are distributed through a network of value-added resellers. After completing the desktop product line extension project about nine months ago, Steve was asked to serve as the project manager for a project to develop a new line of notebook computers.

In asking Steve to serve as the project manager for the notebook computer development project, the Vice-President of Product Development conveyed to Steve the importance of completing the project within a year. To emphasize this point, the Vice-President noted that he personally made the decision to go forward with this project and had not taken the project through the normal project selection and approval process in order to save time. Steve had successfully completed the desktop project in a similar timeframe, and told the Vice-President that this target was quite reasonable. Steve added that he was confident that the project would be completed on time and on budget.

Steve wasted no time in planning the project. Based on the success of the desktop project, he decided to modify the work breakdown structure he had developed for the desktop project and apply it to this new project. He recalled the weeks of planning that went into developing the work breakdown structure for the desktop project. The entire project team had been involved, and that was a relatively straightforward product line extension. The current project was more complicated, and there simply was not sufficient time to involve all team members. What was the point of wasting valuable time and resources to re-invent the wheel?

After modifying the work breakdown structure, Steve scheduled a meeting with the Vice-President of Product

Development to discuss staffing the project. As was typical of other product development projects at Datatech, Steve and the Vice-President agreed that the project should be housed within the engineering division. In his capacity as project manager, Steve would serve as liaison to other functional areas such as marketing, purchasing, finance, and production.

As the project progressed, it continued to slip behind schedule. Steve found it necessary to schedule a meeting each week to address how unanticipated activities would be completed. For example, last week the team realized that no one had been assigned to design the hinge system for attaching the screen to the base.

Indeed, Steve found himself increasingly in crisis mode. For example, this morning the manufacturing group sent a heated email to Steve. The manufacturing group noted that they just learned of the notebook computer project and based on the design presented to them, they would not be able to manufacture the printed circuit boards because of the extensive amount of surface mount components required. Steve responded to this message by noting that the engineering group was doing its job and had designed a state-of-the-art notebook computer. He added that it was the manufacturing group's problem to decide how to produce it.

Just as troubling was the crisis that had occurred earlier in the week. The Vice-President of Product Development had requested that the notebook computer incorporate a new type of interface that would allow the notebook computer to synchronize information with a personal digital assistant Datatech was about to introduce. Steve explained that incorporating the interface into the notebook computer would require changes to about 40 percent of the computer and would delay the introduction by a minimum of several months. Nevertheless, the Vice-President was adamant that the change be made.

As Steve laid down the audit report, he reflected on its conclusion that the project be terminated immediately. In the judgment of the auditing team, the project had slipped so far behind schedule that the costs to complete it were not justified.

QUESTIONS

1. To what extent were the problems facing the notebook computer development project avoidable? What could have been done to avoid these problems?

2. Would it make sense to apply a project selection model such as the weighted scoring model to this project to determine if it should be terminated?

3. In your opinion, are the types of problems that arose in this situation typical of other organizations? If so, what can organizations in general do to avoid these types of problems?

BIBLIOGRAPHY

1. BAKER, N. R., S. G. GREEN, A. S. BEAN, W. BLANK, and S. K. TADISINA. "Sources of First Suggestion and Project Success/Failure in Industrial Research." *Proceedings: Conference on the Management of Technological Innovation.* Washington, D.C., 1983. (A groundbreaking, early empirical paper on predictions of project success and failure.)

2. DEAN, B. V. *Evaluating, Selecting, and Controlling R&D Projects.* New York: American Management Association, 168. (As we noted in the bibliography in Chapter 7, a classic work on selection and evaluation.)

3. INGRAM, T. "Managing Client/Server and Open Systems Projects: A 10-Year Study of 62 Mission-Critical Projects." *Project Management Journal,* June 1994.

4. KIMBALL, R. "Nucor's Strategic Project." *Project Management Journal,* September 1988.

5. MEREDITH, J. R. Private consulting project.

6. PINTO, J. K., and S. J. MANTEL, JR. "The Causes of Project Failure." *IEEE Transactions on Engineering Management,* November 1990.

7. SHENHAR, A. J., O. LEVY, and D. DVIR. "Mapping the Dimensions of Project Success." *Project Management Journal,* June 1997.

Area under the Normal Distribution

Table A-1. Cumulative (Single Tail) Probabilities of the Normal Probability Distribution (Areas under the Normal Curve from $-\infty$ to Z)

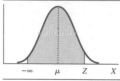

Example: the area to the left of $Z = 1.34$ is found by following the left Z column down to 1.3 and moving right to the .04 column. At the intersection read .9099. The area to the right of $Z = 1.34$ is $1 - .9099 = .0901$. The area between the mean (dashed line) and $Z = 1.34 = .9099 - .5 = .4099$.

z	.00	.01	.02	.03	.04	.05	.06	.07	.08	.09
.0	.5000	.5040	.5080	.5120	.5160	.5199	.5239	.5279	.5319	.5359
.1	.5398	.5438	.5478	.5517	.5557	.5596	.5636	.5675	.5714	.5753
.2	.5793	.5832	.5871	.5910	.5948	.5987	.6026	.6064	.6103	.6141
.3	.6179	.6217	.6255	.6293	.6331	.6368	.6406	.6443	.6480	.6517
.4	.6554	.6591	.6628	.6664	.6700	.6736	.6772	.6808	.6844	.6879
.5	.6915	.6950	.6985	.7019	.7054	.7088	.7123	.7157	.7190	.7224
.6	.7257	.7291	.7324	.7357	.7389	.7422	.7454	.7486	.7517	.7549
.7	.7580	.7611	.7642	.7673	.7704	.7734	.7764	.7794	.7823	.7852
.8	.7881	.7910	.7939	.7967	.7995	.8023	.8051	.8078	.8106	.8133
.9	.8159	.8186	.8212	.8238	.8264	.8289	.8315	.8340	.8365	.8389
1.0	.8413	.8438	.8461	.8485	.8508	.8531	.8554	.8577	.8599	.8621
1.1	.8643	.8665	.8686	.8708	.8729	.8749	.8770	.8790	.8810	.8880
1.2	.8849	.8869	.8888	.8907	.8925	.8944	.8962	.8980	.8997	.9015
1.3	.9032	.9049	.9066	.9082	.9099	.9115	.9131	.9147	.9162	.9177
1.4	.9192	.9207	.9222	.9236	.9251	.9265	.9276	.9292	.9306	.9319
1.5	.9332	.9345	.9357	.9370	.9382	.9394	.9406	.9418	.9429	.9441
1.6	.9452	.9463	.9474	.9484	.9495	.9505	.9515	.9525	.9535	.9545
1.7	.9554	.9564	.9573	.9582	.9591	.9599	.9608	.9616	.9625	.9633
1.8	.9641	.9649	.9656	.9664	.9671	.9678	.9686	.9693	.9699	.9706
1.9	.9713	.9719	.9726	.9732	.9738	.9744	.9750	.9756	.9761	.9767
2.0	.9772	.9778	.9783	.9788	.9793	.9798	.9803	.9808	.9812	.9817
2.1	.9821	.9826	.9830	.9834	.9838	.9842	.9846	.9850	.9854	.9857
2.2	.9861	.9864	.9868	.9871	.9875	.9878	.9881	.9884	.9887	.9890
2.3	.9893	.9896	.9898	.9901	.9904	.9906	.9909	.9911	.9913	.9916
2.4	.9918	.9920	.9932	.9925	.9927	.9929	.9931	.9932	.9934	.9936
2.5	.9938	.9940	.9941	.9943	.9945	.9946	.9948	.9949	.9951	.9952
2.6	.9953	.9955	.9956	.9957	.9959	.9960	.9961	.9962	.9963	.9964
2.7	.9965	.9966	.9967	.9968	.9969	.9970	.9971	.9972	.9973	.9974
2.8	.9974	.9975	.9976	.9977	.9977	.9978	.9979	.9979	.9980	.9981
2.9	.9981	.9982	.9982	.9983	.9984	.9984	.9985	.9985	.9986	.9986
3.0	.9987	.9987	.9987	.9988	.9988	.9989	.9989	.9989	.9990	.9990
3.1	.9990	.9991	.9991	.9991	.9992	.9992	.9992	.9992	.9993	.9993
3.2	.9993	.9993	.9994	.9994	.9994	.9994	.9994	.9995	.9995	.9995
3.3	.9995	.9995	.9995	.9996	.9996	.9996	.9996	.9996	.9996	.9997
3.4	.9997	.9997	.9997	.9997	.9997	.9997	.9997	.9997	.9997	.9998

A · P · P · E · N · D · I · X

B

Probability and Statistics

This appendix is intended to serve as a brief review of the probability and statistics concepts used in this text. Students who require more review than is available in this appendix should consult one of the texts listed in the bibliography.

B.1   PROBABILITY

Uncertainty in project management is a fact of life. The duration of project activities, the costs of various resources, and the timing of a technological change all exemplify the types of uncertainties encountered when managing projects. Each of these *random variables* is more or less uncertain. Further, we do not know when or if a given activity will be successfully completed, a senior official will approve a project, or a piece of software will run without problems. Each *event* is more or less uncertain. We do not know the values that each variable and event will assume.

In common terminology we reflect our uncertainty with such phrases as "not very likely," "not a chance," "for sure." While these descriptive terms communicate one's feeling regarding the chances of a particular event's occurrence, they simply are not precise enough to allow analysis of chances and odds.

Simply put, *probability* is a number on a scale used to measure uncertainty. The range of the probability scale is from 0 to 1, with a 0 probability indicating that an event has no chance of occurring and a probability of 1 indicating that an event is absolutely certain to occur. The more likely an event is to occur, the closer its probability is to 1. This probability definition, which is general, needs to be further augmented to illustrate the various types of probability that decision makers can assess. There are three types of probability that the project manager should be aware of.

- Subjective probability
- Logical probability
- Experimental probability

Subjective Probability

Subjective probability is based on individual information and belief. Different individuals will assess the chances of particular event in different ways, and the same individual may assess different probabilities for the same event at different points in time. For example, one need only watch the blackjack players in Las Vegas to see that different people assess probabilities in different ways. Also, daily trading in the stock market is the result of different probability assessments by those trading. The sellers sell because it is their belief that the probability of appreciation is low, and the buyers buy because they believe that the probability of appreciation is high. Clearly, these different probability assessments are about the same events.

Logical Probability

Logical probability is based on physical phenomena and on symmetry of events. For example, the probability of drawing a three of hearts from a standard 52-card playing deck is 1/52. Each card has an equal likelihood of being drawn. In flipping a coin, the chance of "heads" is 0.50. That is, since there are only two possible outcomes from one flip of a coin, each event has one-half the total probability, or 0.50. A final example is the roll of a single die. Since all six sides are identical, the chance of any one event occurring (i.e., a 6, a 3) is 1/6.

Experimental Probability

Experimental probability is based on frequency of occurrence of events in trial situations. For example, in estimating the duration for a particular activity, we might record the time required to complete the activity on similar projects. If we collect data on 10 projects and the duration was 20 days on 3 of the 10, the probability of the duration equaling 20 days is said to be 0.30 (i.e., 3/10).

$$\text{probability of event} = \frac{\text{number of times event occurred}}{\text{total number of trials}}$$

Both logical and experimental probability are referred to as *objective* probability in contrast to the individually assessed *subjective* probability. Each of these is based on, and directly *computed* from, facts.

B.2   EVENT RELATIONSHIPS AND PROBABILITY LAWS

Events are classified in a number of ways that allow us to state rules for probability computations. Some of these classifications and definitions follow.

1. *Independent events:*   events are independent if the occurrence of one *does not* affect the probability of occurrence of the others.
2. *Dependent events:*   events are termed dependent if the occurrence of one *does* affect the probability of occurrence of others.
3. *Mutually exclusive events:*   two events are termed mutually exclusive if the occurrence of one precludes the occurrence of the other. For example, in the birth of a child, the events "It's a boy!" and "It's a girl!" are mutually exclusive.
4. *Collectively exhaustive events:*   a set of events its termed collectively exhaustive if on any one trial at least one of them must occur. For example, in rolling a die, one of the events 1, 2, 3, 4, 5, or 6 must occur; therefore, these six events are collectively exhaustive.

We can also define the union and intersection of two events. Consider two events A and B. The *union of* A and B includes all outcomes in A or B or in both A and B. For example, in a card game you will win if you draw a diamond or a jack. The union of these two events includes all diamonds (including the jack of diamonds) and the remaining three jacks (hearts, clubs, spades). The *or* in the union is the *inclusive or*. That is, in our example you will win with a jack or a diamond or a jack of diamonds (i.e., both events).

The *intersection* of two events includes all outcomes that are members of *both* events. Thus, in our previous example of jacks and diamonds, the jack of diamonds is the only outcome contained in both events and is therefore the only member of the intersection of the two events.

Let us now consider the relevant probability laws based on our understanding of the above definitions and concepts. For ease of exposition let us define the following notation.

$$P(A) = \text{probability that event } A \text{ will occur}$$
$$P(B) = \text{probability that event } B \text{ will occur}$$

If two events are mutually exclusive, then their joint occurrence is impossible. Hence, $P(A \text{ and } B) = 0$ for mutually exclusive events. If the events are not mutually exclusive, $P(A \text{ and } B)$ can be computed (as we will see in the next section); this probability is termed the *joint* probability of A and B. Also, if A and B are not mutually exclusive, then we can also define the *conditional* probability of A *given that* B has already occurred or the conditional probability of B given that A has already occurred. These probabilities are written as $P(A|B)$ and $P(B|A)$, respectively.

The Multiplication Rule

The joint probability of two events that are not mutually exclusive is found by using the multiplication rule. If the events are independent events, the joint probability is given by

$$P(A \text{ and } B) = P(A) \times P(B|A) \text{ or } P(B) \times P(A|B)$$

If the events are independent, then $P(B|A)$ and $P(A|B)$ are equal to $P(B)$ and $P(A)$, respectively, and therefore the joint probability is given by

$$P(A \text{ and } B) = P(A) \times P(B)$$

From these two relationships, we can find the conditional probability for two dependent events from

$$P(A \mid B) = \frac{P(A \text{ and } B)}{P(B)}$$

and

$$P(B \mid A) = \frac{P(A \text{ and } B)}{P(A)}$$

Also, the $P(A)$ and $P(B)$ can be computed if the events are independent, as

$$P(A) = \frac{P(A \text{ and } B)}{P(B)}$$

and

$$P(B) = \frac{P(A \text{ and } B)}{P(A)}$$

The Addition Rule

The addition rule is used to compute the probability of the union of two events. If two events are mutually exclusive, then $P(A \text{ and } B) = 0$, as we indicated previously. Therefore, the probability of either A or B or both is simply the probability of A or B. This is given by

$$P(A \text{ or } B) = P(A) + P(B)$$

But, if the events are not mutually exclusive, then the probability of A or B is given by

$$P(A \text{ or } B) = P(A) + P(B) - P(A \text{ and } B)$$

We can denote the reasonableness of this expression by looking at the following Venn diagram.

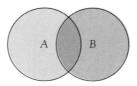

The two circles represent the probabilities of the events A and B, respectively. The shaded area represents the overlap in the events; that is, the intersection of A and B. If we add the area of A and the area of B, we have included the shaded area twice. Therefore, to get the total area of A or B, we must subtract one of the areas of the intersection that we have added.

If the two circles in the Venn diagram do not overlap, A and B are said to be *mutually exclusive* and $P(A \text{ and } B) = 0$. In this case

$$P(A \text{ or } B) = P(A) + P(B)$$

If two events are collectively exhaustive, then the probability of $(A \text{ or } B)$ is equal to 1. That is, for two collectively exhaustive events, one or the other or both must occur, and therefore, $P(A \text{ or } B)$ must be 1.

B.3   STATISTICS

Because events are uncertain, we must employ special analyses in organizations to ensure that our decisions recognize the chance nature of outcomes. We employ statistics and statistical analysis to

1. Concisely express the tendency and the relative uncertainty of a particular situation.
2. Develop inferences or understanding about a situation.

"Statistics" is an elusive and often misused term. Batting averages, birth weights, student grade points are all statistics. They are *descriptive* statistics. That is, they are quantitative measures of some entity and, for our purposes, can be considered as data about the entity. The second use of the term "statistics" is in relation to the body of theory and methodology used to analyze available evidence (typically quantitative) and to develop inferences from the evidence.

Two descriptive statistics that are often used in presenting information about a population of items (and consequently in inferring some conclusions about the population) are the *mean* and the *variance*. The mean in a population (denoted as μ and pronounced "mu") can be computed in two ways, each of which gives identical results.

$$\mu = \sum_{j=1}^{k} X_j P(X_j)$$

where

k = the number of discrete values that the random variable X_j may assume

X_j = the value of the random variable

$P(X_j)$ = is the probability (or relative frequency) of X_j in the population

Also, the mean can be computed as

$$\mu = \sum_{i=1}^{N} X_i/N$$

where

N = the size of the population (the number of different items in the population)

X_i = the value of the *i*th item in the population

The mean is also termed the *expected value* of the population and is written as $E(X)$.

The variance of the items in the population measures the dispersion of the items about their mean (denoted) σ^2 and pronounced "sigma squared"). It is computed in one of the following two ways:

$$\sigma^2 = \sum_{j=1}^{k} (X_j - \mu)^2 P(X_j)$$

or

$$\sigma^2 = \sum_{i=1}^{N} \frac{(X_i - \mu)^2}{N}$$

The standard deviation, another measure of dispersion, is simply the square root of the variance (denoted σ)

$$\sigma = \sqrt{\sigma^2}$$

Descriptive versus Inferential Statistics

Organizations are typically faced with decisions for which a large portion of the relevant information is uncertain. In hiring graduates of your university, the "best" prospective employee is unknown to the organization. Also, in introducing a new product, proposing a tax law change to boost employment, drilling an oil well, and so on, the outcomes are always uncertain.

Statistics can often aid management in reducing this uncertainty. This is accomplished through the use of one or the other, or both, of the purposes of statistics. That is, statistics is divided according to its two major purposes: *describing* the major characteristics of a large mass of data and *inferring* something about a large mass of data from a smaller sample drawn from the mass. One methodology summarizes all the data; the other reasons from a small set of the data to the larger total.

Descriptive statistics uses such measures as the mean, median, mode, range, variance, standard deviation, and such graphical devices as the bar chart and the histogram. When an entire population (a complete set of objects or entities with a common characteristic of interest) of data is summarized by computing such measures as the mean and the variance of a single characteristic, the measure is referred to as a *parameter* of that population. For example, if the population of interest is all female freshmen at a university and all their ages were used to compute an arithmetic average of 19.2 years, this measure is called a *parameter* of that population.

Inferential statistics also uses means and variance, but in a different manner. The objective of inferential statistics is to infer the value of a population parameter through the study of a small sample (a portion of a population) from that population. For example, a random sample of 30 freshmen females could produce the information that there is 90 percent certainty that the average age of all freshmen women is between 18.9 and 19.3 years. We do not have as much information as if we had used the entire population, but then we did not have to spend the time to find and determine the age of each member of the population either.

Before considering the logic behind inferential statistics, let us define the primary measures of central tendency and dispersion used in both descriptive and inferential statistics.

Measures of Central Tendency

The central tendency of a group of data represents the average, middle, or "normal" value of the data. The most frequently used measures of central tendency are the *mean*, the *median*, and the *mode*.

The mean of a population of values was given earlier as

$$\mu = \sum_{i=1}^{N} \frac{X_i}{N}$$

where

μ = the mean
X_i = the value of the *i*th data item
N = the number of data items in the population

The mean of a *sample* of items from a population is given by

$$\overline{X} = \sum_{i=1}^{n} \frac{X_i}{n}$$

where

$\overline{X}$ = the sample mean (pronounced "X bar")
X_i = the value of the *i*th data item in the sample
n = the number of data items selected in the sample

The *median* is the middle value of a population of data (or sample) where the data are ordered by value. That is, in the following data set

$$3, 2, 9, 6, 1, 5, 7, 3, 4$$

4 is the median since (as you can see when we order the data)

$$1, 2, 3, 3, 4, 5, 6, 7, 9$$

50 percent of the data values are above 4 and 50 percent below 4. If there are an even number of data items, then the mean of the middle two is the median. For example, if there had also been an 8 in the above data set, the median would be $4.5 = (4 + 5)/2$.

The *mode* of a population (or sample) of data items is the value that most frequently occurs. In the above data set, 3 is the mode of the set. A distribution can have more than one mode if there are two or more values that appear with equal frequency.

Measures of Dispersion

Dispersion refers to the scatter around the mean of a distribution of values. Three measures of dispersion are the range, the variance, and the standard deviation.

The *range* is the difference between the highest and the lowest value of the data set, that is, $X_{high} - X_{low}$.

The *variance of a population* of items is given by

$$\sigma^2 = \sum_{i=1}^{N} \frac{(X_i - \mu)^2}{N}$$

where

    σ^2 = the population variance

The *variance of a sample* of items is given by

$$S^2 = \sum_{i=1}^{n} \frac{(X_i - \overline{X})^2}{n - 1}$$

where

    S^2 = the sample variance

The *standard deviation* is simply the square root of the variance. That is,

$$\sigma = \sqrt{\sum_{i=1}^{n} \frac{(X_i - \mu)^2}{N}}$$

and

$$S = \sqrt{\sum_{i=1}^{n} \frac{(X_i - \overline{X})^2}{n - 1}}$$

σ and S are the population and sample standard deviations, respectively.

Inferential Statistics

A basis of inferential statistics is the *interval estimate*. Whenever we infer from partial data to an entire population, we are doing so with some uncertainty in our inference. Specifying an interval estimate (e.g., average weight is between 10 and 12 pounds) rather than a *point estimate* (e.g., the average weight is 11.3 pounds) simply helps to relate that uncertainty. The interval estimate is not as *precise* as the point estimate.

Inferential statistics uses probability samples where the chance of selection of each item is known. A random sample is one in which each item in the population has an equal chance of selection.

The procedure used to estimate a population mean from a sample is to

1. Select a sample of size n from the population.
2. Compute $\overline{X}$ the mean and S the standard deviation.
3. Compute the precision of the estimate (i.e., the $\pm$ limits around $\overline{X}$ within which the mean μ is believed to exist).

Steps 1 and 2 are straightforward, relying on the equations we have presented in earlier sections. Step 3 deserves elaboration.

The precision of an estimate for a population parameter depends on two things: the standard deviation of the *sampling distribution*, and the confidence you desire to have in the final estimate. Two statistical laws provide the logic behind Step 3.

First, the law of large numbers states that as the size of a sample increases toward infinity, the difference between the estimate of the mean and the true population mean tends toward zero. For practical purposes, a sample of size 30 is assumed to be "large enough" for the sample estimate to be a good estimate of the population mean.

Second, the central limit theorem states that if all possible samples of size n were taken from a population with any distribution, the distribution of the means of those samples would be normally distributed with a mean equal to the population mean and a standard deviation equal to the standard deviation of the population divided by the square root of the sample size. That is, if we took all of the samples of size 100 from the population shown in Figure B-1, the sampling distribution would be as shown in Figure B-2. The logic behind Step 3 is that

1. Any sample of size n from the population can be considered to be one observation from the sampling distribution with the mean $\mu_{\bar{x}} = \mu$ and the standard deviation

$$\sigma_{\bar{x}} = \frac{\sigma}{\sqrt{n}}$$

2. From our knowledge of the normal distribution, we know that there is a number (see normal probability table, Appendix A) associated with each probability value of a normal distribution (e.g., the probability that an item will be within ± 2 standard deviations of the mean of a normal distribution is 94.45 percent, $Z = 2$ in this case).

3. The value of the number Z is simply the number of standard deviations away from the mean where a given point lies. That is,

$$Z = \frac{(\overline{X} - \mu)}{\sigma}$$

or in the case of Step 3

$$Z = \frac{(\overline{X} - \mu_{\bar{x}})}{\sigma_{\bar{x}}}$$

4. The precision of a sample estimate is given by $Z\sigma_{\bar{x}}$.

5. The interval estimate is given by the point estimate $\overline{X}$ plus or minus the precision, or $\overline{X} \pm Z\sigma_{\bar{x}}$.

In the previous example shown in Figures B-1 and B-2, suppose that a sample estimate $\overline{X}$ was 56 and the population standard deviation σ was 20. Also, suppose that the desired confidence was 90 percent. Since the associated Z value for 90 percent is 1.645, the interval estimate for μ is

$$56 \pm 1.645 \left(\frac{20}{\sqrt{100}} \right)$$

or

$$56 \pm 3.29 \text{ or } 52.71 \text{ to } 59.29$$

This interval estimate of the population mean states that the estimator is 90 percent confident that the true mean is between 52.71 and 59.29. There are numerous other sampling methods and other parameters that can be estimated; the student is referred to one of the references in the bibliography for further discussion.

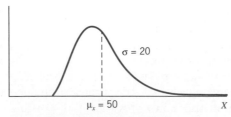

Figure B-1 Population distribution.

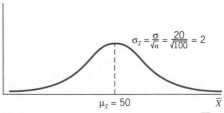

Figure B-2 Sampling distribution of $\overline{X}$.

Standard Probability Distributions

The normal distribution, discussed and shown in Figure B-2, is probably the most common probability distribution in statistics. Some other common distributions are the Poisson, a discrete distribution, and the negative exponential, a continuous distribution. In project management, the beta distribution plays an important role; a continuous distribution, it is generally skewed, as in Figure B-1. Two positive parameters, alpha and beta, determine the distribution's shape. Its mean, μ, and variance, σ^2, are given by

$$\mu = \frac{\alpha}{\alpha + \beta}$$

$$\sigma^2 = \frac{\alpha\beta}{(\alpha + \beta)^2 (\alpha + \beta + 2)}$$

These are often approximated by

$$\mu = (a + 4m + b)/6$$

and a standard deviation approximated by

$$\sigma = (b - a)/6$$

where

a is the optimistic value that might occur once in a hundred times,

m is the most likely (modal) value, and

b is the pessimistic value that might occur once in a hundred times.

Recent research [3] has indicated that a much better approximation is given by

$$\mu = 0.630\,d + 0.185\,(c + e)$$
$$\sigma^2 = 0.630\,(d - \mu)^2 + 0.185\,[(c - \mu)^2 + (e - \mu)^2]$$

where

c is an optimistic value at one in 20 times,

d is the median, and

e is a pessimistic value at one in 20 times.

See Chapter 5 for another method for approximating μ and σ^2.

BIBLIOGRAPHY

1. ANDERSON, D., D. SWEENEY, and T. WILLIAMS. *Statistics for Business and Economics*. 7th ed. Cincinnati, OH: South-Western, 1998.

2. BHATTACHARYYA, G., and R. A. JOHNSON. *Mathematical Statistics*. Paramus, NJ: Prentice-Hall, 1999.

3. KEEFER, D. L., and W. A. VERDINI. "Better Estimation of PERT Activity Time Parameters." *Management Science*, September 1993.

4. MENDENHALL, W., R. L. SCHAEFFER, and D. WACKERLY. *Mathematical Statistics with Applications*, 3rd ed. Boston: PWS-Kent, 1986.

5. NETER, J., W. WASSERMAN, and G. A. WHITMORE. *Applied Statistics*, 3rd ed. Boston: Allyn and Bacon, 1987.

C

Risk Analysis Using Crystal Ball® 2000

As is demonstrated throughout this book, effective project management requires an ability to deal with uncertainty. The duration of project activities, the availabilities and costs of key resources, the timing of technological breakthroughs, the actions taken by competitors, and the whims of a client all exemplify the types of uncertainties encountered in project management. Furthermore, while there are a number of actions that can be taken to reduce the amount of uncertainty, no actions of a project manager could ever completely eliminate it. Therefore, in today's turbulent business environment, effective decision making is predicated on an ability to manage the ambiguity that arises while we operate in a world characterized by uncertain information.

One approach that is particularly useful in helping us to understand the implications of uncertain information is risk analysis. As we note in Chapter 4, the essence of risk analysis is to make assumptions about the probability distributions associated with key parameters and variables and to use Monte Carlo simulation models based on these distributions to evaluate the desirability of certain managerial decisions. Using this approach, a mathematical model of the situation is constructed and a simulation is run to see what the outcomes will be under various scenarios. The model is run (or replicated) many, many times starting from a different point each time based on the probabilities of the variables. Equations in the model are then used to construct a statistical distribution of the outcomes of interest, such as costs, profits, completion dates, or return on investment. The objective is to illustrate to the manager the distribution or *risk profile* of the outcomes associated with the decision. These risk profiles must be considered when making the decision, along with many other factors such as strategic concerns, behavioral issues, fit with the organization, and so on.

This Appendix illustrates how Crystal Ball® 2000 (CB), an Excel® Add-In, can be used to conduct such analyses and thereby obtain a better understanding of the risks associated with managing projects. Our discussion begins in the next section with the topic of project selection. The topics of project budgeting, project scheduling, and resource allocation are addressed in the following sections.

C.1 CONSIDERING UNCERTAINTY IN PROJECT SELECTION DECISIONS

To illustrate the value of considering uncertainty in the project selection decision, consider the experience of a fictitious dot-com startup that needs to upgrade its server computers. Company management has identified the following two options: (1) shift to a Windows-based platform from its current Unix-based platform, or (2) stay with a Unix-based platform. The company estimates that if it migrates to Windows, the new server hardware could cost as little as $100,000 or as much as $200,000. The technical group's best estimate is that the hardware costs will be $125,000 if the Windows option is pursued. Likewise, the company's best guess regarding the cost to upgrade and convert its software to Windows is $300,000 with a range of $275,000 to $500,000. Finally, employee training costs are estimated to range between $9,000 and $15,000, with a best guess of $10,000 if the company moves to Windows.

If the company sticks with Unix, the new server hardware will most likely cost $110,000, but could cost as little as $80,000 or as much as $210,000. Software conversion and upgrade costs are expected to be $300,000 but could be as low as $250,000 or as high as $525,000. Employee training costs should fall between $8,000 and $17,500 with a best guess of $10,000.

In this example, management has developed three estimates for each variable: an optimistic cost, a most likely cost, and a pessimistic cost. Both the beta distribution and the triangular distribution are well suited for modeling variables with these three parameters. However, because the beta distribution is quite complex and not particularly intuitive, we assume that the triangular distribution will provide a reasonably good fit for each variable.

It is worth noting that in contrast to other approaches in which only the most likely value for each variable is considered, tantamount to an assumption of certainty, a major benefit of the risk analysis approach is that the full range of possible values is considered. Therefore, the model developed should provide a closer approximation to the actual situation being modeled. Furthermore, the results will likely be more accurate because it is easier to estimate the range of values a variable may assume than to predict its exact value. To illustrate, would you have more confidence in your single-point estimate of IBM's stock price one week from now or in a range that was bounded by your estimated lowest and highest stock prices? Your estimated range is apt to contain IBM's closing price, while your single-point estimate is likely to be in error.

Returning to the task at hand, the spreadsheet shown in Table C-1 was created in Excel®. The most likely cost estimates were entered in cells B3:C5, while the costs of pursuing each project are calculated in cells B6 and C6 by summing up the hardware, software, and training costs.

Table C-1 Two Web-Server Options

	A	B	C
		Windows	**Unix**
1			
2		**Platform**	**Platform**
3	Hardware cost	$125,000	$110,000
4	Software conversion cost	$300,000	$300,000
5	Employee training	$10,000	$10,000
6	Total Project Cost	$435,000	$420,000

Using CB to run a Monte Carlo simulation requires defining two types of cells in the spreadsheet. The cells that are associated with variables or parameters are defined as *assumption cells*. The cells that correspond to outcomes of the simulation model are defined as *forecast cells*. Forecast cells typically contain formulas that depend on one or more assumption cells. Simulation models can have multiple assumption and forecast cells, but they must have at least one of each. Referring to Table C-1, the variables that we will make assumptions about are contained in cells B3:C5. Likewise, the outcomes of interest, or in this case project costs, are calculated in cells B6 and C6—the forecast cells.

To illustrate the process of defining an assumption cell, refer to cell B3 corresponding to the hardware costs for the Windows-based platform project. Recall that the most likely cost for hardware if the firm migrates to a Windows-based platform is estimated to be $125,000 with a range of $100,000 to $200,000. Also recall our decision to model all costs with a triangular distribution.

The process of defining an assumption involves the following six steps:

1. Click on cell **B3** to identify it as the cell the assumption applies to.

2. Select the menu option **Cell** at the top of the screen.*

3. From the dropdown menu that appears, select **Define Assumption**. CB's Distribution Gallery dialog box is now displayed as shown in Figure C-1.

4. As you can see, CB allows you to choose from a wide variety of probability distributions. Double-click on the **Triangular** box to select it.

5. CB's Triangular Distribution dialog box is now displayed as shown in Figure C-2. In the Assumption Name textbox at the top of the dialog box, enter a descriptive name such as *Hardware cost - Windows* to label the assumption. Then enter the optimistic, most likely, and pessimistic costs of $100,000, $125,000, and $200,000 in the Min, Likeliest, and Max textboxes, respectively.

6. Click on the **OK** button.

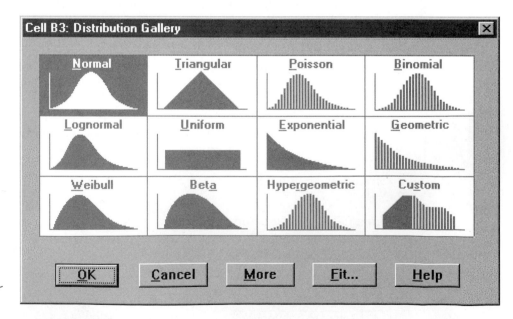

Figure C-1 Crystal Ball® 2000's Distribution Gallery.

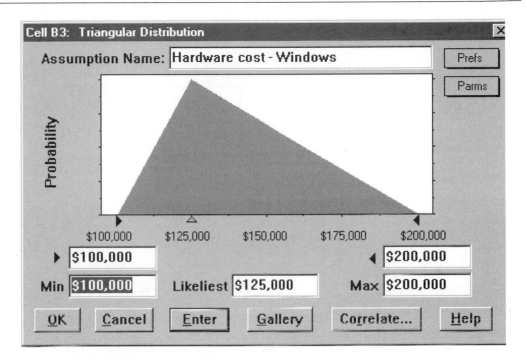

Figure C-2 Triangular Distribution dialog box.

Repeat steps 1–6 for the other five assumption cells (i.e., cells B4:B5 and cells C3:C5). Note the information entered in step 5 will vary for each assumption cell.

Having defined the assumption cells, we now turn our attention to defining the forecast or outcome cells. In our example, we are interested in comparing the costs of the two projects. The process of defining a forecast cell involves the following five steps:

1. Click on cell **B6** to identify it as containing an outcome we are interested in.
2. Select the menu option **C**ell at the top of the screen.
3. From the dropdown menu that appears, select **Define F**orecast . . .
4. CB's Define Forecast dialog box is now displayed as shown in Figure C-3. In the Forecast Name: textbox, enter a descriptive name such as *Total Project Cost - Windows* to label the result. Then enter a descriptive label such as *Dollars* in the Units: textbox.
5. Click **O**K.

Repeat steps 1–5 for cell C6.

One iteration of the simulation model involves randomly generating a value for each assumption cell based on the specified probability distributions and then calculat-

Cell B6: Define Forecast

Forecast Name: |Total Project Cost - Windows|

Units: |Dollars|

| OK | Cancel | More >> | Help |

Figure C-3 Define Forecast dialog box.

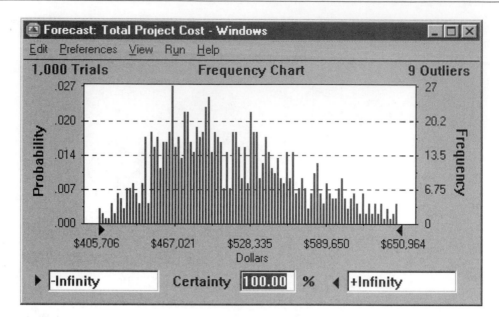

Figure C-4
Frequency chart for
total project costs
(Windows-based
platform).

ing the total project costs. By repeating this process hundreds or thousands of times we can get a sense of the distribution of possible outcomes.

To simulate the completion of these projects 1,000 times, select the **Run** menu item at the top of the screen. Next, in the dropdown dialog box that appears, select **Run Preferences**. In the Run Preferences dialog box that appears, enter **1,000** in the Maximum Number of Trials textbox and then click **OK**. Next, to replicate the simulation model 1,000 times, select the **Run** menu item again and then **Run** from the dropdown menu. CB summarizes the results of the simulation models in the form of frequency charts as the model is being executed, as shown in Figures C-4 and C-5.

CB provides other summary information about the forecast cells in addition to the frequency chart including percentile information, summary statistics, the cumulative chart, and a reverse cumulative chart. For example, to see the summary statistics for a forecast cell, select the **View** menu option in the Forecast window and then select **Statistics** from

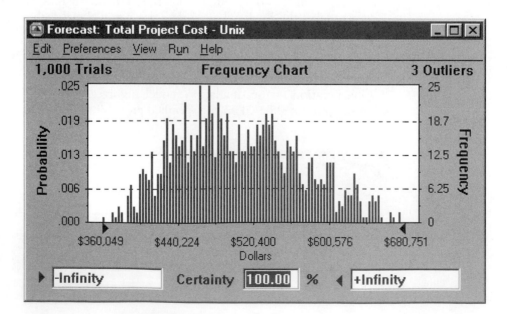

Figure C-5
Frequency chart for
total project costs
(Unix-based
platform).

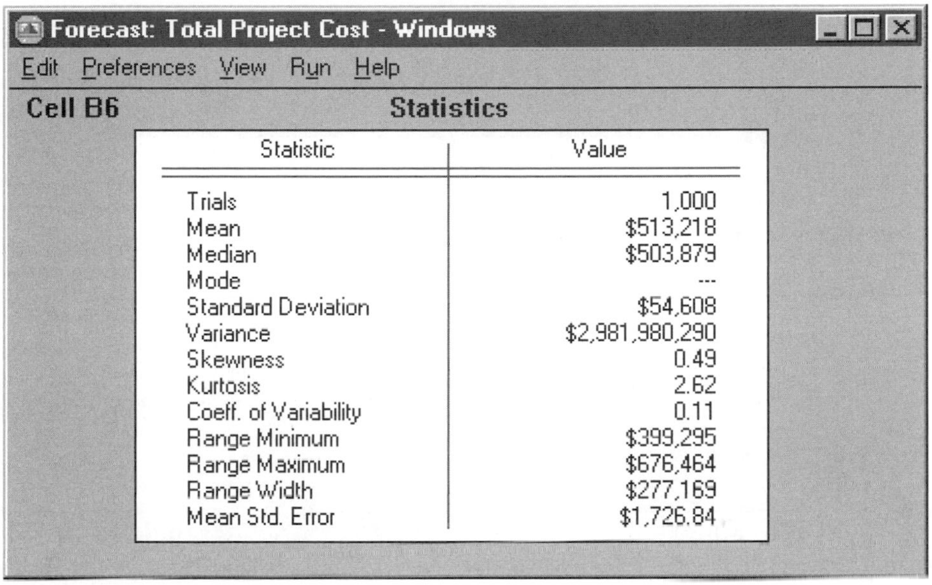

Forecast: Total Project Cost - Windows

Edit   Preferences   View   Run   Help

Cell B6   **Statistics**

Statistic	Value
Trials	1,000
Mean	$513,218
Median	$503,879
Mode	---
Standard Deviation	$54,608
Variance	$2,981,980,290
Skewness	0.49
Kurtosis	2.62
Coeff. of Variability	0.11
Range Minimum	$399,295
Range Maximum	$676,464
Range Width	$277,169
Mean Std. Error	$1,726.84

Figure C-6
Summary statistics
for Windows-based
platform project.

the dropdown menu that appears. The Statistics view for both the Windows-based platform and Unix-based platform projects are shown in Figures C-6 and C-7, respectively.

Reviewing Figures C-6 and C-7 we observe that the average total cost of the Windows project across the 1,000 replications of the simulation model is $513,218, while
the average cost of the Unix project is $506,365. On this basis alone, the Unix project
appears to be the lower cost project.* Figures C-6 and C-7, however, show that the total
cost of the Windows project is expected to range between slightly less than $400,000
and slightly more than $676,000. In contrast, the Unix project might cost as little as

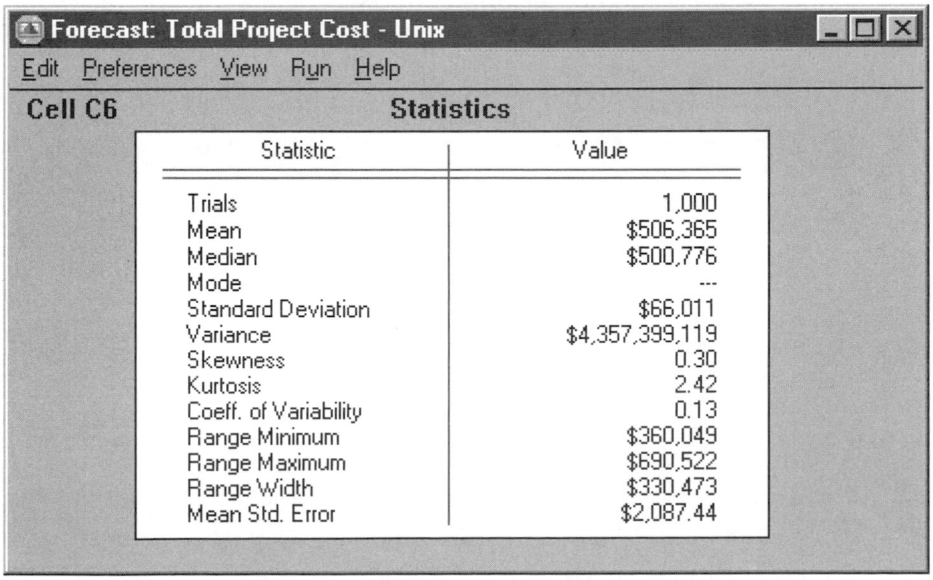

Forecast: Total Project Cost - Unix

Edit   Preferences   View   Run   Help

Cell C6   **Statistics**

Statistic	Value
Trials	1,000
Mean	$506,365
Median	$500,776
Mode	---
Standard Deviation	$66,011
Variance	$4,357,399,119
Skewness	0.30
Kurtosis	2.42
Coeff. of Variability	0.13
Range Minimum	$360,049
Range Maximum	$690,522
Range Width	$330,473
Mean Std. Error	$2,087.44

Figure C-7
Summary statistics
for Unix-based
platform project.

*The ranges shown in the Total Project Cost statistics windows, Figures C-6 and C-7, are slightly different
from the ranges shown in the Total Project Cost frequency charts, Figures C-4 and C-5. The reason for this is that
the frequency charts exclude some outlier data points. The number of outliers excluded is shown in the upper-right-
hand section of each chart.

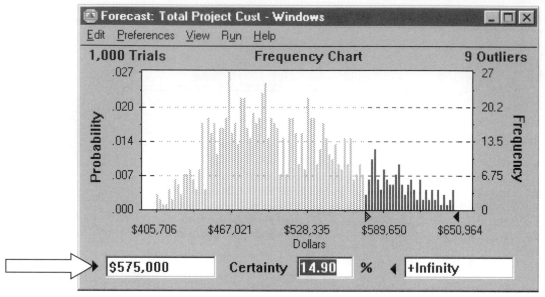

Figure C-8   Calculating the probability that the Windows project total cost exceeds $575,000.

$360,000 or as much as $690,000. The wider range of possible costs associated with the Unix project is an indication of greater uncertainty and therefore greater risk. What should management do in this case? Should it select the Unix project and ignore the risk that it could potentially end up costing over $690,000? Or should it select the Windows project knowing that it is very unlikely that the project costs will exceed $676,000? Clearly, these types of questions only become apparent when the distributions of possible outcomes are considered.

CB provides a feature that helps answer these questions. For example, assume that the firm cannot afford to spend more than $575,000. Then, one dimension to compare the two projects on is the probability that they will exceed the $575,000 budget limitation. We can use the Forecast window provided by CB to answer these questions. More

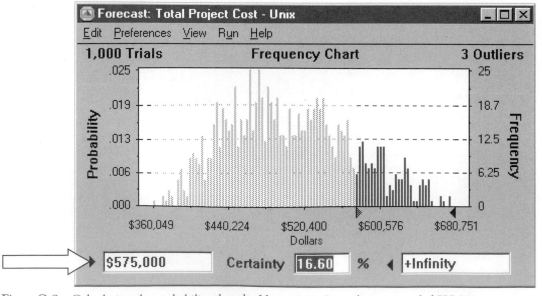

Figure C-9   Calculating the probability that the Unix project's total cost exceeds $575,000.

specifically, in this case we are interested in finding the probability that either project's total cost will exceed $575,000—that its total costs will be between $575,000 and infinity. To calculate this probability for each project, the information shown in Figures C-8 and C-9 was entered in the textboxes at the bottom of each Forecast window. According to the calculations, the Windows project has a 14.9 percent chance of exceeding the maximum available funds, while the Unix project has a slightly higher 16.6 percent chance.

C.2 CONSIDERING UNCERTAINTY IN PROJECT BUDGETING

In this section we address the issue of uncertainty in project budgeting. To illustrate, imagine that a consulting company is asked to prepare a budget for a project to develop a relationship management software program to be used by customer service representatives working in a bank's branch locations. Having completed a number of projects of similar scope, the consulting firm accumulated a fair amount of historical data about the time required to complete each of the five major steps typical of these projects. Analysis of this data indicates that the first phase, requirements planning, requires 80 hours of software engineering time on average with a standard deviation of 15 hours. A summary of this data for all five major phases is provided in Table C-2. Further analysis of the data indicates that the distribution of times to complete each phase is approximately normal.* Software engineers are paid an average of $60 per hour including benefits in this particular firm.

The spreadsheet shown in Table C-3 will help you understand the implications of the uncertainty surrounding the budget for this project. In this spreadsheet, cells B5:B9 were defined as assumption cells with their corresponding assumptions documented in the adjacent cells in column C. Furthermore, the result of interest in this case is the Total Cost of the project, which is calculated in cell B2. Hence, cell B2 was defined as a forecast cell.

Because this is our first time dealing with the normal distribution, we illustrate the process of defining an assumption cell based on this distribution for the Requirements Planning phase (cell B5). After clicking on cell **B5**, selecting the **Cell** menu option, and selecting the **Define Assumption** option the Distribution Gallery is displayed as shown in Figure C-1. In this case we want to define an assumption cell based on the normal distribution. After selecting **Normal** from the Distribution Gallery, the Normal

Table C-2　Software Engineer Time Required

Phase	Average Time (hours)	Standard Deviation
Requirements Planning	80	15
Design	160	25
Prototype Development	320	70
Final Development	640	100
Test	120	20

---

*Note that although we do not demonstrate it here, Crystal Ball® 2000 can fit distributions to historical data. This is accomplished by selecting the **Fit** button in CB's Distribution Gallery window (see Figure C-1) and then specifying the location of the historical data. In completing this task, CB considers a wide variety of probability distributions and offers the user options regarding the goodness-of-fit test used. The interested reader is referred to the Crystal Ball® 2000 *User Manual* for additional details.

Table C-3   Spreadsheet to Investigate Project Budget

	A	B	C	D	E	F	G	H
	Wage Rate ($/hour)	60						
	Total Cost	$79,200	=B1*B10					
	Phase	**Time**						
	Requirements Planning	80	Normal distribution with mean of 80 and std. dev. of 15.					
	Design	160	Normal distribution with mean of 160 and std. dev. of 25.					
	Prototype Development	320	Normal distribution with mean of 320 and std. dev. of 70.					
	Final Development	640	Normal distribution with mean of 640 and std. dev. of 100.					
	Test	120	Normal distribution with mean of 120 and std. dev. of 20.					
10	Total Time	1320	=SUM(B5:B9)					

Distribution dialog box is displayed as shown in Figure C-10. Crystal Ball will automatically fill in the Assumption Name textbox with "Requirements Planning" based on the label entered in cell A5. Therefore, the only information that needs to be entered is the two parameters for the normal distribution, the mean and standard deviation.

Referring to Table C-2, we see that the Requirements Planning phase is expected to have a mean of 80 hours and standard deviation of 15. These values were entered in the Mean and Std Dev textboxes, respectively, as shown in Figure C-10. Note that after clicking the **Enter** button the shape of the distribution changes based on the parameters entered. You can use this feature to visually inspect the distribution and to verify that it provides a reasonable approximation of the variable being modeled.

Referring to Figure C-10 we see that according to the parameters entered, the Requirements Planning phase could take anywhere from 35 to 125 hours, but will most likely require approximately 80 hours. Because the distribution is symmetrical, we also assume that it is just as likely for this phase to require more than 80 hours as it is for it to require less than 80 hours. If based on past experience, one or more of these conditions

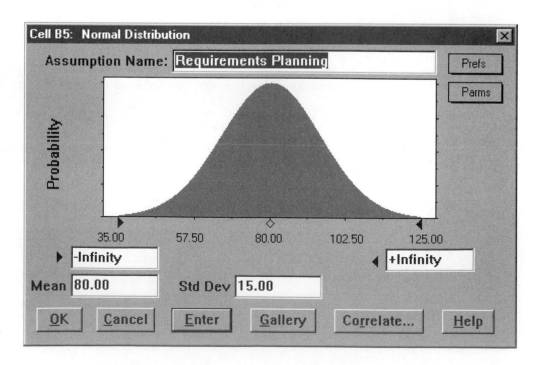

Figure C-10
Normal Distribution
dialog box.

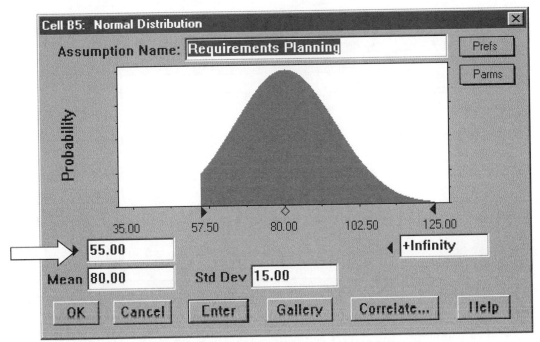

Figure C-11   Changing the lower bound of a distribution.

do not seem reasonable, then one or both of the distribution parameters could be altered to try to obtain a better approximation or perhaps a new distribution should be used to model the variable. Also, values can be entered in the textboxes to truncate the upper and lower values returned. For example, if past experience suggests that the Requirements Planning phase never takes less than 55 hours, 55 could be entered for the lower bound as shown in Figure C-11.

A summary of the results after replicating the model 1,000 times is shown in Figures C-12 and C-13. Analysis of the simulation results indicates that the average or expected

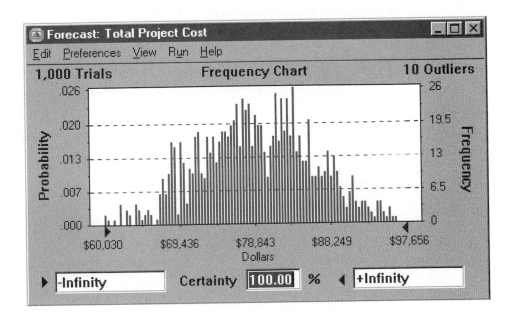

Figure C-12
Frequency chart for
total project cost.

Figure C-13
Summary statistics
for total project cost.

Forecast: Total Project Cost

Edit Preferences View Run Help

Cell B2   **Statistics**

Statistic	Value
Trials	1,000
Mean	$79,037
Median	$78,885
Mode	---
Standard Deviation	$7,342
Variance	$53,909,479
Skewness	-0.00
Kurtosis	3.05
Coeff. of Variability	0.09
Range Minimum	$49,536
Range Maximum	$104,282
Range Width	$54,746
Mean Std. Error	$232.18

cost of completing this project across the 1,000 trials is $79,037. This is very close to the expected value obtained by simply adding up the average times for each phase and multiplying by the $60 per hour rate, that is, $(80+160+320+640+120)\,60 = \$79,200$, which serves to validate our results. Further analysis of the results suggest that on one trial the cost of the project reached $104,282 while on another trial the costs were only $49,536 (see Figure C-13). It is exactly the distribution of likely project costs that determines the risk associated with the project. We would consider a project to have relatively little risk if across all trials of the simulation model the project costs varied little from the average or expected value. As the results from the simulation analysis become more spread out, however, the amount of uncertainty, and therefore, risk increases.

One way to quantify the amount of risk associated with a given project is to calculate the standard deviation. For example, across the 1,000 trials of the simulation model, the standard deviation of the project cost was $7,342. You may recall from a statistics course that 95 percent of the observations fall within plus or minus two standard deviations of the mean for normally distributed data. Based on this, if we are willing to assume that the project completion costs follow a normal distribution, then we can conclude that there is a 95 percent chance that this project will cost between $64,353 and $93,721 ($79,037 $\pm$ 2 $\times$ 7,342). Observe that the width of this interval increases as the standard deviation increases, again indicating greater uncertainty and more risk.

Another way to help quantify the risk associated with a project is to create a frequency chart of the simulation results as shown in Figure C-12. Using CB, we can use this frequency chart to calculate the probability for any number of scenarios. For example, in Figure C-14 the probability that total project costs exceed $85,000 was calculated to be 20.8 percent.

In particular, two characteristics of the frequency chart should be examined. First, the amount of variation or how spread out the observations are should be noted. As was discussed earlier, higher levels of variation correspond to higher levels of risk. The second characteristic that should be observed is the shape of the frequency chart. A symmetrical distribution such as the normal distribution indicates that the project is just as likely to be completed under budget as it is to be completed over budget. A right-skewed distribution suggests that there is a chance that the project will require a much

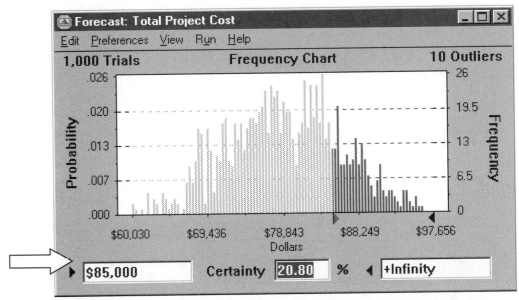

Figure C-14 Calculating the probability that the project's total cost exceeds $85,000

larger than expected budget to complete while a left-skewed distribution suggests that there is a chance that the project will require much less than is expected. The frequency chart shown in Figure C-12 appears to be basically symmetrical.

C.3 CONSIDERING UNCERTAINTY IN PROJECT SCHEDULING

The methodology and advantages of using simulation to analyze projects with probabilistic time estimates were overviewed in Chapter 5. In this section, we take this analysis one step further and demonstrate how CB can greatly facilitate this analysis.

For the purpose of this example, the network diagram in Figure C-15 will be used. In addition to identifying six activities and their precedence relationships, the optimistic, most likely, and pessimistic time estimates for each activity are listed. Further analysis of the diagram indicates there are three paths: **A-C-E, B-D-E,** and **B-F**.

In a similar fashion to the approach used in Chapter 5, the spreadsheet shown in Table C-4 simulates the completion of the project. Rather than using Excel's Random Number Generation Tool to generate random activity times, however, we define cells A3:F3 as assumption cells and use CB to generate the random activity times. Furthermore, since we are given the optimistic, most likely, and pessimistic time estimates for

Figure C-15
Sample project network diagram with optimistic, most likely, and pessimistic time estimates.

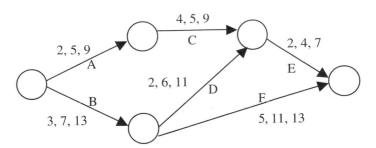

Table C-4   Simulating Project Completion Times

	A	B	C	D	E	F	G	H	I	J
1	Activity	Activity	Activity	Activity	Activity	Activity	Path	Path	Path	Completion
2	A	B	C	D	E	F	A-C-E	B-D-E	B-F	Time
3	5	7	5	6	4	11	14	17	18	18
4										
5	*Key Formulas:*									
6	Cell G3	=A3+C3+E3								
7	Cell H3	=B3+D3+E3								
8	Cell I3	=B3+F3								
9	Cell J3	=MAX(G3:I3)								

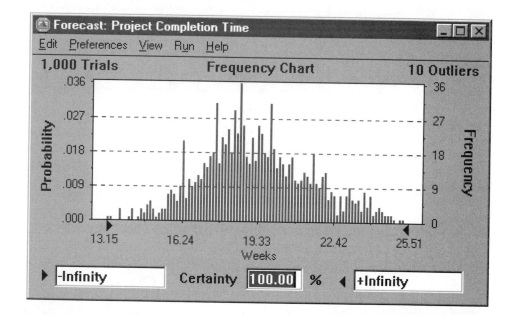

Figure C-16
Frequency chart for project completion time.

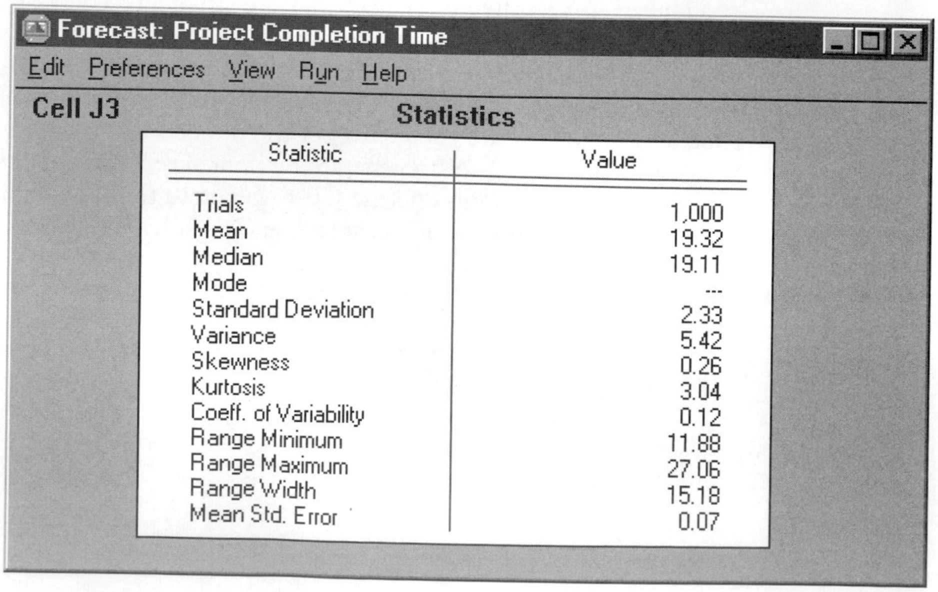

Figure C-17
Summary statistics for project completion time.

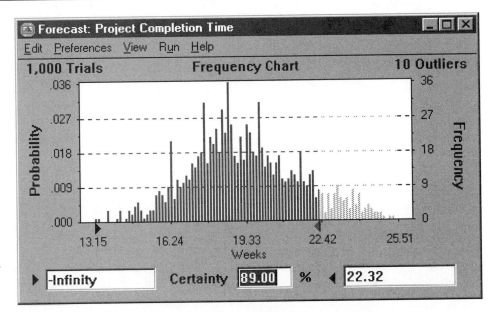

Figure C-18
Sensitivity analysis of project completion time.

each activity in Figure C-15, we will use the triangular distribution to generate the random activity times. Finally, since the result we are interested in is the project completion time, we define cell J3 to be a forecast cell.

A summary of the results after replicating the model 1,000 times is shown in Figures C-16 and C-17. Analysis of the simulation results indicates that on average the project required 19.32 weeks to be completed. Further analysis of the results suggests that the project could be potentially completed in less than 12 weeks or take in excess of 27 weeks.

If you were the project manager for this project, how much time would you tell your supervisor you needed to complete this project? Intuitively, you know that if you request 19.32 weeks you will have a 50 percent chance of completing the project late. Suppose you add three weeks to the project's mean duration. What is the probability the project could be complete in 22.32 weeks? To answer this question, 22.32 was entered as an upper bound in CB's Forecast window as shown in Figure C-18. As it turns out, there is an 89 percent chance the project could be completed in 22.32 weeks or less. Similar analyses can be quickly performed to determine the probability that the project is completed on or before other times, the probability that the project is completed after a specified time, and the probability that the project is completed within a specified timeframe (e.g., the probability the project will take between 17 and 21 weeks).

C.4 CONSIDERING UNCERTAINTY IN RESOURCE ALLOCATION

In this final section we demonstrate the use of risk analysis to investigate issues related to resource allocation. For example, in our discussion of the Critical Chain in Chapter 6, it was noted that in some organizations there can be a negative incentive for project team members to report that activities were completed ahead of schedule. If this is indeed true, what are its implications?

To explore this issue, we utilize the example data given in Figure C-15 making one key modification. Namely, to reflect our hypothesized practice that early completion times go unreported, we will truncate the distributions so that the lower bound is equal

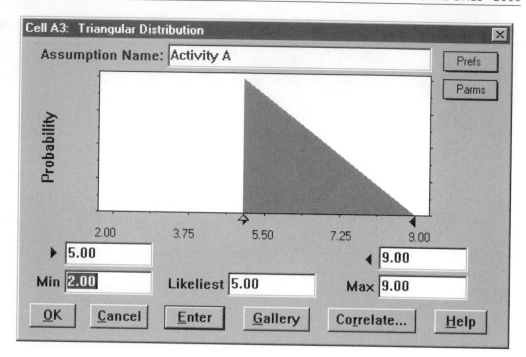

Figure C-19 Truncated triangular distribution for activity. A reflecting assumption that early completion times go unreported.

to the most likely time estimate. This in effect means that if a random time estimate is generated that is less than the most likely value, the time to complete the task is reported as the most likely time estimate. To illustrate, the triangular distribution for activity A with optimistic, most likely, and pessimistic time estimates of 2, 5, and 9 weeks, respectively, is truncated so that randomly generated activity times that are less than five weeks are reported as taking five weeks as shown in Figure C-19.

The results of simulating the project shown in Figure C-15 with the truncated triangular distributions are summarized in Figures C-20 and C-21. In comparing the results

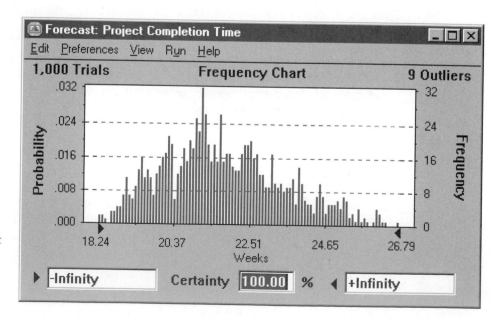

Figure C-20 Distribution of project completion times when early activity completion times go unreported.

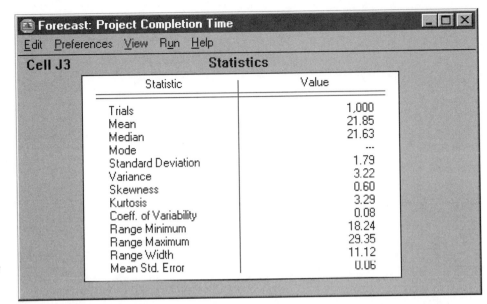

Figure C-21
Summary statistics for project completion times when early activity completion times go unreported.

when early activity times are reported (Figures C-16 and C-17) with the results when early completion times are not reported (Figures C-20 and C-21) we observe that not reporting early activity completions increases the duration of the project by almost three weeks on average or more than 10 percent.

In this Appendix we utilized several examples to illustrate the process of analyzing risk using CB. It is not our intention to either provide a comprehensive treatment of CB or make you experts in risk analysis. Rather, our purpose is to introduce you to this topic and this user-friendly software as a way of demonstrating both the importance and ease of considering risk in project management. As you can likely imagine, the techniques discussed in this Appendix are not limited to the applications discussed here and indeed can be applied in a similar fashion to a wide variety of other project management issues [1].

BIBLIOGRAPHY

1. **Crystal Ball® 2000 User Manual.** Denver: Decisioneering Inc., 2000. (An excellent and readable manual, full of information about statistics and statistical distributions in addition to use of the software.)
2. EVANS, J. R., and D. L. OLSON. *Introduction to Simulation and Risk Analysis.* Upper Saddle River, NJ: Prentice Hall, 1998. (This book is an excellent, readable text on a wide range of applications of simulation and risk analysis to organizational problems. It includes a student copy of Crystal Ball® software.)

AUTHOR INDEX

Hughes, T. P., 53
Hulett, D. T., 157

Ibbs, C. W., 203, 237
Ingram, T., 237, 250

Jandt, F. E., 25
Johnson, R. A., 267
Johnson, R. V., 203

Kamburowski, J., 157
Kandt, D. B., 237
Kaplan, R. S., 25
Keefer, D. L., 157, 267
Keelin, T., 25
Kefalas, A. G., 54
Kharbanda, O. P., 54
Kimball, R., 250
Kloppenborg, T. J., 25
Knutson, J., 81
Koppleman, J. M., 237
Kotter, J. P., 53
Kretlow, W. J., 25
Kurstedt, H. A., Jr., 109
Kurtulus, I., 203
Kwak, Y.-H., 237

Langley, A., 81
Lavold, G. D., 81
Lawrence, A. O., 109
Lawrence, J. A., Jr., 157
Lee, S. A., 203
Levine, H. A., 53
Levy, O., 250
Li, J. I., 203
Liberatore, M. J., 109
Littlefield, T. K. Jr., 157

Mallak, L. M., 109
Mandelbaum, A., 203
Mantel, S. J., Jr., 25, 53, 109, 157, 250

Martin, J. E., 110
Martin, M. G., 81
Martin, P. K., 81
Matson, E., 53
McGuigan, J. R., 25
McLaughlin, F. S., 81
McMahon, C. S., 157
Mendenhall, W., 267
Meredith, J. R., 25, 110, 157, 203, 237, 250
Moyer, R. C., 25

Narula, S. C., 203
Netter, J., 267
Nixon, T. R., 237
Nguyen, V., 203

Olson, D. L., 109, 283

Pasternak, B. A., 157
Patterson, N., 53
Patzak, G. A., 109
Pells, D. L, 81
Peters, T., 55
Peterson, M., 74
Pinto, J. K., 53, 54, 250
Prentis, E. L., 81
Pritsker, A. A. B., 157
Pyron, T., 157

Raiffa, H., 25
Randolph, P. H., 157
Reif, W. E., 81
Reith, W. D., 237
Ruskin, A. M., 157

Sasieni, M. W., 157
Schaeffer, R. L., 267
Schoderbek. C. G., 54
Schoderbek, P. P., 54
Schwerer, E., 203

---

*Decisioneering's Crystal Ball® 2000 is referenced frequently throughout the book, and page entries will not be cited except for discussions of the use of the software.

*Microsoft Excel® 2000 is referenced so frequently throughout the book, that page entries will not be cited except for discussions on the use of the software.

---

*Microsoft Project® is referenced so frequently throughout the book that page entries will not be cited except for discussions on the use of the software.